THE COMPLETE IDIOT'S GUIDE® TO

American Government

Second Edition

by Melanie Fonder and Mary M. Shaffrey

ALPHA

A member of Penguin Group (USA) Inc.

For Marilyn and John Ihlenfeld
—Melanie Fonder
For my parents and Anne Price
—Mary M. Shaffrey

ALPHA BOOKS

Published by the Penguin Group

Penguin Group (USA) Inc., 375 Hudson Street, New York, New York 10014, USA

Penguin Group (Canada), 90 Eglinton Avenue East, Suite 700, Toronto, Ontario M4P 2Y3, Canada (a division of Pearson Penguin Canada Inc.)

Penguin Books Ltd., 80 Strand, London WC2R 0RL, England

Penguin Ireland, 25 St. Stephen's Green, Dublin 2, Ireland (a division of Penguin Books Ltd.)

Penguin Group (Australia), 250 Camberwell Road, Camberwell, Victoria 3124, Australia (a division of Pearson Australia Group Pty. Ltd.)

Penguin Books India Pvt. Ltd., 11 Community Centre, Panchsheel Park, New Delhi—110 017, India

Penguin Group (NZ), 67 Apollo Drive, Rosedale, North Shore, Auckland 1311, New Zealand (a division of Pearson New Zealand Ltd.)

Penguin Books (South Africa) (Pty.) Ltd., 24 Sturdee Avenue, Rosebank, Johannesburg 2196, South Africa

Penguin Books Ltd., Registered Offices: 80 Strand, London WC2R 0RL, England

International Standard Book Number: 978-1-59257-328-8
Library of Congress Catalog Card Number: 2005922485

09   08   8   7   6

Interpretation of the printing code: The rightmost number of the first series of numbers is the year of the book's printing; the rightmost number of the second series of numbers is the number of the book's printing. For example, a printing code of 05-1 shows that the first printing occurred in 2005.

Printed in the United States of America

Note: This publication contains the opinions and ideas of its authors. It is intended to provide helpful and informative material on the subject matter covered. It is sold with the understanding that the authors and publisher are not engaged in rendering professional services in the book. If the reader requires personal assistance or advice, a competent professional should be consulted.

The authors and publisher specifically disclaim any responsibility for any liability, loss, or risk, personal or otherwise, which is incurred as a consequence, directly or indirectly, of the use and application of any of the contents of this book.

Most Alpha books are available at special quantity discounts for bulk purchases for sales promotions, premiums, fundraising, or educational use. Special books, or book excerpts, can also be created to fit specific needs.

For details, write: Special Markets, Alpha Books, 375 Hudson Street, New York, NY 10014.

Publisher: *Marie Butler-Knight*
Product Manager: *Phil Kitchel*
Senior Managing Editor: *Jennifer Bowles*
Acquisitions Editor: *Paul Dinas*
Development Editor: *Michael Thomas*
Production Editor: *Megan Douglass*

Copy Editor: *Ross Patty*
Cartoonist: *Shannon Wheeler*
Cover/Book Designer: *Trina Wurst*
Indexer: *Brad Herriman*
Layout: *Angela Calvert*
Proofreading: *John Etchison*

Contents at a Glance

Part 1:   **Building a Government**   1

   1   Putting It in Writing   3
The documents that led to freedom, democracy, and the American way.

   2   A More Perfect Union   19
A closer look at the main body of the Constitution, the oldest document of its kind in use in the world today.

   3   The Bill of Rights   31
How the framers of the Constitution ensured the basic rights of all Americans.

   4   Keeping the Constitution Alive   41
How the Constitution has changed over the years, largely in response to perceived shortcomings in the governing process.

Part 2:   **The Buck Stops Here**   51

   5   Hail to the Chief   53
Why we call the central figure responsible for American government "Mr. President" instead of "His Highness."

   6   Second in Command—The Vice President   63
History hasn't been especially kind to the role of the vice president. Here's a look at some of the 46 men who have served in this position.

   7   Advising the President   73
All about the members of the president's cabinet—some of the most influential people in government.

   8   Shaping the Presidency   85
Each president has left some mark on the office and the nation. Some were noteworthy for what they did for both; others were infamous for what they did to both.

Part 3:   **Checks and Balances**   99

   9   The Lower House   101
How the House of Representatives differs in form and function from the Senate.

10   The Upper House   117
     *Where some of the most important debates in American
     government take place.*

11   Congressional Authority   133
     How bills become laws.

12   Congress at Work   145
     A day in the life of a member of Congress.

13   Congressional Elections   157
     How candidates for Congress are chosen.

Part 4:   An Even Higher Authority   167

14   Hear Ye, Hear Ye   169
     The role of the judicial branch of government.

15   Supreme Players   179
     *The men and women who wear the black robes, and other
     key players in the judicial system.*

16   First Monday in October   197
     *How cases get to the Supreme Court and what the justices
     do with them when they get there.*

17   Setting Precedents   209
     *Groundbreaking decisions that have helped define the law
     of the land.*

Part 5:   Follow the Money   225

18   Fed Money   227
     The power of the purse—the federal purse, that is!

19   Campaigns and Money   239
     *All about how campaigns are financed and the rules govern-
     ing how candidates raise money.*

20   Campaign Finance Reform   251
     *What campaign finance reform is all about, and the scandals
     that have fueled calls for changing the way campaigns are
     run.*

21   Fundraising   263
     How politicians raise the money necessary for success.

22   The Right to Petition   273
     Giving voice to special interests.

Part 6:   State and Local Government   **285**

23 Governors and Other State Leaders   287
    The numerous roles filled by the people who govern the states.

24 Reapportionment and Redistricting   297
    How the federal government ensures that your voice will be heard.

25 Another House, Another Senate, and What They
    Do for You   305
    The similarities between state and federal government.

26 Local Government   315
    All about counties, townships, towns, and more.

27 The Power of One   327
    The role and responsibilities of the individual in government, and how you can get involved.

Appendixes

A Glossary   339

B Branches of the Federal Government   345

C Recap of the 2004 Elections   349

D Resources   361

   Index   369

Contents

Part 1:   Building a Government   **1**

1   Putting It in Writing   **3**

The Great Charter 4

Bringing Self-Government to America 5

Saying Good-Bye to Royal Control 6

   Declaring Rights 6

   War Time 8

Uniting the Colonies 9

The Constitutional Convention 11

   Key Issues of Debate 12

   Getting to Yes 13

   Other Points of Contention 13

Taking It to the States 14

Federalists vs. Anti-Federalists 15

2   A More Perfect Union   **19**

Success from Failure 19

Constitution by Committee 20

A Framework for Democracy 21

Keeping Control in Balance 21

Inside the Constitution 22

Article 1: Creating Congress 22

Article 2: Ordering the Executive 24

Article 3: You Take the High Court, I'll Take the Low Court 27

Article 4: States' Rights vs. the Fed's Rights 28

Article 5: Making Changes 29

Article 6: The Law That Reigns Supreme 30

Article 7: Getting the States' Approval 30

3   The Bill of Rights   **31**

Protecting the People's Rights 32

Ch-ch-ch-ch-changes 33

Inside the Bill of Rights 34

First Amendment: Ensuring Civil Liberties 34

Freedom of Speech *35*

Freedom of Assembly *36*

Freedom of Religion *36*

Second Amendment: Keeping and Bearing Arms 37

Third Amendment: Protection from the Military 38

Fourth Amendment: Search and Seizure 38

Fifth Amendment: Protection Against Self-Incrimination 38

Sixth Amendment: The Right to a Defense 39

Seventh Amendment: The Right to Trial 39

Eighth Amendment: Barring Cruel and Unusual Punishment....39

Ninth Amendment: Ensuring Fundamental Rights 40

Tenth Amendment: Protecting States' Interests 40

4 Keeping the Constitution Alive   **41**

Protecting Government from Lawsuits: Amendment 11 42

Redoing Veep Elections: Amendment 12 42

The Civil War Amendments: 13, 14, and 15 43

The Beginning of Income Taxes: Amendment 16 45

Tweaking the Election Process: Amendments 17, 20,
22, and 25 45

The Whiskey Amendments: Amendments 18 and 21 46

Giving Women the Right to Vote: Amendment 19 47

Further Expanding the Electorate: Amendments 23, 24,
and 26 48

Granting Raises to Congress: Amendment 27 48

Amendments Tried and Failed 49

Part 2: The Buck Stops Here   **51**

5 Hail to the Chief   **53**

Why They Made Washington President Instead of King 54

Requirements for Office 55

Candidates—Typical and Not 55

Businessmen *55*

Nader the Raider *55*

A Woman's Place Is in the Oval Office? *56*

Anything Other Than White Anglo-Saxon Protestant Male *56*

Primary Battles 56

Delegates and Conventions 58
The Fall Campaign 59
Going to College—The Electoral College, That Is! 59
Victory … and Defeat 60
Who's in Charge? 60

6 Second in Command—The Vice President   **63**

Defining the Office—Sort Of 64
Early Tumult 64
Who Is This Guy? 66
The Role Transformed 67
Playing Checkers with Office Space *67*
Co-President Ford? *67*
Becoming Major Players 68
Selecting a Vice President 69
Basic Considerations *69*
Regional Support *70*
Balancing Perspectives *70*
Swinging the States *70*
Adding Some Sizzle *71*
Working 9 to 5—And Beyond 71

7 Advising the President   **73**

Establishing the "Kitchen Cabinet" 73
Choosing His Advisors 74
The First Four 74
Global Challenges and Diplomacy: The State Department *75*
Minding Money and Security: The Department of Treasury *75*
Defenders of Peace: The Department of Defense *76*
The Enforcers: The Justice Department *77*
New Kids on the Block 77
Farm Aid: The Department of Agriculture *78*
Supporting the Economy: The Department of Commerce *78*
Meeting Workers' Needs: The Department of Labor *79*
*Minding the Country's Health: The Department of Health
and Human Services* *80*
*Ensuring House and Home: The Department of Housing and
Urban Development* *80*

*Getting from Point A to Point B: The Department
of Transportation* *81*
The Department of Energy *81*
Investing in the Future: The Department of Education *81*
Taking Care of Veterans: The Department of Veterans Affairs *82*
Keeping America Safe: The Department of Homeland Security....*82*
Cabinet Level, but Not Cabinet *83*

8 Shaping the Presidency   85

The Father of the Nation: George Washington (1789–1797)....86
Who's in Charge Here? 86
The Expansionist: Thomas Jefferson (1801–1809) 88
Buying Louisiana 89
Shaping Foreign Policy: James Monroe (1817–1825) 89
Expanding the Power of the Presidency:
  Andrew Jackson (1829–1837) 90
The Peacemaker: Abraham Lincoln (1861–1865) 93
A Better Tailor Than President: Andrew Johnson
  (1865–1869) 94
Creating the Bully Pulpit: Theodore Roosevelt (1901–1909) 95
Global Thinker: Woodrow Wilson (1913–1921) 96
Making America Great: Franklin D. Roosevelt (1933–1945) 97

Part 3: Checks and Balances   99

9 The Lower House   101

Representation Based on Population 102
Calling All Voters, Calling All Voters 102
A Woman's Place Is in the House 104
Requirements for Representatives 105
Leaders of the House 106
Mr. Speaker, Mr. Speaker! 107
Other Key Players 109
Committees 110
Committee Sizes *112*
Committee Assignments *112*
Further Divisions *113*
Committee Staffs *113*
Committee Leadership *113*
Minding the Money 113

10 The Upper House   **117**

The Beginning of the "Debater's Society" 118
A Changing Profile 118
Rising Tensions 119
    Compromises Made and Broken *119*
    Edging Toward War *120*
The Senate Gains in Power 121
Becoming Truly Representative 121
Operating in the Shadow of Presidents 122
    Aiding the New Deal *122*
    Shifts in Policy *123*
    Taking Up the Question of Rights *123*
    Debates over War Again *123*
Who Wants to Be a Senator? 124
    Ascending the Ladder *124*
    Rules and Requirements *125*
    Terms and Limits *125*
    "Elected by the People Thereof" *126*
Power over the President 126
    Advice and Consent over Treaties *126*
    Advice and Consent over Presidential Appointees *127*
"High Crimes and Misdemeanors" 128
Leadership and Procedure 129
Committees 131

11 Congressional Authority   **133**

Beginning the Process 133
Types of Legislation 135
    Joint Resolutions *135*
    Concurrent Resolutions *136*
    Simple Resolutions *136*
Building Support 136
Going to Committee 137
We Hear You 138
Calling Witnesses 138
Playing by the Rules 139
Hearings at Home and Away 139
Marking Things Up 139
Reporting Back 140
Floor Debate 140
Passage 142

12 Congress at Work   **145**

From a Part-Time Job to a Full-Time Career 146
Job Perks 146
A Day in the Life 149
On the Weekends 152
The Staff of Life 152
  Top Dogs *152*
  Getting the Word Out *153*
  Working the Cases *153*
The Youngest Staffers 154
Staffing the Committees 155

13 Congressional Elections   **157**

Beginning the Process 157
Picking the Candidates 158
The Primary Process 159
The Lobby Factor 160
The Presidential Push 161
Going for the Vote 162
Appointments and Special Elections 162
  Filling Senate Seats *162*
  Filling House Seats *163*
Bad Congressman, Bad Congressman 164

Part 4: An Even Higher Authority   **167**

14 Hear Ye, Hear Ye   **169**

The Federal Court System 170
The Structure of the Federal Courts 170
The Jurisdiction of the Federal Courts 172
The Federal Court's Interaction with the Executive
  and Legislative Branches 173
The Buck Stops Here 174
Supreme Court Rules and Requirements 175
  Rules of the Supreme Court *175*
  Who Can Argue Before the Supreme Court? *176*

15 Supreme Players   **179**

The Chief Justice 180
The Early Court: Jay Through Ellsworth 181
  The Jay Court (1790–1795) *181*

The Rutledge Court (1795) *182*
The Ellsworth Court (1796–1800) *182*
The Nineteenth-Century Court 182
The Marshall Court (1801–1835) *182*
The Taney Court (1836–1864) *183*
The Chase Court (1864–1873) *183*
The Waite Court (1874–1888) *183*
The Fuller Court (1888–1910) *184*
The Twentieth-Century Court 184
The White Court (1910–1921) *184*
The Taft Court (1921–1930) *185*
The Hughes Court (1930–1941) *185*
The Stone Court (1941–1946) *186*
The Vinson Court (1946–1953) *186*
The Warren Court (1953–1969) *186*
The Burger Court (1969–1986) *186*
The Supreme Court Today 187
Other Responsibilities of the Chief Justice 188
The Role of the Associate Justices 189
The Current Associate Justices 190
Justice John Paul Stevens *190*
Justice Sandra Day O'Connor *190*
Justice Antonin Scalia *191*
Justice Anthony Kennedy *191*
Justice David Souter *192*
Justice Clarence Thomas *193*
Justice Ruth Bader Ginsburg *194*
Justice Stephen Breyer *194*
The Solicitor General 195
Law Clerks 196

16 First Monday in October   **197**

Terms of the Court 197
Who Gets Heard? 199
From Federal or State Courts 200
Four Ways to Arrive at the Supreme Court 202
Petition for a Writ of Certiorari *202*
Appeal *202*
Request for Certification *203*
Petition for an Extraordinary Writ *203*

Following a Case Through the Process 203
Do's and Don'ts for Lawyers Before the High Court 205
And the Winner Is … 206

17 Setting Precedents **209**

Judicial Review 210
Marbury v. Madison 210
Bush v. Gore 211
Due Process of Law 212
The "Slaughter-House Cases" 213
Chicago, Burlington, and Quincy R.R. v. Chicago 213
Palko v. Connecticut 215
The Question of Civil Rights 215
Scott v. Sandford 216
Plessy v. Ferguson 216
Brown v. Board of Education 217
Freedom of Speech and of the Press 218
Schenck v. United States 218
Gitlow v. New York 218
Near v. Minnesota 218
New York Times Co. v. Sullivan 219
Brandenburg v. Ohio 220
Rights of Suspected Criminals 220
Mapp v. Ohio 220
Gideon v. Wainwright 221
Escobedo v. Illinois 221
Miranda v. Arizona 221
Right to Privacy and Roe v. Wade 222

Part 5: Follow the Money **225**

18 Fed Money **227**

The Federal Budget Process 228
Major Budget Laws 229
Gramm-Rudman-Hollings Act 229
The Federal Budget Timeline 230
Creating a Framework 231
Preparing the Budget on Time 232

Appropriations 232
   The Power of 13 ....*233*
   Appropriations Timeline *234*
Pass Me the Pork! 235
Agency Implementation 236

19 Campaigns and Money   **239**

War and Chests 240
Following the Rules 240
   Complicated Contributions Rules *241*
   Critical Deadlines *241*
Who Can't Give? 242
In-Kind Contributions 243
Volunteering for Campaigns 243
Campaign Committees, PACs, and 527's 245
Presidential Coffers 246
Tracking the Money 248

20 Campaign Finance Reform   **251**

Soft and Hard Money 252
What's the Beef? 253
Teapot Dome 255
FECA: Reform for Real 256
Constitutional Questions Arise 257
Bipartisan Campaign Reform Act of 2002 260

21 Fundraising   **263**

Fundraising Strategies 263
Thinking Outside of the Box 265
   Variety Is Key *266*
   Raising Money Online *267*
Single-Issue Influences 267
Going to the Stars (for Money, That Is!) 269
Union Influence 270
Corporate Influence 271

22 The Right to Petition   **273**

What Is a Lobbyist? 274
Recipe for Success 277
Influence of Lobbyists 278

Rules of the Game 280
Blurring the Lines 282

Part 6: State and Local Government   285

23 Governors and Other State Leaders   287

From Figurehead to Elected Official 287
Going to Higher Ground 289
Getting to Gov 289
Governing 291
Executive Role *291*
Legislative Role *292*
Judicial Role *292*
Second in Command: The Lieutenant Governor 293
The Attorney General 294
The Secretary of State 295
State Treasurer and Comptroller 295

24 Reapportionment and Redistricting   297

The Census 298
Redistricting 298
Drawing the Lines 299
Unequal Districts 300
Unusual Boundaries 301

25 Another House, Another Senate, and What They Do for You   305

State Legislatures and Constitutions 306
The People Who Serve 307
Powers of the State Legislature 309
Police Powers *309*
Power of the Purse *309*
State Spending 310
Education *310*
Highways and Byways *311*
Public Health and Welfare *312*
Conservation *312*
Law Enforcement and Corrections *313*

26 Local Government **315**
Counties 315
County Duties 316
Other County Officials 318
Towns and Townships 319
Special Districts 320
Cities, Small and Large 321
City Charters 322
   Mayor-Council Cities *324*
   Council-Manager Cities *324*
   Commission Cities *325*

27 The Power of One **327**
The Major Parties 327
   Minimum Wage *328*
   Abortion *329*
   Gun Control *330*
   Other Issues *331*
Other Parties 331
Registration Requirements 332
   Registering to Vote *333*
   Election Day *333*
   Voting Away from Home *335*
Get Involved 335

Appendixes
  A Glossary **339**
  B Branches of the Federal Government **345**
  C Recap of the 2004 Elections **349**
  D Resources **361**
  Index **369**

Foreword

For those of us who remember the McGuffy Reader, stiff lessons in penmanship, and rote memorization as the only way to learn what was then called "civics," meaning politics and government, it would have been not only enlightening but far more enjoyable if we had been provided with a textbook that was readable and informative.

The Complete Idiot's Guide to American Government, Second Edition, by Melanie Fonder and Mary Shaffrey is that book. It is an essential and mandatory-read book for every student from middle and high school to colleges and universities as well as for any foreign nationals wishing a better understanding of the nature of American government. Its clearly organized chapters are enormously informative and interesting reading. In fact, it should be mandatory reading not only for our students but for all our citizens, including every one of our elected leaders.

Writing in clear, jargon-free language, Fonder and Shaffrey have created what amounts to an authoritative and comprehensive guidebook to the American government. From the history behind the structures and mechanisms of our government to the key events and people who shaped them, from the electoral process and the ever-elusive Electoral College to the often byzantine channels through which bills must travel to become laws, *The Complete Idiot's Guide to American Government, Second Edition,* describes in admirable detail not only how our government became the organization it is today but how it actually functions.

Each branch of the government is broken down into its parts and players. The Houses of Congress, its committee system, and its relationship to the constituencies represented come to life. The authors explain the role and power of the Presidency and the executive branch in general, with an exhaustive description of its cabinet and other agencies. Finally, the role of the judicial branch, so often shrouded in the complex nuances of its legal traditions, is clearly explained as an equal and vital piece in this august mechanism of checks and balances designed by our forefathers.

In this post-September 11 age, when government must balance global concerns of security and peace with domestic pressures of the economy and environment, Americans expect an ever-increasing level of effectiveness from our representatives in Washington. The best way for us to truly participate in our democratic system is for every citizen to understand how our political system operates. This book affords us a powerful tool to acquire this vital knowledge with ease, and a bit of amusement as well.

—Harlan Ullman

Harlan Ullman is an advisor, author, and lecturer and Senior Advisor at the Center for Strategic and International Studies in Washington, DC. His latest book, *Finishing Business—Ten Steps to Defeat Global Terror*, was published in October by the Naval Institute Press. He is a columnist for the Washington *Times* and a contributor for Fox News, BBC, and Japanese and Australian television.

Introduction

From the start of a great experiment more than 200 years ago, American democracy has evolved into what might seem like a complicated web of divisive politics that does not really affect everyday life. But the arguments made by lawmakers today are often the very same as they were then. How much control does a government have over its people? When is the government responsible for providing for its people? What rights are inherent and what rights supersede protections for other citizens?

At times, it might seem like the laws discussed on the evening news have no direct impact on you. But practically every federal law does matter to many everyday occurrences. To understand their impact, the basic history and knowledge of how the laws came to be is critical.

There is one United States government, upon which all the other state and local governments are based in principle and in administration. All branches of government—federal, state, and local—make laws that affect your daily life. Simple, everyday things such as parking restrictions, education standards, banking procedures, and even liquor store hours of operation are controlled by laws. Without these laws and others, society would be chaotic, at best.

The American government is not complicated. When the framers wrote the Constitution, they set forward a document establishing a governmental structure that, despite 27 amendments, is still the most powerful document in the world. It guarantees the rights of all Americans and establishes for them due process under the law, as well as the ability to take part and make change.

If you do not like a certain law, you have the ability to amend it. Write to your representative or senator. Petition your local councilmember and call your governor. When the American public—or any society, for that matter—becomes apathetic, everyone in the society loses out. Furthermore, the ultimate control of the many can be dictated by the few when too few citizens participate in their political society.

The Complete Idiot's Guide to American Government, Second Edition, is by no means the final word on the way American government is run. What it does tell you, though, is how American government affects your life and your children's lives, and what you can do to make a difference in the political process. It highlights the importance of all the federal, state, and local jurisdictions and explains their significance in a twenty-first-century world.

The Complete Idiot's Guide to American Government, Second Edition, is organized into six parts.

Part 1, "Building a Government," goes back to the beginnings of democracy and details how the seminal documents that define and govern the nation were created.

Part 2, "The Buck Stops Here," discusses the executive branch of the federal government and the roles played by the president, the vice president, and the cabinet.

Part 3, "Checks and Balances," details the legislative branch of the federal government and gives an insider's look at how laws are made.

Part 4, "An Even Higher Authority," discusses the judicial branch of the federal government and how cases make it to the Supreme Court, and details some of the most important legal precedents set by the justices who have sat there.

Part 5, "Follow the Money," charts the federal budget process and details how money is raised and spent by political candidates.

Part 6, "State and Local Government," delves into the similarities and differences between the federal government and these levels, and discusses the rights and privileges given to all U.S. citizens.

In the back of the book are appendixes containing the terms used in this book, suggestions for further reading, charts showing the branches of the federal government, and a recap of the 2004 elections.

In addition to the main narrative of *The Complete Idiot's Guide to American Government, Second Edition*, you'll find other types of useful information. Here's how to recognize these features:

On the Record

Quotes by American leaders about American government.

We Hold These Truths

Facts, trivia, and information about American government.

Inside the Beltway

Definitions of terms related to American government. (Italicized words in the text appear in bold here.)

Acknowledgments

We extend our sincerest thanks to Dr. Richard Grace, Dr. Lawrence McAndrews, and John Sherry for lending us their expertise and reading many of our first drafts. A sincere thanks is overdue to Michael Funk. We would also like to thank Sonia Weiss; without her patience, understanding, and guidance, this book never would have been possible.

Special Thanks to the Technical Reviewer

The Complete Idiot's Guide to American Government, Second Edition, was reviewed by an expert who double-checked the accuracy of what you'll learn here, to help us ensure that this book gives you everything you need to know about American government. Special thanks are extended to Ken Uva.

Trademarks

All terms mentioned in this book that are known to be or are suspected of being trademarks or service marks have been appropriately capitalized. Alpha Books and Penguin Group (USA) Inc. cannot attest to the accuracy of this information. Use of a term in this book should not be regarded as affecting the validity of any trademark or service mark.

Part 1

Building a Government

Guided by a belief that they could build a better government than the one they left behind, colonists who came to America were intent on protecting basic rights, such as freedom of religion and freedom of speech. Today, we take such freedoms very much for granted, but in the seventeenth and eighteenth centuries, giving ordinary individuals such power over their lives was a revolutionary idea.

Creating a democracy, however, didn't happen overnight. The process was long and laborious, fraught with conflict, and marked by clashes between various factions with differing agendas. When all was said and done, however, the result was a strong central government that serves as an example for the rest of the world.

Putting It in Writing

In This Chapter

- Laying the groundwork for democracy
- Saying good-bye to royal rulers
- Writing new laws for a new land
- Federalists versus Anti-Federalists

In modern times, the United States has been the one and only super-power, with a strong central government serving as a model of democracy for the rest of the world. Ever wonder how this came to pass?

The United States Constitution, ratified in 1789, is the oldest written constitution still in use, and without it the American government would be powerless. Getting to this point, however, was the result of tedious negotiations and power struggles. The road to freedom was long and began in the thirteenth century. But as the adage says, you have to crawl before you walk, and the process to outright democracy and freedom took many baby steps.

The Great Charter

The British laid the groundwork for American democracy and individual freedoms nearly 800 years ago with the Magna Carta, also known as the Great Charter. It became a source of great inspiration to the American colonists five centuries later, but in its infancy it seemed almost irrelevant because the king who signed it into law in 1215 virtually ignored it.

King John, poor and unpopular as a result of military defeat at the hands of the French, attempted to levy a *scutage* on the barons who had not joined in his campaign against the French. The barons protested and sides were drawn. While the king had far more resources than the barons did, they unexpectedly captured London, and with that John had to listen to them.

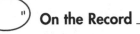

On the Record

The Magna Carta is a "shameful and demeaning agreement [that was] forced upon the king by violence and fear."

—Pope Innocent II, *The Magna Carta and Its American Legacy.* The National Archives and Records Administration, 1996.

Inside the Beltway

Dating back to feudal law, a **scutage** is a fee paid in lieu of military service.

What the barons wanted was simple: traditional rights to be recognized, written down, and confirmed by the Royal seal, and sent to be read to all the freemen in the counties in England. What they got was a different thing altogether. Instead of granting universal protection of the ancient liberties to freemen, the Magna Carta was seen as a document that granted protection to the rights and property of the few powerful families living in England. Its primary purpose was to call for majority rule and recognize the rights of the masses as opposed to the few. It included an enforcement council or parlemenz.

In September 1215, a mere four months after signing the document, which was first known as the Article of the Barons, King John asked Pope Innocent II to void it, saying that it had been forced on the king by violence and fear.

A year later, in the midst of civil war, King John died and his nine-year-old son was crowned King Henry III. With the nobles restless, the king's regents reissued the charter. It would be revised and reissued again several times, with the final version coming in 1225. But this final version omitted one of the most important aspects of the original document, the need for an advisory council. This removed one of the important gains the nobles had made. While the document and the idea behind it are important in the view of history, the Magna Carta was virtually irrelevant in its own time.

We Hold These Truths
Each time a revision was made to the Magna Carta or a copy was sent out to a county, a brand new copy was created. Of the numerous copies that were made, 17 have survived. Billionaire businessman, founder of the Reform Party, and two-time presidential candidate H. Ross Perot owns one of them, which is on permanent loan to the National Archives.

Over the next 400 years, the Magna Carta was relegated to obscurity until Sir Edward Coke, the attorney general for Queen Elizabeth I, resurrected it in an effort to thwart the power of the rival Stuart kings in Scotland. Coke said even the monarchy must obey common law. It was Coke's interpretation that helped the colonists to start demanding rights and privileges for themselves, and helped to start the ball rolling toward independence—and ultimately to the written Constitution that America has today.

On the Record

"In the name of God, Amen. We whose names are underwritten, the loyal subjects of our dread sovereign Lord King James, by the grace of God, of Great Britain, France, and Ireland ... do by these presents solemnly and mutually in the presence of God and of one another, covenant and combine ourselves together into a civil body politic for our better ordering ..."
—The Mayflower Compact, 1620

Bringing Self-Government to America

Settlers to the New World began coming to America on a regular basis in the early seventeenth century. Among them were the Pilgrims, who fled England in 1620 in hopes of finding religious freedom and tolerance in the new land.

The Pilgrims wanted to protect the rights of all the men who came to America (women did not receive full rights, including the right to vote, until the Nineteenth Amendment was ratified in 1920). These rights included religious freedom and rested on the consent of the governed. To this end, 41 members of their contingent wrote and signed the Mayflower Compact, the first written agreement for self-government in America. They agreed to obey the officers they would elect and the laws these officers might pass.

Inside the Beltway

A **charter** is a formal written statement describing the rights and responsibilities of a territory or a state and its citizens.

Over the next 150 years, the various colonies began establishing different rules, depending on the status of their *charters*. For the most part, these charters included some variation of free elections, no taxation without representation, the right to trial by jury, as well as other things.

Saying Good-Bye to Royal Control

In the eighteenth century, relations between the colonies and Great Britain began deteriorating at a fast pace. To punish the colonists for a wide variety of defiances, including not paying taxes and hosting the Boston Tea Party, the British Parliament passed the Coercive Acts of 1774. Called the Intolerable Acts by the colonists, they restricted the rights of colonists in Massachusetts to hold town meetings, among other things, and required all colonists to provide food and housing to British soldiers living in the colonies.

Tired of having to bend to rules and regulations passed by a government in which they had no representation, the colonists decided to take things into their own hands and convened the First Continental Congress in September 1774 in Philadelphia. Delegates to the congress, including representatives from all of the colonies except Georgia, decided to take several actions, including a boycott of British goods. They also drafted a declaration to King George III and the English Parliament outlining the position of the congress. This work is known as the Declaration of Rights and Grievances.

Declaring Rights

Among other things, the Declaration of Rights and Grievances said that the foundation of English citizenry is the people's right to participate in their legislative council. Since the English colonists were not represented—and couldn't properly be represented in the British Parliament—they were entitled to free and exclusive power of legislation in their provincial legislatures. The Declaration went on to say the Intolerable Acts were null and void in the colonies, and until the colonists received representation in the Parliament, all laws passed on their behalf would not be recognized.

On the Record

"That our ancestors, who first settled these colonies, were at the time of their emigration from the mother country, entitled to all the rights, liberties, and immunities of free and natural born subjects within the realm of England.

That by such emigration they by no means forfeited, surrendered, or lost any of those rights, but that they were, and their descendants now are entitled to the exercise and enjoyment of all such of them, as their local and other circumstances enable them to exercise and enjoy ...."

—The section of the Declaration of Rights and Grievances detailing the rights of British subjects

Before leaving Philadelphia, the delegates agreed to meet again the following spring to discuss new developments and reassess the situation.

Naturally, the British government and the monarchy didn't like the colonists' action. They were concerned that the settlers in North America aimed to separate themselves from the mother country. If they succeeded, it would be a serious blow to England's reputation, not to mention a decrease in revenue due to taxes that would no longer be collected.

The delegates to the First Continental Congress met again in May 1775. This meeting came to serve as the first national government of the new United States of America. It met in one chamber and had both legislative and executive functions. During this convention, which lasted until the end of the Revolutionary War in 1781, delegates issued paper money, borrowed funds to finance the war, purchased supplies, and raised an army and a navy. George Washington of Virginia was named the first commander in chief of the colonial army.

Over the next year, tensions between England and the colonists accelerated. At Lexington and Concord, British regulars and colonial militia fired at each other. Two months later, British troops attacked colonists at Breed's Hill (in reports, however it was misidentified as Bunker Hill), with both sides suffering heavy casualties.

King George III, now furious, sent more troops across the Atlantic, including 10,000 German soldiers he hired to quash the Americans.

War Time

Until the spring of 1776, most colonists thought they were fighting unjust laws, not fighting for independence. Most were reluctant to attempt a final break with England. If they lost, they could be tried for treason.

By June 1776, the colonists and the delegates at the convention had had enough of British oppression. Richard Henry Lee, a delegate from Virginia, introduced a resolution on behalf of the entire congress, stating that these "United States are and of right ought to be, free and independent states."

On the Record

"Let this happy day give birth to an American republic. Let her arise, not to devastate and to conquer, but to reestablish the reign of peace and of law. The eyes of Europe are fixed upon us: she demands of us a living example of freedom, that may exhibit a contrast in the felicity of the citizen to the ever-increasing tyranny which desolates her polluted shores. She invites us to prepare an asylum, where the unhappy may find solace, and the persecuted repose ...."
—Richard Henry Lee, in a speech before the Continental Congress, June 7, 1776

Three days later, Lee, a prominent Virginian whose family had lived in the colony for generations, was unexpectedly called home for a family emergency. The congress, so as not to waste time, postponed debate on his resolution but ordered a committee, headed by fellow Virginian Thomas Jefferson, to prepare a declaration in support of it.

The committee presented its draft to the congress on June 28. Lee was still detained in Virginia, so Jefferson stood in his place and oversaw the debate. The congress adopted Lee's proposal on July 2 and signed Jefferson's Declaration of Independence two days later.

For the delegates and for the new nation, the Declaration of Independence served three purposes:

◆ It established the principle of equality for all. The most moving lines start at the very beginning of the second paragraph: "We hold these truths to be self-evident, that all men are created equal." While at the time the document intended to mean only white men, these lines helped pave the way for freedom for minorities and women in the nineteenth and twentieth centuries.

◆ It enumerated the colonists' reasons for separating from England. The delegates called King George III an "absolute tyrant" and painted him as a horrible leader with no thought or care for the rights of the colonists. In addition, they outlined more than 25 major areas of disagreement, distrust, and objection to his behavior and expressed their need to separate from him.

◆ It served as a declaration of war. By pledging their loyalty to the new nation, the signers turned their backs on the British government.

Communication between the colonies was primitive, as was communication between the new nation and its old government. Formal reaction to the Declaration was limited. The British believed they would easily win and would have to deal with the traitors after the war. In the meantime, battles between the two nations began almost immediately. The outcome is well known, but it took five years to accomplish and many lives were lost.

Uniting the Colonies

The Declaration of Independence said what the colonists were willing to fight for, but it said nothing about how they would be administered. With the formal declaration made, the colonists now needed a document to unite the colonies under one central government.

The first attempt at forming a central government was a document called the Articles of Confederation. It was introduced within days of the Declaration of Independence, but the congress only approved it after 16 months of strenuous debate by the delegates. Some wanted a strong central government with an executive authority. Others, including Benjamin Franklin, wanted to make sure that the new American government was no stronger than the governments of the individual states.

Ultimately, the states' rights backers prevailed. They wanted to retain the power and influence of their own states, and they feared that too much government control or influence would be reminiscent of the monarchy in England.

When all was said and done, the Articles of Confederation both established the first government for the new nation and gave it its new name—the United States of America. Each state, however, kept its "sovereignty, freedom and independence" from the other states regarding powers not expressly given to the new federal government.

The new government would have only one branch, the legislative. This congress, with only one house, would be composed of delegates selected from their respective state legislatures. Each state could have anywhere from two to seven delegates, but when they came to vote, all must vote as one. The legislative branch would also administer executive and judicial functions. When the congress was in recess, a Committee of the States—a group of delegates selected from each state legislature— would be in charge.

We Hold These Truths

By any measure, the Articles of Confederation were weak and flawed. The nation was poor and needed resources, but the Articles didn't give the federal government the power to levy taxes. A two-thirds majority vote would be required to decide important matters. Amending the Articles would take unanimous support from all 13 states—not an easy task when the new states all had different agendas. Finally, the Articles didn't establish a national trade policy, so the federal government had no control or authority over trade and commerce between the states and each other, or between the states and foreign governments.

While the war was going on with England, another battle brewed between the states regarding ratification of the Articles of Confederation. Different states had different interests and continually squabbled with one another. Slavery was an issue; the northern states didn't want it, and southern states claimed they needed it. Agricultural states such as North Carolina and Massachusetts had different needs than more industrial states such as New York and New Jersey. Other states, such as Maryland and Virginia, were almost always in a battle over state boundaries.

On March 1, 1781, five years after it was introduced, the Articles of Confederation were finally ratified by all 13 states.

Four months later, American forces handed the British their final defeat at the Battle of Yorktown. While the formal treaty was not signed until 1783, British General Sir Charles Cornwallis surrendered his entire army on October 19, 1781. The Revolutionary War was over.

> ### We Hold These Truths
>
> Another roadblock to getting all the states to ratify the Articles was the question of western lands. Some states, such as New York and Virginia, had claims to lands outside their borders, including present-day Michigan and Tennessee. Smaller states, such as Maryland, did not have the land claims and worried that their influence would suffer as a result. Ultimately, the states gave up their land claims.

The Constitutional Convention

The Articles of Confederation was a good start to making sure that America stood tall and proud in the New World. But the document remained relatively weak in power and scope. For example, it lacked the power to regulate finances, so each state had its own currency. It also couldn't control trade, so the states set their own policies with foreign nations. And the document lacked the power to enforce treaties.

Representatives of five states—New York, New Jersey, Pennsylvania, Delaware, and Virginia—met in Annapolis, Maryland, on September 11, 1786, to amend the Articles of Confederation. However, they realized that substantive work couldn't take place with only five states represented, so they decided to suspend their efforts and reconvene the following summer.

The national convention was slated to start on May 14, 1787, in Philadelphia, where the Declaration of Independence had been signed 11 years earlier. Because of weather and difficult terrain, however, it took 11 days for a majority of the delegates, meaning 7 states, to arrive.

Representatives from 12 states (Rhode Island, or Rogue Island, as some delegates called it, refused to send a representative) eventually made it to Philadelphia to work on a new governing document for the country. After a long, hot summer, the supreme law of the land was born.

The delegates set strict rules for their work at the convention. Fearing discord among the states, they decided to keep their discussions private, thinking it best to present a united front by ironing out their differences behind closed doors.

> ### We Hold These Truths
>
> The secrecy surrounding the Constitutional Convention kept official records from being released until 1818, years after it was adjourned. James Madison, considered a chief architect of the final document, kept his own personal record of the events, which proved much more beneficial than the official record, but it wasn't released until his death in 1836.

Key Issues of Debate

The delegates had every right to be concerned as they engaged in many heated debates. One key issue regarded congressional representation. Two plans were presented: one from Virginia, a larger state, and the other from New Jersey, a smaller state. The plans were very different, and the debate over them raised tensions to high levels.

Virginia's plan, introduced by its governor, Edmund Randolph, and primarily written by James Madison, established the three branches of government that we have today. Its legislative branch was a Congress with two houses—a lower house elected by those qualified to vote and an upper house whose members would be nominated by the legislatures in each state and approved by the lower house.

Under Virginia's plan, the Congress would elect the chief executive, who would serve only one term and could be removed only in the event of an impeachment. The judicial branch would have a supreme court and lower courts. Judges would be appointed by the Congress and would serve for life.

On the Record

"I will never consent to the present system, and I shall make all the interest against it in the state which I represent that I can. Myself, or my state will never submit to tyranny or despotism."

—William Paterson, in a speech before the delegates at the Constitutional Convention, 1787

William Paterson, a fiery delegate from New Jersey, flatly refused to have any part of Virginia's plan, saying it benefited solely the larger states and that smaller states would eventually crumble as a result. He also strongly objected to the idea of one chief executive, fearing it would bring back the kind of tyranny that caused many to flee from England.

Paterson's plan, which became known as the New Jersey Plan, called for only one congressional house, with all members elected by the state legislatures, not by individuals. Each state would have only one vote, with no proportional representation.

Instead of a single chief executive, there would be at least two, who would be elected by the Congress and would serve one term. These executives could be removed if the majority of states dictated it.

Finally, a supreme court would be the only governing judicial body, with its members appointed for life by one of the chief executives.

Getting to Yes

Throughout the course of the summer, many compromises would be made between the delegates on a wide variety of issues. Of them, the Great Compromise, or the Sherman Compromise, named after Roger Sherman of Connecticut, proved to be the most vital. Without it, the larger and smaller states would never have come to agreement, and the convention would have folded.

Sherman, an attorney and judge, devised a compromise that took elements from both proposed plans. It called for two congressional houses—a lower house that would be proportional to the size and population of eligible voters, with each state having at least one representative, and an upper house composed of senators, with two from each state, no matter how large or small, thus giving each state equal representation.

On the Record

"We were on the verge of dissolution … scarce held together by the strength of a hair, though the public papers were announcing our extreme unanimity."

—Maryland delegate Luther Martin on the congress's mood before the Great Compromise, *Miracle at Philadelphia*, 1986

Other Points of Contention

The delegates faced other contentious issues during that long, hot summer. Those related to slavery were the most divisive. While many despised slavery and felt it inherently evil, they also believed their hands were tied. Many in the South did not want slavery discontinued, for fear that it would hurt their economy and make them weaker than their northern neighbors.

George Mason, an aristocratic plantation owner from Virginia, was an exception to the rule. He owned more than 200 slaves, and he wanted to see slavery abolished so he could free them.

Several northern delegates felt slavery needed to continue because their states had benefited from the trade of slaves on ships in their ports.

Without the support of the southern states, the emerging document had little chance of being effective. Recognizing this, delegates agreed to postpone the elimination of the slave trade and proposed a 21-year cool-down period, lasting until 1808, during which the slave trade could continue as it was. Many felt slavery was dying out anyway and would die on its own.

Another issue concerned how people of color would be counted when it came to their representation in Congress and taxation. Southern delegates wanted slaves counted for the purposes of representation but not taxation. Northerners, on the other hand, wanted slaves counted strictly for tax reasons and not for representation.

On the Record

"We ought to attend to the rights of every class of people … [and] provide no less carefully for the … happiness of the lowest than of the highest order of citizens."

—George Mason, *Miracle at Philadelphia*, 1986

We Hold These Truths

The delegates assumed that the popular vote of the country would be in line with the vote totals of the electoral college. For the most part, it has been. Of the more than 50 presidential elections since the electoral college was established, in only three of them—1824, 1876, and 2000—has the winner of the popular vote not won the electoral vote.

In the end, the delegates approved what is known as the three-fifths compromise, which would remain in place until after the Civil War. It stipulated that each slave would count as three-fifths of a person for purposes of both taxation and representation. If a community had 25,000 free citizens and 25,000 enslaved, according to the compromise, 40,000 would be the number used in assessing their taxes and their representation.

Selection of the chief executive, or president, also posed a difficult question for the delegates. Many feared giving too much control to the people, who were generally viewed as uneducated and uninformed, and wanted him selected by either the Congress or only a limited number of people. Other delegates wanted direct election of the president by the people and only the people.

After much debate, the delegates decided to compromise by creating a separate body of electors equal to the number of delegates each state had in Congress, plus two for the senators. The electors would be selected by the state legislatures, and these people—the electoral college—would ultimately vote for the president.

Taking It to the States

With all their differences ironed out, the delegates adjourned on September 17, 1787. Of the 55 delegates who attended the Constitutional Convention, 39 signed the new document, now known as the Constitution. The reasons for dissension varied. Some delegates feared giving too much power to the common man, while others did not like the omission of a Bill of Rights.

The next round involved presenting the Constitution to the states, which had to ratify it in order to make it law. Nine of the 13 states were needed for approval. Fearing that the states' legislatures would turn down the document because they didn't want to cede any more power to the federal government, the framers of the Constitution decided to call special conventions in each state to explain the Constitution and to have the conventions themselves, rather than the state legislatures, decide on ratification.

Federalists vs. Anti-Federalists

Opinions regarding the Constitution were widely divided. Some farmers in the west were afraid urban cities would get all the attention while they would be taxed through the roof. Then there were city dwellers who worried that the federal government would be too centralized and that the powers would be taken away from the states.

Those who supported the Constitution and the new framework it established came to be known as Federalists, meaning they supported a strong central government with shared powers between the states and the national government. Those who were opposed were known as Anti-Federalists.

The three main Federalists were Alexander Hamilton, James Madison, and John Jay. Together they wrote a series of anonymous essays about the Constitution that appeared in newspapers. Writing under the pseudonym Publius, in reference to Publius Valerius Publicola, a founder of the Roman Empire, their essays, today referred to as *The Federalist Papers*, or simply *The Federalist*, laid out the foundational principles of the Constitution—representation of the people in the government, separation of powers, checks and balances, and the inherent freedom of a nation's people—and are often cited in court cases, legal arguments, and presidential directives.

Meanwhile, the Anti-Federalists published their own series of essays to argue for a looser coalition of the states and a weaker national government. Led by some of the most prominent Americans who had fought against the British during the War for Independence—including

---

We Hold These Truths

Widely respected since its publication, *The Federalist* has been used by lawmakers, judges, and scholars to interpret the Constitution. The first 77 articles were published in newspapers, many in New York, in an effort to garner that state's crucial support. The complete set was published in 1788. Hamilton wrote the majority of the essays, with 51 total. Madison wrote 29, while Jay wrote only 5.

New York Supreme Court Justice Robert Yates, who signed his essays Brutus, and Richard Henry Lee of Virginia, who used the pen name The Federal Farmer—they took issue with the Federalists on many points.

Patrick Henry, the leading legislator from Virginia, feared the presidency would become nothing more than a tyrant's soapbox, where the executive would be beholden to no one other than himself. John Hancock, the man who so largely displayed his signature for the king to read when he signed the Declaration of Independence, agreed. Others felt that the provision for a vice president, outlined in the second article of the Constitution, was useless, unnecessary, or even scary.

The Federalists and Anti-Federalists disagreed on several other critical points, including what representation of the people in government meant. Anti-Federalists argued that representatives must be a true representation of the people—and only smaller governments could truly understand the desires of its people. They also said representatives would be too far physically removed to adequately represent the interest of their states. Laws would not be followed, the Anti-Federalists said, unless there was a military presence nearly everywhere.

Federalists were adamant, however, that representatives act on behalf of the people as well as have independent judgment. This way, the Federalists argued, the long-term national interest would be first served over immediate public sentiment. They also scoffed at the notion that force would be necessary because of the distance between representatives and their constituents, with Hamilton arguing that one central government would be better able to serve the people than several competing governments.

Anti-Federalists and Federalists also wrote about the threat of tyranny, or one power-hungry group ruling over the people unjustly. The Anti-Federalists were most concerned with those institutions that did not have any direct link to the people to be held accountable—such as the president and the Senate. The Federalists were concerned with a popular majority working in concert to override justice. But Madison explained that checks and balances of each branch of government on the other would alleviate the threat of that tyranny.

A final area of dispute the Anti-Federalists and Federalists wrote about was what, exactly, limited government meant. How would powers be limited between the states and the national government? Anti-Federalists argued that the national government should be more limited than state governments. But the Federalists said that the national government should have broad authority, with checks and balances to stop potential abuses of the powers.

The Anti-Federalists were also concerned that the Constitution created a centralized government at the expense of states' rights. While the states fought for independence together, they viewed each other as separate. Many feared too much control at the hands of the national government, which at that time was located in New York City.

The biggest problem that many seemed to have with the new Constitution was that it did not provide for a bill of rights, laws that were expressly granted and stated for all citizens in the United States. The public wanted these rights listed so that no one would question or dispute the fundamentals such as freedom of speech or religion. Many feared that if they were not written in stone, the government would start to control aspects of their daily lives. As a way to calm these fears, the framers agreed that the newly created congress would write a bill of rights, addressing such issues as freedom of religion, speech, and assembly and the right to bear arms, after the Constitution was ratified. (See Chapter 3 for more on how this document came about and what it contains.)

On the Record

"There will be no checks, no real balances in this government. What can avail your specious, imaginary balances, your rope dancing, chain rattling, ridiculous ideal checks and balances!"

—Patrick Henry, in a speech before the Virginia ratifying convention, June 5, 1788

Delaware was the first state to ratify the Constitution, doing so on December 7, 1787. New Jersey and Pennsylvania followed shortly afterward. By early June 1788, nine states had ratified the Constitution. But the critical states of New York and Virginia had not. Of the two, Virginia had the most spirited debates regarding ratification. Patrick Henry led the charge against it and had an answer for any question or counterpoint produced.

But on June 25, by a narrow 10-vote margin, the Virginia convention voted to approve the document. One month and one day later, by just a three-vote margin, New York, despite the efforts of upstate farmers fearing excessive taxation, approved the document as well. Rhode Island, which had not sent any delegates to the convention, became the last state to ratify the Constitution, approving it by a 34–32 vote in May 1790.

The Least You Need to Know

- The Constitution is the oldest written constitution still in use, and it is also one of the shortest, using approximately 6,700 words to establish the supreme law of the land.

- The Declaration of Independence served three purposes: It established a new theory of government, listed the reasons for separation from England, and declared war.

- While there were 13 states at the time of the Constitution's drafting, only 12 took part in its development because Rhode Island refused to send a delegate.

- It took four months to compile a document that a majority of the delegates could agree on, and it took another nine months to get the necessary number of state conventions to approve it.

2

A More Perfect Union

In This Chapter

- ◆ Learning from failure
- ◆ Balancing control
- ◆ Creating congressional authority
- ◆ Stipulating what a president can and can't do

For more than 200 years, the Constitution has survived as a model of limited government. It is the oldest written constitution of a nation in use in the world today. In this chapter, we take a closer look at the main body of the Constitution—the Articles—and discuss some of its more important points.

Success from Failure

As you read in Chapter 1, the Articles of Confederation represented the first step in putting together the foundational principles of the Constitution. While this document was relatively weak in power and scope, it served an important purpose. From its failures, the framers of the Constitution learned what worked and what didn't work.

On their second try, the framers got it right. They realized they needed to secure basic rights and specific freedoms, but to not be so specific as to overstate their general meaning.

Constitution by Committee

Ten days before the Constitution was signed, the members of the Second Constitutional Convention formed a Committee of Style and Arrangement to revise the articles that had been drafted and to put them into a presentable form. William Samuel Johnson, Alexander Hamilton, Gouverneur Morris, James Madison, and Rufus King were chosen for the committee.

We Hold These Truths

Of the five men responsible for the Committee of Style and Arrangement, only two—Madison and Hamilton—are well-known names. Who were the other men?

William Samuel Johnson, who chaired the committee, came to the convention as a delegate from Connecticut, despite having recently accepted the post of president of Columbia College in New York. He was well respected by all, and one contemporary described him as "the tout ensemble of a perfect man, in face, form and proportion."

Gouverneur Morris was not the friendliest of the delegates at the convention, yet he talked more at the convention than any other delegate. Morris believed that in order to write history one must be able to fill it with prose. One Constitutional observer noted that Morris believed it was better for the history writer to be familiar with the works of William Shakespeare than political theorists at the time.

Rufus King came to the convention with very low expectations. He was a congressman and believed that the Congress that the Articles had established was the proper forum for changing them—not a special convention. During the hot summer months, however, his opinion would change and he became one of the most adamant defenders of the Constitution.

Written and reworked by these five men, the Constitution was to be included with a letter for presentation to Congress. The men also condensed the work of the convention from 23 articles into 7. Morris, who had given more speeches at the Constitutional Convention than any other delegate, was credited with the majority of the actual rewriting and the style of the words the committee presented to the Convention four days after they first formed in September 1787.

The five committee members styled the preamble of the Constitution with little notion of the future significance of the words:

> We the People of the United States, in Order to form a more perfect Union, establish Justice, insure domestic Tranquility, provide for the common defence, promote the general Welfare, and secure the Blessings of Liberty to ourselves and our Posterity, do ordain and establish this Constitution for the United States of America.

A Framework for Democracy

For all the arguments throughout the long summer of 1787 that took place concerning it, the Constitution ended up emerging as a fairly brief seven-*article* document. It set up a three-tiered structure—the executive, legislative, and judicial branches—and outlined the powers and requirements of each. Its general framework is intended to serve as a guide for democracy, but it does not account for the minute details of running the government on a daily basis.

Keeping Control in Balance

The entire structure of the Constitution is based on a system of *checks and balances*—that is, each of the three branches of government has controls to prevent any one branch from holding too much power.

The system the framers set up requires all three branches to work together to achieve any goal—often a tough feat in government today. For example, the president can recommend legislation, but only Congress can make laws. The president can veto laws, but Congress can override the veto. The judicial branch has power over cases that arise from laws or executive orders. Congress can overturn Supreme Court decisions by amending the

Inside the Beltway

Articles are sections of a legal document that deal with particular points.

Checks and balances refers to branches of the government keeping watch over each other's powers.

On the Record

"[T]he great security against a gradual concentration of the several powers in the same department consists of giving those who administer each department the necessary constitutional means and personal motives to resist encroachments of the others."

—James Madison, "The Federalist No. 51"

Constitution. The president appoints heads of agencies and federal judges, but the Senate must confirm these appointments. The president can make treaties with foreign nations, but the Senate must approve them. Congress can impeach the president and federal judges.

Inside the Constitution

The founders knew they could not have possibly predicted everything that was needed to run a country. Therefore, they crafted a document that was comprehensive yet made allowances for future changes. The entire document of the Constitution, which in its current form consists of 7 articles and 27 amendments, can be read in a brief period of time. But interpretation of its meaning continues more than 200 years after its inception.

On the Record

"If men were angels, no government would be necessary. If angels were to govern men, neither external nor internal controls on government would be necessary. In framing a government which is to be administered by men over men, the great difficulty lies in this: you must first enable the government to control the governed; and in the next place, oblige it to control itself."

—James Madison, "The Federalist No. 51"

You'll find a discussion of how the Constitution has been changed since its drafting in Chapter 3.

Article 1: Creating Congress

All legislative Powers herein granted shall be vested in a Congress of the United States, which shall consist of a Senate and a House of Representatives.

In the first—and longest—article of the Constitution, the legislative branch, its powers, and the requirements of its members are designated. Learning from their experiences with the Articles of Confederation, the framers made sure the legislative governing body of America had the ability to enforce the laws it made. Creating a strong federal government among the states did this.

This article also allowed for the taxation of U.S. citizens so that the federal government would have money to fulfill its obligations to the states. The first article authorized Congress to create a military, declare war, establish a court system, and create money for the states.

Here, the Constitution also places requirements on members of Congress, such as the required age to serve and how long members must have been citizens, among others. A census to be conducted every 10 years to ensure members of Congress are representing the required number of constituents is also detailed here.

The powers of impeachment are also granted in the first article. Only the Senate can try all impeachments and, to be convicted, two thirds of the members must vote to impeach. While not explicitly stated in the first article, the president, vice president, cabinet members, and federal judges are all subject to impeachment.

Members of Congress themselves are exempt from impeachment, but they may be *censured* or removed from office. The vice president presides over all impeachment trials in the Senate, except for the impeachment trial of a president, in which case the Chief Justice of the Supreme Court presides.

Inside the Beltway

Censure is expressing official disapproval or condemnation of somebody or something, usually by vote.

Because the Senate is a continuing body, specific requirements in the article detail how a vacant seat in the Senate must be filled. One clause of the first article gives governors of states the authority to fill a congressional vacancy until "the next meeting of the legislature, which shall then fill such vacancies." Also known as a writ of election, it allowed governors to fill the vacant seat as well as call a special election to fill the vacancy. However, as you'll read in Chapter 3, this article was changed by the Seventeenth Amendment.

Specific powers that Congress holds are also listed in the first article, including the right to collect taxes and tariffs, borrow money from itself, regulate commerce, coin money, regulate immigration, investigate counterfeit, establish post offices and roads, promote sciences and "useful arts," grant inventors exclusive rights to their ideas, create courts lower than the Supreme Court, and protect U.S. ships and citizens when they are not in the country. The right to declare war, raise and support armies, maintain a navy, regulate those armed forces, call up a "militia"—now known as the National Guard—to execute laws, aid states in supporting their militia, and have control over the District of Columbia are all included in these explicit powers.

Perhaps most significant, the first article of the Constitution contains the "elastic clause," which says that Congress can "make all laws which shall be necessary and proper for carrying into execution the foregoing powers, and all other powers vested by this Constitution in the Government of the United States, or in any Department or Officer thereof." This clause of the Constitution authorizes the use of *implied powers* and has often been the basis for controversy. Arguments have often been made based on this clause to stretch the document's meaning from those powers that are specifically noted.

Inside the Beltway

Implied powers are powers assumed by Congress under the Constitution even though the document does not explicitly state them.

James Madison had earlier noted the need for such powers under the Constitution in "The Federalist No. 44" when he wrote, "Without the substance of this power, the whole Constitution would be a dead letter." However, the key interpretation of the elastic clause was determined by the Supreme Court case *McCulloch v. Maryland* in 1819, in which Chief Justice John Marshall deemed "necessary and proper" as the key terms of the clause.

In 1816, Congress passed a law to create the Second Bank of the United States under the assumption of implied powers, even though such a bank was not stated explicitly in the Constitution. The bank was the only one in Maryland not chartered by the state and was very unpopular. The state placed a high tax on any bank that it didn't charter, a tax that David McCulloch, a clerk at the national bank, refused to pay. The state sued McCulloch and won, but the U.S. Supreme Court overturned the ruling. The court was unanimous in its ruling of *McCulloch v. Maryland* that Congress could indeed create a national bank. Marshall's broad interpretation explained the precedent this way: "Let the end be legitimate, let it be within the scope of the Constitution, and all means which are appropriate, which are plainly adapted to that end, which are not prohibited, but consist with the letter and spirit of the Constitution, are constitutional."

Article 2: Ordering the Executive

The executive Power shall be vested in a President of the United States of America.

The second article of the Constitution creates the executive branch of the government and explains the powers of the president. It also contains the specific requirements for the president's election.

Article 2 has always been particularly controversial, though, for what it doesn't explicitly state. For example, it does not say that the president alone can create his own budget or exclusively choose his cabinet officials. It also does not grant the president the power to dismiss government officials. But a president does have the power, according to this article, to fill a vacancy when Congress is not in session (you'll read more about this in Chapter 10).

This article also allows presidents to make treaties with foreign nations, with the advice and consent of the Senate. The second article requires the president to take an oath of office, which must be administered by the Chief Justice of the Supreme Court.

Because the first article grants Congress the right to create government agencies through the passage of laws, the legislative and executive branches have perpetually clashed over the issue. Congress also holds the power to fund all government agencies—another dilution of presidential power.

In the past 100 years, however, the interpretation of the powers granted to the president has grown substantially. For example, presidents have submitted their annual budget recommendations to Congress for approval since 1921. Presidents were granted authority in 1926 to remove department heads, and Congress later allowed the president to reorganize departments with its consent.

Presidential duties are also outlined in the second article. They include …

♦ The delivery of information to Congress.

♦ The ability to convene both houses on "extraordinary occasions."

♦ The duty of receiving ambassadors from other countries.

♦ Acting as commander in chief of the armed forces.

♦ Oversight of making sure that all laws are carried out.

Although it's not expressly mentioned in the Constitution, the practice of *executive privilege* developed as a result of the continuing conflict

Inside the Beltway

Executive privilege is the practice of withholding presidential information from Congress or other entities. Although it dates back to the earliest days of the presidency, the term was first used during the Eisenhower administration when officials refused to turn over military personnel records to the Senate Government Operations during the heated communism hearings held by Wisconsin Sen. Joe McCarthy.

between the Congress and the presidency, which began almost immediately after the Constitution was ratified.

Presidents from Washington through Bush have argued that the separation-of-powers provision implies that the executive branch is separate from the legislative and judicial branches, and therefore enjoys certain privileges the other branches do not.

The main issue surrounding executive privilege is whether or not documents, correspondence, transcripts—just about anything, really—obtained or developed through the White House is open to the public. For example, presidents have long argued that their advisors need to be assured their remarks are confidential so that they can speak in a free manner, as opposed to having to tailor their remarks and advice, thinking of how they might play out on the evening news.

And not surprisingly, presidents often attempt to claim executive privilege because speaking or releasing information would help their political enemies.

Andrew Jackson withheld information from the Senate for records on his fight with the Bank of the United States, saying, "I have yet to learn under what constitutional authority that branch of the legislature has to require of me an account of any communication."

Richard Nixon invoked executive privilege in 1974 to try to keep White House tape recordings that contained information about the break-in at the Watergate secret. But Nixon lost his fight in the Supreme Court—and resigned his presidency 17 days after the high court ruled the tapes must be released.

The second article also creates the electoral college, or presidential electors who equal the number of representatives and senators of a state. When people vote in a presidential election, they aren't voting directly for the president but instead are voting for electors from their states. Still, nearly every state has a system by which the candidate who wins the popular vote wins all the state's electoral votes.

How electors are chosen for the electoral college is determined by each state. Today, every state except Maine and Nebraska has a "winner take all" system, which means that the candidate who receives the most popular votes in a state receives the votes of all the electors. The Maine and Nebraska systems require a plurality (a candidate must have the most votes but does not have to win a majority) in each congressional district, and its electoral votes can then be split based on district totals.

Votes from the electoral college are counted by a joint session of Congress in January after a presidential election. If neither candidate receives a majority of the electoral college, the House has the power to decide the presidency. Each state has one vote in such cases.

The concept continues to be relatively misunderstood by the American people. But the 2000 election provided a crash course in the electoral college for many, when on election night they learned that then-Vice President Al Gore had won the popular vote, but then-Texas Gov. George W. Bush was leading (and eventually won) the electoral college.

> **We Hold These Truths**
>
> In his second term beginning in 1936, President Franklin Delano Roosevelt attempted to "pack" the Supreme Court by proposing the idea that he should be allowed to add one justice for every one currently serving over 70 years old. If Congress had not objected in 1937, Roosevelt would have been able to add six new justices.

> **We Hold These Truths**
>
> Because the outgoing vice president (who also serves as the president of the Senate) is required to count the electoral college ballots during the joint session and announce the winner, Al Gore was forced to announce his opponent, George W. Bush, as the next president in the tightly contested 2000 election. The same thing happened to Richard Nixon in 1960 when he lost to John F. Kennedy, and to Hubert Humphrey, who lost to Nixon in 1968.

Article 3: You Take the High Court, I'll Take the Low Court

The judicial Power of the United States, shall be vested in one supreme Court, and in such inferior Courts as the Congress may from time to time ordain and establish.

Article 3 establishes the judicial branch of government through the establishment of the nation's highest court and a lower federal court system.

Cases brought before the Supreme Court are decided upon the basis of what has become known as the "supreme law," or the law according to the Constitution. Through precedent, under the three-part government structure, the judiciary branch has the final say on whether laws made by the legislative branch and enacted

Inside the Beltway

Judicial review gives the court system the power to declare a law unconstitutional.

Federalism is the ability for both state and federal governments to devise their own laws.

On the Record

"I have sought for a middle ground which may at once support a due supremacy of national authority, and not exclude [the states]."

—James Madison, in a letter to George Washington, April 16, 1787

by the executive branch are constitutional. Judicial power must be based on actual cases brought before the courts, not hypothetical ones.

Although the Constitution does not state this in its third article, the Supreme Court consists of nine justices, who are nominated by the president and confirmed by the Senate. Appointments must be made with the advice and consent of the Senate, as listed under Article 2.

The Constitution stipulates that cases brought before the Supreme Court must fall into one of two categories. First, the case may be a dispute between the United States and an opposing party, between a state and the federal government, or between two states. The other option is if the dispute involves an interpretation of the Constitution, federal statutes, or treaties.

The only crime defined explicitly in the Constitution is treason, which is defined as a citizen having waged war against the United States or having given "aid and comfort" to its enemies. A conviction of treason must be made from the testimony of two witnesses to a single act, unless the person confesses to treason.

Although not stated explicitly in the Constitution, the concept of *judicial review* has evolved as the most significant power of the judiciary branch. Judicial review often involves some of the most controversial issues the Supreme Court has ever had to address, including abortion rights, affirmative action, civil rights, and religious freedom (more about this in Chapter 17).

Article 4: States' Rights vs. the Fed's Rights

Full Faith and Credit shall be given in each State to the public Acts, Record and judicial Proceedings of every other State.

The fourth article of the Constitution came as a relief to many of the Convention's signers, who worried considerably over the federal government's power over the individual states. Here, the Constitution defined *federalism*, or the ability for both the state and federal governments to devise their own laws. The federal government is granted certain powers, such as the ability to declare war. The state governments also are granted particular powers, such as the ability to conduct local elections. Both branches share other powers, such as the right to tax citizens.

Even though the federal government operates under limited powers, as set up by the Constitution, it has an upper hand over the states: No law created by the states can contradict a federal law. Still, because the authors of the Constitution did not explicitly detail this relationship, the rights of the federal government and those of the states have long been debated.

Laws created by both the states and the federal government are subject to the supreme law of the land—the Constitution. A state can, however, impose certain restrictions on citizens of other states, such as residency requirements to vote.

The final three articles of the Constitution — all brief articles with no separated sections— dealt with how the document could be changed and what provisions were necessary for it to be approved.

> **We Hold These Truths**
>
> According to Article 5, there's another way the Constitution can be amended, although it has never been used. If the legislatures of two thirds of the states request one, a constitutional convention can be convened to change the document. Because there are no limits on subjects addressed at such a constitutional convention, many have advised against them.

Article 5: Making Changes

In Article 5, the Constitution deems that two thirds of the Senate and the House must approve an amendment to the Constitution. Three fourths of all states' legislatures must then ratify an amendment for it to be adopted.

Two areas of the Constitution can't be amended, according to this article. The first, now obsolete, restricted any changes made before 1808 on two sections of the first article that deal with taxing individuals. The second, still guaranteed today, is that no state can be denied equal representation in the Senate.

Article 6: The Law That Reigns Supreme

Article 6 established the Constitution as the supreme law of the land and states that all state and federal officials must abide by it, either by oath or affirmation. Referred to as the supremacy clause, it bound state judges to the supreme law even if state laws or constitutions conflicted with it.

This article also upheld the validity of all debts and engagements held by any of the states before the adoption of the Constitution.

Article 7: Getting the States' Approval

Finally, the seventh article of the Constitution required that 9 of the then 13 states must approve the Constitution for it to be ratified. The framers never expected to achieve signatures from 13 states—Rhode Island hadn't even sent delegates to the Constitutional Convention!

The Least You Need to Know

- ◆ The Constitution of the United States has served as a model of limited government for more than 200 years and is the oldest written constitution in use today.

- ◆ The Articles of Confederation, while weak and ineffective, played an important step in the Constitution's development.

- ◆ The Constitution, in its current form, consists of 7 articles and 27 amendments. Interpretation of its meaning continues to this day.

- ◆ The first three articles of the Constitution give the parameters for establishing the three branches of the U.S. government—the legislative, executive, and judicial branches. The fourth governs matters pertaining to the states. The last three articles stipulate how the Constitution can be amended and what it would take to put the document into effect.

The Bill of Rights

In This Chapter

- ◆ How the Constitution can be changed
- ◆ Ensuring basic rights
- ◆ Protecting basic freedoms
- ◆ Reserving states' rights

The framers of the nation understood this: They could not predict what they did not know. The future of the fledgling country was unclear, but what *was* clear was that it would change. The document structuring the nation would need to be flexible enough to change with it throughout time. As Alexander Hamilton wrote in "The Federalist No. 49," "There is certainly great force in this reasoning, and it must be allowed to prove that a constitutional road to the decision of the people ought to be marked out and kept open, for certain great and extraordinary occasions."

The framers included Article 5 of the Constitution to allow for changes to the document governing the land. For all the changes that have occurred in the United States since its founding, it is remarkable that the governing law of the land is relatively unchanged today. In fact, of the more than 10,000 amendments that have been proposed since 1789, only 27 have been added.

In this chapter, we look at the first 10 amendments, which were added during the arduous process of ratifying the Constitution.

Protecting the People's Rights

Known today as the *Bill of Rights*, this document often is confused with the Constitution.

George Washington, too, was a strong supporter of allowing future generations to have the power to amend the Constitution. In a letter written in 1787 to his nephew, Bushrod Washington, he wrote:

> And as there is a Constitutional door open for it, I think the people (for it is with them to judge) can, as they will have the aid of experience on their side, decide with as much propriety on the alterations and amendments which shall be found necessary, as ourselves; for I do not conceive that we are more inspired—have more wisdom—or possess more virtue than those who will come after us.

Inside the Beltway

A **bill of rights** generally is defined as a set of agreed-upon freedoms granted to a people who are governed—a set of rights that can never then be taken away by that government.

We Hold These Truths

One of the two amendments rejected by the state legislatures said there would be one member of Congress per 50,000 people, which would have resulted in over 5,000 House members today.

The second doomed amendment would have stopped, until after an election, salary raises that members of Congress gave themselves.

Most of the framers felt the Constitution generally stood on its own. Some had even suggested that a bill of rights was too much like the rules a king granted to his people. Still, Thomas Jefferson, upon receiving the completed Constitution while serving as an ambassador in France, lamented that it did not have a bill of rights. In letters to James Madison, Jefferson worried that without a bill of rights, freedoms of the people could be overrun by the strong central government.

This was also a common complaint from many of the states as they considered whether to ratify the constitution, several of which already had their own bills of rights. During the debate over ratification, Anti-Federalists were strongly in favor of a bill of rights because they feared strong national control. In an Anti-Federalist essay, Brutus wrote, "There are certain things which rulers should be absolutely prohibited from doing, because if they should do them, they would work an injury, not a benefit to the people."

Madison, at the convening of the first Congress, promptly took up the issue. Twelve amendments were written and adopted by Congress in 1789. The states ratified 10 of them in 1791.

In his first inaugural address to the nation in April 1789, George Washington issued his strong support for a bill of rights but cautioned the people on an excess use of the ability to amend the Constitution.

After warning against making changes that might endanger the benefits of a united and effective government, Washington encouraged the citizenry to be patient and "await the future lessons of experience." He said he was confident that "a reverence for the characteristic rights of freemen and a regard for the public harmony will sufficiently influence your deliberations ...."

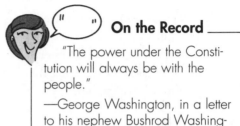

On the Record

"The power under the Constitution will always be with the people."

—George Washington, in a letter to his nephew Bushrod Washington, November 10, 1787

Ch-ch-ch-ch-changes

As you read in Chapter 2, there are two ways to change the Constitution, although only one has been used.

The first way, which has never been used, allows for two thirds of the states to call for a national constitutional convention. The second way is for two thirds of Congress and three fourths of the states to approve the change.

The first method was created to protect against a situation in which Congress itself was reluctant to change problems with its own laws. The ratification of the Seventeenth Amendment—which called for the direct election of senators—is the closest this process has ever come to being used.

A constitutional convention was nearly called because the Senate refused to pass the measure. But a strong *grass-roots* movement in the states

Inside the Beltway

Grass roots refers to the power of ordinary people to influence their political leaders. Grass-roots campaigns are often used today to lobby members of Congress on a particular issue through mail, e-mail, fax, and phone-call campaigns.

finally resonated with the Senate, and it passed the measure on to the states for ratification in 1912, avoiding a constitutional convention.

Although it might sound fairly simple, the process of passing amendments is truly a difficult task. For example, the Nineteenth Amendment, which grants the right to vote to women, was introduced in Congress 118 times from 1866 until its passage in 1920.

Inside the Bill of Rights

As previously mentioned, the first set of changes to the Constitution resulted in the document that we know as the Bill of Rights. Consisting of 10 amendments, it protects our civil rights and liberties from intrusion by the government and other citizens. The framers followed the same format as the Constitution and referred to the amendments as articles.

First Amendment: Ensuring Civil Liberties

Congress shall make no law respecting an establishment of religion; or prohibiting the free exercise thereof; or abridging the freedom of speech, or of the press; or the right of the people peaceably to assemble, and to petition the Government for a redress of grievances.

The First Amendment sets up the foundation of central civil liberties to Americans and guarantees freedom of speech, freedom of the press, freedom of religion, and the right to peaceable assembly. It also says that Congress can pass no laws that would restrict those freedoms. People are also granted the right to "petition the government for a redress of grievances"—in other words, to complain about whatever they choose to any government official.

As mentioned previously, part of the success of the Constitution and its amendments is their very brevity. But within the framework of the limited government, the interpretation of those concise amendments can then become the basis for how they are carried out. Most of the interpretation has come from court rulings.

While the First Amendment is only one sentence long, the resulting interpretation of it in court cases and scholarly interpretations could fill room upon room with case law. But these rights—freedom of speech, religion, assembly, and the press—often come into conflict with other rights expressed elsewhere in the Constitution or its amendments. The same can be said for many amendments, but the Bill of Rights, in particular, has been the basis for necessary and ongoing interpretation.

The notion of balancing any of the freedoms guaranteed by the First Amendment with those that inherently would limit them, such as national security and freedom of the press, has led to wide and varying interpretations. Supreme Court Justice Hugo Black, who was on the high court from 1937 until he retired in 1971, believed the phrase "no law" meant exactly that—no law could be passed limiting those freedoms in the First Amendment. But Supreme Court Justice Felix Frankfurter, who was a justice from 1939 until he retired in 1962, believed that the rights guaranteed by the First Amendment are no more valuable than any other freedoms and require a careful balance—a notion that has come to be known as the *balancing doctrine*.

Inside the Beltway

The **balancing doctrine** is the belief that the rights guaranteed by the First Amendment are no more valuable than other freedoms.

Freedom of Speech

One of many cases that clearly illustrate this division between the right to free speech and the need to protect the nation came before the Supreme Court in 1919. During World War I, Congress passed what was known as the Espionage Act, a law that prosecuted people who opposed actions of the federal government. Charles Schenck was convicted under the Espionage Act for mailing materials to draftees during the war that urged them to avoid military service.

In *Schenck v. United States*, the court upheld the conviction and said that even though in "normal times" Schenck's actions would have been protected by the First Amendment, the war was clearly a different situation. His words created a "clear and present danger" in the manner in which they were used. However, the interpretation of clear and present danger has continued until today (see Chapter 17 for more on this).

Today, freedom-of-speech issues are continually being interpreted in the area of mass communications, including the Internet and e-mail. For example, the 1997 Supreme Court decision *Reno v. American Civil Liberties Union* struck down an earlier law that would have prohibited sending "indecent" messages via e-mail or on the Internet.

The ever-present conflict between freedom of the press and national security is perhaps best exemplified in *The New York Times'* printing of the Pentagon Papers after a Department of Defense employee, Daniel Ellsberg, quit his job because he opposed U.S. involvement in the Vietnam War. In 1971, Ellsberg gave *The New York Times* top-secret documents that detailed the United States' role in the war, including deception government officials had been involved in.

Seeking to stop *The New York Times* from publishing the controversial papers, the Nixon administration secured a temporary injunction against the publication, arguing that the printing would endanger national security. But the Supreme Court ruled in favor of *The New York Times* and printing was allowed to continue. The court's decision was based on a precedent, set in another case—*Near v. Minnesota* in 1931—that an injunction to prevent the publication of information is unconstitutional.

Freedom of Assembly

Another First Amendment right—the right to freedom of peaceable assembly—often clashes with established laws. The Fourteenth Amendment, which guarantees due process under state laws in addition to the due process outlined in the Fifth Amendment, is often invoked to protect the right of citizens to organize, even if they are breaking an existing law.

During the Vietnam War, several students in Iowa wore black armbands adorned with a peace symbol to their high school, even though the school had said such demonstrations could not occur. The three students were suspended but sued the school in federal court. In ruling on the case, *Tinker v. Des Moines Independent Community School District*, the court found that the school district had violated the students' First Amendment and Fourteenth Amendment rights based on freedom of speech and due process. The court ruled in favor of the students, saying, "They are possessed of fundamental rights which the State must respect, just as they themselves must respect their obligations to the State." Still, while the court has consistently ruled in favor of "peaceable assembly," it is necessary to note that demonstrators or anyone invoking their right to assemble do not have free reign over any given situation and these people must not infringe on the rights of those who do not agree with them.

Another form of usually "peaceable assembly" has occurred frequently in recent years, with demonstrators surrounding world trade meetings to protest the meeting's purpose. This form of assembly is known as civil disobedience, a deliberate breaking of laws that protesters believe to be unjust.

Freedom of Religion

The First Amendment's religious freedom has undergone frequent interpretation as well. An ongoing debate has been where exactly the framers intended to draw the line between the separation of church and state. In what is known as the establishment clause, Supreme Court Justice Hugo Black clearly defined that the federal government cannot create a church or national religion and cannot force a citizen to attend church or believe a certain faith.

Religious freedom has become problematic in two ongoing debates: religious expression in public schools and federal or state funding to parochial schools. Can the government fund parochial schools for nonreligious materials and supplies? Can it help fund teachers' salaries in religious schools? The Supreme Court has ruled "no" on those two questions, but it has allowed funding to bus students to religious schools on the grounds that it adds to the overall well-being of the student, without expressing support for the religion being taught at the school. For the most part, prayer in public schools has been ruled as a violation of the separation between church and state. The court has ruled that religion can be taught in public schools, as long as it expresses a neutral position on the teachings.

The exact meaning of "free exercise" of religion has been interpreted as the free exercise clause. While a belief of faith has always been protected by the First Amendment, actions on the belief, if they conflict with other laws, may not be protected. One example involves religions that do not believe in certain forms of medical treatment. While an adult of that faith may refuse medical treatment, the court has sometimes ruled that, regardless of religious convictions, a child must receive medical treatment even if it is in opposition to the parents' wishes.

Second Amendment: Keeping and Bearing Arms

A well regulated Militia, being necessary to the security of a free State, the right of the people to keep and bear arms, shall not be infringed.

The exact meaning of the Second Amendment is unclear—does it mean everyone has the right to own any kind of gun they want to? Or does it mean the country has the right to organize a "well regulated Militia" and those people can have guns?

Always a source of friction, the Second Amendment has long pitted gun owners against those who favor a strict interpretation of the amendment, meaning only the military has the right to bear arms. However, both Congress and state legislatures have passed laws regulating the private ownership and use of weapons by individuals.

Third Amendment: Protection from the Military

No soldier shall, in time of peace be quartered in any house, without the consent of the owner, nor in time of war, but in a manner to be prescribed by law.

The Third Amendment is a result of the constant takeover of citizens' homes by the British during the Revolutionary War. To stop this, the Third Amendment protects individual homes from the military and says that, during peacetime or wartime, "no Soldier shall … be quartered in any house, without the consent of the owner."

Fourth Amendment: Search and Seizure

The right of the people to be secure in their persons, houses, papers, and effects, against unreasonable searches and seizures, shall not be violated, and no warrants shall issue, but upon probable cause, supported by oath or affirmation, and particularly describing the place to be searched, and the persons or things to be seized.

The Fourth Amendment requires the use of search and arrest warrants from a judge to search either a person or a home. Warrants must be issued by a judge, be issued on the basis of probable cause, and detail what exactly will be searched and where. In addition, an officer who asks for a warrant must take an oath backing up the reasons the warrant is requested. The Supreme Court has ruled that items seized without a warrant cannot be used in court.

Fifth Amendment: Protection Against Self-Incrimination

No person shall be held to answer for a capital, or otherwise infamous crime, unless on a presentment or indictment of a Grand Jury, except in cases arising in the land or naval forces, or in the militia, when in actual service in time of war or public danger; nor shall any person be subject for the same offense to be twice put in jeopardy of life or limb; nor shall be compelled in any criminal case to be a witness against himself, nor be deprived of life, liberty, or property, without due process of law; nor shall private property be taken for public use, without just compensation.

Inside the Beltway

Usually referred to simply as "due process," **due process of law** guards individual rights from infringement by state or federal governments.

The Fifth Amendment protects people from testifying against themselves in a criminal trial. It also says that a person cannot be tried for the same crime twice or be denied *due process of law*. In trials, this amendment is often heard when a defendant is said to be "taking the Fifth."

Sixth Amendment: The Right to a Defense

In all criminal prosecutions, the accused shall enjoy the right to a speedy and public trial, by an impartial jury of the State and district wherein the crime shall have been committed, which district shall have been previously ascertained by law, and to be informed of the nature and cause of the accusation; to be confronted with the witnesses against him; to have compulsory process for obtaining witnesses in his favor, and to have the assistance of counsel for his defense.

The Sixth Amendment gives the right to every defendant to be aware of any charges against him, as well as the right to an attorney, regardless of whether the defendant can afford one, and a jury trial.

Seventh Amendment: The Right to Trial

In suits at common law, where the value in controversy shall exceed twenty dollars, the right of trial by jury shall be preserved, and no fact tried by a jury, shall be otherwise reexamined in any Court of the United States, than according to the rules of the common law.

The Seventh Amendment establishes the right to a federal trial in which one person sues another over anything more than $20. Not all civil cases are brought before a federal court, however.

Eighth Amendment: Barring Cruel and Unusual Punishment

Excessive bail shall not be required, nor excessive fines imposed, nor cruel and unusual punishments inflicted.

The Eighth Amendment guards against any excessive bail, fines, or cruel and unusual punishment for criminals and alleged criminals. The interpretation of this amendment has been expanded by Supreme Court rulings to prevent the securing of confessions through such "cruel and unusual punishment."

Ninth Amendment: Ensuring Fundamental Rights

The enumeration in the Constitution, of certain rights, shall not be construed to deny or disparage others retained by the people.

The Ninth Amendment dictates that the rights retained by the people can be contradicted by the Constitution. It was added to ensure fundamental rights of the people that are not included in the Constitution. The right to privacy is not explicitly stated in the Ninth, or any, amendment. But over time, the interpretation of the Ninth Amendment has come to include the right of citizens to privacy. The generally agreed-upon parameters are that all citizens have the right to think whatever they want, to not be spied upon by the government, and to keep personal data collected by the government (which is also limited in the type of records it may obtain) from the eyes of the general public. Still, the lack of detail surrounding a right to privacy has long created conflicting interpretations. The congressional and national debate over the Patriot Act, a measure that strengthened law enforcement investigative techniques after September 11, 2001, is a clear example of this ongoing discussion.

Tenth Amendment: Protecting States' Interests

The powers not delegated to the United States by the Constitution, nor prohibited by it to the States, are reserved to the States respectively, or to the people.

The Tenth Amendment, the final amendment of the Bill of Rights, protects states from the federal government.

The Least You Need to Know

- While the framers of the Constitution felt they had created a comprehensive and enduring document, they also knew it would have to be flexible enough to change with the times.

- More than 10,000 amendments to the Constitution have been proposed since 1789, but only 27 have been added.

- The First Amendment, dealing with freedom of speech, religion, assembly, and the press, is the most debated and interpreted because the rights it protects often come into conflict with other rights expressed in the Constitution or its amendments.

- The Fifth Amendment, protecting people against testifying against themselves during trial, is invoked when a witness says that he or she is "taking the Fifth."

Keeping the Constitution Alive

In This Chapter

◆ Changing the election process

◆ Giving women the right to vote

◆ Trying—and failing—to legislate a social problem

◆ Amendments that failed to pass

As noted in Chapter 3, the framers of the Constitution knew the document they were creating had to be flexible enough to change as necessary over time.

While the first 10 amendments to the Constitution were passed as a package defining basic immutable rights, the remaining 17 have arisen throughout the history of the United States, usually in response to a perceived shortcoming in the governing processes.

In this chapter, we look at the remaining 17 amendments as well as the interesting cases of some that failed to become ratified.

Protecting Government from Lawsuits: Amendment 11

Ratified in 1798, the Eleventh Amendment expands the power of both the state and federal governments by protecting them from lawsuits. The first amendment to be added to the Constitution after the Bill of Rights was approved, the Eleventh Amendment, came about as a direct result of a controversial Supreme Court case.

In 1793, Alexander Chisholm, a will executor living in South Carolina, sued the state of Georgia on behalf of the estate of Robert Farquhar, a merchant. Farquhar had sold goods to the state. When he died in 1784, it appeared that Georgia owed him money. When Chisholm tried to collect payment, Georgia officials countered that they had paid agents for the merchandise and they owed nothing to Farquhar's estate.

Could a person in one state sue another state? Yes, the court ruled. In a 4–1 decision (the lone dissenter, Justice James Iredell, felt that a state could not be sued by an outside entity unless the state consented to the lawsuit), the justices decided that Chisholm could sue the state of Georgia on Farquhar's behalf. Chisholm eventually received bonds from Georgia to cover the money owed to Farquhar.

> ### We Hold These Truths
>
> The case of *Chisholm v. Georgia* was one of the first tests of the newly created federal court system.

> ### On the Record
>
> "The Constitution, in all its provisions, looks to an indestructible Union, composed of indestructible States."
>
> —Supreme Court Justice Salmon P. Chase, writing in Supreme Court opinion *Texas v. White*, April 12, 1869

Interestingly enough, no one from Georgia went to the Supreme Court to represent the state or hear the case, and state officials argued that a citizen of another state had no legal right to sue another state.

Congress, too, was outraged, with each chamber eventually voting overwhelmingly to approve an amendment that, if ratified, would overrule the decision. When all was said and done, the Eleventh Amendment, which says a foreign country or person in another state cannot sue a state in federal court without the state's permission, reversed the Supreme Court's decision.

Redoing Veep Elections: Amendment 12

The Twelfth Amendment, added in 1804, was a response to the presidential election of 1800, in which Thomas Jefferson and Aaron Burr received the same number of electoral votes. According to the second article of the Constitution, whoever received the most votes (and a majority) would be president, and the person who came in second would be vice president. But if there were no majority, the House would then decide the election by choosing the winners from a pool of the top five candidates. But the Constitution did not explicitly state that the House electors must designate in their two votes which was for president and which was for vice president.

Congress needed 36 ballots to determine who would be president after Aaron Burr and Thomas Jefferson tied in the 1800 election. The entire process lasted six days and involved heavy lobbying by supporters of both candidates to swing the election in their favor. Burr, too, tried to outwit the system by claiming that even though he was the vice presidential candidate, he should be considered for president because he had received an equal number of votes. Finally, James Bayard, a congressman from Delaware, switched his vote from Burr to Jefferson and placed the man who drafted the Declaration of Independence into the presidency.

To prevent a similar situation, the Twelfth Amendment separated the ballots for president and vice president.

We Hold These Truths

A little-known second aspect of the Twelfth Amendment says that, in the event of a tie for the office of vice president, the Senate will decide between the two top candidates. This has happened only once. In the 1836 election, Richard Mentor Johnson, Martin Van Buren's running mate, received one electoral vote less than the majority needed to elect him. The Senate met on February 8, 1837, and elected Johnson vice president by a vote of 33–16.

The Civil War Amendments: 13, 14, and 15

The next set of three amendments wasn't passed for more than 50 years. Known as the Civil War amendments, the Thirteenth, Fourteenth, and Fifteenth Amendments were all enacted to protect former slaves.

The Thirteenth Amendment, ratified in 1865, simply outlawed slavery and gave former slaves the same rights as other citizens. It also represented a decrease in the power of state governments—and an increase in federal power.

The Fourteenth Amendment, ratified in 1868, gave all foreign-born citizens who were naturalized the same rights as those born in the United States, and made it clear that citizens of the United States were also citizens of the states where they lived. As with the Thirteenth Amendment, the Fourteenth clearly expanded federal power and reduced state power.

The stage for the Fourteenth Amendment was set in 1833 with the Supreme Court case *Barron v. Baltimore*. In the case, Barron, who owned a commercial wharf, charged that his wharf couldn't be used because of the debris the city of Baltimore deposited when it paved the streets. Barron sued the city under the Fifth Amendment, arguing that the city had deprived him of property. The Supreme Court decision said that if the federal government had caused the deprivation, Barron would be right. But because Maryland's constitution did not protect Barron the same way, he had no case.

Inside the Beltway

The **equal protection clause** of the Fourteenth Amendment stipulates that no state can "deny to any person within its jurisdiction the equal protection of the laws."

At the close of the Civil War, though, the Fourteenth Amendment was an attempt to change that decision and specifically differentiated states' rights from rights protected on the national level in the Bill of Rights. Included in the amendment is the due process clause and what has come to be known as the *equal protection clause*.

The times after the Civil War, however, were still mired in conflict, with many whites looking for a way to keep the status of blacks lower than their own. What the amendment said and what it actually provided to former slaves were very different ideas. Racial discrimination continued for nearly a century and, in some cases, Supreme Court cases even strengthened racism.

Although intended mainly for protection of the rights of former slaves, the equal protection clause came to be used in countless cases involving unequal protection of any grouping of citizens, as well as for the guarantee of due process under state and federal law. Case after case made the question of how the Fourteenth Amendment protected citizens of states under the Bill of Rights increasingly unclear.

In *Plessy v. Ferguson*, decided by the Supreme Court in 1896, the justices found that segregation was legal and the Fourteenth Amendment's equal protection could segregate on the basis of race as long as the facilities were equal. The equal protection clause was also the basis for the court's decision in the landmark case that essentially reversed the *Plessy v. Ferguson* ruling, *Brown v. Board of Education*, in 1954 (see Chapter 17 for more on this).

Approved in 1870 (but not fully enforced for nearly a century), the Fifteenth Amendment stopped state and federal governments from denying a citizen the right to vote based on race, skin color, or status as a former slave. Women were still not given the same privilege, but their concerns would soon be addressed.

The Beginning of Income Taxes: Amendment 16

The Sixteenth Amendment, the first to be passed in the twentieth century, allowed income to be taxed and was a clear response to a Supreme Court decision, *Pollock v. Farmers' Loan & Trust Company*.

Congress had passed an income tax law in 1894 that the Supreme Court found to be unconstitutional on the basis that it should be divided among the states by population. The national government, however, just like a business, needed a way to raise money to pay its operating costs and debts. The legislators believed they could tax income to use for whatever they needed to without having to divide it according to population.

Article 1 of the Constitution, which says Congress can "lay and collect Taxes, Duties, Imposts and Excises, to pay the Debts and provide for the common Defence and general Welfare of the United States," made it clear that the founding fathers agreed that the nation's government should have broad powers to tax its people. The Constitution did differentiate between two kinds of taxes that Congress could employ: direct and indirect. Direct taxes should be apportioned on the basis of population, while indirect taxes had to be laid equally according to geography.

After *Pollock v. Farmers' Loan & Trust Company*, income taxes were labeled as direct taxes, making it virtually impossible to impose them through reapportionment. As a result, there were no income taxes for almost 20 years until the Sixteenth Amendment was ratified in 1913.

Tweaking the Election Process: Amendments 17, 20, 22, and 25

Four amendments passed in the twentieth century dealt directly with elections.

The Seventeenth Amendment, also passed in 1913, had a significant impact on the electoral system. Before the amendment was passed, state legislatures elected the state's two U.S. senators, giving voters little control over their representation in the Senate. Now citizens vote directly for their state's senators.

In 1933, the Twentieth Amendment set noon on January 20, following a presidential election, as the time for a term of office for the president to end. Terms for senators and representatives end at noon on January 3, following an election. This amendment also sets up the line of succession in the event that a president dies before being sworn into office.

After Franklin Delano Roosevelt's unprecedented four terms in office, during which he exponentially grew the size of government and, with it, the power of the executive office, legislators approved the Twenty-second Amendment in 1951 to limit the number of terms served by any future president to two. If a president dies or is incapacitated, the vice president may succeed to the presidency, serve up to two years of that unexpired term, and then be elected to two full terms, for a total of 10 years, or two and one-half terms.

In 1967, the Twenty-fifth Amendment set rules for a vacancy in the vice presidency. Although the president can nominate anyone for the vacancy, his choice must be approved by a majority of both the House and the Senate.

The Whiskey Amendments: Amendments 18 and 21

Prohibition did little to stop the Roaring Twenties—even though the Eighteenth Amendment outlawed the production, sale, or transportation of alcohol in 1919. The period of great prosperity—and indulgence—between the two great wars didn't stop the social problems caused by liquor any more than lawmakers could. "Speakeasies" were private clubs that defied the law by serving alcohol, which, for the most part, was illegally brought into the United States from Canada and other foreign countries. They were immensely popular and proved to be quite lucrative for the owners who knew how not to get caught.

Of all the amendments to the Constitution, the Eighteenth is the only one that has been repealed. Its failure is largely attributed to the fact that it was an attempt to legislate a societal problem.

We Hold These Truths
Even the White House broke the rules. During the Harding Administration, known for its many social gatherings, liquor was available in the White House library.

Passed in 1933, the Twenty-first Amendment repealed the Eighteenth. It protected the states' rights, however, to make their own laws regarding the manufacture, sale, and transportation of liquor. If a state wants to be "dry" and to prohibit such things as transportation or importation of liquor, the Twenty-first Amendment backs it up.

Giving Women the Right to Vote: Amendment 19

Fifty years after former male slaves were guaranteed the right to vote, women received the same right with the passage of the Nineteenth Amendment in 1920. The timing of the amendment doubled the electorate in time for the presidential election that year. Its passage was a long time coming.

In 1777, New Jersey had given women the right to vote but later revoked the right. In the mid-nineteenth century, a powerful women's movement evolved that began the decades-long battle for the right to vote. The first call for women's *suffrage* came during the Seneca Falls Convention in 1848. A "Declaration of Sentiments," introduced by Elizabeth Cady Stanton, played on the Declaration of Independence by granting women and men equal rights under the Constitution and included a list of grievances endorsed by the burgeoning movement.

Suffrage for women suffered setbacks after the Civil War, when lawmakers focused their efforts on ensuring the rights of the newly freed slaves. Still, a constitutional amendment granting women the right to vote was first presented to Congress in 1878. It would come before Congress a total of eight times before it was approved.

Inside the Beltway

Suffrage, also known as franchise, refers to the right to vote.

On the Record

"Marriage, to women as to men, must be a luxury, not a necessity; an incident of life, not all of it. And the only possible way to accomplish this great change is to accord to women equal power in the making, shaping, and controlling of the circumstances of life."

—Susan B. Anthony, in a speech delivered in Chicago, Illinois, on March 14, 1875

We Hold These Truths

One method used by members of the women's suffrage movement, including Susan B. Anthony, was to head to the polls on election day and attempt to vote. Anthony was even arrested and convicted without any evidence being presented at her trial.

Another member of the movement, Virginia Minor, sued the registrar in St. Louis, Missouri, for not allowing her to register to vote. The case went to the Supreme Court, which ruled that not all citizens were granted the right to vote under the Constitution.

Several Western states had already begun to grant women the right to vote, beginning with Wyoming in 1890. Colorado, Idaho, and Utah soon followed. The women's movement then focused its attention on getting other state legislatures to follow suit—a grass-roots strategy that slowly proved effective. By the time Congress began actively considering the idea of women's suffrage, 11 other states had given women full voting rights and 14 had granted limited suffrage.

Even with the right to vote, women didn't have the same privileges as men in the eyes of the law. Shortly after their successful battle to pass the suffrage vote, the women's movement began pushing for an equal rights amendment, which was not taken seriously for another 50 years (and, as you'll later see, was never passed).

Further Expanding the Electorate: Amendments 23, 24, and 26

In the twentieth century, three more amendments were passed to protect the rights of voters and expand the size of the electorate. District of Columbia citizens were granted the right to vote in presidential elections when the Twenty-third Amendment was ratified in 1961. Residents there, however, are still pushing for another constitutional amendment that would give their delegate in Congress a vote, as well as two senators, which all the states have.

In 1964, the Twenty-fourth Amendment stopped those who could not pay from being eliminated from the system by abolishing *poll taxes*. Until then, districts throughout the country had indiscriminately used poll taxes both to raise income and to stop poorer classes of people from exercising their constitutional right.

Inside the Beltway

Poll taxes were fees levied at polling places used to raise money and stop poor people from voting.

The Twenty-sixth Amendment, passed in 1971, gave citizens 18 years or older the right to vote. A response to the political activism of youth the decade before, the amendment was in part an attempt to soothe generational tensions.

Granting Raises to Congress: Amendment 27

The most recent amendment to be ratified (in 1992), the Twenty-seventh Amendment, makes effective after the following election any pay raise that Congress passes for itself. Ironically, the same amendment was originally introduced in 1789 by the first Congress but failed to receive the support of the state legislatures.

Amendments Tried and Failed

Although only 27 amendments have been added to the Constitution, more than 10,000 have been proposed since 1789. Thirty-three have passed both houses of Congress and gone on to the states for ratification. For various reasons, 6 of those 33 died in this process. Several came fairly early in history. They include …

◆ An amendment proposed with the Bill of Rights that would have provided 1 representative for every 30,000 people, until there were 100, at which point Congress would regulate the number.

◆ An amendment that would have revoked citizenship for any person who accepted a title of nobility.

◆ An amendment to allow any amendment or Act of Congress to abolish slavery.

Two others, one regarding the right to prohibit the employment of anyone under 18 and one that would grant full representation in Congress to the District of Columbia, were approved in 1926 and 1978, respectively.

Of the six that failed to become laws, the Equal Rights Amendment is the best known and the subject of the most protracted battle. The amendment was the result of decades of pressure from the women's movement and was ratified by 28 states in the first year after Congress approved it. But opponents of the amendment began an effective campaign to stop other states from ratifying it. By 1974, five more states had ratified it, but three others that had previously ratified the amendment voted to rescind it.

We Hold These Truths

The case of states rescinding their ratification of a constitutional amendment was unprecedented. Idaho, Nebraska, and Tennessee all voted to rescind their ratification of the Equal Rights Amendment. The Supreme Court did not hear a case involving it because the justices believed it to be a political concern that should be decided by Congress. But Congress never had to decide whether the states' reversal would be counted in the 38-state minimum for ratification.

The failure of the Equal Rights Amendment, which was intended to grant men and women equal rights under the law, demonstrated the difficulty of the two-part ratification process. Once Congress approves the amendment, there is a seven-year period for the required 38 states to approve the amendment.

The process got messier still when Congress controversially extended the seven-year ratification period in 1979 by three years. But the ratification period expired in 1982, and the amendment died, with only 35 of 50 states ratifying it.

The Least You Need to Know

♦ The 17 amendments passed after the Bill of Rights was approved affirm the goal of the framers of the Constitution, who wanted to ensure that the Constitution maintained its power by keeping up with the times.

♦ The majority of amendments that have been ratified deal with a perceived shortcoming in the governing processes.

♦ The Eighteenth Amendment, prohibiting the manufacture, transportation, and sale of liquor, is the only amendment that was ratified and later repealed.

♦ Of the six Constitutional amendments that failed to pass muster, the Equal Rights Amendment, which would have ensured that all men and women have the same rights, is the best known.

Part 2

The Buck Stops Here

The monarchy was a difficult institution for early Americans—including the framers of the Constitution—to let go of, as it was the only form of government they knew. Clearly, however, there was some out-of-the-box thinking going on even then, and enough people were ready to try something else—within reason. While they were willing to vest executive power in one individual, they didn't want to give this person unbridled authority. Instead, they put the executive office at the same level as the legislative and judiciary branches. Each was given broad authority, including the ability to stop potential abuses of that authority.

While the president and the role he plays in government often come to mind first when we think of the executive branch of the government, other important people and offices also make their home in this branch. You'll get to know more about all of them and what they do in this part.

Chapter 5

Hail to the Chief

In This Chapter

- ◆ Why the United States has a president
- ◆ Becoming a candidate
- ◆ Recent contenders
- ◆ Who's in control (if the president can't be)

In the fall of 2000, when then-Governor George W. Bush of Texas and then-Vice President Al Gore were campaigning all over the country, pleading for votes and posing with babies at staged "photo opportunities," the press extensively covered everything they said or did. When it was revealed that Bush had been arrested for drunk driving in the late 1970s, it was front-page news. Likewise, when it was inaccurately reported that Gore claimed to have invented the Internet, it was the subject of all the late-night talk shows. How did Bush and Gore get to that point? In this chapter, we look at the road to the presidency along with the requirements of office.

Why They Made Washington President Instead of King

While it is difficult for most Americans now to even think of a king in control of the government, this was a very real consideration during the Constitutional Convention of 1787. The delegates debated at length about who should be the central figure responsible for American government. Should there be a king? Should there be a president? Should the president serve only one term? Should this person be impeachable? Hugh Williamson, a delegate from North Carolina, went as far as to say (midway through the convention, no less) that he was "pretty certain at some time or other [the United States should] have a king." This idea horrified Thomas Jefferson, who wrote in a letter to a friend that he was astonished that the delegates were considering a monarchy as the solution.

During the convention, the delegates voted on the matter no less than 60 times. Sometimes they supported an appointed president. Other times they supported an elected president, but then the question was by whom, state legislatures or the people? The issue dominated the convention and even occasionally halted the proceedings.

The issue finally reached boiling-point levels when a British loyalist in Connecticut decided to start a rumor that the convention delegates were considering appointing one of King George III's sons as the king of America. This enraged many of the new Americans throughout the colonies. Recalling that the delegates had pledged secrecy, they released a statement saying that while they could not say what they were doing, they *could* say what they weren't doing, and appointing the king's son as King of America was not a notion they had ever considered. The public uproar over this idea provoked the delegates to drop the king idea.

We Hold These Truths

The monarchy was something that Americans deeply held on to. When the Senate was debating a title for Washington, the phrase "His Highness the President of the United States and Protector of their Liberties" was proposed by none other than John Adams. The House did not accept this, however, and Washington and his successors became known simply as "Mr. President."

We Hold These Truths

Who was the youngest president? Did you guess John F. Kennedy? Good guess, but wrong. Kennedy was the youngest elected president, at age 43. But 60 years earlier, Vice President Theodore Roosevelt became president at age 42 when President William McKinley was assassinated.

Requirements for Office

To be president, a candidate must meet three basic requirements. First, the candidate must be a native-born American citizen. Although there is no such requirement for serving in Congress, the framers of the Constitution wanted to make sure that the person who held this office had loyalties to no one other than the United States of America.

The other two requirements deal with age and residency. The candidates must have lived in the United States for the last 14 years and must be a minimum of 35 years old.

Candidates—Typical and Not

Most people who run for president have at least some previous elected office experience, such as having served as a governor, a senator, or a member of the House of Representatives. However, over the course of history some famous, well-established candidates have run for president, as have some not-so-famous candidates without prior elective office experience.

Businessmen

Over the last 20 years, wealthy businessmen have tested the waters, some with more success than others. In 1992 and 1996, H. Ross Perot, a Texas billionaire, ran as an independent candidate for president. He had never run for, much less served in, elected office. However, he had an enormous following among many in the electorate who were frustrated with both major candidates and their respective parties. Even after withdrawing and re-entering the 1992 race, Perot garnered 19 percent of the popular vote. He was less successful in 1996, drawing only 8 percent.

Nader the Raider

Ralph Nader, the best recent example of a nonelected official running for office (and, to many, a huge spoiler in the 2000 election), has run for president on the Green Party ticket twice, and was an independent candidate in the 2004 election. Widely known, if not universally respected, for his work as a consumer advocate, he ran in 2000 because many Democrats, particularly those on the liberal side of the party, were upset with Democratic candidate Al Gore. Many liberals believed Gore was too moderate and not much different from Bush, the Republican candidate. Gore's support of permanent normal trade relations with China, something the labor unions adamantly opposed, created significant tension within the Democratic Party.

A Woman's Place Is in the Oval Office?

While all major party candidates for president have been men, women have given the top office a shot, too. The first woman to run for president was Victoria Woodhull in 1872 on the Equal Rights Party ticket. The stockbroker could not vote for herself (women didn't have the right to vote yet), but she still managed to garner nearly 4,000 votes nationwide. Ironically, had she won, she would have been ineligible to serve because she was only 34 years of age at the time.

Anything Other Than White Anglo-Saxon Protestant Male

Of the 43 presidents, only one—John F. Kennedy—was not a Protestant. Kennedy was the first (and so far the only) Catholic to hold that office. During his campaign, he spent a considerable amount of time convincing voters he could separate his religion from his politics and that he would not be beholden to the pope in Rome, as many southern Christians feared he would.

No Jewish candidate has ever been nominated by a major party for president. In 2000, however, the Democrats made history by nominating Connecticut Sen. Joseph Lieberman as their vice-presidential nominee. Lieberman's wife is the daughter of Holocaust survivors, and both are devout in their religion. His nomination symbolized that Americans had, for the most part, come to terms with religious differences and were not concerned about someone other than a Protestant male potentially holding that office.

Lieberman competed for the presidency in 2004, but withdrew from the race after poor showings in the early primaries. However, his nomination and general public acceptance bodes well for more minority candidates running in the future. Neither party has had an American of African, Asian, or Hispanic descent run successfully.

Primary Battles

In recent years, candidates have been announcing their presidential ambitions earlier. As a result, it seems like the road to the White House gets longer during every election cycle, although in reality the primary season lasts only from late January through June of a presidential election year. In recent years, primaries held after mid-March have had virtually no effect on the eventual outcome of the nomination.

From the time they announce their candidacy until the first *primary* or *caucus*, the candidates spend a great deal of time in various parts of the country, but their focus always is on two key states: Iowa and New Hampshire.

Inside the Beltway

In a **primary,** members of a registered party choose among candidates in their own party to nominate them to be the ultimate party nominee. Most times only registered members of a party may vote in the primary. In some cases, though, there is an open primary, and members of third parties (but usually not the major opposition party) may vote for a candidate. **Caucuses** are held when local party officials or delegates gather to vote on behalf of all the registered voters in that state to select the winner.

What makes these two relatively small states so important? Different states have different election dates, and Iowa and New Hampshire are first on the election calendar. Winning (or losing) one or both of these can make or break a candidacy.

As the winter weeks pass by and various states have their own primary, the number of candidates seeking the nomination dwindles. Some see the writing on the wall fairly early and drop out after a devastating loss, while others will hold on until the bitter end. Party committees usually discourage the latter because they say it hurts party unity. By *Super Tuesday*, the first Tuesday in March, the party's nominee is normally selected, thus giving him (or her, although as mentioned that has never happened) four months to campaign before "officially" accepting the party's nomination at the National Convention.

Sitting presidents are not immune from intraparty challenges. In 1992, President George H. W. Bush lost the New Hampshire primary to conservative commentator Pat Buchanan.

Inside the Beltway

Super Tuesday is the first Tuesday in March, when ten states—California, Connecticut, Georgia, Maryland, Massachusetts, Minnesota, New York, Ohio, Rhode Island, and Vermont, hold primaries and caucuses to determine who their nominee is.

While Bush eventually went on to win the party nomination, the loss did not bode well for him. He went on to lose the general election to Arkansas Gov. Bill Clinton.

Delegates and Conventions

During each primary, each state party establishes a set number of *delegates* that are available for a candidate. These delegate totals are ultimately combined with those of other states at the national convention, and they determine who the presidential nominee is going to be. By winning a state with a large number of delegates, a candidate helps further his or her chances of becoming the nominee at the convention.

In the past, conventions have been very contentious, with candidates and delegates duking it out to see who would receive the majority of the required number of delegates. Floor debates and multiple delegate votes were regular events. Parties were fractionalized and the outcome uncertain until the end.

Inside the Beltway

Delegates are party loyalists who are selected by their local parties to represent the state at the national convention. Democrats have 4,336 delegates, and a candidate must receive 2,170 votes—exactly half plus 1—to win. Republicans have 2,065 delegates, and 1,034 votes are needed to capture the nomination.

Modern-day party conventions, however, are anti-climactic affairs. They are a chance for candidates to show off themselves and their ideology, but they offer little in the way of substance or true surprise. Usually hosted in a city that is either a swing city (meaning the voters could go one way or the other) or a safe city (meaning they are located in a state that is defined as clearly red [Republican] or blue [Democrat], such as Texas [red] or Illinois [blue]), the four-day event brings together thousands of people (as well as countless journalists) from all over the country for what can best be described as a big party.

Rank-and-file party members compete for prime-time speaking engagements with the hope of bolstering their careers. When the Democrats nominated Gov. Michael Dukakis of Massachusetts as their standard bearer in 1988, Bill Clinton, at the time a little-known southern governor, gave the nomination speech. While the speech itself was widely panned as too long and boring, the exposure introduced him to a large number of delegates who would be of great aid to him four years down the road, when he was running in a crowded primary. U.S. Sen. Barack Obama of Illinois, who was then just a candidate, gave the keynote address at the 2004 Democratic convention. His speech was very well received and as a result, his name—which was not known outside his small state senate district in Illinois—immediately became famous. He won his U.S. Senate race in a landslide, and is often mentioned as a possible presidential contender in the future.

The Fall Campaign

Both conventions are usually over by the end of the summer, with the party out of power holding its convention first. Once the parties select their candidates, the campaigns shift into high gear.

The major party candidates and their running mates venture across the country, giving speeches; eating breakfast, lunch, and dinner, sometimes more than once a day; and meeting as many people as possible. It is not unusual for candidates to spend a considerable amount of time in the large swing states such as Pennsylvania, Florida, and Michigan, and ignore the large safe states such as New York, California (both safe Democrat), and Texas (safe Republican).

Going to College—The Electoral College, That Is!

Why do the candidates need to worry about some big states and not others? Because they are concerned with the electoral votes of each state just as much, if not more so, than the popular votes of the states.

As discussed in Chapter 2, each state, as prescribed by the Constitution, has a set number of electors. This figure is determined by combining the number of congressional representatives a state has (at minimum one) with its senators (two). Delaware, for example, has three electors and electoral votes, while California, as a result of the 2000 census and reapportionment, has 56. The total number of electors never changes, but it may change from state to state every 10 years.

We Hold These Truths

As seen in 2000, all the electors, no matter how big or small, are important. Bush won by the barest of margins in the electoral college (and actually lost the popular vote by over 500,000 votes, according to the Associated Press), winning 271 votes to 266 votes—one delegate abstained from voting. A candidate must receive half plus 1 (270). If three votes had gone the other way, Bush would have remained governor of Texas and Gore would have been president.

The total number of electors is set at 538: 435 for the House of Representatives, 100 for the Senate, and 3 from the District of Columbia.

The popular vote from each state determines who receives the electoral votes. Forty-eight states combine the popular vote to total and award the winner all the electoral votes—known as the "winner take all" approach. Two states, Maine and Nebraska, split the electoral votes by congressional districts and award the electors individually. Whoever wins the majority of the state vote also receives the two votes that represent the number of senators.

Victory ... and Defeat

On election night, in the past, the major television networks all competed to make the first call. But as a result of 2000, when some networks called Florida for Gore before the panhandle region of the state, which is in a different time zone, had completed its voting, they have become more cautious.

Now the networks double- and oftentimes triple-check their numbers. Some have said they would rather be last than come out first and be wrong.

Under traditional circumstances, the loser of the election speaks first, giving a concession speech to his supporters and congratulating the victor. This usually elicits boos and hisses from his supporters but is viewed as the statesmanlike approach. The victor then speaks to his supporters, announces that he is pleased to be known as the president-elect, and pledges to serve all Americans, not just those who voted for him.

The victor begins almost immediately assembling a cabinet and working on the transition. Inauguration is just over two months away on January 20, and the next 10 weeks are critical to ensure that he is ready to take over at noon on this day.

For all his hard work, long hours, and the chance to be arguably the most powerful person in the entire world, the president receives an annual salary of $400,000.

Who's in Charge?

If the president is unable to complete his term, the vice president becomes president. But what if something catastrophic happened and both the president and the vice president were unable to serve?

The Presidential Succession Act of 1947 set up a power of succession in the event that both of these officials are unable to carry out their responsibilities. It specifies the following order of succession:

1. Speaker of the House

2. President pro tempore of the Senate

3. Congressionally approved cabinet officials, in the order in which the cabinet departments were created (for more on this, see Chapter 6).

The Twenty-fifth Amendment, ratified in 1967, took away a great deal of the need for the Presidential Succession Act because it called for the nomination of a vice president if this office becomes vacated. The president would nominate a candidate for vice president, and a majority vote in both houses of Congress would be required for approval.

Despite the Twenty-fifth Amendment, every time the president gives a *State of the Union address*, at least one member of the cabinet remains away at an undisclosed location, in case of a national disaster.

In peacetime, a president gives only one address to a joint session of Congress. When this State of the Union address takes place, traditionally in late January, one member of the president's cabinet does not attend and is taken to an undisclosed location. The vice president and the Speaker of the House are always immediately behind the president in the House chamber.

To highlight the significance of President Bush's September 20, 2001, speech before Congress—which came nine days after the terrorist attacks of 9/11—both Vice President Richard Cheney and Secretary of Health and Human Services Tommy Thompson remained away. This was the first time in recent memory that a vice president was not present during a president's address to a joint session of Congress.

Inside the Beltway

The **State of the Union address** is the annual speech given by the president to a joint session of Congress, usually in January or February.

We Hold These Truths

Although the Constitution requires that a president give an address to Congress outlining the condition of the union, it does not specifically state that he must do so in person. In fact, Thomas Jefferson began what would become a 112-year tradition of delivering the address via letters to Congress in 1801. Woodrow Wilson resurrected the practice started by Washington of delivering the address in person.

The Least You Need to Know

◆ If not for delegates arguing against the monarchy during the 1787 Constitutional Convention, Americans could be referring to the highest figure of authority in the land as "His Highness" instead of "Mr. President."

◆ Presidential candidates must be native-born American citizens, must have lived in the United States for the 14 years prior to their candidacy, and must be at least 35 years old.

◆ Although the primary season extends from late January through June of a presidential election year, primaries held after mid-March now have virtually no effect on the eventual outcome of the nominee.

◆ During every State of the Union address, presidential succession is protected by having at least one member of the cabinet remain away at an undisclosed location.

Chapter 6

Second in Command– The Vice President

In This Chapter

♦ The history of the vice president

♦ How the office has changed

♦ Famous and infamous vice presidents

♦ Responsibilities and duties

What do Elbridge Gerry, John C. Calhoun, William Wheeler, Theodore Roosevelt, and Dan Quayle have in common? All of these men served as vice president. Chances are, if you are like most Americans, you know who two of those people are, and you may remember a third from your high school civics class. History has not been especially kind to the role of the vice president, and most of the 46 men who have served in this position are forgotten names from the past. Some vice presidents have had active roles within their respective administrations, while others have been left in the dark on virtually all decisions. Over time, however, the job of the vice president has evolved from being the fifth wheel to the major engine under the hood.

Defining the Office—Sort Of

The Constitution makes only two references to the duties of the *veep*. The document's vagueness on the responsibilities of the office created an official whose role has greatly changed over time. The first mention, in Article 1, Section 3, says that the "Vice President of the United States shall be the President of the Senate, but shall have no Vote, unless they be equally divided." The other mention, in Article 2, Section 1, says the president and the vice president cannot be from the same state. As for vice-presidential duties, it states that the president of the Senate shall "in the presence of the Senate and the House of Representatives, open all the certificates and the votes [for president and vice president] shall be counted."

Inside the Beltway

Veep is the slang term often used when referring to the vice president.

Alexander Hamilton wrote in "The Federalist No. 68" that, similar to the role of lieutenant governor in a state, the new nation should "authorize the vice president to exercise the authorities and discharge the duties of the president" if the president can no longer serve.

Early Tumult

The first two elections after Washington completed his two unanimous selections as president proved difficult for the new republic in selecting the vice president. In the election of 1796, some Federalist electors did not like their chosen presidential candidate, John Adams, so they voted for their vice-presidential candidate instead. The result: For the first (and only) time in American history, the president (John Adams—Federalist) was from one party and the vice president (Thomas Jefferson—Republican party, no relation to the modern Republican party) was from the other. No one expected Jefferson to be Adams's top advisor, and four years later Jefferson ran for the top job again.

Selecting the vice president did not get any easier in the election of 1800. The Federalists renominated Adams. The Republicans put forward the same ticket as before, with Jefferson for president and Aaron Burr for vice president. When all the ballots were counted, Jefferson and Burr were tied!

In the case of a tie, the Constitution says that the House of Representatives has the final say. While the Republicans controlled the House, the Federalists were a strong enough minority that they devised a plan to muddy the water. They preferred Burr because he was more moderate than Jefferson and was not as committed to Republican ideals as the presidential nominee was.

Over the next three and a half months (remember, it was not until the Twentieth Amendment was ratified in 1933 that the president was inaugurated in January—until this point, he was inaugurated on March 4), the House voted 35 times, with no clear winner. With less than three weeks before the inauguration, on the 36th ballot, Jefferson was declared the winner and Burr was selected as vice president.

We Hold These Truths

Aaron Burr, the vice-presidential nominee, was not supposed to be a presidential candidate in 1800, but because of a fluke he became one. It took three and a half months to resolve the situation, and when it was over a bitter Burr served as vice president. Burr blamed his defeat on Federalist Alexander Hamilton. Four years later, he challenged Hamilton to a duel, the proper way to settle a fight in the early nineteenth century. Burr won when he shot and killed Hamilton in Weehawken, New Jersey. While he was indicted for murder in both New York and New Jersey, he was never tried. He returned to Washington and completed his term as vice president. As if that wasn't enough, three years later, Burr was arrested for treason when he tried to form a new republic in the southwest for which he would be leader. He was acquitted and later returned to practicing law. He died in 1836.

As you read in Chapter 4, the Twelfth Amendment was written to end such confusion. After its ratification in 1804, electors were required to vote for the positions on separate ballots, with candidates specifically running for the separate positions.

We Hold These Truths

A little-known second aspect of the Twelfth Amendment says that in the event of a tie for the office of vice president, the Senate will decide between the two top candidates. This has happened only once. In the election of 1836, Martin Van Buren was elected president. His vice-presidential candidate, Richard Mentor Johnson, however, received one electoral vote less than the majority needed to elect. The Senate met on February 8, 1837, and elected Johnson vice president (33–16) over his closest rival. Johnson, hardly a household name in vice-presidential circles, was a colorful character. His wife was a former slave and they had several mixed-race daughters. Furthermore, he cared more about tending to the needs of his customers at a local saloon than his vice-presidential duties!

Who Is This Guy?

The public was, for the most part, ambivalent toward the vice president for much of the early nineteenth century. Apparently so were some of the officeholders of the job. In 1841, John Tyler was the first sitting vice president to become president due to a president's death. Exactly one month into office, President William Henry Harrison died of pneumonia and Tyler became president. Some questioned his authority, and Tyler routinely returned mail unopened if it was addressed "Acting President."

On the Record

"My country has in its wisdom contrived for me the most insignificant office that ever the invention of man contrived or his imagination conceived."

—John Adams, in a letter to his wife, Abigail, during his second term as Washington's vice president

"Worst damnfool mistake I ever made was letting myself be elected vice president. The vice presidency ain't worth a pitcher of warm spit."

—John Nance Garner, FDR's first veep, who gave up his role as Speaker of the House to be vice president

At least four presidents—John Tyler, Millard Fillmore, Andrew Johnson, and Chester Arthur, all former vice presidents themselves—served without a vice president, when they became president as a result of presidential death.

The job has been referred to as the "do-nothing" job, and President Franklin Pierce's vice president, William R. King, did exactly that. He simply never reported for duty. At the time of his election in November 1852, King was living in Cuba for medicinal purposes (he was sick with tuberculosis and hoped the warm climate would help). He did eventually return to his native Alabama, only to die a month into Pierce's term.

Numerous vice presidents died in office, and boredom is just as probable a cause as any medical diagnosis. Henry Wilson, vice president during Ulysses Grant's second term, had so much free time on his hands that he managed to write a three-volume history of slavery—before dying in his Capitol Hill office.

Other vice presidents were selected in an effort to shut them up. Theodore Roosevelt, arguably one of the most charismatic presidents to serve, was selected in part because New York Republican leaders wanted to get rid of him. As governor, he was a vocal thorn in their side, but as vice president, he would be nearly invisible—so they thought. Had they been able to see into the future and learn that McKinley would be shot in 1901, thus elevating Roosevelt to the presidency, it is unlikely Roosevelt ever would have been chosen as the running mate.

The Role Transformed

It wasn't until the mid-twentieth century that the role of vice president was transformed into a stronger executive position instead of the purely legislative one it had been before. Richard Nixon may be remembered for the Watergate scandal, but before he was president, he was vice president. Some historians credit him as the author of the modern vice-presidential era.

Playing Checkers with Office Space

Nixon was the first vice president to have an office in the Eisenhower Executive Office Building (EEOB), which is right next to the White House on the corner of Pennsylvania Avenue and 17th Street. He also traveled extensively on behalf of the president and, through the new medium of television, was able to introduce himself to the American public in a way previous vice presidents could have only dreamed of.

Vice President Walter Mondale, a former senator from Minnesota, provided valuable insight to President Jimmy Carter during their four years in office (1977–1981). Carter, who had no Washington, D.C., experience, relied heavily on Mondale, who had strong Capitol Hill ties. Carter referred to Mondale as his "equal partner" and "chief staff person." Mondale also became the first vice president to have an office in the West Wing, primarily because he felt that his office space in the EEOB was too far from the action.

The tradition of presidents and vice presidents meeting (at least) once a week for lunch also began with Carter and Mondale.

> **On the Record**
>
> "When you are there, you might as well be in Baltimore."
> —Walter Mondale, commenting on the office in the EEOB

Co-President Ford?

In 1980, the office of the vice president came dangerously close to becoming one of co-president. Republican nominee Ronald Reagan and his advisers were in deep discussions with former president Gerald Ford about giving him the number-two spot. Ford wanted unprecedented authority as veep, asking for veto control over potential Reagan appointments and actions. If successful, it would have become a power-sharing deal that the framers never envisioned.

During a six-hour window, when conversations between the two camps were at a standstill, aides to Reagan and George H. W. Bush (Bush had been a key primary rival) began talking. They struck a deal for Bush, instead of Ford, as Reagan's running mate.

Becoming Major Players

Vice presidents during the last 20 years have exercised an increasingly important role within their administrations. President George Bush placed Vice President Dan Quayle in charge of the Task Force on Regulatory Reform, which Quayle renamed the Council on Competitiveness. He also headed the then-Cabinet-level National Space Council.

While President Bill Clinton dissolved these vice-presidential duties for his own veep, he nonetheless made sure that Vice President Al Gore had a very active role in his administration. Gore monitored relations between the U.S. and Russia and was the administration's go-to man on issues concerning the environment, technology, and telecommunications.

Dick Cheney, George W. Bush's vice president, is widely regarded as one of the most hands-on vice presidents in American history. Bush placed him in charge of the presidential transition team in late 2000 to oversee the change of power between Bush and Clinton. Currently, Cheney is in charge of the administration's energy task force and is responsible for planning the budget. (Cheney is the one who says yes or no to cabinet budget proposals; Bush never sees them, according to one report.)

We Hold These Truths
When George H. W. Bush was elected president in 1988, it was the first time in 152 years that a sitting vice president immediately succeeded his boss by election. Other veeps made the transition from veep to president, but they initially became president either because of a president's death or, in Nixon's case, after an eight-year hiatus.

Finally, in light of the severity of current events surrounding the war on terrorism, Cheney has been active behind the scenes but has not been in the public eye that often. While consulting daily with the president, he has often been shuttled to undisclosed locations to protect his safety as well as the succession of power.

Selecting a Vice President

When a presidential nominee has locked up the support of his party and is preparing for the summer convention, it becomes time to search for a running mate. The running mate, who becomes the vice president if the ticket wins, is usually someone who brings a critical aspect to the ticket that the nominee himself lacks in order to create balance.

Basic Considerations

The selection of vice president is not a chance event. Once the nominee has secured the delegates necessary for the summer convention, he appoints a selection committee to help him search for the ideal running mate. This committee will vet potential candidates and look for glitches in the personal and political resumés that could potentially harm the ticket. They look for inconsistencies in voting records, poor statements in the past regarding controversial issues, as well as whether the individual has any drinking, drug, depression, or adultery problems that could trigger voters. The ticket does not want any surprises late on the campaign trail, and you can be sure if either nominee has any skeletons in their closet, the press will find out.

We Hold These Truths

There was not always a need for the search committee. The press exercised more restraint when it came to personal matters until the late 1960s. In 1972, the press uncovered that Democratic vice-presidential nominee Sen. Thomas Eagleton of Missouri had been hospitalized for emotional illness. Democratic presidential nominee Sen. George McGovern of South Dakota initially continued to support his embattled selection, but eventually he asked Eagleton to step aside. The initial selection worried voters who questioned his judgment, and even though his eventual running mate and Peace Corps founding director Sargent Shriver was widely respected, the debacle crippled the ticket and President Richard Nixon was re-elected.

Regional Support

In 1960, Sen. John Kennedy of Massachusetts selected Sen. Lyndon Johnson of Texas, who was coincidentally a primary rival for the nomination, as his running mate. Johnson, a southern senator, helped the Democrats carry an important region of the country in what was a very close election.

Balancing Perspectives

Another consideration for a candidate is ideology. In 1988, Vice President George Bush (the current president's father) selected a little-known but widely respected senator from Indiana, Dan Quayle. Quayle, a true conservative, brought balance to the ticket and helped Bush solidify his Republican credentials because he was viewed by many in the party as too moderate.

Swinging the States

If a race is particularly close, a nominee might select a running mate who comes from a state with a large number of electoral votes in hopes of carrying that state. President Lincoln used this strategy twice. The first was in 1860, when the Republicans selected Hannibal Hamlin of Maine, giving the ticket a New England balance. Four years later, in the height of the Civil War, Maine was a safe Republican seat and Hamlin was dropped. He was replaced by Sen. Andrew Johnson of Tennessee, very much a swing state, and Lincoln was re-elected.

We Hold These Truths

Choosing a running mate on the basis of the votes that he can potentially secure doesn't always work. In 1988, Democratic nominee Massachusetts Gov. Michael Dukakis selected popular Texas Sen. Lloyd Bentsen as his vice president, in hopes of capturing the Lone Star State (the adopted home state of Republican nominee George H. W. Bush). The plan did not work: The Republicans easily carried Texas, and the rest of the nation as well.

Adding Some Sizzle

A final strategy is to select a running mate who brings an intangible form of excitement to the ticket because of who he is. Like the electoral strategy, however, it has not been as successful in the past as candidates had hoped.

In 1984, Walter Mondale, the Democratic nominee, selected three-term New York Congresswoman Geraldine Ferraro as his running mate. He knew incumbent President Ronald Reagan was incredibly popular, but he hoped adding a woman to the ticket would mobilize female voters to make history and elect the first woman vice president. While her nomination was historic—it was the first time a major party had nominated a woman for vice president—it did little to galvanize that voting base, and Reagan carried every state except Mondale's home state of Minnesota.

Working 9 to 5—And Beyond

After all the hard work and the complete and total invasion of privacy, the person who becomes vice president makes $202,900 a year. Depending on how influential the vice president is, that can be the easiest money a person ever makes (if he is all but ignored) or the hardest job, paying less than minimum wage (when all the hours are counted). But most men and women who enter public service don't do it for the money.

In addition to his office in the West Wing, the vice president maintains a suite of offices in the Eisenhower Executive Office Building, which is located next to the West Wing on the White House premises. The vice president's office in the EEOB is called the Vice President's Ceremonial Office. This restored, historical office served as the Navy secretary's office when the EEOB housed the State, Navy, and War departments. Today it is used for meetings and press interviews.

> ### We Hold These Truths
>
> There are several items of note in the Vice President's Ceremonial Office, but the most interesting may be the vice president's desk. This desk is part of the White House collection and was first used by Theodore Roosevelt in the Oval Office in 1902. Several other important veeps and even presidents have chosen to use this desk—including presidents Wilson, Coolidge, and Eisenhower. It was placed in storage from December 1929 until 1945, when President Truman used it. Vice President Johnson and all subsequent vice presidents have used the desk. The various users have signed the inside of the top drawer since the 1940s.

The vice president's staff, while smaller, is in essence the same as the president's. He has a chief of staff, a press secretary, and policy advisors.

> ### We Hold These Truths
>
> It has been widely reported that President Harry Truman, FDR's third vice president, who served with the legendary president for less than four months, had no knowledge of the atom bomb project. He was not informed of its existence until after he was sworn in as president in April 1945. Less than four months later, he had to make the important decision to drop the bomb on Japan, which, in essence, ended World War II.

The Least You Need to Know

♦ Seemingly added to the executive branch as an afterthought, the office of the vice president was once viewed as a do-nothing job.

♦ Unless they ascended to the presidency, the majority of the men who have held the second-highest office in the land have faded into obscurity.

♦ The position was held in such low esteem during the 1800s that at least one of the men elected to the vice presidency didn't bother to fulfill the commitment.

♦ At times likened to "standby equipment," the office of the vice president has gained in power and authority in recent years.

Advising the President

In This Chapter

- ◆ The president's closest advisors
- ◆ The selection process
- ◆ Roles of the departments
- ◆ Cabinet level, but not cabinet

Some of the most influential members of the government are members of the president's cabinet. Dating back to President Andrew Jackson's administration, these individuals are the closest advisors to the president. They are usually experts in their given departments and have the president's ear when it comes to matters that concern their specific agency.

In this chapter, we take a look at the various cabinet departments and agencies, along with their history and their function.

Establishing the "Kitchen Cabinet"

While he was president, Andrew Jackson wanted to bring the government closer to the people, so he assembled a group of informal advisors to meet with on a regular basis. His enemies, who were shut out of these meetings, dubbed the advisors members of the "kitchen cabinet." The term implied that they met in private and snuck in through the back door of the White House.

In 1789 there were only four cabinet departments established—State, Treasury, War, and the Office of the Attorney General. Today the president's cabinet includes 15 departments.

We Hold These Truths

Unlike modern cabinets, Andrew Jackson's cabinet was stuffed with influential newspaper editors, in an effort to curry favor with the press. He fired members of his advisory "kitchen cabinet" for arbitrary reasons, many not having anything to do with governmental affairs. The most bizarre reason for a Jackson cabinet official being relieved of his duties: refusal to speak to another cabinet member's wife!

On the Record

"They have seen in his [Douglas's] round, jolly, fruitful face, post offices, land offices, marshalships and cabinet appointments ... bursting and sprouting out in wonderful exuberance, ready to be laid hold of by their greedy hands."

—Abraham Lincoln, speaking out against the spoils system during a campaign speech on July 17, 1858

Choosing His Advisors

The process of choosing members of the president's cabinet has changed substantially since Jackson's day. His informal selection process has evolved into what is often a long, drawn-out procedure that by no means ensures the president will end up with his top choices.

The president selects his department heads at the beginning of his term (or midterm, if someone resigns) with the consent of the Senate. Selecting these cabinet officials can be a very easy or trying time, depending on the nominee. As you read in Chapter 2, the Senate has the authority to confirm or reject any of the president's cabinet selections. While the Senate has rejected only 9 appointments over the last 200 years, numerous nominees have withdrawn their names from consideration because their confirmation seemed in doubt.

Cabinet appointments are usually given to people who have a specific interest or expertise in the selected area. Often these individuals are also political (as well as personal) friends of the president.

The First Four

As previously mentioned, the president's cabinet began with four departments: State, Treasury, War, and the Office of the Attorney General.

Global Challenges and Diplomacy: The State Department

The oldest of the cabinet departments, the Department of State was established in September 1789. The main function of the State Department is to handle diplomatic ties between the United States and foreign nations. In the event of a national disaster, the person who heads this department is the first cabinet official in line for the presidency. The Secretary of State and his or her staff travel extensively, building coalitions, promoting human rights and democracy, and mediating conflicts abroad. During the Clinton administration, the State Department was active in working to resolve conflicts in the Middle East and the Balkans. The department also works to bring nations together to address global challenges such as terrorism, international crime, and communicable diseases, among many other issues.

> **We Hold These Truths**
>
> Colin Powell, who served as President George W. Bush's Secretary of State from 2001–2005, was the first African American to hold the post. The first woman was his immediate predecessor, Madeleine Albright.

In addition to working on diplomatic issues, the Department of State holds custody of the Great Seal of the United States of America. The red and white stripes of the shield represent the states united under and supporting the blue, which represents the president and Congress. White symbolizes purity, red signifies hardiness and valor, and blue represents vigilance, perseverance, and justice. The sole support of the American eagle represents the belief that Americans should rely on their own virtue. The olive branch and the arrows display the power of peace and war. "E Pluribus Unum" expresses the union of the 13 states. It has evolved in form several times since its original design in 1782, but the message is the same.

Minding Money and Security: The Department of Treasury

The Department of the Treasury oversees the monetary concerns of the federal government. It has numerous bureaus and agencies. Some might surprise you, but others you have certainly heard of.

The Treasury Department oversees the Bureau of Engraving and Printing, which makes paper money, as well as the U.S. Mint, which distributes coins. This department also oversees the Internal Revenue Service, which collects income taxes. And up until March 2003, the Treasury Department had a law-enforcement arm, which administered the U.S. Customs Service and the U.S. Secret Service, and the Bureau of Alcohol, Tobacco, and Firearms.

After 9/11 the world changed, and how America viewed protecting itself changed as well. Before this time, however, it made perfect sense that the U.S. Secret Service was under the discretion of the Treasury Department—because its original purpose when formed in the mid-nineteenth century was to seek out counterfeit money launderers. During the Civil War, nearly 30 percent of all the currency in circulation was counterfeit. There were 1,600 state and local banks printing their own money, and there were more than 4,000 varieties of counterfeit notes to go along with the more than 7,000 legitimate notes produced by the banks. To help investigate the countless counterfeit claims, the Secret Service became a part of the Treasury Department in 1865.

Over the next 40 years, the United States lost two more presidents to assassination (Lincoln died three months before the Secret Service was established), and the public wanted a protection agency put in charge of the president. At the time, the Secret Service was the only law-enforcement agency within the federal government. While Secret Service agents still work on counterfeit money concerns, since 1906 protecting the president has been a top priority.

The Secret Service was one of many federal agencies that became part of the Department of Homeland Security in 2003 (see "Keeping America Safe: The Department of Homeland Security" later in this chapter).

We Hold These Truths

Sure, the Secret Service takes care of the president and the vice president, but those are not the only people protected by the agency. The Secret Service is authorized to guard the immediate families of the president and the vice president, as well as former presidents and their spouses; minor children of former presidents until the age of 16; major presidential and vice presidential candidates; the spouses of these major candidates within 120 days of the election; as well as visiting foreign heads of state and others authorized by the president. Often these others include cabinet officials and members of Congress.

Defenders of Peace: The Department of Defense

The Department of Defense was originally called the War Department. It was founded at the same time as the Departments of State, Treasury, and Justice. In 1798, the Navy separated from the agency and created its own department to oversee Naval and Marine Corps concerns. The departments remained separated until after World War II, when military experiences proved the armed forces should be under a single unified command.

In 1949, Congress established a single civilian Secretary of Defense to oversee the Army, Navy, Air Force, and Marines. The purpose of the Department of Defense is to strengthen American military resources and work with allies around the world. American military forces have served as peacekeepers and humanitarians, as well as traditional defenders against oppressors and defenders of American interests around the world.

The Enforcers: The Justice Department

The Justice Department, the last of the original four departments, oversees the largest law office and is responsible for enforcement of all federal laws. In recent years, the department has taken up high-profile cases against major industries, including tobacco companies and software giant Microsoft, for health and antitrust concerns on behalf of the American public.

If there are allegations of misconduct on the part of executive-level officials, it is the responsibility of the attorney general, who is the head of the Justice Department, to appoint an independent counsel to investigate the situation.

The Office of the Solicitor General also comes under the jurisdiction of the Justice Department because the Solicitor General is the one responsible for representing U.S. interests in cases before the Supreme Court. (For more information on the Solicitor General, see Chapter 15.)

In light of the terrorist attacks on Washington and New York City, the Justice Department has asked for greater authority to investigate suspected criminals. Some are concerned that this authority might trample on civil rights, while others are concerned that not enough is being done to find and capture criminals.

> **We Hold These Truths**
>
> Originally the position of attorney general—like most jobs in government at the time, including those in Congress—was considered a part-time job.

New Kids on the Block

As the country grew, more departments and agencies were established and added to the president's cabinet. Of this new group, the Department of the Interior, established in 1849, is the oldest. Charged with handling the budding nation's growing domestic affairs, it initially had a wide range of areas to address, ranging from the penal system in the District of Columbia to the management of hospitals, universities, and public parks.

Over the next century, the responsibility of the department grew, and subsequent departments—notably the departments of Labor and Health, Education, and Welfare (more about them later)—were established to meet the changing needs of the country. Today the Department of the Interior focuses primarily on national parks and conservation of wildlife and natural resources.

Farm Aid: The Department of Agriculture

President Lincoln, who described this agency as the people's department, founded the Department of Agriculture in 1862. During the height of the Civil War, 90 percent of Americans were farmers and were in desperate need of accurate information regarding their crops. While the number of people who farm has greatly decreased—now it's approximately just 2 percent of the American workforce—the agency continues to serve their needs as well as the needs of the remaining 98 percent of Americans.

Currently the department administers a wide variety of programs, most of which directly or indirectly relate to food, including the Food and Nutrition Service, the Center for Nutrition Policy and Promotion, the Food and Safety Service, and the Animal and Health Plant Inspection Service. People in larger cities also have access to USDA programs, most notably the Women, Infants, and Children program, or WIC, as it is commonly known, as well as food stamp distribution.

The department deals with the concerns of rural Americans, particularly because most farmers come from these regions. The Farm Service Agency offers disaster assistance, farm loans, and other resources to farmers nationwide to deal with fluctuations in the economy.

Supporting the Economy: The Department of Commerce

The mission statement of the Department of Commerce states its goals to be the promotion of job creation, economic growth, sustainable development, and improved living standards for all Americans. It works to accomplish its goals by joining forces with businesses, communities, and workers. In addition to working to achieve the obvious goals of economic development and increased workplace technology, the Secretary of Commerce works with the U.S. Trade Representative to increase global trade.

We Hold These Truths
The Department of Commerce is responsible for making sure weather reports are available every morning in every city across the country. The National Weather Service falls under the jurisdiction of the Commerce Department and issues warnings and alerts. Next time you hear the weather report in the morning and the radio station tells you it was brought to you by Company XYZ, remember it was the Commerce Department that gave it to the radio station in the first place.

The Commerce Department has a wide range of responsibilities. It regularly releases data pertaining to new home sales, the job market, and the overall economic condition of the country. Every 10 years, one of its agencies, the U.S. Census Bureau, releases statistics on the makeup and size of the American nation. And if you invent something and want to have it registered, you need to go through the Patent and Trademark Office, also administered by the Commerce Department.

Meeting Workers' Needs: The Department of Labor

Congress established the Department of Labor in 1913 to help "foster, promote, and develop the welfare of working people, to improve their working conditions [and] to enhance their opportunities for profitable employment." The growing Department of Interior had previously addressed these issues.

As its name indicates, the department focuses a great deal of attention on workers. This agency stipulates how long you can work and sets age restrictions for certain jobs. It also has oversight of the hiring practices of employers to ensure that discrimination against minority groups does not exist.

We Hold These Truths
Elaine Chao, appointed Secretary of Labor in 2001 by George W. Bush, was the first woman of Asian descent to head a cabinet-level position.

We Hold These Truths
The Department of Labor was the first department to be chaired by a woman. Franklin Roosevelt appointed Frances Perkins Secretary of Labor in 1933. Perkins served 12 years, longer than any other labor secretary to date.

Minding the Country's Health: The Department of Health and Human Services

What is now known as the Department of Health and Human Services was created by Dwight D. Eisenhower in 1953 and was called the Department of Health, Education, and Welfare. The department has more than 300 programs focusing on a wide range of topics, including medical and social science research, infectious disease prevention, financial assistance for low-income families, the Head Start program for young children, and substance-abuse programs, as well as comprehensive health services delivery for Native Americans.

We Hold These Truths
The Department of Health and Human Services is the largest grant-making agency in the federal government, issuing an average of more than 60,000 grants a year. Like the other departments, it affects the daily lives of Americans who probably don't realize it. For example, the national Medicare program is the largest health insurer in the country, dealing with more than 900 million claims a year.

HHS also administers the nation's Food and Drug Administration. The FDA works to determine the safety of foods and cosmetics, as well as the safety of pharmaceuticals, biological products, and medical devices. The Center for Disease Control also comes under the jurisdiction of HHS and monitors the health and well-being of the nation. It keeps medical statistics on the health of the country and analyzes whether medical science is helping to decrease the number of deaths related to specific diseases.

Ensuring House and Home: The Department of Housing and Urban Development

The Department of Housing and Urban Development, established in 1965 as the result of Congressional action, is responsible for ensuring that all Americans have a roof over their heads. The department aims to create opportunities for home ownership and provides funding assistance for low-income persons.

In July 2001, then-HUD Secretary Mel Martinez announced that he was reactivating the Interagency Council on the Homeless, which directs 15 different agencies to streamline the delivery of federal services to homeless individuals and families.

The agency also has a law-enforcement arm because it is responsible for ensuring fair housing laws. It is especially active in securing housing for people living with HIV/AIDS who are often discriminated against in their housing applications. Many AIDS patients wind up homeless or are in immediate danger of losing their homes. HUD works to find affordable as well as medically acceptable housing for them through Housing Opportunities for Persons with AIDS/HIV.

Getting from Point A to Point B: The Department of Transportation

The Department of Transportation has oversight of every road, airport, train, metro, boat, and other form of transportation imaginable. Established by an act of Congress in 1966, the agency aims to develop and coordinate polices that will provide an efficient and economical national transportation system.

> **We Hold These Truths**
>
> Norman Mineta, named Secretary of Transportation in 2001 by George W. Bush, was the first American of Asian-Pacific descent to serve in the cabinet. He previously served as the Secretary of Commerce in the Clinton administration.

The Department of Energy

The Department of Energy was established in 1977 and immediately took on the responsibilities of the Federal Energy Administration, the Energy Research and Development Administration, and the Federal Power Commission. These were federal agencies in place dealing with a wide range of topics that, when joined to create the Department of Energy, centralized the research and productivity of energy directives.

The Department of Energy promotes secure, competitive, and environmentally responsible sources and production that work to meet the needs of the public. It also supports national security to promote international nuclear safety and reduce the global danger from weapons of mass destruction.

Investing in the Future: The Department of Education

The Department of Education was created when it broke off from the Health, Education, and Welfare Department in 1980. The goal of the department is to improve the quality of education nationwide. Some see that role as just focusing on the public school system, while others want the government to assist the needs of private schools as well.

The department has come under scrutiny from many sides in the political arena. Some conservatives for years wanted to abolish the department, claiming it caused too much intrusion into the lives and jurisdictions of diverse communities. How can one agency, based in Washington, D.C., adequately address the needs of urban students in south central Los Angeles at the same time it is dealing with the concerns of rural students in Saranac Lake, New York, conservatives asked.

Others have argued that only through the watchful eye of Washington, D.C., can the nation's educational standards and scores improve.

Another issue that has caused divisions within the department and the political arena is the concept of vouchers. Vouchers would give parents who send their children to private schools, whether they are religiously affiliated or not, money that could go toward their children's education. Critics say this policy would take needed resources away from public schools and, if the students attend religiously affiliated schools, violates the separation of church and state. Proponents argue that parents of children in private schools pay twice.

Taking Care of Veterans: The Department of Veterans Affairs

Established in 1989, the Department of Veterans Affairs administers benefits and programs to the nation's military. As of May 2001, the latest period for which statistics are available, more than 518,000 servicemen and women, as well as their spouses, received benefits. A very small number of children of Civil War veterans still receive benefits as well.

The Department of Veterans Affairs monitors the care of veterans. This includes everything from ensuring they receive their military benefits to overseeing the quality of their care at veterans hospitals around the country and helping them with prescriptions, housing, and even funerals.

Keeping America Safe: The Department of Homeland Security

Established in the aftermath of the September 11, 2001, terrorist attacks, the Department of Homeland Security is charged with making America more secure by developing and coordinating a comprehensive national strategy for protecting against terrorist threats or attacks. The department has three primary missions:

- To prevent terrorist attacks in the United States
- To make the United States less vulnerable to terrorism
- To minimize damage from attacks that do occur

The department was established in November 2002 by the Homeland Security Act, and began operating in January 2003. It is composed of a number of government security functions that were previously parts of other departments, including customs and border protection, immigration and customs enforcement, and emergency preparedness and response. On March 1, 2003, some 180,000 personnel from 22 government agencies became part of the department. It was the largest government reorganization since the Defense Department was created.

Cabinet Level, but Not Cabinet

In addition to the preceding departments, there are seven cabinet-level agencies whose heads are formally recognized as part of the president's administration. The president's Chief of Staff knows everything the president knows and everything the president *needs* to know. He is the captain of the White House ship and is in constant contact with the president. Did you ever wonder who whispered in the president's ear that the second World Trade Center tower had been hit by a plane? That was Chief of Staff Andrew Card.

Others who have cabinet status include …

♦ The Director of the Environmental Protection Agency, responsible for protecting human health and safeguarding the natural environment.

♦ The Director of the Office of Management and Budget, who assists the president in preparing the federal budget. This individual also helps formulate the administration's spending plans and evaluates the effectiveness of agency programs.

♦ The U.S. Trade Representative, who works to promote growth and international open-market policies at home. This person also takes a leading role in negotiating commodity and direct investment programs with other countries.

♦ The Director of the Office of National Drug Control Policy, who works to reduce drug use and drug-related crime. The office was established in 1988 as a result of congressional action.

♦ The vice president.

The Least You Need to Know

◆ The group of advisors known as the president's cabinet was established during the Jackson administration.

◆ The president can select whomever he wants to head the agencies that comprise his cabinet—subject, however, to confirmation by the Senate.

◆ Over time, various agencies have been established to meet the growing needs of the young country, and the people who headed them have been added to the president's group of advisors.

◆ Today the president's cabinet includes 15 departments—the most recent addition, the Department of Homeland Security, was created in response to the terrorist attacks of September 11, 2001, on New York and Washington.

Chapter 8

Shaping the Presidency

In This Chapter

- Presidential firsts
- Testing presidential authority
- Expanding presidential power
- Influencing the international arena

Leader of the Free World—the title doesn't appear on the door of the President of the United States' office, but it could. The framers of the Constitution didn't know what would happen when they came to the revolutionary decision to make the chief executive of the United States a president instead of a king. The section of the Constitution that established the office gave some general guidelines concerning what the president had to do and could do. Anything beyond that was unclear.

Each president, no matter how important or obscure his administration, has left some mark on the office and the nation. Some presidents were noteworthy for what they did for both; others were infamous for what they did to them. In this chapter, we take a look at the actions of more than a dozen presidents and see how they shaped a position and a nation that today rank as the most powerful in the world.

The Father of the Nation: George Washington (1789–1797)

George Washington wanted to retire to his farm at Mount Vernon after the Revolutionary War ended in 1781. But duty to the new nation he had fought so hard for came first. Realizing, like many others, the inadequacies of the Articles of Confederation, Washington served as president of the Constitutional Convention in Philadelphia in 1787. After the new Constitution was ratified, he became the first president of the United States of America.

Everything that happened during Washington's administration was a first, both for him and for the nation. The first treaty, the first law, the first dispute, the first cabinet officials ... the list goes on.

After the first electoral college unanimously elected him president (the first and only time, to date, that this has happened), Washington took the first presidential oath of office on April 30, 1789, in New York City, the capital of the United States at the time. In the years that followed, he worked to build a solid foundation for future presidents. Hoping to prevent sectionalism from dividing the new nation, he toured the New England states shortly after his inauguration and visited the South two years later.

While the Constitution laid out the foundation for the judicial branch of the government, it didn't address what its structure should be. That came later in the Judiciary Act of 1789. Washington, who signed the act into law, also appointed the first Chief Justice of the Supreme Court, John Jay, and the first five associate judges (you'll read more about the early years of the Supreme Court in Chapter 14).

We Hold These Truths

A firm believer in the Constitution (although he privately said he didn't think it would last more than 20 years, according to notes from the Constitutional Convention that were made public in 1987), Washington refused to appoint anyone to his staff who opposed the document.

Who's in Charge Here?

The first real test of presidential authority also came during Washington's administration. To help pay off American debt and establish good credit for the new nation, Treasury Secretary Alexander Hamilton encouraged Congress to pass—and Washington to sign—an *excise tax* on alcohol.

Alcohol was becoming big business in the young country, especially in rural areas where grain farmers often converted their corn into alcohol to avoid the high costs of transporting their crops to market. At the time, western Pennsylvania was the center of alcohol production, and the farmers there refused to pay the tax. In 1794, warrants were issued for their arrest, after which a riot broke out. A federal officer was killed during the skirmish, and the farmers set fire to the home of the revenue collector.

Inside the Beltway

An **excise tax** is an internal tax levied on the manufacture, sale, or consumption of a commodity within a particular country.

Washington ordered the farmers to stop their resistance, but they refused to listen. Deciding that the situation was beyond the control of federal marshals, Washington asked the governors of Pennsylvania, Virginia, New Jersey, and Maryland to mobilize their militias—15,000 militiamen in all. This show of force was all it took to end the "Whiskey Rebellion," as the farmers' rebellion came to be called. The office of the president had demonstrated its strength.

Washington, who believed that the Constitution was clear on government's policy-making aspects, preferred not to interfere with congressional affairs. The one arena in which he felt the president should act, however, was foreign policy. When the French Revolution led to a major war between France and England, Washington refused to side with either party, preferring instead that the United States remain neutral until it could grow stronger.

On the Record

"The alternate domination of one faction over another, sharpened by the spirit of revenge, natural to party dissension, which in different ages and countries has perpetrated the most horrid enormities, is itself a frightful despotism. But this leads at length to a more formal and permanent despotism. The disorders and miseries which result gradually incline the minds of men to seek security and repose in the absolute power of an individual; and sooner or later the chief of some prevailing faction, more able or more fortunate than his competitors, turns this disposition to the purposes of his own elevation, on the ruins of public liberty.

"Without looking forward to an extremity of this kind (which nevertheless ought not to be entirely out of sight), the common and continual mischiefs of the spirit of party are sufficient to make it the interest and duty of a wise people to discourage and restrain it."

—George Washington, on the evils of political partisanship in his Farewell Address of 1796

Washington's health began to decline toward the end of his second term, and he decided not to seek a third term. In his farewell address, Washington became reflective and warned the nation about the ill will of political parties and the factions they develop. His words, more than 200 years old, could easily be applied to twenty-first-century America.

Washington left office in March 1797 with the foundation that he had hoped to build well in place. With Hamilton's help, the country's financial system was well established. Washington's contacts and knowledge of the American landscape and peoples had helped secure frontier lands east of the Mississippi from raids by Native Americans.

The Expansionist: Thomas Jefferson (1801–1809)

Like Washington—and most early presidents—Thomas Jefferson was no stranger to the American people when he was elected president in 1800. Best known as the chief architect of the Declaration of Independence, Jefferson had been active in local and state politics in his home state of Virginia, where he also practiced law. He served in the Continental Congress twice and as the U.S. minister to France before accepting George Washington's appointment as Secretary of State, a post he held from 1790 to 1793.

In 1796, Jefferson was nominated as a presidential candidate. Retired and living at Monticello, his renowned classical estate, he did little to promote his own campaign, yet he finished second to John Adams. Under the rules of the day, he became vice president. Adams and Jefferson did not see eye-to-eye on most matters, so Jefferson ran again for president four years later. After a protracted electoral college battle, caused when Jefferson and his running mate, Aaron Burr, both received enough electoral votes to win the election, Jefferson was eventually selected and took office on March 4, 1801.

Inside the Beltway

The **strict construction** interpretation of the Constitution holds that powers not explicitly mentioned there belong to the people.

Jefferson, an ardent Federalist, believed in the *strict construction* interpretation of the Constitution, which governed many of his beliefs and actions both before and during his terms as president. When it came to the biggest decision he faced as chief executive—expansion of the new nation—it also caused him a fair number of sleepless nights.

Buying Louisiana

Of everything Jefferson did during his time in office, his decision to purchase the Louisiana Territory from the French was by far his biggest achievement. This act had a great impact on the young country. With a stroke of his hand, he doubled the size of the United States, adding 800,000 square miles in what remains the largest land acquisition in U.S. history. The country's border, which had been the Appalachian Mountains, now stretched to the Rocky Mountains.

Although he believed his decision to buy the Louisiana Territory was in the country's best interest because it protected the large shipping port at New Orleans, a vital component of American commerce, Jefferson also was troubled by it. The Constitution was very specific in the roles outlined for the executive, and buying land from foreign governments wasn't one of them. Technically, the way to go about such a purchase was to amend the Constitution, but Jefferson knew he risked losing the land through that lengthy process.

Even though it went against his interpretation of the Constitution, Jefferson went directly to the Senate and asked for immediate ratification of the treaty. Every Federalist sitting in the Senate voted against Jefferson's request on the grounds it was unconstitutional, but the Senate did as Jefferson asked and added the land of the Louisiana Purchase to the United States in 1803.

> **On the Record**
>
> "The Constitution has made no provision for our holding foreign territory, still less for incorporating foreign nations into our Union. The Executive, in seizing the fugitive occurrence which so much advances the good of their country, has done an act beyond the Constitution."
>
> —Thomas Jefferson on the merits of buying the Louisiana Territory

Shaping Foreign Policy: James Monroe (1817–1825)

James Monroe, who served as minister to France, envoy to France, and minister to Britain before being elected president, is best known for establishing the tenets of foreign policy called the Monroe Doctrine.

By the early 1800s, a number of Latin American countries had won their independence from Spain and Portugal. However, concern was mounting over the future of the former Spanish colonies, especially when it appeared that an alliance of European countries, including Austria, Prussia, France, and Russia, was preparing to invade them. In his annual address to Congress in 1823, Monroe outlined a bold agenda for keeping American states free from interference from European countries. In no uncertain terms, he proclaimed that …

♦ The western hemisphere was no longer open to colonization.

♦ Any new attempts at colonization, or attacks on countries within the western hemisphere, would be viewed as attacks on the United States and would be subject to reprisal from the American government.

♦ The United States would not interfere in the affairs of any nation that at that time already had a colony in the region.

♦ In return for this last concession, Europeans would not interfere in any way in the politics or policies of any free nation in the region.

The policy Monroe outlined that day became known as the Monroe Doctrine and quickly became the foundation of U.S. foreign policy.

On the Record

"We owe it, therefore, to candor and to the amicable relations existing between the United States and those powers to declare that we should consider any attempt on their part to extend their system to any portion of this hemisphere as dangerous to our peace and safety …."
—From James Monroe's address to Congress on December 2, 1823

Expanding the Power of the Presidency: Andrew Jackson (1829–1837)

Old Hickory, as Andrew Jackson was called, was a war hero who had fought the British during the War of 1812 and famously defeated them at the Battle of New Orleans in 1815 (after the war had ended, interestingly, because news of the treaty didn't reach him until well after it was signed).

Unlike previous presidents, all of whom had come from wealth and privilege, Jackson's family was poor Scotch-Irish farmers who had settled in the hills of Tennessee. His election proved that any white man (politics was still considered a single-sex profession, and elected office was still restricted to whites) could ultimately reach the highest office, regardless of his upbringing.

Unlike most of his predecessors, Jackson didn't defer to Congress on policy-making decisions. Instead, he insisted on using the power and influence of his office to expand the power of the presidency. He was the first president to replace federal officeholders who disagreed with his policies with people who had supported his candidacy. Often the placements were awarded because of loyalty to Jackson, not merit or ability. At the time, many people criticized his moves, giving rise to the term "spoils system" from the phrase "to the victor belong the spoils."

Jackson defended his right to appoint new people to office and believed that bringing fresh blood into the administration brought the common man closer to the government. While historians have been critical of Jackson for other reasons, most notably his treatment of Native Americans, many admit he made government more representational and accessible for the common man.

Inside the Beltway

The term **kitchen cabinet,** used to describe members of a presidential administration, comes from the Jackson era. He often met privately with his advisors—most of them unofficial—in his kitchen. His detractors, who felt the meetings should be held in public and were angered by the secrecy, began calling Jackson and his cronies the kitchen cabinet.

Jackson was a staunch defender of the Union. He didn't like the National Bank because he felt it favored the rich, but he did believe that the nation as a whole was bound by laws passed by Congress and signed by the president.

On the Record

"Our Federal Union—it must be and shall be preserved."

—Andrew Jackson, to his vice president, April 1830, *Triumph of the American Nation,* 1986

"The Union—next to our liberty, the most dear! May we always remember that it can only be preserved by respecting the rights of states."

—John C. Calhoun, in reply

Tariff taxes were another issue on which Jackson stood firm. Enacted to protect American merchants from foreign competition, tariff tax rates had risen steadily since the end of the War of 1812. Many southern merchants, who depended on trade with colonies outside the United States, particularly in the Caribbean, opposed the tariffs. Vice President John C. Calhoun, who was from South Carolina, also opposed the tariffs.

In 1828, after Congress passed another tariff act—called the Tariff of Abominations by its detractors—Calhoun issued an unsigned statement urging the states to nullify any action by Congress that they felt was unconstitutional. The South Carolina legislature took Calhoun's comments to heart and passed legislation calling the tariff unconstitutional and unjust. Georgia, Tennessee, and Virginia passed similar laws shortly thereafter.

When word of the states' actions reached Jackson, he sided with Congress and supported the tariffs. Predictably, relations between Jackson and Calhoun became rocky after Jackson found out that his vice president's actions had caused the southern states to oppose laws passed by Congress. By the 1832 presidential campaign, their relationship had deteriorated to the point that Jackson replaced Calhoun with Martin Van Buren as his vice-presidential running mate.

Over the next three years, tensions between the South and the government in Washington, D.C., continued to grow over the tariff issue. They reached a boiling point when South Carolina threatened to secede from the Union following the passage of the Tariff Act of 1832. The state eventually backed down, but as a result, the Compromise Tariff of 1833 was passed; along with it, the federal government was given the power to use the military to enforce federal tariff laws.

We Hold These Truths

The ninth and tenth presidents hold the dubious distinctions of being the first president to die in the White House and the first vice president to complete a presidential term.

William Henry Harrison's inauguration in March 1841 came on a particularly cold, damp day. Not only did Harrison ride hatless to the Capitol, but he then gave the longest inaugural speech on record, clocked at 1 hour and 45 minutes. He caught a severe cold and died of pneumonia one month later.

John Tyler, Harrison's vice president, was never popular enough to run as president on his own steam, and he only served out Harrison's term. Most people in Washington didn't think that Tyler was capable of being president—in fact, at one point all but one of his cabinet members resigned in protest over one of his vetoes. The veto, on tariff legislation, also brought the first charge of impeachment against a sitting president.

The Peacemaker: Abraham Lincoln (1861–1865)

Abraham Lincoln was a great man whose life was filled with enormous tragedy. His only brother died in infancy, his mother died when he was 10, and his sister died in childbirth. His first love died of fever before they could marry. His second love turned him down when he asked for her hand in marriage. His road to marriage with Mary Todd was rocky, and he even called off their first engagement. Only one of his four sons reached adulthood. With all this baggage, it's a wonder that Lincoln was able to get up in the morning, let alone save the United States from complete dissolution.

On the Record

"… I had been oppressed nearly ever since the battles at Gettysburg, by what appeared to be evidences that yourself, and Gen. Couch, and Gen. Smith, were not seeking a collision with the enemy, but were trying to get him across the river without another battle…."
—Letter from Lincoln to Union Gen. George Meade, July 14, 1863

In 1860, Lincoln was chosen as a compromise candidate by the Republicans, who were looking for a way to take advantage of a split in the Democratic Party. Although Lincoln had served only one term in the U.S. House of Representatives, he was well known in Republican circles as a grass-roots party organizer in his home state of Illinois, and he had narrowly lost a Senate race to Democrat Stephen Douglas in 1858.

Lincoln believed in the Union above all else. He was opposed to slavery, but he didn't carry the passion that many abolitionists did. He didn't buck the issue like his predecessor, James Buchanan, and he recognized that his election in 1860 likely meant a Civil War. He was right. Even before he could take office, seven states—South Carolina, Mississippi, Florida, Alabama, Georgia, Louisiana, and Texas—had seceded from the Union. By June 1861, that number had increased to 11.

Lincoln knew the war was going to be long and hard-fought, but he continued to maintain that the Union would prevail in the end. Slowly, though, he also realized that the war was just as much about slavery as it was about the Union. Four times he issued separate proclamations ending slavery in certain regions before the final Emancipation Proclamation on January 1, 1863.

The war waged on until April 9, 1865, when Gen. Robert E. Lee surrendered to Union Gen. Ulysses S. Grant at the courthouse in Appomattox, Virginia. Lincoln hoped to peacefully readmit the Confederate states, with compassion and not strife. This, however, wouldn't happen. Six days later he was dead from a gunshot wound to the head from southern sympathizer John Wilkes Booth.

A Better Tailor Than President: Andrew Johnson (1865–1869)

Andrew Johnson, who followed slain president Abraham Lincoln into office, is the only president who never spent a day in school. Born into abject poverty, he supported himself and his family as a tailor, and the only education he received was from the people who read to him and his fellow workers during his apprenticeship.

Johnson's talent at tailoring, however, led to a successful business venture as the town tailor in Greeneville, Tennessee. Johnson's small shop became a favorite hangout for locals—including area politicians—and he gained another education from listening to them chew the fat over local issues. By the time he was elected mayor of Greeneville, Johnson had become a skilled orator and debater. From mayor, he ascended to the office of military governor of Tennessee, then to the U.S. Senate, and then to the vice presidency.

Johnson believed that the Constitution reigned supreme over everything, including states' rights. He was also fervent about preserving the Union. When the southern states seceded, he was the only southern senator to remain in Washington.

As president, Johnson tried hard to carry out Lincoln's vision of a peaceful transition back to a restored Union. With Congress out of session, he began reconstructing the South on his own terms. Radical Republicans from the North, as well as other members of Congress, didn't approve of Johnson's actions, nor did they trust him. When they returned to Congress the following year, they repealed many of his plans.

Over the next three years, Johnson squabbled repeatedly with Congress, leading to his becoming the first president to be impeached. Members of the House of Representatives, angry over Johnson's dismissal of Secretary of War Edwin Stanton, charged him with violating the Tenure of Office Act, which his Republican enemies had passed to prevent him (or other presidents) from dismissing any federal officials without prior approval from the Senate. The House voted 11 articles of impeachment against Johnson. He was then tried by the Senate in the spring of 1868 and was acquitted by one vote.

Historians are divided on Johnson's presidential legacy, but most agree he left the office in worse shape than he found it. It has been noted, however, that his acquittal helped preserve the independence and power of the presidency.

> ### We Hold These Truths
>
> Richard Nixon, like Andrew Johnson a century before him, left the White House in shambles. The Watergate scandal and Nixon's eventual resignation brought down the president and made the nation more skeptical of its national leaders and the actions of government. The personal activities of presidents and presidential candidates were never issues before 1974. Since then, no candidate can run for any office without having every word and action scrutinized.

Creating the Bully Pulpit: Theodore Roosevelt (1901–1909)

Theodore Roosevelt wasn't elated over being nominated as William McKinley's vice presidential running mate in early 1900. Already an enigmatic, forceful leader, he had concerns over holding what was then one of the most obscure positions in American politics. But he lacked the support he needed from the Republican Party to seek another office, so he accepted the offer. When McKinley was shot and killed six months after Roosevelt was inaugurated as vice president, another man whom no one ever thought would become president did.

Roosevelt was a patriot and a fiercely independent thinker who used the *bully pulpit* of his office to fight for his beliefs. He argued tirelessly for the people and against big business, and he used antitrust legislation to regulate firms and corporations that he felt were reducing or threatening competition. He also espoused internationalist policies and believed American imperialism and expansion were good practices. He never hesitated to get involved in affairs he felt were of national importance to the United States.

Inside the Beltway

Bully pulpit was the term Teddy Roosevelt used to refer to the power and influence given to him as a holder of public office.

One of Roosevelt's most lasting legacies, however, was his conservationism. A former "Rough Rider" who loved the Dakota country of the West as well as the Adirondacks of upstate New York, Roosevelt set aside huge tracts of land for federal protection. He is considered by many to be the father of the modern conservationist movement.

Global Thinker: Woodrow Wilson (1913–1921)

Woodrow Wilson is noted for having the vision that would position the United States as a key player in international politics. Wilson did not come to this position easily, though. Initially an isolationist who campaigned for re-election in 1916 as the man who had kept America out of the war in Europe, Wilson eventually realized how the world was globally connected. He would become a leading proponent of international cooperation among the nations of the world.

One of our most learned presidents—he is the only president to date to hold a doctoral degree—Wilson worked hard to keep the United States out of World War I, believing, like most Americans, that the conflict between European countries had little to do with American interests. However, Germany's continued aggression left him little choice, and he reluctantly brought the United States into what was known then as the "Great War" in 1917.

Believing it was necessary to make the world safe for democracy, Wilson used his 1918 State of the Union address to announce what he called a "general association of nations" to give "mutual guarantees of political independence and territorial integrity to great and small states alike." Campaigning for an international organization to keep global peace would become his signature issue.

Under the Treaty of Versailles signed in 1919, a League of Nations was formed under Wilson's direction. He had worked hard to convince the leaders of France, Italy, and England to come together and not totally divide the defeated Germans. Unfortunately for Wilson, the battle to get his own country to buy into the plan was much harder. Wilson was a Democrat, and both the House and the Senate were controlled by Republicans, who found weaknesses in the League's plans, including a provision that pledged unconditional support for member nations if attacked from someone outside the League.

Wilson's brainchild, the League of Nations, was formed without him and without American backing when the Senate rejected the treaty. It eventually went on to include more than 60 member nations, but it was too weak to prevent the outbreak of another "great war," as Wilson had hoped.

Making America Great: Franklin D. Roosevelt (1933–1945)

Franklin Delano Roosevelt, a distant cousin to Teddy Roosevelt, built on his cousin's bully pulpit to help his country become a twentieth-century superpower.

FDR became president during the greatest economic downturn in American history. The Roaring Twenties had ended with massive unemployment, hunger, and despair; more than 12 million Americans were out of work. FDR pledged to fix the economy, and while it is unclear whether his policies or World War II ended the Depression, FDR is credited with helping America gain back its economic and military strength.

Almost immediately, FDR helped restore Americans' faith in themselves. In his first inaugural address, he told the struggling nation, "The only thing we have to fear is fear itself." During his first four months, he proposed—and Congress enacted—the New Deal, a revolutionary program aimed at bringing economic recovery and relief to the nation.

Two years later, the country was getting back on its feet. But not everyone was pleased with recovery. Businessmen were particularly irked that FDR had taken the United States off the gold standard. In an answer to these criticisms and others, Roosevelt established new reform programs: Social Security, with heavier taxes on the wealthy; new controls over banks and public utilities; and an enormous work-relief program for the unemployed.

In 1936, FDR was re-elected by a wide margin (in fact, he received no less than 432 electoral votes in all 4 of his presidential elections). Such a wide margin of victory, he felt, showed that the electorate had given him a mandate to do whatever he wanted. When the Supreme Court began ruling against him and his policies, FDR decided to "pack" the court with his favorites. The scheme failed and is considered a low point in his administration. (For more on Roosevelt's court-packing agenda, turn to Chapter 14.)

We Hold These Truths

Roosevelt's decision to seek an unprecedented four terms in office led to the creation of the Twenty-second Amendment, which limits the number of terms a president can serve to two. If a president serves more than two years of another president's term as a result of succession, he may run for election only once.

Roosevelt had tried to keep America out of World War II, much like Wilson had tried 20 years earlier, but all that changed when the Japanese attacked Pearl Harbor shortly before 8 A.M. on December 7, 1941. Roosevelt declared war on Japan the following day, and his wartime legacy began.

In another move similar to Wilson's, FDR spent a great deal of time considering a plan to bring the world—particularly the United States and Russia—together in a global organization. While the war would drag on for four years—and American victory was not always a guarantee—FDR remained strong and confident for the people. He built strong alliances with European allies and, despite declining health, traveled the globe to promote the Allied cause. He made secret deals with Russia and England that some historians have criticized, but for the most part, he is viewed as a solid American war president who steered the nation through one of its worst times.

The presidents who followed FDR faced a world carved up by communism and threatened by nuclear war. While many of their actions by necessity focused on making the world safe from both, they also enacted legislation that changed the face of the United States. It is still too early to view their accomplishments in historical terms, although President Ronald Reagan is widely credited with helping to bring down communism in Europe in the 1980s. Like the presidents who came before them, though, their unique talents and visions shaped both the office they held and the world we live in.

The Least You Need to Know

◆ George Washington, the first president, established many of the precedents that would guide the United States and the office of president.

◆ Of everything Thomas Jefferson did while in office, his decision to buy the Louisiana Territory had the greatest impact on the young country.

◆ While many people disapproved of Andrew Jackson's "spoils system," he is noted for making government more representational and accessible.

◆ Beginning with Teddy Roosevelt, the office of the president has become increasingly concerned with international issues.

Part 3

Checks and Balances

When it came to establishing a lawmaking body for the United States, the framers of the Constitution had quite a job on their hands. They had to come up with a model that would give each state—no matter its size or population—equal representation and equal say in how the country was run.

After much wrangling and compromising, they settled on two chambers—an upper chamber, or Senate, where each state had the same number of representatives; and a lower chamber, or House of Representatives, where representation was based on state size and population.

Although partisan posturing often occupies more of the spotlight than the issues in question do, there's no denying Congress's importance and authority as the chief lawmaking body in the United States. From approving treaties with foreign nations to setting the annual appropriations for governmental agencies, what happens on Capitol Hill affects all Americans in some way.

Chapter 9

The Lower House

In This Chapter

- ◆ Women in the House
- ◆ Leaders of the House
- ◆ Key committees
- ◆ Managing the country's money

As you read in Chapter 1, delegates to the Constitutional Convention differed significantly on how states would be represented in the new government they were forming. Some representatives, especially those from smaller states, wanted the same number of representatives for every state, regardless of size—meaning they all would have equal representation. Those from larger states wanted representation based on population, with the larger states having more influence.

The delegates ended up striking a compromise that established the upper house, or Senate, with equal representation, and the lower house, or the House of Representatives, with members chosen based on state size and population. Each state, no matter how small, would have at least one member in the lower house.

In this chapter, we take a closer look at the House of Representatives and how it differs in form and function from the Senate.

Representation Based on Population

Originally, members of the House represented districts with populations of roughly 30,000 to 40,000 people. Under current law, the House has a set number of 435 representatives. Instead of representing districts of 40,000, they represent districts that average nearly 600,000 citizens. If the population numbers had remained the same since the eighteenth century and not changed with the times, today there would be over 6,900 members of the House of Representatives alone!

We Hold These Truths

The House is often referred to as the "People's House" because the members who serve here often have more contact with their constituents than their counterparts in the Senate. Also, unlike the Senate, in which members were appointed rather than elected until the early twentieth century, House members have always been elected by the people.

Representation is based on population. As a result, Alaska, the largest state in the union, and Delaware, the second smallest state, each have only one representative. On the other hand, Rhode Island, the smallest state, has 2 representatives, and Massachusetts, the sixth smallest state, has 10 representatives. California, the third largest state in land size, has the most representatives, 53. (See Chapter 24 for more information on how the district lines are drawn and what determines the number of representatives for a state.)

Calling All Voters, Calling All Voters

There has always been direct election of the representatives by the people. The election of representatives takes place every two years, and many members often complain they start their re-election campaign the day after the election because two years goes by very fast.

The definition of who is eligible to vote, however, has changed over time. At first, only white men who owned property could vote. Later the property restriction was lifted, but it was not until the Fifteenth Amendment was ratified in 1870 that minority men were given the right to vote.

We Hold These Truths

The first black American to serve in the U.S. House of Representatives was Joseph Rainey, a Republican from South Carolina. Rainey, a former slave, was elected in 1870. He served four terms and then was appointed an internal revenue agent for the state of South Carolina in 1879. Other black Americans went on to serve in both the House and the Senate, but after Reconstruction ended in 1877, many of the freedoms they had won as a result of the Civil War were severely limited by restrictive and bigoted laws of southern states.

The Fifteenth Amendment clearly paved the way for black men to vote. By the late nineteenth century, however, Southern states began to turn back the clock. They passed oppressive laws, such as the poll tax, charging free men a fee to vote, and the literacy test, making sure the men who were voting could read. With most black men poor and illiterate due to little or no education, they were disenfranchised.

When it became apparent that many white men were poor and illiterate as well, some states passed *grandfather clauses*. Under the grandfather clause, if a man could not pay the tax or read, he was eligible to vote if he, his father, or his grandfather had been eligible to vote on or before January 1, 1867. Because minority men were not given the right to vote until the Fifteenth Amendment was ratified more than three years after this date, the grandfather clause all but ensured that very few blacks would be voting.

Inside the Beltway

The **grandfather clause** was a clause in some southern states' constitutions that waived electoral literacy requirements for descendants of those allowed to vote before 1867, in effect enabling illiterate white people to vote while excluding illiterate black people.

The Supreme Court did not rule the grandfather clauses unconstitutional until 1915, in the case of *Guinn and Beale v. United States*. However, it was not until the Voting Rights Act of 1965 was signed into law by President Lyndon Johnson that the remaining poll taxes, which had still been considered legal, were outlawed.

The 1965 law is considered by many to be one of the most important legislative achievements of the twentieth century. The legislation also mandated federal supervision of voter registration in minority districts, where those registered to vote were less than half of those who were eligible to vote. Literacy tests were eventually made illegal. The effect was instant and great. Many southern counties saw a rise in voter participation, and blacks saw an increase in power.

A Woman's Place Is in the House

Women comprised another population that wasn't originally allowed to vote for members of the House. Although the federal government was not guaranteeing the rights of women in the democratic process, however, individual states were. Wyoming was the first, granting women the right to vote while it was still a territory in 1869. Several other western states followed suit as well, including Utah, Colorado, and Idaho. In a four-year period between 1910 and 1914, women suffragists—people supporting the right of women to vote—convinced seven more states, all west of the Mississippi River, to give women the vote.

Jeanette Rankin, a Republican from Montana, was the first woman elected to the House of Representatives, winning her seat in 1916. She was the only member to oppose American entry into both World War I and World War II. Ironically, she served only two terms. During her first term, she announced that she would vacate her House seat and run for Senate in the next election. She lost in the primary. For the next 20 years, she remained active in politics and ran again in 1940, defeating an incumbent. Unable to address the House as a whole, she repeated her solitary vote against entry into the war. She did not even try for re-election.

Since Rankin's historic election, more than 130 women have served in the House of Representatives. Some served for barely two months. Rep. Veronica Grace Boland, a Democrat from Pennsylvania, won a special election to finish out her late husband's term on November 3, 1942, but she did not run to be the next representative. Her term expired on January 3, 1943, just two months later. Boland received no committee assignments and never participated in any debates.

Twenty years earlier, Winnifred Mason Huck had also been elected during a special election to succeed her late husband. Huck, a Republican from Illinois, served only four months. During this time she was appointed to several committees and was known to be a firebrand with various viewpoints. On one hand, she supported self-government for Cuba, Ireland, and the Philippines; on the other hand, she introduced legislation calling for a direct referendum by the people to participate in any war declarations. She ran for another open seat in February 1923 but was defeated in the primary.

We Hold These Truths

The longest-serving woman in the House was Rep. Edith Nourse Rogers, a Republican from Massachusetts. She was initially elected to finish out the term of her late husband in June 1925. Unlike most of the other widowed congresswomen, Rogers had a lengthy and successful career on Capitol Hill. She did extensive work for veterans' affairs including serving as chairwoman of the Veterans' Affairs Committee during two separate sessions. Her major legislative accomplishments included a Women's Army Corps and sponsorship of the GI Bill. Rogers died in office three days before what would have been her nineteenth primary election on September 10, 1960. She was 79.

Currently, there are more than 50 women in the House of Representatives, serving in all capacities. Both Republicans and Democrats have women in leadership. U.S. Rep. Nancy Pelosi, a Democrat from California, is the highest woman serving in elected leadership. She was elected House Minority leader—a first for a woman—in 2002.

Requirements for Representatives

To be elected a member of the House of Representatives, a candidate must first meet several federal requirements. He or she must be 25 years old at the time they are sworn in (meaning that a candidate could be 24 on election day, provided that he or she turns 25 by the time service begins) and must be a resident of the state in which the election occurred.

Yes, you read that last part correct: A candidate must be a resident of the state he or she runs in, but the person does not necessarily have to be a resident of the district they hope to represent. Most candidates, however, do not live outside their districts, or they would be subject to *carpetbagger* criticism.

It is important to note, however, that most members do have a second home in the Washington, D.C., area. Sessions run for long periods of time; sometimes members do not get out until late at night and need to have somewhere they can sleep. With few exceptions, these homes are sparsely furnished apartments within walking distance of the Capitol used only as a place to shower, change, and sleep.

Inside the Beltway

Carpetbagger is a term used to describe an outsider whose only interest in coming to a place is to win it as a political seat.

The final requirement for a House member is to have been a citizen of the United States for the last seven years.

We Hold These Truths

Article 1, Section 5, of the Constitution says "each house of Congress shall be the judge of the elections, returns, and qualifications of its own members." Before a 1969 Supreme Court ruling, Congress had occasionally used this power to refuse seating to a number of seemingly qualified candidates. The Supreme Court ruled, however, that these words referred only to the age, residency, and citizenship requirement and Congress could not refuse to seat an elected member for any other reason.

Although there is no educational requirement for serving in Congress, many who serve on the House side have less-professional backgrounds than those in the Senate, who are traditionally lawyers, business executives, or career government officials.

Members who serve in the House have varied professions. In the 109th Congress, which began January 3, 2005, there are teachers, public relations consultants, real estate agents, and farmers. Some members have a law degree, while others have earned a two-year community college degree.

Leaders of the House

As detailed in the following table, the House is divided into two sets of leadership—majority and minority. The Republicans, who hold a six-seat advantage, currently control the majority leadership. The Democrats control the minority leadership. The Republicans have been in control since 1995. Before the 1994 midterm election, the Democrats had been in control for 40 years.

Majority Leadership	Minority Leadership
Speaker of the House	Minority leader
Majority leader	Minority whip
Majority whip	Deputy whips*
Deputy whips*	Caucus chairman
Conference chairman	Caucus vice chairman
Conference secretary	Assistant to the minority leader

Not elected positions—appointed by the leadership to serve as lieutenants in the party army.

House leaders are responsible for maintaining party organization; scheduling the business affairs of the chamber, including the legislative sessions and debate times; and providing members with the most current and up-to-date information on national affairs as well as legislation. Those chosen as leaders are traditionally members who have served for an extended period of time, who understand the way the system works, and who have widespread respect within their own caucus—and sometimes even on the other side of the aisle.

Mr. Speaker, Mr. Speaker!

The leader of the House of Representatives is known as the Speaker of the House. Traditionally, he (there has never been a woman Speaker) is selected by his majority caucus to be their leader and Speaker nominee, and then the entire House as a whole votes for the position. Having a majority of the votes, he wins.

The minority party also nominates a Speaker candidate, but it is only a formality. The vote for Speaker is often what defines a member and his party affiliation. It is not unheard of for a member to vote for someone other than the party's nominee, provided that the person is voting for someone within the party.

We Hold These Truths

Typically, members vote for someone from their own party to be the leader. While they do not have to vote for one of the designated candidates or nominee, they need to vote for a fellow party member or face consequences. For example, at the start of the 107th Congress, two Democrats did not vote for the party's nominee. James Traficant, a representative from Ohio, voted for the Republican nominee and was all but formally expelled from the Democratic caucus. The party didn't seat him on any committees. Gene Taylor, a representative from Mississippi, voted for another Democrat, Rep. John Murtha of Pennsylvania. Because he voted for another Democrat, he didn't suffer the same consequences as Traficant.

The Speaker is responsible for recognizing members on the floor of the House when they want to speak. Most times, because of his other duties, a designate is appointed to take his place.

The Speaker has broad powers when it comes to committee assignments and legislation. He appoints members of the select and conference committees and assigns legislation to the standing committees. Committee assignments for legislation can be key to its eventual outcome because some committees may look more favorably toward certain bills than others. If a bill has several contentious aspects to it, the Speaker may also decide to send it to more than one committee for recommendation.

For the most part, the power and influence of the Speaker largely depend on the member himself. If he is charismatic and has a good deal of political skill, he can use his influence and power to help vulnerable members bring home favorable projects—and, therefore, hopefully win re-election. But if his lieutenants have a lot of power, he can serve as little more than a puppet.

In addition to the Speaker, the majority party has three other key leaders within the caucus:

- ◆ The majority leader is the person who speaks for the party and often has a highly visible role. The Speaker is meant to be a less partisan individual, so even though the Speaker is technically the leader of the party, he sits back and allows the majority leader to be more combative and to freely tout the party philosophy.

- ◆ Next in line of the majority party leadership is the majority whip. The whip is the person who works behind the scenes to control the agenda. He has several deputy whips whom he appoints to help with his mission. He is the person responsible for making sure all members vote a certain way on key party line votes. He also is responsible for generating enthusiasm and support for party initiatives. Sometimes, as is currently suspected, the majority whip wields more control within the caucus than the majority leader, just by the secret nature of his job.

- ◆ While there are more than four leaders within the majority party, the final leadership role of significance is the conference chair. The conference chair is responsible for getting the party message out to the members, coordinating meetings, and helping to set the agenda.

We Hold These Truths

When members of the House of Representatives file into the chamber, they do not have assigned seats. Members of the leadership traditionally sit at the desks on their respective sides, but unlike their counterparts in the Senate, whose seats are assigned, the House members can sit wherever they want and can change seats daily if they choose.

On the minority side, the leadership system is much the same. The minority leader takes on the role of both the Speaker (because he speaks for his party) and the leader for his party. At times he can be very political or more statesmanlike, depending on the situation. Some minority leaders have been complacent with their standing within the House and often worked well with the majority leadership, while others have been more aggressive and assertive in trying to get their message out in partisan tones.

The minority whip could be considered the pit bull of the House. He or she is responsible for keeping party members on message as well as preventing any members from straying to the majority side on key votes. Like the majority side, the minority whip has several deputy whips to help with this process. Often, if the issue is controversial, or if the issue divides the party, the minority whip will be the one out front making the case (or the attacks) and trying to create unity.

The final member of the leadership of note is the Democratic caucus chairman. His role is almost identical to that of the Republican conference chairman, with minimal differences due to his current minority status.

Leadership races within the House are often some of the most highly contested and divisive races during an election year, even if they are played out in virtual secrecy to anyone living outside the beltway. Members will lobby each other, sometimes hourly, to vote for a certain candidate. Having a member of your delegation, even if not of your party, in the leadership can bring significant amounts of resources back to your state. Also, members in the leadership are exposed to classified information and top security measures, as well as a significant amount of money in the event of a tough re-election campaign. They are the go-to people for the party and can turn an obscure member into a national leader overnight. For example, in the early 1990s there was a little-known minority whip by the name of Rep. Newt Gingrich of Georgia, who went on to become one of the most powerful and influential Speakers in modern-day American government.

Other Key Players

Other members of the House play important roles even though they are not part of the elected leadership of either party. Groups also known as caucuses form due to common interests. Often these caucuses have members of both parties working together. Some caucuses are well known, such as the Women's Caucus or the Pro-Life Caucus. Other caucuses are less known and deal with the geographic or professional concerns of members. Most caucuses are bipartisan, but the two most well known are not. The Congressional Black Caucus is made up entirely of Democrats, as is the Hispanic Caucus. These caucuses deal primarily with partisan issues and most fall on the Democratic side.

Nonpartisan caucuses include these:

- Congressional Mining Caucus
- Congressional Boating Caucus
- Congressional Steel Caucus
- Congressional Travel and Tourism Caucus
- Congressional Children's Caucus
- Federal Government Service Caucus

Other caucuses include the Vietnam Era Veteran's Caucus, the Rural Health Coalition, the Urban Caucus, the Congressional Arts Caucus, and the Sportsmen's Caucus.

Committees

Committees in both the House and the Senate are divided into three categories: standing, select, and joint.

Standing committees are permanent committees with legislative authority within Congress. They are specific in nature, such as the Education Committee or the Budget Committee, but they deal with a large range of issues within these parameters. Currently, there are 20 standing committees.

Standing committees are further broken down into three separate categories: exclusive, nonexclusive, and exempt. If a committee is considered exempt, a member may serve on this committee and it will not affect his or her standing or service on other committees. An exclusive committee is one that requires a great deal of time and energy, such as Appropriations or Commerce. A member may only serve on one exclusive committee.

Standing committees (nonexclusive):

- Agriculture
- Armed Services
- Banking and Financial Services

- Budget

- Education and Workforce

- Government Reform

- House Administration (Democrats only)

- International Relations

- Judiciary

- Resources

- Science

- Small Business

- Transportation and Infrastructure

- Veterans' Affairs

Standing committees (exclusive):

- Appropriations

- Commerce

- Rules

- Ways and Means

- Exempt

- Select Intelligence

- Standards of Official Conduct

- House Administration (Republicans only)

As a rule, a member may not serve on any more than two standing committees and four subcommittees, for a maximum of six slots.

In addition to the preceding committees, there are two additional types:

- Select committees are also known as special committees. They are temporary panels established for a set amount of time to handle a specific mandate. Most select committees do not have a legislative authority. They are created by a simple resolution.

◆ Joint committees are made up of members from both houses of government. They are permanent panels with study, housekeeping, and administrative authority.

Committee Sizes

Committee sizes in the House, as in the Senate, are negotiated between the party leaders before and during organizational meetings before the beginning of each Congress. The committee assignment process and delegation is handled by the steering committees for both the Democrats and the Republicans. Steering committees are made up of leadership, as well as other members from various regions of the country with competing interests, to recommend which members should be placed on which committees. While the recommendations of the steering committees are subject to a vote by the entire party caucus, it is very rare for a committee assignment to be overturned.

We Hold These Truths

Committee sizes are not listed anywhere in House rules; instead, they are allocated in the aggregate. The allocation is based on the total number of committee slots available on all committees instead of on a committee-by-committee basis. This is done to ensure that a working majority is in place for the most important committees.

Committee Assignments

Members are given committee assignments based on their individual areas of expertise, their interests, the interests of their district, and their availability. Committee assignments can often determine the course of a member's career. Once a member has served at least one term, he or she has more flexibility and seniority and therefore can carry more weight when requesting specific committee assignments. He or she is likely to move up and over to new assignments once committee slots open up due to retirement, resignation, or larger committee sizes.

The ratios for these committees are dependent on the difference between the majority and minority sides. Therefore, they fluctuate with each new Congress, but usually by no more than a few seats.

Further Divisions

Each committee is further divided into subcommittees that deal with specific areas within the committee. House rules limit the number of subcommittees to five per parent committee; the exception to this is the Appropriations Committee, which is discussed later in this chapter.

Committee Staffs

In addition to having staff members who work in their individual offices, the members have separate committee staffs at their disposal. These staffers often work tirelessly (and thanklessly, to the general public at large) behind the scenes on pending legislation and proposals. While unknown to most people outside the Capitol Hill area, these staffers are enormously influential.

Committee Leadership

Committee leadership on House committees varies depending on which party is in power. There is always a committee chairman or chairwoman and a ranking member on each committee and subcommittee.

Republicans, who came to power for the first time in 40 years as a result of the November 1994 elections, take many factors into consideration when appointing their committee leadership. These factors include seniority, strength (or vulnerability) at home, fund-raising abilities, and expertise. Republicans also put in place term limits for service as a committee chairman. Instead of members serving for 10 or 20 years as chairmen, they are limited to 6 years for a given committee. This was done to bring new blood into the fold, with new thoughts and ideas.

Democrats choose their committee leadership solely on the basis of seniority. The member who has served the longest on a given panel is the ranking member. If the Democrats retake the House in the 2006 midterm elections, the same process would presumably be in place for selecting chairmen.

Minding the Money

Article 1, Section 7, of the Constitution reads as follows: "All Bills for raising Revenue shall originate in the House of Representatives, but the Senate may propose or concur with Amendments as on other bills."

Article 1, Section 8, continues by saying, "The Congress shall have Power to lay and collect Taxes, Duties, Imposts, and Excises to pay debts and … to borrow Money on the credit of the United States."

In other words, with these two parts, the framers of the Constitution set up a system by which any and all money-raising bills, including taxes and tariffs, need to originate in the House. The theory is that the House is more in tune with the average citizen because its members were elected by them, as opposed to the Senate, whose members were appointed up until the early twentieth century.

The Ways and Means Committee was first established in 1789. For the next 76 years, it oversaw all business associated with appropriations, banking, and currency. On March 2, 1865, at the tail end of the Civil War, the House of Representatives separated these duties into two new committees, the Appropriations Committee and the Banking and Currency Committee.

You may have never heard of the Ways and Means Committee, but you certainly have heard of legislation that has passed through the committee. The most recent significant legislation to go from the committee to the president's desk was the bill granting permanent normal trade relations with China in 2000. The bill, which was hotly debated, caused divisions within both parties. (The president at the time was Bill Clinton, a Democrat who strongly supported it. The Republican House leadership, both the minority leader and the minority whip, opposed it.) The bill originated in the Ways and Means Committee because it dealt specifically with eliminating any tariffs on goods coming to the United States from China, as well as vice versa, on a permanent basis. It was passed and signed into law in late 2000.

The Appropriations Committee, which is in both the House and the Senate (note that the Senate does not have a Ways and Means Committee), is responsible for the expenditures of the country. All appropriations bills must start in the House, but they can be debated in the Senate any time after House introduction. When the nation was first born, there was only one appropriations bill that met the needs of the entire country. Things have greatly changed since then, and during each fiscal year of the 107th Congress, October 1 through September 30 of the following year, the Appropriations Committee deals with 13 different spending bills!

These are not cheap tabs, either. To give you an idea, Congress passed 13 appropriations bills in 1997, totaling more than $794.9 billion! Compare this with the total from the first year that the new Appropriations Committee reported the general bills, 1867: a mere $357.5 million! Note the million with an "m" in 1867, compared with the billion with a "b" 130 years later!

The Least You Need to Know

♦ All 435 members of the House of Representatives are up for election (or re-election) every two years.

♦ The leader of the House is known as the Speaker of the House.

♦ Members of the House of Representatives each represent approximately 600,000 people.

♦ Members often join together in a bipartisan manner in caucuses that deal with common concerns or interests.

♦ All tax bills and money bills must originate in the House.

Chapter 10

The Upper House

In This Chapter

- ◆ Meeting behind closed doors
- ◆ Powers over the president
- ◆ Requirements for being a senator
- ◆ Impeachment power

Often described as the statelier chamber, the Senate is known for its deliberateness and thoughtful approach to legislative issues, especially when compared with the livelier House of Representatives.

Over the years, the Senate has been the venue for some of America's most deeply divisive debates, including slavery, voting rights for women and minorities, federal versus state control, treaties, and judicial appointments to the Supreme Court.

The exclusive powers over presidential appointees and control over approval of treaties with foreign nations are part of the reason for the Senate's distinct way of handling legislation.

The Beginning of the "Debater's Society"

Before the Senate became known as a debater's society or the upper house of Congress, the body made its way into the Constitution as a bargaining chip.

Designed to represent the states equally, the Senate was part of the "Great Compromise" between large and small states. As you read in Chapter 1, the goal was to have each state represented equally with two members each, as opposed to the population-based House of Representatives.

> **We Hold These Truths**
>
> Since the Senate's first session in 1789, it has met in two venues outside of Washington, D.C.: New York City (1789–1790) and Philadelphia (1790–1800).

Before Washington, D.C., became the nation's capital, Senate sessions were held in New York and Philadelphia. Many of those first meetings were held secretly, in contrast with the House sessions, during which members of the public were always allowed to view proceedings.

In those days, many senators believed their proceedings would be used mainly as an advisory body to the president. But the public increasingly demanded to hear what the Senate discussed, and in 1795 a small visitors' viewing area was opened. Visitors to both the Senate and the House were afforded the same privilege when Congress moved to Washington in 1800.

> **We Hold These Truths**
>
> Some of the most commanding figures from the nineteenth century—including Daniel Webster, Henry Clay, Stephen Douglas, and John C. Calhoun—were senators during this period. The setup of the Senate offered the perfect forum for intense debate between these expert orators.

A Changing Profile

The Senate's beginning years, even after opening the chamber to the public, were relatively uneventful. Initially, much of the public attention was focused on the House, which had far more lively proceedings and more members. Part of the Senate's early years were slow moving because its members realized that much of what they did would serve as a model for years to come.

The Senate began to shed its low profile shortly after the turn of the nineteenth century. It changed drastically with the presidential election of 1824, when then-Senator Andrew Jackson won the popular vote and the electoral college but lost the presidency because he did not garner a simple majority of either.

Jackson's bitterness over that loss caused him to resign from the Senate the following year to begin planning his second bid for the presidency in 1828. This time he won overwhelmingly. But the Jackson administration fought with Washington insiders over nearly everything, including the division between the Senate and presidential powers.

The issues being debated in the first half of the century were by no means insignificant ones, and they included the expanding nation, interpretation of federal authority versus states' rights, and, of course, slavery.

Rising Tensions

Tensions rose over the most contentious issue of all: slavery. The founders of the country had not dealt with the issue, and numerous compromise attempts only delayed the war.

Decided in 1820 by Congress, the Missouri Compromise was the first major attempt to settle the slavery question in the lands acquired in the Louisiana Purchase. The number of slave and free states was equal and both sides were worried about upsetting that fragile balance. Missouri was eventually allowed to enter the Union as a slave state, while Maine entered at the same time as a free state. Except for Missouri, the compromise also said slaves were free above the 36 degree, 30 minutes north latitude line.

Compromises Made and Broken

Breaking the Missouri Compromise, the Compromise of 1850 was passed by Congress to deal with whether slavery should exist in several new states entering the Union. California was admitted without slavery, but the territories of Utah and New Mexico would be allowed to decide for themselves whether to allow slavery. The new compromise also created stiffer penalties, known as fugitive slave laws, for those who aided escaped slaves. Webster, Clay, and Douglas led the side supporting the compromise, while Calhoun led the southern states that opposed the measure.

In 1854, the Kansas–Nebraska Act was passed on similar grounds. The two new territories would be permitted to decide for themselves the question of whether to allow slavery, a decision that also directly conflicted with the Missouri Compromise.

We Hold These Truths

Perhaps one of the most startling examples of the deep divisions during the time involves Sen. Charles Sumner, a Republican from Massachusetts and an ardent opponent of slavery, and Rep. Preston Brooks, a Democrat from South Carolina, a defender of slavery. In 1856, after Sumner finished a speech arguing against allowing slavery in the Kansas territory, a furious Brooks stormed onto the Senate floor and began beating Sumner with his cane because Sumner had directly criticized Brooks's uncle.

Sumner was severely injured, and his Senate desk sat empty for two years—a clear symbol of the battle between the North and the South. After the House tried to censure Brooks but ended up with a straight party-line vote, Brooks resigned. His constituents immediately re-elected him.

Edging Toward War

In 1857, the Supreme Court decided the Dred Scott case, concerning the freedom of a slave whose owner had died. The Court ruled that Scott could not sue his owner's widow because he was not a citizen. The decision enraged the North.

As the nation edged closer to the Civil War, several senators made last-ditch attempts to preserve the Union. One such effort, known as the Crittenden Compromise, was introduced by Sen. John Crittenden of Kentucky. The agreement would have allowed slavery to continue where it already existed and was an attempt to keep southern states from seceding. But the House voted down the proposal, and the country began preparing for war.

When southern senators began resigning as their states seceded from the fledgling Union, the effects on the Senate were immense. When Mississippi decided to secede in 1861, shortly after South Carolina, one of its United States senators—Jefferson Davis—resigned from the Senate. A month later, he became president of the Confederacy.

Sadly, Davis, in a speech on the Senate floor on January 21, 1861, told his colleagues,

> I am sure I feel no hostility toward you, Senators from the North. I am sure there is not one of you, whatever sharp discussion there may have been between us, to whom I cannot now say, in the presence of my God, I wish you well; and such, I feel, is the feeling of the people whom I represent toward those whom you represent. I, therefore, feel that I but express their desire when I say I hope, and they hope, for peaceable relations with you, though we must part.

We Hold These Truths

At the beginning of the Civil War, Abraham Lincoln demanded that federal employees must retake an oath of office, which Congress expanded with a clause supporting the Union. This addition became known as the Ironclad Test Oath because it required federal employees and military personnel to swear future loyalty as well as assert that they had never been disloyal in the past. In 1884, the part of the oath known as the Ironclad Test Oath was repealed, leaving the same oath of office taken by every senator today.

The Senate Gains in Power

As you read in Chapter 3, three constitutional amendments granting rights to slaves were passed after the Civil War. President Andrew Johnson, a southern Democrat, was lenient on southern states and officials who had fought against the Union in the Civil War. This enraged slavery opponents.

Johnson also vocally opposed the Fourteenth Amendment—granting former slaves citizenship—which Congress passed anyway. After Johnson began removing government officials and replacing them with his allies on reconstruction policies, Congress passed the Tenure of Office Act, requiring Senate consent before the president could make such changes. Johnson vetoed the measure, but Congress overrode the veto.

Escalating the battle, Johnson then asked for the resignation of his Secretary of War, Edwin Stanton. Stanton refused. When the Senate refused to take Johnson's side, the president fired Stanton, leading to the first impeachment of a president. Congress nearly succeeded in convicting Johnson in his impeachment trial. The House impeached Johnson, but the Senate failed to convict him, falling one vote shy of the two-thirds majority necessary.

For the rest of the nineteenth century, the Senate became a much stronger body than at any other time in its history. This was a result of two factors: the weak presidents who followed Johnson, and because the Senate believed the primary role of the chief executive was to enforce the laws that Congress passed.

Becoming Truly Representative

The body was also slowly becoming more representative of the rest of the country by this time. While African Americans, Hispanics, Native Americans, and Asian

Americans have all had representation in the Senate, the first was an African American. Hiram Revels of Mississippi was in the Senate for only one year, from 1870 until his death in 1871. Later, Charles Curtis of Kansas was the first Native American elected to the Senate; he served from 1907 to 1913 and again from 1915 to 1929. Curtis also served as vice president under Herbert Hoover from 1929 to 1933.

We Hold These Truths

Thirty-one women have served as senators since the brief appointment of Rebecca Latimer Felton. As of 2001, there are 13 women in the Senate—the most at any point in history. Among them is Sen. Hillary Rodham Clinton, a Democrat from New York, who made history as the first former first lady to serve in the Senate.

But Hispanics, Asian Americans, and women all had to wait longer to hold a Senate seat. Octaviono Larrazolo of New Mexico was the first Hispanic and held office for one year, from 1928 to 1929. Hiram Fong of Hawaii was the first Asian American to hold office, from 1959 to 1977.

The first woman to hold a Senate seat was Rebecca Latimer Felton of Georgia, who was appointed to fill a vacancy for only two days in 1922. Hattie Caraway of Arkansas was the first woman elected to the Senate in her own right. Following the death of her husband in 1931, Caraway was appointed to the seat and won the special re-election in 1932. That fall, she was re-elected to serve her own full term.

Operating in the Shadow of Presidents

Larger-than-life presidents such as Theodore Roosevelt and Woodrow Wilson, who appeared in the first half of the twentieth century, partially overshadowed the Senate. Congress as a whole was a weaker body under strong executives. Still, the Senate had the yea-or-nay power over many presidents' top priorities. It rejected Wilson's Treaty of Versailles in both 1919 and 1920. The other exclusive power of the Senate—over presidential appointees—was also exercised in this period. The Supreme Court nominee John Parker was the first in the twentieth century to fail to be approved by the Senate. The Senate did not vote down another Supreme Court nominee for almost 40 years.

Aiding the New Deal

During the Great Depression in the 1930s, the Senate played a critical role in passing many of Franklin Delano Roosevelt's *New Deal* programs.

Inside the Beltway _____

The **New Deal** was Roosevelt's legislative response to the Great Depression. It was launched by a nationwide bank holiday, which Roosevelt called for on his first day in the White House, and a special four-month emergency session of Congress, during which a number of measures were passed that created a host of new federal agencies to help bolster the country's flagging economy.

Shifts in Policy

After the attack on Pearl Harbor in 1941, a major policy shift occurred in the Senate (and the rest of the government), and what had been bitter internal strife mostly evaporated as senators turned their attention to foreign shores.

In 1936, the Supreme Court case *United States v. Curtiss-Wright Export Corp.* had granted to the president exclusive power over foreign affairs without an act of Congress needed. The case stemmed from a war between Bolivia and Paraguay, both of which wanted to purchase weapons from the United States. Trying to stop the war, Congress passed a measure that would give President Roosevelt authority to ban the sale of weapons to the countries, which Roosevelt then signed. But Curtiss-Wright sold the weapons anyway, under the claim that the Constitution did not give the president embargo power. Since that time, Congress and the president have perpetually clashed over foreign policy, especially because Congress often has much less access to information regarding these policies.

Taking Up the Question of Rights

In the 1950s, the Senate began furiously debating civil rights policies, which finally resulted in the landmark legislation of the Civil Rights Act of 1964. This legislation outlawed discrimination in hiring on the basis of race, color, religion, or sex. The following year, the Voting Rights Act of 1965 made discrimination by state governments against minorities illegal.

Debates over War Again

Soon afterward, the Senate became embroiled in what much of the country was debating during this time—the United States' involvement in the Vietnam War.

Although the war resolution, called the Gulf of Tonkin Resolution, passed overwhelmingly in 1964, there were soon fissures that resulted in a repeal of the resolution.

In 1973, Congress passed the War Powers Act, over the veto of President Nixon, to give Congress more say over U.S. military involvement in other countries. Successive presidents, however, including Ford, Carter, Reagan, and George H. W. Bush, have ignored part or all of the measure, citing it as unconstitutional.

Who Wants to Be a Senator?

A common phrase inside the Beltway is that every senator is said to look in the mirror each morning and see a President of the United States. Because they represent an entire state instead of a single district, and because there are only 100 senators compared to 435 members of the House, members of the upper body often receive more public attention.

While many senators run for president, only the 15 in the following list have succeeded in ascending to the highest office in the land.

Senators who have also been president:

- James Monroe
- John Quincy Adams
- Andrew Jackson
- Martin Van Buren
- William Henry Harrison
- John Tyler
- Franklin Pierce
- James Buchanan
- Andrew Johnson
- Benjamin Harrison
- Warren G. Harding
- Harry S. Truman
- John F. Kennedy
- Lyndon B. Johnson
- Richard M. Nixon

Ascending the Ladder

Most politicians work from the bottom up and follow a fairly predictable pattern from local office to the House, and then to the Senate and perhaps even the presidency. But not everyone adheres to this pattern.

Claude Pepper, a Democrat from Florida, is the only senator to conclude his career in government in the House. A senator from 1936 to 1951, Pepper was a representative from 1963 until his death in 1989. Meanwhile, Andrew Johnson had a slightly reversed political track. Johnson was elected to the Senate in 1875—a sweet victory for the former president who barely escaped impeachment in the same chamber.

Rules and Requirements

The Constitution sets down several requirements of individuals wanting to be senators:

- ◆ They must be at least 30 years of age.
- ◆ They must have been citizens of the United States for the previous nine years.
- ◆ They must be residents of the state they represent.

But one senator broke the first requirement of the Constitution. The record for youngest senator goes to John H. Eaton of Tennessee, who was sworn in when he was only 28 years old—breaking the requirement by two years! Eaton was appointed to fill a vacancy created by Sen. George W. Campbell in 1818. Eaton was re-elected in 1821.

Terms and Limits

Senators serve six-year terms, with one third of the upper chamber facing re-election every two years. The architects of the legislative system decided on a lengthy term (compared to two-year terms in the House) to help its members be less affected by immediate political pressure. There is no limit on the number of terms a senator can serve.

We Hold These Truths
Sen. Strom Thurmond of South Carolina easily holds the record for longest-serving senator. Thurmond served 46 years in the Senate when he retired in January 2003. First appointed to fill a vacancy in December 1954, Thurmond was elected as the only write-in candidate to ever win a U.S. Senate race a month earlier, but he was not sworn in. He resigned in April 1956 to keep a promise to voters, but he was re-elected to fill his own vacancy later that year. In 2003, he died at the age of 100, less than a year after he completed his final term.

"Elected by the People Thereof"

Citizens not only weren't allowed to watch the Senate in action, they also couldn't directly vote for their senators until 1913, when the Seventeenth Amendment was passed. Before then, senators were elected by state legislatures.

Part of the reason for originally giving state legislatures that power was to increase the number of states that would ratify the Constitution. But problems began with the system before the Civil War, when some legislatures could not agree on a senator because of opposing opinions in different parts of one state. Later, more difficulties developed and Congress passed a law creating regulations for each state to follow to be consistent in the election of senators. Problems were rampant, however, and support began building for reform of the system.

On the Record

"The Senate of the United States shall be composed of two senators from each state, chosen by the legislature for six years; and each Senator will have one vote." (A constitutional amendment was required to allow constituents to vote directly for their senators.)

—Article 1, Section 3, of the U.S. Constitution

In 1907, Oregon became the first state to use direct election to select its senators, and other states slowly began to follow. In response to growing public opinion, the Senate passed a resolution requiring direct election in 1911, which the House passed in 1912. Three fourths of the states had ratified the Seventeenth Amendment by 1913. Aside from senators being "elected by the people thereof," the amendment allowed the governor of a state to appoint a senator of his or her choice to a vacant senate seat until the next general election.

Power over the President

Two significant powers that rest with the Senate often allow the body to exercise critical power over the president.

Advice and Consent over Treaties

First, the Senate has exclusive power to approve or deny treaties the president seeks with foreign nations. Article 2, Section 2, of the Constitution says the president "shall have Power, by and with the Advice and Consent of the Senate, to make Treaties, provided two thirds of the Senators present concur."

One treaty that established boundaries for future treaties was debated during the Washington administration. Washington sent Supreme Court Chief Justice John Jay to Great Britain to negotiate a treaty and settle disputes with the nation left over from the Revolutionary War. But Washington had not alerted the full Senate. Senators were angry on two fronts: They had not been consulted or involved in the negotiations, and they opposed some of its clauses.

Because the Senate was not able to exercise its "advice and consent" over the treaty, several senators argued vehemently that they would approve the treaty only if the Senate was involved in framing future treaties. Although that measure was defeated, "Jay's Treaty" was approved in 1795. Far-reaching results of its passage, however, highlighted the need for presidents to ensure bipartisan support on treaties, and some have even included senators in the negotiation stage.

We Hold These Truths

Only 21 treaties have been wholly rejected by the Senate; the first was a treaty with the Wabash and Illinois Indians in 1794. But perhaps the most famous example of the Senate brutally exercising its power was its rejection of the Treaty of Versailles twice, in 1919 and 1920, which dealt a huge blow to Woodrow Wilson's presidency.

Wilson had proposed a League of Nations to prevent a second world war, but the 49–35 defeat meant that the United States would not become a member of the league. Part of Wilson's failure was attributed to his exclusion of any senators during the rounds of negotiations. The defeat was also credited to the opposing party controlling the Senate at the time.

Advice and Consent over Presidential Appointees

Second, the Senate has control over every presidential appointee—a power that often pits a president of one party and a Senate controlled by the other in direct opposition. Article 2, Section 2, of the Constitution says the Senate has advice-and-consent power over "Ambassadors, other public Ministers and Consuls, Judges of the Supreme Court, and all other Officers of the United States, whose Appointments are herein otherwise provided for."

We Hold These Truths

Throughout history, the Senate has most often rejected appoint-ees of the Supreme Court because jus-tices are granted lifetime seats. Twenty-seven of 148 Supreme Court nominees have been rejected, but only 9 out of more than 700 presidential cabinet appointees have been rejected.

The Senate must approve more than 1,000 positions to fill the Cabinet each time a new president is elected. Some 4,000 civilian appointments and 65,000 military appointments are subject to Senate approval in each session.

Senate committees (more about them later), especially the Judiciary Committee, play influential roles in the confirmation process because some nominations languish in committee and never even make it to the Senate floor for a vote.

We Hold These Truths

Meanwhile, the Constitution's intent is widely interpreted, with some senators finding that a nominee ought to be confirmed unless he or she is grossly unqualified. Others, however, believe the Senate can reject a nominee for any particular reason. The only way for a president to sidestep the Senate's power is to use recess appointments, which means that the president authorizes the appointee when Congress is in recess. The term for those appointed during a recess expires at the end of the next session of Congress, and this is a tactic commonly used by outgoing presidents.

"High Crimes and Misdemeanors"

Although the Senate does not hold the exclusive power to impeach, its role in one of the most powerful tools of the legislative body is unique. While the House has the power to impeach an official, the Senate must hold the trial and decide whether to convict. The president, vice president, and all civil officers, including federal judges, are subject to impeachment for "treason, bribery, or other high crimes and misdemeanors." A conviction in the Senate means automatic removal from office, with no opportunity to appeal.

The Senate has convicted government officials of impeachable offenses only seven times (all were federal judges) since 1789. Sixteen impeachment cases have been sent to the Senate from the House. Seven were acquitted, and in two cases the officials had already vacated their office.

The framers were deliberately vague in their choice of impeachable offenses, and Congress has frequently debated over its powers in the relatively few impeachment cases it has experienced. Two, in particular—resignations and definitions of the impeachable offenses—have been furiously debated throughout the country's history.

When Richard Nixon became the focus of impeachment proceedings in 1974, he resigned and the case was dropped. But in 1876, Secretary of War William Belknap tried to resign before he was impeached. The House voted to impeach him the same day he resigned, although the Senate later voted for his acquittal because members believed they did not have the power to convict a private citizen.

The impeachment trial of Supreme Court Justice Samuel Chase in 1805 was also precedent setting. Chase, a partisan Federalist, often criticized Jeffersonian Republicans. When Jefferson was elected president and a majority of Republicans were in Congress, the House voted to impeach him. The Senate, however, did not convict. Thus, the precedent was set that officials could not be impeached based solely on their political views.

Throughout Bill Clinton's impeachment trial, the issue of what exactly constituted an impeachable offense was particularly unclear. *Narrow constructionists* view impeachable offenses as those crimes that are considered to be indictable offenses. *Broad constructionists* tend to view the impeachment power as a political weapon and expand the meaning of "high crimes and misdemeanors." President Andrew Johnson used the defense of the lack of an indictable crime in his impeachment trial, although he avoided conviction in the Senate by only one vote.

Inside the Beltway

Narrow—or strict—**constructionists** interpret the Constitution based on the framers' intentions and generally take a more literal meaning from the document. **Broad**—or loose—**constructionists** apply the intentions of the framers to a changing society.

Leadership and Procedure

In 1789, during the Senate's first session, John Langdon of New Hampshire was selected as the first president pro tempore. Vice President John Adams was the Senate's first president. Today, it's rare for the vice president to regularly preside over the Senate, but occasionally he does have to cast a deciding vote in the case of a 50–50 tie in the chamber.

The president pro tempore presides over the Senate when the vice president is absent. Throughout most of the twentieth century, common procedure for electing the position has been to choose the most senior member of the majority party. The president pro tempore is fourth in line to the presidency behind the vice president and the Speaker of the House.

While the House has a Speaker who is the most visible leader in that chamber, the Senate does not have a singular leader. Instead, the two most powerful leaders are the majority leader and the minority leader. There was not a majority leader in the

Senate until 1913, when the post then known as "majority floor leader" was created by Democrats in response to a division in the Republican Party.

Elected by their respective caucuses at the beginning of each session, the two leaders are primarily responsible for pushing their parties' agendas. The majority leader also schedules debates over legislation on the floor. *Unanimous consent* agreements are developed between the two leaders to govern how legislative debates will be run. The term also refers to the agreements worked out between majority and minority leaders to govern a debate, including how many and what kind of amendments will be debated, the time limit for debate on each one, and the time for the final vote on the measure, all of which must be agreed to by unanimous consent.

Inside the Beltway

Unanimous consent refers to agreements that are used to allow generally routine motions to pass.

Cloture is the only way to stop debate in the Senate without unanimous consent.

But the majority leader can file for *cloture* if debate rules cannot be agreed upon. Three fifths of those present and voting must agree to cloture, which then limits senators to one hour of debate each. If a debate appears deadlocked, the majority leader may also file a motion for cloture on a bill, which ends debate if two thirds of the Senate approves.

In debate, senators are allowed to speak as long as they want on a particular topic unless cloture is invoked. Hoping to block legislation, senators often use the *filibuster*, in which they debate a topic for hours. The Senate maintains unlimited debate, unless a motion for cloture passes. Teams of senators often work a joint filibuster, either by objecting to a motion for unanimous consent or by reading aloud the previous day's Congressional Record. The filibustering record goes to Sen. Strom Thurmond, from South Carolina, who spoke continuously for 24 hours and 17 minutes against the Civil Rights Act of 1957. When a senator takes part in a filibuster, he or she does not have to speak on the matter at hand. Instead, the only rule is that he or she must remain standing and remain talking.

Inside the Beltway

Filibusters are tactics used to delay or block legislation by delivering long speeches.

Another way to delay debate is through the use of a quorum call—or roll call of every senator's name. Quorum calls are also used to demonstrate that a majority of the Senate is present to conduct business.

Both parties also elect whips, whose responsibilities include counting the votes of the party's members to ensure passage or defeat of a bill. Whips are also given the task of finding additional votes, if needed.

Committees

When the Senate first began meeting, temporary rather than permanent committees were used. Those committees, which typically had between three and five senators, were set up after the chamber had already passed a bill; the committee would then hammer out specific details of the measure. Because temporary committees were set up as they were needed, chairmen of the committees were often changing and had little overall power. In comparison, committee chairmen today are often some of the most powerful senators.

But by the War of 1812, senators realized that permanent committees needed to be established. First organized in 1816, the 11 committees created were based on the categories of the president's agenda and were known as standing committees. Each committee had five members except for two committees, which had only four.

Three types of committees exist in the Senate today: standing, select or special, and joint. There are 16 standing committees, 4 special or select committees, and 4 joint (with members of the Senate and the House) committees. Committees are also ranked according to their importance and are labeled Class A (most important), Class B, and Class C. Members are limited to serving on two Class A committees and one Class B committee. Today there are 12 Class A committees and 4 Class B committees. Special or select committees are Class B or C committees.

Committees have dual roles and are authorized to conduct far-reaching investigations and hammer out the details of legislation before it reaches the floor of the Senate. When senators are first elected to the Senate, a priority system guarantees that each senator is allowed to make one committee selection before any other new senator is allowed to make a second choice. Party leaders have approval over which other committees senators sit on.

Often the background for some of the most famous investigative hearings ever held in Congress, high-profile committee hearings have included organized crime, the Vietnam War, Watergate, and, most recently, campaign finance reform.

The Least You Need to Know

- ◆ The term of a senator is six years.
- ◆ The Senate has been the venue for some of America's most divisive debates, such as slavery and voting rights for women and minorities.

◆ Originally thought to be merely an advisory group to the president, the Senate steadily gained in power and influence over the years.

◆ Thirty-three women have served as senators; some filled in for their deceased spouses, but the majority were elected in their own right.

◆ Senators must be at least 30 years old, must have been citizens of the United States for 9 years, and must be residents of the state they represent.

Chapter 11

Congressional Authority

In This Chapter

- ◆ How Congress creates legislation
- ◆ Types of bills
- ◆ The committee process
- ◆ Taking it to the floor

On average, thousands of pieces of legislation, or bills, are introduced in each session of Congress. Yet just a fraction of them eventually become law.

Understanding the process by which a bill becomes a law does not require a degree in advanced political theory. But understanding the system by which a bill becomes a law requires about the same amount of patience as the study of this technical science.

In this chapter, we look at the process a bill must go through to become a law.

Beginning the Process

Ideas for laws first originate in the minds of members of Congress, usually in response to an event or a constituent suggestion that something needs to be changed. In some cases, a constituent or special-interest group may have complained about an archaic rule or may be concerned that some policy is not as strong as it could be. Wherever the idea comes from, most legislation comes as the result of civic action on the part of individuals or lobbying groups (more about them in Chapter 22).

When it comes time to draft legislation, members seek the advice of their staffs, who are experts in selected areas. In fact, committee staffers are often the authors of the first drafts of measures, which are then changed by members. They also have access to the *Office of Legislative Counsel* in their respective chamber. These attorneys, who are nonpartisan, offer technical expert assistance in the crafting of legislation, resolutions, and amendments.

Inside the Beltway

The **Office of Legislative Counsel** consists of attorneys who offer nonpartisan advice and assistance on crafting legislation, resolutions, and amendments. Both the Senate and the House have these offices.

In the second session of the 106th Congress (January to December 2000), Rep. Martin Frost, a Democrat from Texas and fourth in Democratic House leadership, co-sponsored more legislation than any other representative. His name appeared as a co-sponsor on 920 measures initiated in the House.

After the drafting process, members may hold a press conference to announce their plans and proposed legislation. This is especially true if the proposed bill deals with a hot-button issue. It is sometimes also done in an effort to garner publicity for the measure, if it is not as high on the radar screen as the member would like. Often bill sponsors will be joined by colleagues, or co-sponsors, who will be working with them to help pass the legislation.

Press conferences are not always held to announce legislation. If members think their objective might be too controversial, they will occasionally try to get legislation passed with as little fanfare as possible by doing their work behind the scenes.

In rare cases, members will try to pass legislation in complete secrecy. In 2000, Utah Sen. Orrin Hatch, then chairman of the Judiciary Committee, was the secret author of a bill that, if passed, would help drug manufacturer Schering-Plough Corp. in its efforts to extend the patent on its top-selling allergy drug Claritin. For weeks Hatch was referred to as "Senator Anonymous" as everyone on Capitol Hill tried to figure out who the author of the legislation was. Hatch eventually came forward and revealed himself to a Capitol Hill reporter. The legislation was never passed.

Types of Legislation

Members may introduce several types of legislation. The most common is a bill. Bills may be introduced simultaneously in both the House and the Senate. For a bill to become law, however, it must be passed with identical language in both Houses. If the houses pass similar but not completely identical versions, conference committees are called. (More about these later in this chapter.)

When bills are introduced into the House, they are given the title H.R., for House of Representatives, plus an assigned number. When they are introduced into the Senate, the title is simply S., plus the number. The number the bill is assigned refers to the order in which it was introduced during the session. There are more members in the House than the Senate, and therefore far more bills are introduced there.

> **We Hold These Truths**
>
> In the second session of the 106th Congress (January to December 2000), the House introduced 2,701 measures and the Senate introduced 1,546. Of this number, 372 eventually became public laws.

Joint Resolutions

Another process by which members can legislatively conduct business is through a joint resolution. Similar to a bill, a joint resolution enforces laws, but it also can be used for the purpose of proposing amendments to the Constitution. When this is done, the joint resolution must pass both chambers by a two-thirds vote; then it is directly submitted to the states, instead of the president, for approval. Joint resolutions carry the designation H.J.Res. or S.J.Res.

An example of a joint resolution relates to the activities that took place immediately following the terrorist attacks on September 11, 2001. Members of both chambers unanimously passed legislation condemning the attacks and calling for an end to terrorism. It put the lawmakers on record as supporting increased resources "in the war to eradicate terrorism" and extended condolences to the victims and their families.

Concurrent Resolutions

Members do not just legislate laws that affect the nation, but are also responsible for dealing with the internal affairs of Congress. When dealing with these matters, they may pass concurrent resolutions, designated as H.Con.Res. or S.Con.Res. Concurrent resolutions must pass both chambers but are not sent to the president for final approval. While they do not have the force of law behind them, they can be used to express *nonbinding* opinions for the Congress.

Inside the Beltway

Nonbinding refers to opinions that do not create legal or moral obligations.

When Bill Clinton was under investigation by independent counsel for lying under oath in 1998, many members of Congress floated the idea of offering a concurrent resolution by both chambers to censure, or publicly rebuke, the actions of the president instead of seeking impeachment. While the idea was eventually dropped, the theory behind it was that members were allowed to go on record for disapproving of what Clinton did without punishing him for it.

Simple Resolutions

Finally, members can introduce simple resolutions, known as H.Res. or S.Res., again followed by a number. They are used to deal with internal matters of the individual chambers, for reasons such as establishing special committees and funding resolutions for special committees, and for special rules coming from the House Rules Committee (more about this group later).

One example of a simple resolution was one introduced in 1999 by Rep. Nancy Pelosi, a Democrat from California, in memory of the tenth anniversary of the Tiananmen Square massacre in China. While Congress was in no way officially sanctioning China for its actions in regard to the events, it was publicly saying it would not forget the communist regime's crackdown on civil and human rights.

Building Support

Members and co-sponsors often send out "Dear Colleague" letters to garner support for their given issue. These letters are used to raise awareness of the issue with their colleagues, as well as give them the opportunity to become co-sponsors themselves.

Co-sponsors in both chambers can be added throughout the legislative process until a measure is reported from committee. In the Senate, they may also be added through unanimous consent.

Going to Committee

Bills may be introduced at any time during the congressional session. Once a bill is introduced into the House or Senate, it is almost always sent to the relevant committee for review. On very rare occasions, bills are sent directly to the floor for review.

We Hold These Truths

In September 2000, the Republican House leadership decided to bring a bill to the floor that surprised many, especially considering its topic and chance for passage. Rep. Lynn Woolsey, a Democrat from California, had introduced legislation that would revoke the federal charter given to the Boy Scouts. Woolsey was angered by the private organization's decision to exclude homosexuals from membership, which the Supreme Court had upheld earlier that year. The bill, never debated before committee, was extensively debated on the floor. It failed miserably, 12–362.

The process by which bills are referred to committees in both the House and Senate is similar. According to the rules used to administer proceedings in each chamber, the bills are referred to the committee that has the most relevance to the given subject matter.

In the House, the Speaker has the authority to assign a primary committee to review and analyze the legislation. Sequential committees may be added later to assist with the review. The Speaker has the authority to mandate and impose a time limit on the committee for review. This limit can be set either at the time of the referral or after it has been referred.

In the Senate, legislation is referred to the committee that the subject matter of the legislation predominates. Unlike the House, no one person directs which committee gets specific legislation; instead, it comes under the jurisdiction of the Rules Committee. Legislation can be referred to two committees if there is no predominant subject matter.

We Hear You

Like so many aspects of government, there are multiple types of committee hearings. (You'll read about the others in Chapter 12.) The legislative hearing, the most common type, is responsible for reviewing legislation under consideration by the committee. Witnesses testify in support of or in opposition to legislation and are asked questions by the members in attendance. Witnesses can be industry lobbyists, celebrities, cabinet or administration officials, or even ordinary citizens who would be affected by the legislation. Just because a committee hearing is taking place, however, does not mean that all members will attend. Often, especially if the subject matter is not high on the public radar, there will be only a few members of a committee in attendance.

Hearings are typically open to the public. If the matter is related to security, intelligence, or other sensitive areas, however, it might be restricted. To close a hearing, members must record a vote saying they want the matter kept private and internal. Testimony during the closed hearings may be released only if a majority of the members supports it.

Calling Witnesses

During any committee hearing, the members have the right to subpoena witnesses, very much like jury trials. They may also subpoena documents. Each committee has a different set of rules that dictates how it may obtain subpoenas. It is important to note that while the committees have this power, they rarely use it, and subpoenas are not common.

We Hold These Truths
Recent celebrity testifiers have included Michael J. Fox (Parkinson's disease), Olivia Newton-John (breast cancer research), Alec Baldwin (animal rights), and Pearl Jam (Ticketmaster disputes), among many others.

Witnesses who come to testify before committees have varying experience. Some come because they are experts in a given area. Others are invited at the behest of the committee to shed new light. Often celebrities will testify. Even Elian Gonzales, the little Cuban boy whose boat capsized on his way to America with his mother, was asked to appear before a Senate committee, although he never did. While these people may not be as knowledgeable as some of the experts with whom they testify, they bring immediate media attention to issues that otherwise may not have received any.

Committees must announce their plans to hold hearings at least one week in advance, to give witnesses, the press, and staffers enough time to plan. Newspapers, both exclusive to Capitol Hill and those in Washington, D.C., publish committee schedules during this time, announcing their location and expected testifiers.

Playing by the Rules

The chambers have rules (surprise, surprise) that dictate when hearings may be held. The House is permitted to hold committee hearings at any time while Congress is in session, except when Congress is holding a joint session. Joint sessions are typically held for State of the Union addresses and other presidential or diplomatic addresses to Congress.

However, the Senate rules are a bit complicated. They stipulate that a committee is forbidden from holding a committee hearing after the Senate has been in session for two hours, or after 2 P.M. when the Senate is in session, depending on which time is earlier. However, another rule says that this scheduling rule may be waived by unanimous consent on the Senate floor or by mutual agreement between the majority and minority leaders.

Hearings at Home and Away

Most committee hearings are held in Washington, D.C., on Capitol Hill. The Senate and the House both have office buildings that have personal offices for the members, as well as committee offices for the committee members and their staffs. Committee rooms are usually large so that members, witnesses, the press, and even visitors can come in and watch. If a hearing is over a particularly divisive issue or controversial nomination, it is not unusual for the room to be overflowing with people, with lengthy lines outside.

Committees will occasionally hold field hearings away from home. This allows the members to go to areas of the country that might be significantly affected by proposed legislation.

Marking Things Up

After the hearings are completed, all the witnesses have had their say, all the questions have been asked and hopefully answered, committees proceed to the *mark-up* phase.

Inside the Beltway

The **mark-up** phase of the legislative process is when committee and subcommittee members refine a bill through amendments and debates.

In this phase, members of a committee or subcommittee debate, offer, and vote on amendments to a given measure. The final product that comes from this meeting is what the entire House will debate on the floor at a later time.

That is, of course, assuming the committee passes the bill. If the committee fails to pass the bill, it dies there. The bill can be rewritten and reintroduced, but the likelihood for passage after a committee votes it down is slim.

Reporting Back

Regardless of whether a committee passes a bill, the committee is still required to file a report on the bill as a whole. These reports include …

- ◆ The purpose of the bill
- ◆ Defense of committee action on the bill
- ◆ Specifics of potential changes in existing laws
- ◆ The perspective of any executive branch agencies

Those on the opposing side of the eventual outcome are also given the opportunity to file supplemental reports. While the committees' reports are often more than 1,000 pages long (that is not a misprint!), they are the official method of communicating the decision of a committee to the entire House or Senate. If a committee passes a bill, it is required, in both the House and the Senate, to include a five-year cost estimate, oversight findings, and regulatory statements.

Floor Debate

Now that the bill has passed the committee, it is well on its way on the long journey of legislation, but the bill is still a far cry from becoming law. The leadership in both chambers is responsible for bringing bills to the floor for debate. They set the time frame, with the help of their respective *Rules Committee*, for which members on both sides of a given issue can speak. Usually the chairman or chairwoman of the committee that approved the bill stands alongside the primary sponsor during the debate and watches, listens, and answers questions.

Inside the Beltway

Both the House and the Senate have separate **Rules Committees,** whose functions are similar but not identical. The House Rules Committee serves as the gatekeeper for legislation coming to the floor. This committee decides who can offer amendments and how much time will be allotted for debate on each bill and amendment. Finally, it also decides what opportunities the minority side will have to offer amendments on the floor.

The Senate Rules Committee is not quite as powerful as its House counterpart, but it nonetheless has official jurisdiction over Senate organization relative to rules and procedures, including those that govern the floor and the gallery. In this regard, it, too, decides which bill or amendment will come up for consideration at a given time.

Traditionally, bills are debated in the order in which they were approved out of committee. However, both the Senate Unanimous Consent Agreement and the House Special Rule dictate that bills requiring immediate attention can be taken out of order and immediately brought before the chamber for a vote.

During a regular debate, there are often fewer than 10 members in the chamber when debate is going on—quite a different scene from events such as the State of the Union address, when the chamber is packed beyond capacity. Rest assured, however, that all the member offices have C-SPAN and C-SPAN 2 on at all times when Congress is in session.

The Senate is a bit better when it comes to turnout for debate, with more members stopping in and taking part in the dialogue. But do not take low turnout to mean the representatives and senators are not interested in what is going on. The truth is quite the opposite. The members' days are filled with committee hearings, visits with constituents, lobbying groups, lunches, speeches, and a variety of other issues (more about this in Chapter 12).

During the debate, members can offer further amendments to the legislation, at the discretion of the Rules Committee. These amendments are considered separate from the bill and are voted on individually. Amendments in the House must be germane to the bill, while amendments in the Senate may have nothing to do with the given issue and are just tacked on to ensure passage. On noncontroversial measures, debate is nonexistent, but on divisive issues, debate can last well into the night, with every member wanting to have a say.

The Rules Committee sets the time for debate and the order of amendments offered. While it is a small committee and has the smallest committee room, it is the most powerful committee and can almost single-handedly determine the fate of a bill or amendment before they get to the floor.

Passage

After all debate is finished and the votes are cast, the hard work of the members and the staff either continues further down the line of democracy or is over in less than a half hour. One disgruntled Democratic staffer said at the end of the 106th Congress that he was fed up with 18-hour days or nonstop work on important legislation with nothing to show for it—so he left.

If similar bills pass both the House and the Senate (unless they are identical), a conference committee is established to iron out the differences. By law, the committee may discuss only the differences between the two bills and do not consider additional revisions. The Speaker of the House, along with the presiding officer of the Senate, formally appoints conferees to the committee. Here Democrats, Republicans, senators, and representatives come together to work on the final product. Most conference committees are small in size, with two dozen or so members.

> **We Hold These Truths**
>
> The largest conference committee in history was held in 1981 for the budget-reconciliation bill— 258 senators and congressmen were in attendance—nearly half of all the elected officials in Washington!

When a majority of the conferees from both chambers agrees on a final package, the committee staffs prepare a final report. This report, or the final bill, is then passed by the committee and sent back to both chambers. When both chambers pass the bill, it then lands on the president's desk, hopefully garnering his signature.

The president has two choices when the bill arrives at his desk: He can either sign it or veto it. If he signs it, everyone goes home—sometimes happy, sometimes not. The bill became a law. If the president opts for a veto, he has two options. The direct veto occurs when he turns it down within 10 days of passage and sends it back to the House and the Senate. If the House and the Senate each fail to pass the bill with a two-thirds majority, the bill is dead. However, if they are able to get the two-thirds majority necessary to override the veto, the bill becomes a law. The president can also exercise a pocket veto, in which he vetoes the bill after Congress has adjourned and, therefore, it cannot override him.

During the second session of the 106th Congress (January to December 2000), President Bill Clinton vetoed six bills that had been passed by Congress. One such bill would have made it a crime, punishable by up to three years in prison and/or a fine, for any government official or employee, active or retired, to willfully disclose classified information knowing the person receiving it was not authorized to have it. The veto was praised by an unusual group of opponents that included Republicans, Democrats, and civil libertarians, as well as members of the press.

The Least You Need to Know

◆ Thousands of pieces of legislation are introduced during each Congressional session, but only a small percentage of them become laws.

◆ Bills may be introduced simultaneously in both the House and the Senate; however, for a bill to become law, it must pass with identical language in both houses.

◆ Celebrities are sometimes called to testify in front of Senate or House committees, often because they can bring media attention to issues that may otherwise escape notice.

◆ The arduous task of getting a bill passed by both houses of Congress can be wiped out in a pen stroke if the president decides to veto it.

Congress at Work

In This Chapter

- ◆ Perks and benefits
- ◆ A typical day
- ◆ Aiding the effort
- ◆ The youngest helpers

When Congress is in session, Capitol Hill is a veritable beehive of activity. Days begin early and end late. Practically every minute of every day is accounted for—often with several events coinciding. Committee hearings, votes, press conferences, fundraising, and meetings with lobbyists and constituents fill members' days.

Still, there are plenty of benefits to being a member of Congress. Even though they are not all recognized by the majority of Americans, each and every one is guaranteed at least a footnote in history. And some, whether for a positive or a negative reason, end up with entire chapters written about their political careers.

From a Part-Time Job to a Full-Time Career

In the early Congresses, being a representative or a senator was viewed as a part-time job, with most members living in Washington for only a few months and then returning to their regular lives, families, and jobs for the rest of the year. But as the institution grew, so did the number of members who began to view Congress as a singular, full-time career.

By the turn of the twentieth century, the average length of service for representatives was three terms. Today the average is between four and five terms. Part of the reason for serving in Congress longer is to attain top party positions or key committee chairmanships. But reforms in the past 20 years have somewhat decreased the need for seniority to attain higher posts. Likewise, the *term limits* movement has reduced the number of members viewing Congress as a singular career.

Inside the Beltway

Term limits dictate the number of years elected officials may serve. Occasionally, candidates pledge to serve anywhere from three to six terms in Congress before retiring, although many have broken their pledges.

For their work, members receive an annual salary of $158,100, with a $3,000 annual tax deduction for travel to and from the district.

Members in the leadership in both houses receive higher salaries than other members. The vice president and the Speaker of the House receive a salary of $203,000. The president pro tempore and the House and Senate majority and minority leaders all receive $175,600.

While their salaries might seem high compared to the average salaries of many Americans, most members of Congress have taken significant pay cuts from their previous careers. Many must also maintain two households—one in their district and an apartment or house in or near Washington. Whenever Congress votes to give its members a pay raise, the change does not take place until after the next election.

Job Perks

Are there any? Well, there probably would not be 535 members of Congress if the work were all drudgery and no reward. In addition to their compensation, members are given office space, furniture, supplies, and allowances to hire staff (you'll read more about them later in this chapter). In recent years, the amount each House office can use for staff salaries in district and Washington offices, office expenses, and their *franking privilege* has hovered around $1 million.

Senators, meanwhile, have greater resources allotted to them because they are representing an entire state. If the state has a high population, more financial resources are made available to the senator. Senators' offices may draw from three separate funds:

Inside the Beltway

- ◆ An administrative allowance (based on population)

- ◆ A legislative assistance allowance (same regardless of population)

- ◆ An expense allowance (based on population and distance from Washington), which pays for travel and other office expenses

Instead of using postage, members are allowed to use a frank, or signature, to send newsletters or related materials to their constituents. The **franking privilege** prohibits members from using the system for personal mail or for campaign literature.

The total amount available ranges on average from just under $2 million to more than $3 million. Although it's hard to quantify, real power—and, in some cases, proximity to real power—is another integral perk for many members of Congress. Being able to talk to the President of the United States in person about anything can be a heady experience, much less having the president ask *you* for advice on a piece of legislation.

If a member of Congress is lucky, a major piece of legislation with his or her name on it might become part of the general lexicon and instantly raise his or her profile. Campaign finance reform—or McCain-Feingold—is practically a household term. And while Sen. John McCain, a Republican from Arizona, was already a relatively well-known senator, Sen. Russ Feingold, a Democrat from Wisconsin, was a virtual unknown outside his own state before campaign finance reform came along.

Members also know they might be lucky enough to get a federal building or even a monument named after them. Perhaps surprisingly, there is no law that can stop such naming of buildings for members who are still in office.

Even though the travel schedule can be exhausting, the opportunity to take "learning" trips—also known as junkets—to nearly every corner of the world is an additional perk for members of Congress. Members typically take such trips during recesses of Congress, during holidays or longer breaks, also known as district work periods.

We Hold These Truths

Here's what members can and cannot do on a junket (although it's hard to enforce the rules): They cannot use their office budget on any travel outside their district; their travel must be sponsored by a "qualified" private group or corporation for food, transportation, and lodging. The member can bring a spouse or a child, but not both. To make the trip legitimate, a member has to participate in a "fact-finding" event, give a speech, or attend a topical meeting. Domestic trips are limited to four days, while international trips are limited to one week. Still, members can extend any trip at their own expense. All expenses that the government pays for are read into the Congressional Record several times a year.

If a House delegation and a Senate delegation travel together to a location, the trip is known as a co-del, or congressional delegation. One or two staffers usually go along on co-dels.

Such trips usually have all expenses paid—a factor that often leads to a negative image in the media for many prime locale trips. Often in press reports, members are shown to travel frequently to places used as vacation spots by the rest of the world, including California, Florida, Italy, and any number of tropical islands.

Because lobbying groups or large corporations often fund such trips, the public views them as old-fashioned political schmoozing trips (which is not always inaccurate). But garnering such one-on-one time with a key legislator, no matter what the location, is a top priority for lobbyists (more about them in Chapter 22).

Other perks for members include these:

◆ Members get great parking privileges (including free parking at two Washington-area airports, Reagan National and Dulles International).

◆ They can accept free tickets to national sporting events such as the Super Bowl, or any gift from any lobbying group or association under $50.

◆ Because the Capitol Complex is arranged as its own small city, several simple everyday perks exist for members in terms of proximity (they are located in the basement of the complex). There are several restaurants, a barber shop and hairdressers, and a dry-cleaning service, all of which members must pay for.

◆ In the Senate, a treasured perk is a "hideaway," or private office. Hideaways, which do not appear on Capitol floor plans, are given out on the basis of seniority. While senators will happily take any hideaway, those most sought after are located within seconds of the Senate floor or have an exquisite view of the National Mall.

But the few rewards offered members of Congress, at least lately, seem to have more politicians serving for only a few terms and then returning to more lucrative careers, either in their home state or in Washington. Less collegiality has also become evident as more families choose to stay in the home district, especially for House members. Fewer members meet their colleagues' families or have get-to-know-each-other gatherings.

A Day in the Life

Looking at the schedule of a typical member on a day when Congress is in session isn't pretty. Practically every minute of every day is accounted for—often with several events happening at the same time. Often separated from their families throughout the congressional workweek, members usually have to schedule time just to talk to their families.

In helping to set policy for the nation, representatives and senators must fight for not only what their constituents want, but also what their party wants. The varying roles that members must play throughout the day to accomplish their goals are enormous— from campaigner, debater, colleague, and fundraiser to regular-old-fashioned legislator—and they must be talented at each one. Each activity of their day can be a factor in whether they will be re-elected. Was the member able to efficiently answer constituent requests? Could he bring home dollars, or *pork*, to improve his district? Could she solve problems for her constituents? Does he have standing among his colleagues? Can she effectively maneuver the legislative process? Can he raise money for the party?

The House is traditionally in session from Tuesday to Thursday, with most of Monday and Friday reserved for district work and travel to and from D.C. The Senate is typically in session for the full week, but this, too, can change from week to week, depending on the legislative and political calendars.

Inside the Beltway

Pork, coming from the term "pork barrel," is the millions of dollars attached to spending bills for individual projects in members' home districts. Members who successfully attach money to provide for costly projects in the district are able to "bring home the bacon."

A "normal" day is likely to begin at 7 or 8 A.M. with a breakfast reception or meeting, which could be a panel discussion on a particular topic during which the member might be asked to make a few remarks. Next there is often a meeting of the party caucus in the Capitol to discuss the strategy of the latest major bill being brought up for a vote, or an agenda-setting meeting for the remainder of a session.

Committee hearings usually begin at 9:30 or 10 A.M. Members of Congress may attend three types of hearings:

♦ Investigative hearings are conducted by committees wanting to exercise their power to investigate any program or federal official. These are not connected to legislation. Instead, they are held to examine a subject that the committee has a particular interest in. Often these hearings are the result of wrongdoing by government officials.

♦ Oversight hearings are hearings conducted by Congress that review the executive branch agencies. They are done to ensure that the agencies are administering their programs in the way Congress intended. In 2000, while the Census was being conducted, several hearings took place to make sure that all citizens were being represented fairly. Republicans questioned some of the questions asked by the Census and pressured the Census director on the motives for the questions. Democrats felt that not everyone would answer the Census and likewise pressed for alternative methods of counting traditionally undercounted (and Democrat-leaning) areas.

♦ Confirmation hearings, the final type of hearing, are typically held during the first few months of a new administration. The House does not confirm presidential appointees, but the Senate does. Often these hearings can be confrontational, especially if the majority party in the Senate is the opposition party to the president. Confirmations are necessary for thousands of government jobs, as well as cabinet-level appointments.

Hearings are typically open to the public. If the matter is related to security, intelligence, or other sensitive areas, however, it might be restricted. In order to close a hearing, members must record a vote saying they want the matter kept private and internal. Testimony during the closed hearings may be released only if a majority of the members supports it.

Once the House and Senate convene, which can be at varying times depending on the day of the week, *roll-call* votes are called throughout the day, forcing members to stop whatever they are doing and rush to their respective chambers and cast their votes before the time limit expires.

All members carry a special pager that has greater range than most, which announces when votes are being called. A member then has 15 minutes to make it to the floor to vote—usually no problem if they are somewhere in the Capitol Complex. But if they are at a reception anywhere in Washington, making votes can certainly be a challenge. In those instances, a member's entourage is allowed to break traffic laws to get there.

A press conference on a bill the member is sponsoring might be held midmorning, before a lunch with an outside interest group or another key lawmaker. Party leaders have their own press conferences, often called *dugouts*, which usually address a wide range of topics. Committee hearings continue in the afternoon, and smaller caucuses may also meet.

Inside the Beltway

Roll-call votes are votes during which each member's name is called and recorded.

Dugouts are similar to press conferences, except that they are held by members of the party leadership, usually to address a broader range of topics than just one.

Constituents, lobbyists, and other groups have 10- or 15-minute meetings scheduled throughout the afternoon with the member, for most of which the member is late. Receptions for any number of causes begin in the late afternoon, and the member is often expected to at least make an appearance to show support for the cause.

Receptions and events often continue until 8 P.M. Afterward, the member might have dinner with a colleague or a lobbyist. Or the member might have to return to the Capitol for late-night votes, which have been known to occur after midnight, especially near the end of a session. Some members have even been known to sleep on the office couch and shower in the Capitol gym.

Weekly—and sometimes daily—staff meetings must be held. If the president is signing a bill the member strongly influenced, he or she might also take a trip to the White House Rose Garden for a signing ceremony.

The number of assorted task forces or caucuses the member might serve on can further complicate members' schedules. Aside from scheduled press conferences, the member might have to

We Hold These Truths

Members are prohibited from fundraising on Capitol Hill. But because fundraising is an essential part of a lawmaker's political career, many take a brief walk off the grounds to make fundraising pitches from other phones.

schedule television interviews or individual interviews with print, radio, or electronic media reporters. The never-ending fundraising cycle also must be worked into the schedule, whether the money being raised is for the member's own coffers, for a colleague, or for the member's political party.

On the Weekends

Weekends provide little downtime for members, especially for newer members, who often must spend every available minute campaigning when they are in their home districts. Whenever votes end for the week, usually on Thursday evenings or Friday mornings, an exodus from the Capitol occurs. Most members, except those who have permanently moved their families to the Washington region, head home by plane, train, and car to see their families—and work.

Just because members are "home" does not mean they can relax. Once in their districts, members have meetings with local political leaders, town hall meetings for constituents to air their views, more fundraisers and receptions, parades, and other local events to attend. While they are usually able to stick to their weekend schedules more easily than their Washington schedules, there is a problem for many in terms of the ever-changing floor schedule in determining when Congress will recess.

The Staff of Life

Aside from the many congressional services that assist members of Congress, each member has a support staff to do everything from answering constituent mail to planning and adjusting daily schedules.

Congressional staff has existed since nearly the beginning of Congress, but the number of paid staff grew rapidly in the mid-twentieth century to help the growing number of committees after World War II. Today, more than 10,000 congressional staffers are working in district offices and in the Capitol. And each congressional office is set up similar to a small business, with the member acting as the boss of the company.

Top Dogs

In most offices, the top job—financially and in terms of access to the member—is the chief of staff. This person usually oversees much of the day-to-day operations in a congressional office, under the supervision of the member. The chief of staff has oversight of almost every detail in a member or senator's life, from the legislative strategy in an office to scheduling in the district, even to where he or she eats breakfast. This staffer has usually worked on the election campaign for the member or has known and worked with his or her boss for years.

Other senior positions include deputy chief of staff and legislative directors, who oversee key measures the member works on, as well as legislative assistants, who typically work in one or two specialty areas. For example, if the member sits on the Judiciary or Agriculture committees, there will usually be at least two legislative assistants, one who focuses solely on issues related to each committee. In many offices, the legislative assistants are the first to draft legislation or amendments that the member wants to submit on a bill.

Outside Washington, the top staffer is usually referred to as the district or state director. This position entails coordinating all district staff and events with the member's activities in the Capitol.

Getting the Word Out

Each office has a press secretary or communications director, who serves as the chief medium between the omnipresent press and the member. As the spokesperson, the press secretary or communications director drafts speeches, press releases, and op-eds, and keeps close contact with local and sometimes national reporters and producers. The press secretary is also responsible for "getting out the message" for the member on legislation and the member's positive activities. In a scandal, the task of defending and diluting negative press typically falls first to the spokesperson.

Working the Cases

Each office employs case workers, who are assigned to handle specific cases of the member's constituents. Responsibilities of the case workers vary in each office but usually involve coordinating federal, state, and local offices that are trying to solve a problem involving a constituent who has little experience in unraveling the mountain of red tape that precludes action.

A recent example of casework is a fishing boat called the *Linda E* that disappeared with three men off the coast of Lake Michigan in December 1998. Then-freshman Rep. Mark Green, a Republican from Wisconsin, coordinated the search operation for the vessel with the U.S. Coast Guard and the U.S. Navy, even reopening the search on behalf of the families of the missing when the Coast Guard recommended closing the investigation in December 1999. The boat was found six months later, and an investigation later determined that a barge likely had struck the *Linda E.* In 2001, Green introduced legislation called the Maritime Disaster Family Assistance Act, which would require lengthier searches by the Coast Guard as well as appoint a family liaison in similar disasters.

Working closely with the legislative assistants is typically a legislative correspondent, who is responsible for drafting communications for the member specifically related to bills. Each office also has an office manager, who oversees general office tasks such as hiring, handling payroll, and managing equipment and supply needs in the office. The task of organizing and handling the constantly changing schedule of the member falls to the scheduler. Most offices also employ a systems manager, who keeps the member's website and other technology equipment running and up to date.

The Youngest Staffers

Finally, at any time during the year, offices have college (and sometimes even high school) interns helping the member in any number of ways. Internships enable interested students to experience government and the political process firsthand. Usually unpaid, the work is not glorious, but it can often lead to employment on Capitol Hill or in government after the student graduates. And most important, an internship provides a front-row seat for democracy in action.

In many cases, internships are divided into the usual administrative-type work and the more exciting legislative work, with interns conducting initial research for bills, speeches, or testimony. Most of the summer or semester spent in Washington is probably grunt work. Some interns rarely even see the member of Congress they work for. Many spend their days doing mundane duties, such as answering the phone, responding to constituent requests, or even taking tour groups around the Capitol.

We Hold These Truths

Among the thousands of pages who have served since Congress began is Microsoft founder Bill Gates.

But as time passes, successful interns usually get assigned more significant tasks and gain a critical inside look at how Congress works.

To the offices they work in, interns are viewed in varying ways. Yes, the office gets free help for the least favored tasks, but many offices also make sure they include qualified interns in the process more as the internship progresses.

Even though most internships are unpaid, many interns receive college credit for their labor. Interns are often the first beneficiaries of the numerous receptions held at the Capitol every day. Even if a member attends, interns typically are also allowed to go and can usually scrape much-needed free meals out of the numerous events.

Not all interns are college students; some are graduate students and others are even mid-career professionals who go to work in Congress for a sabbatical or as a fellow. Depending on the agency or specific program they are with, these interns are usually granted higher status because they enter offices with specific policy backgrounds.

> **We Hold These Truths**
>
> Before electric signals were installed to let members know when votes began, pages would run throughout the Capitol telling members there was a vote.

On Capitol Hill, pages, dressed in navy blue uniforms, do everything from delivering messages to members to working on the floor of each chamber.

High school students between the ages of 16 and 18 can spend a semester, a year, or a summer working on the Hill, serving as a page. These students attend school from 6:15 A.M. to 10:30 A.M. in a special school set up for them near the Capitol. The pages live together in a dormitory.

Although both girls and boys serve as pages today, girls did not serve with any frequency until the 1970s. In 1939, the daughter of Rep. Eugene Cox (a Democrat from Georgia), Gene, served as a page for one day.

Staffing the Committees

Aside from each member's immediate office staff, each committee employs its own staff, on both the Republican and Democratic sides. Whichever party has control of the chamber has a larger staff and more resources to use for the committees (just as members in the majority party get more seats on the committees). Some committees have their staff work jointly, while others divide their staffs according to subcommittee.

When Congress passed the Legislative Reorganization Act of 1946, congressional committee staffs grew exponentially and permanent professional staff positions were created. But when Republicans were swept into power in the landmark 1994 election, committees were affected drastically by the changes made the following year. As part of the "Contract with America," House Republicans vowed to restructure the committee system. In doing so, most committees were renamed, committee budgets were reduced, and one third of all permanent committee staff were eliminated in 1995. Term limits were also established for GOP committee chairmen, creating another upheaval six years later when they were first imposed on sitting chairmen. The Senate, also controlled by Republicans at the time, cut committee staff by 20 percent.

Similar to individual offices, a committee usually has a staff director and a minority staff director, which is closest to the chief of staff position. Most committees also have a counsel, who can advise the member of any legal background that may be required for legislation. Larger committees also have communications directors or press secretaries as well as permanent administrative support staff.

However, the role of committee staff on public policy is usually much greater than that of an office staff. Committee staffs prepare materials for hearings, including who will testify and in what order. Committee staff is usually doing the groundwork on any legislative proposal, including meeting with lobbyists and special-interest groups as well as coordinating the political strategy for any major legislation. Ideas they favor are more likely to be passed on to the chairman or ranking member, while those they do not favor are discarded more easily.

Both office staff and committee staff can use several congressional agencies to do their extensive research (and provide a critical nonpartisan viewpoint), including the General Accounting Office, the Congressional Budget Office, and the Congressional Research Service.

The Least You Need to Know

- Rank-and-file members of Congress receive an annual salary of $158,100, plus a $3,000 annual tax deduction for travel to and from their districts.

- In addition to their pay, members receive office space, furniture, supplies, and allowances to hire staff, in addition to other perks such as free parking, franking privileges, and the ability to go on junkets.

- Each member of Congress hires a full contingent of staffers who are responsible for making sure that the member's days run like well-oiled machines.

- Interns and pages are the youngest congressional staffers, and they often receive little or no recognition or compensation for their assistance beyond the chance to see democracy in action.

Congressional Elections

In This Chapter

- ◆ Choosing the candidates
- ◆ Behind-the-scenes players
- ◆ The primary process
- ◆ Filling vacancies

How does someone get elected to Congress? If you think it begins with a primary, think again. And if you think you pick your local candidate, think again.

The road to Congress is a long process, with a lot of behind-the-scenes players who have a great deal more to do with choosing the candidates than you may think.

Beginning the Process

When you see Jane Smith or Jim Rogers running to be your representative or senator, there is a good chance that someone in Washington, D.C., had something to do with their entry into the race.

Both major political parties have committees whose main purpose is to ensure that the party's candidates are victorious in November. The

National Republican Congressional Committee, NRCC, and the Democratic Congressional Campaign Committee, DCCC, oversee candidates running for House races all over the country. On the Senate side, there is the Democratic Senatorial Campaign Committee, DSCC, and the National Republican Senatorial Committee, NRSC.

> ### We Hold These Truths
>
> In the 2004 elections, with control of both chambers, as well as the White House, hanging in the balance, the national parties raised record amounts of money to be dispersed to candidates. The Republicans, for the most part, had the upper hand. The Republican National Committee raised $330,016,950, while the Democratic National Committee raised $299,131,034. The parties also have fundraising arms specifically for House and Senate races. The National Republican Congressional Committee raised $159,162,870, while the Democratic Congressional Campaign Committee raised about half as much with $76,030,016. On the Senate side, the Democratic Senatorial Campaign Committee raised $76,355,981 to the National Republican Senatorial Committee's $68,689,712.

Analysts with both parties become familiar with the local mores, history, and events in different regions. They are plugged in to the issues of importance in districts that are as diverse as they are different, and they spend countless hours focusing on issues of significance in the states that otherwise might not be in the national spotlight.

Committees on both sides are made up of current House and Senate members, party loyalists, and strategists. They have a leadership structure of their own, similar to that of Congress. The chairs of each committee are appointed by their party leadership. They often play a critical role in the policy and agenda shaping of the parties during an election year, and they have the ear of their entire caucus as the big day draws closer.

Picking the Candidates

The committees often research potential candidates to be their nominees in districts across the country. Committee officials talk to local party officials to determine the most viable candidates, taking into consideration whether they are running against an incumbent who may be vulnerable or whether they are running for an open seat.

In open-seat contests, the committee does not generally endorse or favor one candidate over others if the local area is unable to unite behind a selected nominee. There are two reasons for this. First, the candidates do not want to leave themselves open to attacks from opponents who could charge them with being the puppet of bureaucrats back in D.C. Second, party leaders and candidates know that people in the district know more about what's important to them than officials living up to 3,000 miles away.

Once a viable candidate is identified, the committee then encourages other potential candidates to step aside so that the party can present a unified ticket. Many potential candidates resent this involvement from national leaders but have little say in the matter, and they generally remain quiet in their criticism of the process.

The Primary Process

Prior to the general election, a primary election is held to determine the nominees for each of the parties. Depending on the state and the year, this election can take place in September, June, or even March. The candidate who receives the most votes wins and proceeds to be the party's nominee for the general election. In some states there are also run-off elections in which the top two vote getters in the primary face off a few weeks later. This is to ensure that the party nominee receives a majority of votes, not just a *plurality*.

Inside the Beltway

Plurality refers to the number of votes that the leading candidate obtains over his or her nearest rival.

There are three types of primaries:

- ◆ **Closed primaries.** These are the most common and are restricted to members of a specific party. On election day, the voter shows the poll worker a voter registration card or presents identification that matches the voter's name to a specific list of registered voters with a given party. Then the voter is directed to a booth with his or her party's ballot to vote.

- ◆ **Open primaries.** These are not restricted to members of the same party. Instead, third-party registrants—and sometimes even major opposition-party registrants— are eligible to vote. By voting in one party's primary, however, they forfeit their right to vote in any other primary.

- ◆ **Blanket or wide-open primaries.** In a few states, candidates for the same office are placed together on the same ballot, without noting party affiliation. Voters pick one person for each party, and it is possible to cross party lines and vote for candidates of different parties.

Inside the Beltway

Swing districts are areas that do not have a dominant registration and that could support candidates of either party.

Committees generally shy away from openly endorsing candidates in primaries. When a candidate survives a primary, however, committees pour significant amounts of money into the district, depending on the likelihood for victory. The closer the race is, and the closer election day looms, the more attention a competitive district receives.

With control of the House and the Senate resting on such narrow margins, *swing districts* become imperative. If you live in a swing district, your local election takes on national importance. National leaders descend on these districts, and often these races cost more money than non-swing-district races. With redistricting, however, as a result of the 2000 census, there are relatively few swing districts. Most seats are solidly Democratic or solidly Republican.

It's important to note that there are other parties besides the two central ones, Democrats and Republicans. In addition, there is the Libertarian Party, the Constitution Party, the National Law Party, the Green Party, the Reform Party, the National Women's Party, and others. They often run Congressional candidates in districts where they think they have a good chance of winning. The two third parties that have received the most attention in recent years are the Green Party and the Reform Party. The Green Party of the United States is a federation of state Green Parties. Their top priorities are the environment, social justice, and peace. They are known for their grassroots activism. Oftentimes they will run candidates in congressional elections not with the goal of winning, but to bring added attention to the issues they feel the major party candidates are ignoring.

The Reform Party came to prominence in the mid-1990s with the emergence of Texas billionaire H. Ross Perot. Its philosophy and ideology is closer to that of Republicans. Under Perot's leadership, the party, which also elected a governor (Gov. Jesse Ventura of Minnesota) in 1998, tended to be fiscally and defensively conservative, while socially moderate. The party has fallen on bad times in recent years and has not played a significant role in American presidential politics since 1996.

The Lobby Factor

Lobbyists for major corporations or special-interest groups can also play critical roles in recruiting candidates. Groups such as the National Rifle Association or EMILY's List (a pro-choice Democratic women's organization) will often work with area officials or party activists to find a candidate who best represents their views. With the support of major foundations or interest groups, the candidates are likely to receive significant amounts of outside dollars that they would not otherwise receive.

If an issue or cause receives more play in a given election year, groups associated with that cause are likely to have more influence. They can propel candidates who might otherwise have a slight shot at winning to become serious contenders overnight.

In 2004, groups known as 527's, so called for the section of the tax code that deals with their regulation, spent millions of dollars advocating on behalf of both Republicans and Democrats. The most well known was a group called "Swift Boat Veterans for Truth," which spent millions of dollars in advertisements against Democratic presidential nominee Sen. John Kerry.

The Swift Boat group, as well as groups who were opposed to President George Bush, were not so much about advocating *for* a specific cause or person, but more *against* a specific person. Some had hoped when the McCain-Feingold Campaign Finance Reform legislation was signed into law (more information in Chapter 12) that these groups and their ads would not be as common, but 527's are not regulated under that law.

The Presidential Push

Finally, if lobbying groups and special-interest organizations are not enough, the parties often have one more person they can call on to help persuade a candidate to run or to garner support for a candidate in a given region after they have announced: the president. Receiving a personal phone call from the president telling you "your country needs you" is a very difficult call for potential candidates to walk away from.

Bill Clinton played an instrumental role in getting several Democrats to run for the House and Senate in 2000. More recently, President George W. Bush has been working behind the scenes as well, encouraging candidates to run for office in hopes of securing the House for Republicans and returning the Senate to Republican hands.

> **We Hold These Truths**
>
> Prior to 1845, when the switch was made, elections were held during the first (likely cold) week of December.

Going for the Vote

The focus of all this jockeying around is the congressional elections, which take place the second Tuesday of November in even-numbered years. At this time, all 435 members of the House of Representatives are up for election, as are one third of the members of the Senate. Congressional leaders debated at length in the mid-nineteenth century over what would ensure the highest voter turnout. They finally settled on this date and day because they figured with the harvest just over, turnout would be higher.

In an *off-year election*, the party out of power usually picks up seats. The reason for this is simple: People rarely think everything is going great. As a result, voters want "change." How better to make changes than to elect people different from the party in power? A perfect example of this came in the election of 1994 when the Republicans picked up more than 40 seats in the U.S. House of Representatives and gained control of the chamber for the first time in 40 years. A clear message had been sent: The American public from Maine to California was upset with Democrats and President Bill Clinton. The wake-up call worked, and two years later Clinton was re-elected by a comfortable margin. Democrats were also able to regain some of the seats they had lost two years before.

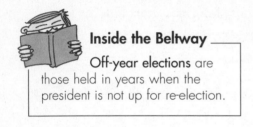

Inside the Beltway

Off-year elections are those held in years when the president is not up for re-election.

Appointments and Special Elections

Up to now, we've focused on the electoral process of choosing members of Congress. There are different procedures for filling a vacancy in the event of a death or resignation midterm for senators and representatives.

Filling Senate Seats

In the Senate, if a member is unable to finish his or her term (usually because of death or sometimes resignation), the governor of the state he or she represents appoints someone to serve until a special election can take place. This special election usually takes place during the first November of an even year that the appointed senator is serving. The governor is under no obligation to appoint someone of the same party as the senator who served previously.

A recent and bizarre case of a Senate appointment can be seen in Missouri. In October 2000, weeks before the general election, the Democratic nominee, Gov. Mel Carnahan, died in a plane crash. The race between him and incumbent Sen. John Ashcroft had been virtually tied, and polls indicated it was going to go down to the wire. Party activists convinced his widow, Jean, to announce that she would accept appointment from the Democratic governor if her husband won posthumously. He did, and Sen. Jean Carnahan was inaugurated on January 3, 2001, with the rest of her new colleagues. However, unlike other senators who won elections in November 2000, Carnahan was forced to defend her seat in November 2002—because she was still serving out the remainder of her husband's posthumous appointment—and lost.

Another strange family appointment came in December 2002. Newly elected Alaska Gov. Frank Murkowski sparked outrage when he appointed his daughter Lisa, a relatively inexperienced state legislator, to the U.S. Senate seat he had vacated when he was elected governor. Many critics charged nepotism, and the younger Murkowski—a Republican like her father—faced an uphill battle in November 2004 when she had to defend her right to serve out the remaining years of her father's term. She narrowly defeated her Democratic opponent, the former governor her father had replaced.

We Hold These Truths

Widows have often served out the terms of their husbands. In the early twentieth century, they were often appointed as diplomatic choices, assuming they would represent the same views as their husbands. Rarely were they expected to run for themselves. Some served less than a year, while others didn't hold office long enough to even make it to Washington. Sen. Rebecca Latimer Felton, a Democrat of Georgia, served just two days in 1922 after being appointed by the governor as a largely symbolic gesture after the death of Thomas Watson.

Filling House Seats

When a member of the House of Representatives is unable to complete his or her term due to death or resignation, it is up to the governor of that state to call for a special election. Usually the election takes place within six months of the vacancy. Sometimes there is just one general election and the top vote getter wins. Other times there is a primary and later a general election. Unlike in the Senate, the governor does not appoint anyone to fill the vacancy. When a district is without a member in Congress, an office remains open on Capitol Hill to deal with constituent concerns.

Members resign for a variety of reasons. Some do so for personal family reasons; others want to spend more time campaigning for another office. Still others do so because of new job opportunities. Finally, a member might resign to avoid a messy investigation into improper behavior.

Bad Congressman, Bad Congressman

The House and Senate both have ethics committees in place to sanction members who behave inappropriately. The definition of "behaving inappropriately," however, is up for wide debate. For the most part, members are hesitant to publicly punish or rebuke colleagues. Instead, they prefer to work behind closed doors and then present united fronts. In recent years, however, there have been several prominent departures from this policy, due to the gravity of the situation as well as party politics.

Sen. Bob Packwood, a moderate Republican from Oregon and the Chairman of the Finance Committee, had long been rumored to be a bit too friendly with women. In 1995, a Senate ethics investigation uncovered his diaries. In his notes, he detailed some of the allegations female staffers and associates had made toward him. In a surprising move, the ethics panel recommended Packwood's expulsion from the Senate, something it had not done since the Civil War—and even then it had been done for treason! Twenty-four hours later, Packwood announced he would resign his seat.

For a while in the fall of 2001, there was talk of removing Rep. Gary Condit, a Democrat from California, from his post on the House Select Intelligence Committee as a result of his reported affair with and his evasiveness with regard to the investigation into missing Washington, D.C., intern Chandra Levy. He was not removed, but when Condit ran for re-election, he lost in the Democratic primary.

The Least You Need to Know

- ◆ When a candidate runs for federal office in your area, he or she has already been in contact with officials in Washington, D.C., whose responsibility it is to find the strongest candidates for specific regions and races across the country.

- ◆ While the Democratic and Republican parties are the most prominent in American politics, numerous others often have direct effects on the outcomes of elections, even if their candidates do not win.

- ◆ When a senator dies in office or resigns, he or she is immediately replaced by an appointment at the hands of the governor of his or her state.

◆ When a member of the House of Representatives dies in office or resigns, a special election is held several months later to replace the member, with no appointment from the governor.

◆ Members are often reluctant to publicly rebuke their colleagues, but there have been rare occurrences in which elected officials have resigned following pressure from other members.

Part 4

An Even Higher Authority

Although their actions generally don't garner as much public attention as do those of the president or members of Congress, the decisions reached by the nine justices who comprise the Supreme Court bear just as much weight and significance. Congress makes the laws, and the president approves them, but it's up to the Supreme Court to interpret them. Since many of the court's decisions deal with questions related to individual rights and liberties, what takes place there plays a significant role in how U.S. citizens live their lives.

The 2000 election, which caused the Supreme Court to make one of its most famous decisions in recent history, served as a vivid reminder of the court's most important function—the ultimate determiner of the law of the land. It's just one of the decisions you'll read about as you go behind the scenes of the judicial branch of the U.S. government in the chapters ahead.

Chapter 14

Hear Ye, Hear Ye

In This Chapter

- ◆ The guardians of the Constitution
- ◆ Federal versus state jurisdiction
- ◆ Special courts
- ◆ The lawyers who argue before the court

Of the three branches of government, the judiciary remains the one most Americans know the least about. The president may make televised or radio speeches to the nation, and Congress's work is seen on C-SPAN with live, gavel-to-gavel coverage. But when it comes to what the federal courts do—especially the Supreme Court—the average person sees or hears little about it, even though almost every part of the federal judicial process is open to the public.

One of the main reasons we know so little about the federal court system is that few of us are ever able to participate in it. For the most part, our disputes are handled at the state court level, which has jurisdiction over virtually all legal disputes, ranging from divorce and child custody matters to criminal cases, contract disputes, and traffic tickets. As you'll read in this chapter, only certain cases fall under the jurisdiction of the federal court system. You'll also learn what rules apply to the ultimate judicial authority—the Supreme Court.

The Federal Court System

The federal court system was established in Article 3 of the Constitution, which called for the judicial branch to serve as one of the new government's three branches. Often called "the guardians of the Constitution" because their rulings protect rights and liberties guaranteed by it, the federal courts have the job of resolving disputes by interpreting and applying the law.

On the Record

"The judicial Power of the United States shall be vested in one supreme Court, and in such inferior Courts as the Congress may from time to time ordain and establish. The Judges, both of the supreme and inferior Courts, shall hold their Offices during good Behaviour, and shall, at stated Times, receive for their Services, a Compensation, which shall not be diminished.during their Continuance in Office."

—Article 3 of the U.S. Constitution

Although the Constitution called for the establishment of the federal court system, it didn't specify how it should be structured. That came later in the Judiciary Act of 1789, which established the Supreme Court—the highest court in the federal judiciary—and two levels of federal courts underneath it: the trial courts and the appellate courts.

In addition to the Supreme Court, the Judiciary Act established the federal circuit court system and the federal district courts, and the Office of the Attorney General.

The Structure of the Federal Courts

Congress has created two levels of federal courts under the Supreme Court: the trial courts and the appellate courts.

Ninety-four federal district courts, also known as the trial courts, exist in the United States. These federal courts have the authority to hear almost every type of federal case, including both criminal and civil concerns. There is at least one district court in each state as well as the District of Columbia and Puerto Rico. Included in each of these district courts is a U.S. Bankruptcy Court as a unit of the court. The three remaining territories—the Virgin Islands, Guam, and the Northern Mariana Islands—hear bankruptcy cases in their own respective district courts.

Two trial courts have a special designation with nationwide jurisdiction of certain cases. These are the Court of International Trade and the U.S. Court of Federal Claims. The Court of International Trade deals with cases concerning trade and customs. The U.S. Court of Federal Claims is responsible for most claims of money damages against the government, as well as disputes over federal contracts and unlawful seizure of private property by the government.

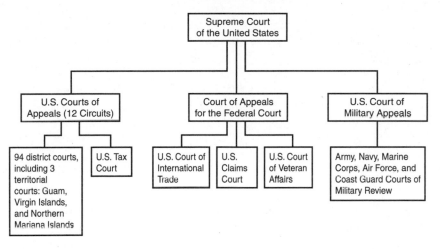

The federal courts.

The U.S. Court of Appeals for the Federal Circuit has nationwide jurisdiction to hear appeals in specialized cases, including all those that involve patent laws and cases decided by the Court of International Trade and the Court of Federal Claims.

The 94 federal courts are divided among 12 regional circuits. These circuits are known as the U.S. Court of Appeals, which are responsible for hearing appeals from the district courts within its circuit. The U.S. Court of Appeals may also hear appeals from decisions made by the various administrative agencies.

Several courts also deal with specialized subject matter, although they are not a part of the judiciary established under Article 3. Their functions are self-explanatory, given their names: the U.S. Tax Court, the U.S. Court of Military Appeals, and the U.S. Court of Veteran's Appeals. While they are not a part of the federal judiciary, appeals of their decisions typically run through the Article 3 courts.

The Jurisdiction of the Federal Courts

When you file a case against the government or someone you feel has wronged you, you cannot just decide to have it heard in federal court. For a federal court to be considered the proper jurisdictional avenue for your dispute, certain conditions must be met:

1. The Constitution says that the federal courts exercise only judicial powers. What does this mean? Well, for a case to qualify, a federal judge must interpret the law through actual legal disputes, not as the result of a hypothetical scenario. In other words, a court cannot attempt to correct a problem on its own, or give an advisory opinion.

2. With the understanding that there is an actual case to be discussed, the plaintiff (the person bringing the case forward) must have legal standing within the court and must have been harmed in some way by the defendant.

3. The case must present a situation that the law in question was established to address, and it must be a complaint that the court has the constitutional authority to correct.

4. The case must be relevant. It can't be a moot issue that has previously been resolved.

Because these four criteria must be met, the federal courts are often referred to as having "limited jurisdiction" because they may decide only certain types of cases.

Understanding the confusing web of details that make up the federal jurisdiction can be mind-boggling. The most important thing for you to take from this section, however, is that two main sources of cases come before the federal courts today: federal question jurisdiction and diversity jurisdiction.

Cases that involve a federal question are cases that involve any one of the following areas:

◆ The U.S. government

◆ The U.S. Constitution

◆ Federal laws

◆ Controversies among the states

Wondering what some of these might be? It could be a claim by an individual for payment of welfare benefits or a charge by the government that a citizen has violated federal law. It could also be a situation in which an individual challenges the actions of a federal agency.

The diversity question deals with *litigants* who are from different states or from another country. To ensure fairness toward the individual who is out of state (or from another country), the Constitution requires that such cases be heard in a federal court. There is a significant stipulation that must be met, however, for this case to be fully accepted as a diversity question: The case must involve more than $75,000 in potential damages.

Inside the Beltway

A **litigant** is a person actively involved in a court case. He or she can be either the plaintiff or the defendant.

Federal courts are located in every state. The vast majority of cases that are discussed in American courts, however, are debated in the state court system. State courts have jurisdiction over divorce proceedings, custody battles, probate- and inheritance-related matters, real estate questions, and juvenile matters. They also handle most criminal cases as well as traffic violations and parking tickets.

The Federal Court's Interaction with the Executive and Legislative Branches

Congress dictates three guidelines regarding the Federal Court system. First, Congress decides where there should be a court and how many judges will sit on it. Second, the Senate approves or denies judges a seat on the federal bench through the nomination process. Finally, and equally important, every year Congress appropriates funds for the federal judiciary and approves its budget.

The Constitution says that the president appoints the federal judges with the advice and consent of the Senate, and it is very unusual for a president not to consult with various members of the Senate before a nomination is made. In twenty-first-century America, special-interest groups have long lists of people they

We Hold These Truths

The judiciary portion of the annual federal budget is less than one percent of the entire federal budget.

support (or don't), so there is little doubt about how these groups feel. The groups, in turn, put pressure on the senators and remind them that election time is right around the corner. Their messages of support or opposition are then brought back to the president.

The nomination of federal judges is not the only interaction that the federal courts have with the executive branch. As you read in Chapter 7, the Department of Justice is responsible for prosecuting federal crimes and representing the federal government in civil cases. As a result, the federal government is the most frequent litigator in the federal court system. Furthermore, the U.S. Marshal's Service is responsible for protecting the federal courthouses and the judges who serve there. Finally, the General Services Administration builds and maintains federal courthouses.

The Buck Stops Here

All the judges who are appointed to the Supreme Court or the various courts of appeals and the district courts are appointed for life and can be removed only through resignation or impeachment. They must be nominated by the president and confirmed by the U.S. Senate. However, judges who are appointed to the bankruptcy courts are given 14-year terms.

Magistrate judges are the judicial officers of the district courts. The judges of these courts appoint them for eight-year terms. It is important to note that, unlike the other justices, bankruptcy and magistrate judges are not selected by the president and the Senate; instead, they are appointed by the courts in which they are serving.

The judge who has served on the court of appeals or the district courts the longest most often is also the chief judge. To be appointed the chief judge, he or she must be under 65. Chief judges can serve for a maximum of seven years and may not serve in this role after the age of 70.

All federal judges are required to abide by a Code of Conduct for United States Judges. This code sets a standard of ethical and moral guidelines that have been adopted by the Judicial Conference of the United States:

- A judge should uphold the integrity and independence of the judiciary.

- A judge should avoid impropriety and the appearance of impropriety in all activities.

- A judge should perform the duties of the office impartially and diligently.

◆ A judge may engage in extra-judicial activities to improve the law, the legal system, and the administration of justice.

◆ A judge should regulate extra-judicial activities to minimize the risk of conflict with judicial duties.

◆ A judge should regularly file reports of compensation received for law-related and extra-judicial activities.

◆ A judge should refrain from political activity.

Supreme Court Rules and Requirements

A long set of rules, which is constantly updated, dictates how the Supreme Court will operate. These rules cover just about every aspect of the court, from who can argue there to the time frame for appeal. The rules are broken down into nine parts. There are too many to examine here, so we look at only the more important ones.

Rules of the Supreme Court

The rules that are associated with the Supreme Court apply to the daily functions of the court, from the clerk to the library. They also establish the times the court will be in session and what constitutes a session in the first place.

The clerk has three responsibilities within the court, as prescribed by law. First, the clerk is responsible for receiving the documents that are to be filed with the court and has the authority to reject any of the submitted filings that do not comply with these rules. Second, the clerk oversees all the records of the court and will not allow them to be removed from the building unless the court has previously authorized them. Finally, the clerk must keep office hours Monday through Friday from 9:00 A.M. to 5:00 P.M., except on federal legal holidays.

The Supreme Court has its own internal library. Only people authorized to use the library may do so. These people include those who have

> **On the Record**
>
> "I [candidate's name] do solemnly swear (or affirm) that as an attorney and as a counselor of this Court, I will conduct myself uprightly and according to the law of the United States."
>
> —The oath/affirmation that each candidate for admission to the Supreme Court must sign

been admitted to the bar for the Supreme Court, members of Congress and their staffs, and lawyers for federal agencies and the United States. The librarian, with the approval of the chief justice, decides the hours for the library. Finally, this is not like a public or school library—only justices and members of their staffs may remove books from this facility.

Like many aspects of government, the year for the court does not begin on January 1. Instead, the term for the court begins on the first Monday in October and can run as late as the Sunday before the first Monday in October of the following year. Typically, however, the court adjourns in late June or early July.

For the court to be in session, six justices must be present, constituting a quorum. Sessions can be public or private and can be held to hear arguments or review cases. When it is necessary to declare a recess, the court directs either the clerk or the marshal to do so.

Who Can Argue Before the Supreme Court?

A person must be a member of the Bar of the Supreme Court to argue a case before the highest court. But to be a member of the Bar of the Supreme Court, a candidate must have been admitted to practice law in the highest court from the state or territory in which he has currently resided (for at least three years) and must not have been involved in any disciplinary action during that time.

Candidates must be of high moral standing and must meet the three-year requirement. Then they must pay a $100 fee for admission, payable to the United States Supreme Court. The attorney then receives a certificate stating that he or she can argue cases before the high court.

We Hold These Truths

Most federal judicial proceedings are open to the public. One of the benefits of going to a hearing is that most of the courthouses are historical structures that tell stories themselves, in addition to the cases at hand. Most times if you want to watch a proceeding, just show up at your local courthouse. If it is a controversial case, you may have to wait or be limited to a certain amount of time; however, with few exceptions, these cases are open to the public. Most are not televised or broadcast on the radio, though.

But what if an attorney on a high-profile case involving constitutional matters in a state or territory in which he or she has not been a member of the highest court for the last three years wants to go before the Supreme Court? Is that attorney out of luck? No. The court has a special circumstance known as *pro hac vice*.

Inside the Beltway

Pro hac vice is a legal term granting a lawyer temporary admission to the bar for a specific case only. It is not restricted to use within the Supreme Court. Provided that the attorney is in good standing in the courts from which he or she comes, pro hac vice is almost always granted. (An interesting side note about pro hac vice is that it is not limited to simply Americans. If an attorney is a member of his or her home country's highest court, that attorney also can be admitted to the Supreme Court for this reason on a temporary basis.)

If during an attorney's tenure on the Supreme Court he or she is disbarred or suspended from another Court, the attorney will likely have privileges revoked from the Supreme Court as well. Immediately after privileges are revoked from the lower court, the Supreme Court begins the process of removing the attorney from its rolls as well. The attorney has 40 days to appeal the order, and then it is up to the court to make a final decision.

The Least You Need to Know

♦ The federal courts resolve disputes by interpreting and applying the law.

♦ Only certain cases fall under the jurisdiction of the federal court system—most disputes are handled at the state court level.

♦ Attorneys wanting to argue cases before the Supreme Court must be of high moral standing, must have been admitted to practice law in the highest court of their home state or territory for three years, and must pay a $100 admission fee.

♦ Attorneys lacking the necessary credentials to argue cases before the Supreme Court can still do so under pro hac vice, which grants them temporary admission to the bar for a specific case only.

Chapter 15

Supreme Players

In This Chapter

- ◆ The men and women who wear the robes
- ◆ The role of the chief justice
- ◆ Majority and minority voices: the associate justices
- ◆ Other key players

The Supreme Court is the highest court in the land, with the best and brightest in American legal circles listening to the cases and presenting the arguments. In this chapter, you learn about the players in the forefront who wear the long black robes, as well as those who play influential roles behind the scenes.

The chief justice is not someone who just has a fancy title, but rather someone who wields enormous power in determining what the court will and won't hear. And when the associate justices sit in the chamber and listen to the arguments presented, they don't just sit next to their best buddy on the court. Their seat assignment is determined by seniority. To give you an idea of how often the seats change, the last time a new member joined the court, Monica Lewinsky and Viagra were not household names, and former Baltimore Orioles player Cal Ripken Jr. was still a year away from breaking Lou Gehrig's consecutive games played record. The year was 1994.

The Chief Justice

The Chief Justice of the Supreme Court is nominated by the president and appointed with the advice and consent of the Senate. Nothing in the Constitution requires this person to be a current member of the Supreme Court.

Like the other justices appointed by the president, the chief justice serves for life as long as he has "good behavior," so says the Constitution. Just because he is chief justice (there has never been a female chief justice), however, does not mean his vote counts any more than the other justices or that he gets extra votes. Although the chief justice ultimately decides which cases are heard by the Supreme Court, he or she does not get to decide which way the vote goes—in fact, the chief justice has been known to be on the dissenting side of a case on numerous occasions.

Regardless of the balance of power on the court, however, the court is often referred to as the chief justice's court. Whether it is the Warren Court, the Taney Court, or the Hughes Court, historians and legal analysts have been able to use the chief justice's name as an adjective to help describe how the court has influenced and affected their lives.

The longest-serving chief justice was John Marshall, who served 34 years (1801–1835). As you can see in the following chart, there have been 16 Chief Justices of the Supreme Court since President George Washington appointed John Jay as the first chief justice in 1789.

> **We Hold These Truths**
>
> John Rutledge (1795), who served for less than a year, held the shortest term of any Supreme Court judge. Most, however, have served for a period of several years.

Chief Justices of the Court

Name	Years	Nominating President	Party Affiliation
1. John Jay	1789–1795	Washington	Pro-Admin.
2. John Rutledge	1795	Washington	Federalist
3. Oliver Ellsworth	1796–1800	Washington	Federalist
4. John Marshall	1801–1835	John Adams	Federalist
5. Roger Taney	1836–1864	Jackson	Democrat
6. Salmon P. Chase	1864–1873	Lincoln	Republican

Name	Years	Nominating President	Party Affiliation
7. Morrison R. Waite	1874–1888	Grant	Republican
8. Melville W. Fuller	1888–1910	Cleveland	Democrat
9. Edward D. White	1910–1921	Taft	Democrat
10. William H. Taft	1921–1930	Harding	Republican
11. Charles Hughes	1930–1940	Hoover	Republican
12. Harlan F. Stone	1941–1946	F. Roosevelt	Democrat
13. Frederick Vinson	1946–1953	Truman	Democrat
14. Earl Warren	1953–1969	Eisenhower	Republican
15. Warren Burger	1969–1986	Nixon	Republican
16. William Rehnquist	1986–present	Reagan	Republican

Next we look briefly at the evolution of the court over the last 200 years and how the chief justices have shaped it and American history.

The Early Court: Jay Through Ellsworth

The early court did not wield much influence or power. The members were still trying to figure out what role this new branch of government was meant to serve in the infant American democracy. In addition to hearing cases at the Supreme Court—wherever it was located, since it changed several times in the early years—the members also had to ride the circuit and visit courts around the country to hear cases before them. As a result, their time was limited, and few cases of any note came out of the Supreme Court during the tenure of these three Supreme Court chief justices.

The Jay Court (1790–1795)

Two important cases came before the court during Jay's tenure. In *Chisholm v. Georgia* (1793), the court held in a 4–1 decision that citizens of another state could sue a state. But that ruling was overturned with the passage of the Eleventh Amendment (see Chapter 4).

A year later, the court ruled unanimously in *Glass v. The Sloop Betsy* that U.S. federal courts have jurisdiction over claims regarding captured foreign vessels brought into American ports. This ruling helped the court and the new nation gain respect.

The Rutledge Court (1795)

This court did not hand down any significant opinions because John Rutledge served as chief justice for a total of four months. He was a recess appointment by President Washington, and when the Senate reconvened later that year, his nomination was ultimately rejected 14–10.

The Ellsworth Court (1796–1800)

Filling John Jay's shoes was a difficult task for Washington. His first choice was rejected by the Senate, and his second, William Cushing, declined the position. Oliver Ellsworth finally was sworn in in 1796. Over the next four years, the court's rulings gave the new nation greater authority, something the Federalists strongly supported. In *United States v. La Vengeance* (1796), the court granted the federal government maritime authority over inland waterways.

The Nineteenth-Century Court

Two prominent individuals—John Marshall and Roger Taney—dominated the court during the nineteenth century. The court grew in influence as well as respect until the Dred Scott decision in 1857. In the second half of the nineteenth century, however, the court took a roller-coaster ride with regard to its significance in American life. At the end of the century it issued *Plessy v. Ferguson*, which like Dred Scott is viewed as one of the low points in American judicial history.

The Marshall Court (1801–1835)

Chief Justice John Marshall served longer than any other chief justice. For the first 30 years of his service, Marshall and his Federalist ideals dominated the court, and it was during his time that the court grew into its position of equal footing with the other branches of government. The Marshall Court also began the practice of releasing unified opinions instead of separate opinions from each justice. Marshall himself was a prolific writer, and he wrote most of the decisions during his time, giving his colleagues little, if anything, to write about.

Federalist ideals were waning toward the end of Marshall's term. President Andrew Jackson, a strong Democrat, had appointed six justices to the court, and its tilt went toward states' rights. Marshall died in office, after having served 34 years, 5 months, and 2 days.

The Taney Court (1836–1864)

Jacksonian Democracy and President Jackson's packing of the court with mostly southern Democrats altered the court dramatically during the most contentious time in American history. If the court was at its high point during the John Marshall years, it was at its lowest during the Roger Taney years. While Taney was able to exercise as much influence over his court as Marshall had, the court's power was seriously undermined with the *Dred Scott* decision of 1857. (You'll read more about this in Chapter 17.)

The Chase Court (1864–1873)

Just as the Taney Court was dominated by the will of the southern Democrats, the court of Salmon P. Chase was dominated by the will of Radical Republicans in the South. These radicals did not carry on the ideals of forgiveness that President Lincoln had hoped to instill in the nation. Congress and the court bickered over supremacy during these years.

In addition to southern concerns, financial matters took on added prominence during this time. The Legal Tender Act of 1862 made paper money acceptable currency for all debts, public and private. However, in *Hepburn v. Griswold* (1870), the court ruled that this act could not be applied retroactively, so debts incurred before the law had to be paid in gold or silver. The law, which the Union had used to finance its war efforts, was thus declared unconstitutional.

The Waite Court (1874–1888)

Morrison Waite is not a household name in America today, but as chief justice in the late nineteenth century, he presided over a court that had long-range effects on civil rights—and not for the betterment of America. In *Minor v. Happersett* (1875), for example, the court ruled that the right to vote was not among the privileges and immunities guaranteed in the Fourteenth Amendment. At issue was whether women were allowed to vote. The decision was unanimous, and it was another 45 years before women won the vote.

Economic cases were also important. In *Munn v. Illinois* (1877), the court ruled that states had the right to regulate business. This decision led to greater government regulation of business.

The Fuller Court (1888–1910)

Melville Fuller ascended to the court after the death of Morrison Waite. During Fuller's tenure, the court reached the high-water mark on *laissez-faire constitutionalism* and helped to fuel the progressive era in America. Fuller often occupied himself with administrative duties and let his associates concentrate on the legal matters before the court.

Inside the Beltway

Laissez-faire constitutionalism is the idea that the government should have a hands-off approach to business and industry with regard to contracts and legal agreements.

Allgeyer v. Louisiana (1897) concerned the legality of citizens to contract with out-of-state insurance companies. A Louisiana statute had prohibited dealings with out-of-state companies unless they met certain preconditions. The court decided the Louisiana law was unconstitutional and for the first time recognized the doctrine of freedom of contract, which the court said was guaranteed by the due process clause of the Fourteenth Amendment.

The Twentieth-Century Court

The Supreme Court evolved into the respected institution it is today during the twentieth century. During this period, the court expanded civil rights and the protection of free speech. While John Marshall still holds the record for the longest service as chief justice, twentieth-century chief justices made indelible marks on the court.

The White Court (1910–1921)

President William Howard Taft wanted to be chief justice after being president. Instead of replacing Fuller with a younger chief justice, such as Charles Evans Hughes, he nominated Edward Douglass White, who was 65 at the time of his nomination. He hoped White would only serve a few years so that he (Taft) could then be appointed to the court as chief justice after his term as president was over.

During his tenure, the White Court made one notable decision—*Standard Oil v. United States* in 1911. The case revived the Sherman Antitrust Act, and White used a "rule of reason" to break up trusts such as the Standard Oil Company. Justice John Marshall Harlan, in a concurring opinion, wrote that the court was essentially increasing judicial powers of legislation at the expense of Congress by making federal courts the arbiters of reasonableness.

The Taft Court (1921–1930)

When Chief Justice White died in 1921, Taft got his wish and was appointed chief justice by President Wilson. Taft is known mostly for his administrative abilities, and it was during his time that funds were appropriated for a permanent home for the court. Although Taft did not live to serve in the current structure, without his pressure on Congress for the funds, it is questionable when the court would have received a permanent home. It was also during this time that law clerks became a permanent feature on the court, with annual funds appropriated.

> ### We Hold These Truths
>
> Taft and his fellow justices believed the Supreme Court was the last check on superfluous legislation passed by rash lawmakers. The Supreme Court invalidated more legislative proposals under Taft than had been done in the previous 50 years.

One important decision cast in 1923 was *Wolff Packing Company v. Court of Industrial Relations*. The court turned back the clock on 50 years of progress made by labor unions and other progressive entities by making it impossible for states to regulate private business.

The Hughes Court (1930–1941)

Charles Evans Hughes was finally appointed chief justice nearly 20 years after his initial appointment to the Supreme Court. Many legal scholars say he played a key role in two very different courts—the first, the Taft Court, was decidedly pro-Republican, and the second, several years after Hughes became Chief Justice, gradually changed to support more of President Franklin Roosevelt's New Deal objectives.

President Roosevelt, angered that the court was striking down critical legislation to bring the country out of the depression, developed a court-packing scheme and hoped to appoint at most seven additional justices to serve alongside those already serving. The plan never materialized because of widespread opposition, but the Hughes Court shifted dramatically in its final five years. With a growing number of legal appointments by FDR, the court solidified the progress the president was trying to accomplish.

In an important First Amendment case, the court ruled unanimously in *Lovell v. City of Griffin* that a city ordinance requiring written permission to circulate flyers violated the First Amendment right to free speech.

The Stone Court (1941–1946)

The chief justice sets the tone for the entire court, and the tenure of Harlan Stone, while a brief five years compared to others in this role, was the most contentious in American history. Egos and opinions of the associate justices ran wild.

The most notable action by the court was not so much the decisions that it rendered, but the back-room bickering that dominated its proceedings. The justices did not get along with each other, neither professionally nor personally, and as a result this time was characterized as one of great disagreement.

The Vinson Court (1946–1953)

When President Harry Truman appointed Fred Vinson, his longtime friend, to be chief justice, he hoped that Vinson would be able to quell some of the fires that were still burning from the Stone Court. Unfortunately, he was not successful. There were few cases of note during his tenure, and unanimous decisions reached an all-time low of 19 percent in 1952. For this reason, and others, historians have ranked Vinson as the least effective of all chief justices.

The Warren Court (1953–1969)

The Warren Court is most fondly remembered for what it did for the advancement of civil rights. While these ideals are often thought of being championed by the Democrats, it was Earl Warren, a Republican, who led the court during these historic times.

The historic cases such as *Brown v. Board of Education* (1954) and *Miranda v. Arizona* (1966) were both decided by the Warren Court. Other important but lesser-known cases include *Yates v. United States* (1957), in which the court upheld the rights of individuals to freely associate without government intrusion. And in *Griswold v. Connecticut* (1965), the court recognized for the first time the right to privacy.

The Burger Court (1969–1986)

The modern Supreme Court owes much of its authority to the Burger Court. Richard Nixon appointed Warren Burger in 1969. Five years later, the Burger Court established the Supreme Court as the ultimate authority on constitutional issues. In *United States v. Nixon* (1974), the court mandated that President Nixon act against his own wishes and forced him to hand over documents pertaining to the Watergate crisis.

In 1973 the Supreme Court handed down *Roe v. Wade*, which became one of the more controversial decisions of its tenure. The court ruled that the right to privacy for a woman protected her right to terminate a pregnancy in the first two trimesters. This decision has become a litmus test for all subsequent potential Supreme Court appointees, and continues to be a lightning rod for all presidential candidates who would appoint justices, and senatorial candidates who would confirm them.

The idea of the separation of powers was further enhanced by *Immigration and Naturalization Services v. Chadha* (1983). In *Chadha*, the court struck down the right of the Congress to have a legislative veto over the actions of agencies.

The Supreme Court Today

President Ronald Reagan appointed Chief Justice William Rehnquist in 1986, upon the retirement of Warren Burger. Rehnquist had served on the court since 1972 and, like Reagan, is conservative in his philosophy.

Rehnquist has said that he likes to model himself after Chief Justice Charles Evans Hughes (1930–1941), who has been regarded as one of the most effective chief justices in American history. Rehnquist has received high marks from his associates, even those he disagrees with, on his administrative abilities.

Rehnquist is a solid conservative and has had several notable opinions during his tenure. On what is considered the most controversial decision of the twentieth century by many, Rehnquist voted in the minority on *Roe v. Wade* (1973) and even wrote his own decision.

In the first case to deal with the rights of the dying, *Cruzan v. Director, Missouri Department of Health* (1990), Rehnquist wrote for the majority and stated that the state has a right to demand clear evidence of an incompetent patient's wishes— something that needed to be present before the patient became incompetent to do so on his or her own. The case revolved around the rights of the parents of Nancy Cruzan, a woman in a permanent vegetative state as a result of a car accident, to turn off her feeding tube. They claimed that Cruzan had previously informally said she did not want to be kept alive by artificial means. While the Court rejected the claims of the Cruzan family, it recognized for the first time the right of the patient to refuse potentially life-saving treatment.

However, Rehnquist will likely be remembered for his role as overseer of the impeachment trial of President Bill Clinton in 1998. Ironically, he had written a

304-page book in 1992 titled *Grand Inquests: The Historical Impeachments of Justice Samuel Chase and President Andrew Johnson.*

Rehnquist's court will also always be remembered for its vote in *Bush v. Gore* that essentially awarded George W. Bush the 2000 presidential election over Al Gore. Following protracted court battles, the U.S. Supreme Court overruled a Florida Supreme Court decision that ordered a hand recount of some 170,000 Florida ballots. That unsigned decision, which came on December 12, 2000, was 7–2. But a 5–4 split of the U.S. Supreme Court existed over whether the recount should continue or not. Regardless, the ruling dealt the final blow to Al Gore—who could not win without Florida's 25 Electoral College votes.

The current Rehnquist Court is considered conservative in many ways, but it is also reflective of the rest of American society. It has clear philosophical lines of disagreement, with strong conservatives and liberals on both sides. The swing votes of two or three moderates often decide the outcome of a case, and anything is possible.

On the Record

"During times such as these, the role of the courts becomes even more important in order to enforce the rule of law … to continue functioning effectively and efficiently, however, the courts must be appropriately staffed."

—Chief Justice William Rehnquist, giving his annual address on the state of the country's courts on January 1, 2002. Rehnquist believes the Senate, which has the power to confirm justices for the federal courts, needs to act faster.

Other Responsibilities of the Chief Justice

Although the chief justice and the associate justices have equal standing with regard to their votes, the chief justice has added responsibilities that you may not have known. He is the permanent chairman of the Judicial Conference of the United States, and he is third in line to meet with visiting dignitaries, after the president and the vice president. He can reassign circuit court justices, and he even sets the hours for the Library of the Supreme Court. And when it comes to decisions that come down from the high court, the chief justice decides who authors them. If he chooses himself, he is likely to ensure he has a prominent place in judicial history: We all know that precedent is one of the key attributes of any court hearing, case, and decision.

The last notable responsibility of the chief justice is to deliver the annual state of the federal courts address. Unlike the president's State of the Union address, this address usually is in the form of a letter. It is published and analyzed by the various media outlets, and it lets the country know what is going on in the judicial branch of the federal government. It can deal with just the Supreme Court, but more often it also discusses the state of the lower courts as well. The announcement is made on January 1 of the given year.

The Role of the Associate Justices

Eight associate justices serve with the chief justice to comprise the Supreme Court. The number of justices is fixed by Congress and has remained at nine since the Judiciary Act of 1869. As noted earlier, the justices all have assigned seats, based on seniority in the court. Each time a new member joins the court, the seats rotate to fill the spot of the member who is no longer serving.

Although the votes of all the justices carry the same weight, the justices do sit and speak in the order of their rank. The most junior justice sits on the far right, the second-most-junior justice sits on the far left, and so on. The chief justice sits in the middle.

Each justice, along with the chief justice, is assigned to at least one of the federal appeals courts. Although the justices usually do not sit on these courts (their time is already precious enough), they are available to grant bail, stay an execution, or issue injunctions for applications to the circuit to which they are assigned.

> **We Hold These Truths**
>
> Although the number of justices has remained at nine since 1869, it did not start out this way. The original court had five justices and one chief justice. It remained this way until 1801, and over the course of the next 68 years, the number of justices fluctuated seven times!

If you visit the Supreme Court while in session, take note of the behavior of the justices. Some may look bored or asleep. Others might be angry and argumentative to the attorneys presenting cases. Others may appear as if they are reading a novel or daydreaming. This is not because the justices don't care—they do. It's just that when a case comes before the court, often the justices either have very specific questions or have already been briefed to such an extent that they don't have any at all.

The Current Associate Justices

The current associate justices range in age from their mid-50s (Clarence Thomas) to their mid-80s (John Paul Stevens). While there is no mandatory retirement age, some have speculated that in the coming years several of the current justices may retire for age or health reasons.

Justice John Paul Stevens

John Paul Stevens, a native of Chicago, was born in 1920. He graduated from the University of Chicago in 1941 and went off to serve in the Navy during World War II. When he returned, he went to Northwestern Law School and earned his degree in 1947. After he graduated from Northwestern, Stevens made his first trip to the Supreme Court. He served as a law clerk to Associate Justice Wiley B. Rutledge for the 1947–1948 term.

We Hold These Truths

Besides John Paul Stevens, only one other justice on the current court has served as a clerk. Justice Stephen Breyer clerked for Justice Arthur Goldberg during the 1964 Supreme Court session.

In 1970, after serving as general counsel to a special commission appointed by the Illinois Supreme Court to investigate the integrity of one of its judgments, Stevens was appointed by President Nixon to the U.S. Court of Appeals for the Seventh Circuit. Five years later, President Gerald Ford appointed him to the Supreme Court where Stevens is responsible for the Sixth and Seventh Circuit Courts of Appeals. This area includes several Midwestern states, including Ohio, Kentucky, Tennessee, Illinois, and Wisconsin.

Justice Sandra Day O'Connor

Sandra Day O'Connor was born in El Paso, Texas, on March 26, 1930. Like Rehnquist, she received her undergraduate and law degrees from Stanford University. She graduated third in her class. (Rehnquist was first!) O'Connor served as the Deputy County Attorney for San Mateo County, California, and later as a civilian attorney for the Quartermaster Market Center in Frankfurt, Germany. In 1969, she was appointed to the Arizona State Senate, and she was re-elected twice as a Republican. Later she was appointed to the Arizona Court of Appeals.

In 1981, President Ronald Reagan made history by nominating O'Connor to be the first woman to sit on the U.S. Supreme Court. She was confirmed 99–0.

Sandra Day O'Connor is part of the swing bloc of justices who can make or break a decision. On the issue of abortion, she is pro-life. However, in 1992 she surprised many by upholding the constitutionality of *Roe v. Wade*. In *Planned Parenthood of Pennsylvania v. Casey*, she wrote for the court that the state has the right to limit access to abortion, provided it does not impose an "undue burden" on the woman's right to an abortion.

In 1995, O'Connor wrote for the majority in *Adarand Constructors, Inc. v. Pena*, in which, in a 5–4 decision, the court retreated from a previous position that favored minority set-asides as a way to remedy past discrimination.

O'Connor is the justice serving on the Ninth Circuit Court of Appeals. This area includes most of the western states as well as the territories of Guam and the Northern Mariana Islands.

Justice Antonin Scalia

Continuing his trend of firsts, Ronald Reagan nominated Antonin Scalia to the Supreme Court in 1986. Scalia became the first American of Italian descent to serve on the court.

Scalia was born in Trenton, New Jersey, on March 11, 1936. He went to Georgetown University for his undergraduate work and received his Doctor of Laws degree—a J.D.—from Harvard University Law School in 1960.

Scalia is considered by many to be the intellectual of the court. This could be partly because of his academic background. He taught at the University of Virginia Law School from 1967 to 1971. After a stint working at the Justice Department and serving as the resident scholar at the conservative American Enterprise Institute, he returned to teaching at the University of Chicago Law School. Later he became a visiting professor at Georgetown and Stanford universities.

Reagan appointed Scalia to the U.S. Court of Appeals for the District of Columbia Circuit in 1982. Four years later, he nominated Scalia to take Rehnquist's position as an associate justice when Rehnquist was appointed chief justice.

Scalia serves on the Fifth Circuit Court of Appeals. This area includes Mississippi, Louisiana, and Texas.

Justice Anthony Kennedy

Anthony Kennedy, no relation to the Kennedy political clan, was Reagan's third choice to replace retiring Justice Lewis Powell in 1986. His first nominee, Robert Bork, was rebuked by the Senate as too conservative, and his second nominee, Douglas Ginsburg, withdrew his name nine days after Reagan nominated him, after allegations arose that he had smoked marijuana while teaching at Harvard.

Kennedy was born in Sacramento on July 23, 1936. Like Rehnquist and O'Connor, he studied at Stanford. He went to Harvard Law School and earned his J.D. in 1961. In 1976, President Ford appointed Kennedy to the U.S. Court of Appeals for the Ninth District. Kennedy is one of the swing justices on the court and, although a Republican, is not a sure vote on conservative issues.

In one of the most significant decisions for the court in its history, *Rosenberger v. University of Virginia* (1995), Kennedy wrote the majority opinion that essentially approved direct state financing of a religious activity. The case involved Ronald Rosenberger, the founder of a Christian newspaper at the University of Virginia. Rosenberger sued the school when it refused to fund his publication—even though the university funded other student publications—on the grounds that it violated the separation of church and state. The court sided with Rosenberger.

Kennedy sits on the 11th Circuit Court of Appeals. This area includes Georgia, Alabama, and Florida.

Justice David Souter

When President George Bush nominated David Souter, a bachelor judge from New Hampshire, in 1990, he said there would be no litmus test on his positions. Twelve years later, that statement is proving true: Souter has evolved into one of the swing members, tilting toward the liberal side of the court, despite his appointment by a conservative Republican president.

We Hold These Truths

Souter was appointed by President George H. W. Bush. Ten years later, when *Bush v. Gore* came before the court to decide the outcome of the election of 2000 between Al Gore and George W. Bush, Souter voted in favor of Gore.

Souter was born in Melrose, Massachusetts, on September 17, 1939. He earned his undergraduate and graduate degrees from Harvard. He spent his entire professional career in New Hampshire, where he served in various capacities, from acting as Deputy Attorney General all the way up to serving on the New Hampshire Supreme Court.

Souter began his service quietly and was more of an observer judge than an activist judge. During his first term, he wrote only three opinions, the fewest of any justice appointed in the last 30 years. Over the years, however, he has begun to exert himself as a moderate and sometimes even liberal member of the court.

Souter sits on the First and Third Districts of the U.S. Courts of Appeals. This area includes Maine, Massachusetts, New Hampshire, Rhode Island, Puerto Rico, Delaware, New Jersey, Pennsylvania, and the Virgin Islands.

Justice Clarence Thomas

You might not be able to name all of the Supreme Court justices—or even a few. But chances are, you can name at least one: Clarence Thomas. Thomas was nominated by President Bush in 1991 to replace Thurgood Marshall. Marshall was the first African American to serve on the court. After a lengthy and contentious battle, Thomas became the second.

Thomas was born into poverty in rural Georgia on June 23, 1948. He is the youngest of the justices currently serving on the court. He graduated from Holy Cross College in 1971 and Yale Law School in 1974. George H. W. Bush then appointed him to the U.S. Court of Appeals for the District of Columbia Circuit.

Thomas's nomination initially received a warm reception. Many felt Bush was appointing Thomas not because he was the most qualified, but because he was the most qualified minority to replace the respected Marshall. Allegations arose shortly before he was to be confirmed that he had sexually harassed a former colleague, Anita Hill. Thomas adamantly denied the charges. After heated testimony from both Thomas and Hill, the Senate narrowly confirmed Thomas, 52–48. This was the smallest margin of confirmation of any Supreme Court justice.

Initially, Thomas was quiet and reserved in his approach to his activities on the court. Alongside Scalia, he is considered the most conservative member of the court. In recent years, he has become more vocal and outspoken on the court, and he is taking on a more activist role. His detractors, primarily liberals, do not acknowledge his ability, which is arguably quite good from a constitutional perspective—if not a philosophical one. His supporters, however, argue that Thomas is growing into the position they knew he would have all along. Thomas serves on the Eighth Circuit Court of Appeals. This area includes Arizona, Iowa, Minnesota, Nebraska, North Dakota, and South Dakota.

Justice Ruth Bader Ginsburg

Ruth Bader Ginsburg became the second woman to serve on the Supreme Court when President Bill Clinton appointed her in 1993.

Ginsburg was born in Brooklyn, New York, on March 13, 1933. After graduating from Cornell University, she entered Harvard Law School as one of only nine women in the class of 1959. In 1963, she became only the second woman to join the faculty at Rutgers University. Nine years later, she was named the head of the liberal American Civil Liberties Union Women's Rights Project. Simultaneously, she left Rutgers and went to the Columbia School of Law, where she became the first female tenured professor.

> **We Hold These Truths**
>
> The old expression that politics makes strange bedfellows could apply to this court. Ruth Bader Ginsburg, a liberal, had at least one long-term friend when she joined the court: Antonin Scalia, a conservative, from his days on the appellate courts. And if Ginsburg was at all concerned about the confirmation process, she no doubt received some pointers from her other good friend: Robert Bork, also a conservative.

In 1980, President Jimmy Carter appointed Ginsburg to the U.S. Court of Appeals for the District of Columbia. She served 13 years, and when conservative justice Byron White retired, President Bill Clinton, a Democrat, jumped at the chance to appoint the first true liberal Democrat to the court in over 20 years. Ginsburg was confirmed 97–3.

Ginsburg, along with Stevens, are the two true liberals on the court. They are often successful in getting Souter and Stephen Breyer, the newest justice, to form a liberal block and then work a bit harder to pick off one of the three swing voters to create a liberal position.

Ginsburg serves on the Second Circuit Court of Appeals. This area includes Connecticut, Vermont, and New York.

Justice Stephen Breyer

Stephen Breyer was born in San Francisco on August 15, 1938. He received a Bachelor of Arts degree from Oxford, and a J.D. from Harvard Law School. He served as an assistant special prosecutor on the Watergate Special Prosecution Force in 1973. Later, he served as Special Counsel to the U.S. Senate Judiciary Committee and as chief counsel from 1979 to 1980.

Breyer also has a strong intellectual background. He was a visiting professor at the College of Law in Sydney, Australia, and at the University of Rome. From 1967 through his appointment in 1994, Breyer was a law professor at Harvard.

Clinton first met Breyer when he was searching for White's replacement a year earlier. Due to an earlier bike accident, Breyer did not make a strong impression on the president, and he was passed over for Ginsburg. Breyer was not the president's first choice the next time around, either; Clinton would have preferred someone with more worldly experience, but he ultimately settled on the academic-leaning Breyer.

While solidly a liberal on the court, Breyer has been known to pull a few surprises, most notably his vote in favor of the Good News Club in the 2000 term. For more information on this, see Chapter 26.

The Solicitor General

The solicitor general is a position that most people have never heard of. In fact, it's possible that some might confuse this position and that of the surgeon general (a health official) because of their similar-sounding names.

The main responsibility of the solicitor general, which is a position administered through the Department of Justice, is to oversee and argue government litigation in the Supreme Court.

The solicitor general decides which cases before the Supreme Court will also have a government review. The president nominates a candidate and the Senate confirms the position in the same vein as is done for Supreme Court justices. Although the solicitor general is one person, he or she has an office that is composed of dozens of attorneys. These attorneys prepare petitions, briefs, and countless other papers prepared on behalf of the United States for Supreme Court litigation. The solicitor general personally assigns the oral argument of government cases before the Supreme Court.

> **We Hold These Truths**
>
> The United States is actively involved in roughly two thirds of all the cases that the Supreme Court decides on a merit basis in a given year.

Another important function of the solicitor general is to review all the cases that went against the government in the lower courts. If the solicitor general determines that the decision was wrong, he or she decides to continue an appeals process and may argue it in front of the Supreme Court.

Law Clerks

The least known but perhaps most influential group of people are the clerks of the court. These clerks, 36 in all, are usually right out of law school—mostly Ivy League schools—are white, and are overwhelmingly male. The process for applying for a position varies. Some justices rely on recommendations from professors or previous law clerks. Ultimately, however, the decision for who is hired rests solely with the justice.

Becoming a law clerk can open many doors down the road. Today clerks perform a wide range of activities for the justices, including summarizing cases, reviewing appeals, and even writing the first drafts of a justice's opinion. The amount of input that a particular clerk has depends on the justice he or she works for.

Law clerks were not always a part of the Supreme Court. Justices initially read each and every case that came before the court on their own. Since 1882, however, all the justices have had at least one law clerk to assist with the growing caseload. In 1972, the court initiated a pool arrangement among the clerks. Under this setup, a single law clerk reviews an incoming petition and summarizes it for all the justices participating in the pool. This clerk then recommends to the court which cases to accept and which to decline.

On the Record

"I had a lot less responsibility than some of the clerks now. They are much more involved in the entire process now."

—Justice John Paul Stevens, in 1999

Today there is concern that the justices allow the clerks to wield too much power. A 1999 study conducted by *USA Today* found that by allowing the clerks to have an influential say in which cases appear on the docket, they are shaping the course of history; consequently, some less glamorous but equally important cases are being ignored.

The Least You Need to Know

- ◆ Supreme Court justices serve for life—or as long as they want to—which means there's very little turnover at this level of the judicial system.

- ◆ The Supreme Court is historically referred to by the name of the chief justice—for example, the Burger Court, the Rehnquist Court, and so on.

- ◆ The solicitor general represents the government's interest in Supreme Court cases.

- ◆ Serving as a Supreme Court law clerk can be an important step in a legal career.

Chapter 16

First Monday in October

In This Chapter

♦ The inner workings of the court

♦ Original vs. appellate jurisdiction

♦ How cases arrive at the Supreme Court

♦ Rules of order

As the nation's top legal court, the Supreme Court is the most centrally secretive body found in the three branches of government. Much of its work is conducted behind closed doors, alleviating the court from the kinds of pressures that are placed on both the legislative and executive branches, and few people besides the nine justices know what is going to happen on a given case. Public opinion and lobbying have much less influence here—although they still have some—than they do in other branches of government. Still, it's possible to see certain aspects of the court's work by either visiting it or researching court decisions.

Terms of the Court

Nearly every aspect of the court follows some of the many traditions set by previous members of the Supreme Court (see Chapter 17). The general public can view *oral arguments*, although there are only 188 seats available for the general public to do so. In the Supreme Court, attorneys make oral arguments on a time limit: 30 minutes per side, unless the court decides differently before they begin. The attorney for the person bringing the argument makes his or her case first. During oral arguments, justices often interrupt to ask questions or make observations.

Inside the Beltway

Each Supreme Court **term**, or **session**, is held within one year beginning the first Monday in October. Terms are referred to by the year in which they started, even though the majority of work is done in the following year.

A court's **docket** is the list of cases it is to hear.

Each court *term* or *session* begins on the first Monday in October and usually ends in midsummer of the next year when the court's *docket* is cleared. However, the term does not technically end until the day before the first Monday of the next October and the beginning of the next court term.

When the court is in session, oral arguments are heard Monday through Wednesday. On Monday and Tuesday, the Court hears the arguments from 10 A.M. to 12 P.M. and from 1 P.M. to 3 P.M. On Wednesday, only a morning session with oral arguments is held. Usually, two cases are heard during each segment.

Inside the Beltway

Oral arguments are arguments made before a court that augment briefs already filed by each side with lengthier materials.

The **Orders List** is a list of the business the court will conduct on each day it is in session. It includes any cases the court is hearing that day, as well as any cases it has just decided to review or not review in the future.

On Tuesday mornings before oral arguments, the court releases any opinions it has rendered and its *Orders List*. (When the Court is not hearing oral arguments, Orders Lists and opinions are issued on Monday.)

On Wednesday afternoons, the court holds a private conference between the justices. Thursday and Friday are the days reserved for justices to conduct their own business, including researching and writing opinions. When the court is in session, the nine justices also meet together in private to discuss pending cases.

Inside the Beltway

Drawn up by the chief justice, the list of potential cases to be heard before the court in oral arguments is known as the **discuss list**.

During Supreme Court conferences, the chief justice presides and is responsible for developing the first *discuss list*. The chief justice also assigns which other justices will write the opinions of the court—or he or she can choose to write them. If justices would like to add to the list, they are allowed to do so. Cases on the list are voted upon by the justices as to whether they will be heard.

During the term, the court holds two-week sessions, each followed by a two-week recess. Recesses, used for the justices to review cases and prepare for the next session, are longer in December and February.

Who Gets Heard?

The Supreme Court can hear a case in two areas: *original jurisdiction* and *appellate jurisdiction*.

Original jurisdiction is a much smaller area of the Supreme Court but is nonetheless very significant. As Article 3, Section 2, of the Constitution laid out …

> The judicial Power shall extend to all Cases, in Law and Equity, arising under this Constitution, the Laws of the United States, and Treaties made, or which shall be made, under their Authority;—to all Cases affecting Ambassadors, other public Ministers and Consuls;—to all Cases of admiralty and maritime Jurisdiction;—to Controversies to which the United States shall be a party— to Controversies between two or more States;—*between a State and Citizens of another State; —between Citizens of different States,—between Citizens of the same State claiming Lands under Grants of different States, and between a State, or the Citizens thereof, and foreign States, Citizens or Subjects.*

It's important to note that the Eleventh Amendment altered the italicized portions to exclude the power of a foreign country or person in another state to sue a state in federal court without the state's permission.

As defined by the Constitution, the Supreme Court has original jurisdiction over any conflict between two states, meaning that the high court can choose to hear and rule on the case first, before any other court. In cases concerning ambassadors, disputes between the United States and a state, or cases filed by states against citizens, the Supreme Court also has original jurisdiction. If any court decides a case out of its jurisdiction, that decision is void.

Inside the Beltway

Original jurisdiction is the power to hear and decide on a case for the first time. **Appellate jurisdiction** is the power of a higher court to correct the decision of a lower court.

The Supreme Court's structure is designed to allow for only the minimal outside influence, which is why lobbyists and groups advocating a particular cause usually focus their energies on the legislative and, to some extent, executive branches. However, there is one way for an outside group to air its views before the justices—through filing an *amicus curiae brief*.

Inside the Beltway

The literal translation of *amicus curiae* means "a friend of the court." An **amicus curiae brief** is usually submitted to a court by a group that has some stake in the outcome of the case being argued; however, it may not be submitted if the person or group filing would be personally affected by the outcome. For example, in the Supreme Court case *Bush v. Gore* in the 2000 session, both sides were supplemented by the filing of amicus curiae briefs by a range of groups, including the Brennan Center for Justice at New York University Law School and the American Civil Liberties Union, among others.

An amicus curiae brief may also be used if a lawyer for one side or the justices ask the group for input because it has relevant experience with the case being debated. An attorney who files the amicus curiae brief may be allowed to state his or her case during oral arguments as well, although time is deducted from the 30 minutes of the relevant side.

In a typical court term, there are only a few cases of original jurisdiction. In the 2000 term, the court heard *Kansas v. Colorado*, which was a case of original jurisdiction because it concerned a dispute between the two states over a compact made regarding the use of the Arkansas River.

In those cases of original jurisdiction, the Supreme Court appoints a master, who listens and reviews evidence in the case before making a recommendation to the justices on what their decision should be.

Most of the high court's cases are the result of appellate jurisdiction, meaning that the court can choose to hear cases already decided by lower federal courts as well as cases from state courts when an issue concerning a federal law is raised.

From Federal or State Courts

If a case goes to the Supreme Court from the federal court system, it follows a very specific path, no matter what the issue:

1. U.S. district courts are the hearing rooms for federal court cases. Their jurisdiction can include a wide variety of cases, from those between citizens of two different states to serious criminal matters relating to federal laws such as counterfeiting or espionage.

2. If the matter is a civil or criminal one, the losing side can make an appeal to a U.S. Court of Appeals by claiming that the district court made an error in the proceedings or issued its judgment unfairly. There are 12 Courts of Appeals in the United States, based on 12 geographic judicial circuits. Each state, as well as Puerto Rico, the Virgin Islands, Guam, and the Northern Mariana Islands, is included in one of the circuits. However, there is a thirteenth Court of Appeals, known as the United States Court of Appeals for the Federal Circuit.

3. After the Court of Appeals decision, the losing side can appeal one final time to the Supreme Court.

> ### We Hold These Truths
>
> There haven't always been Courts of Appeals. They were established in 1891 to stop the Supreme Court from becoming bogged down in deciding on every appeal made from the federal court level. Still, a person who loses at the Court of Appeals can appeal to the Supreme Court if desired.

Each Supreme Court justice is assigned to one or more of the circuits, where he or she might be asked to stay an execution, issue an injunction, or respond to other unique emergencies.

The process is slightly different if a case heads to the Supreme Court from a state court system instead of the federal court system:

1. Because each state has its own system, the original hearing might be held in a circuit court, a district court, a court of common appeals, or whatever the particular state calls the trial court that first hears the case in the state.

2. After the case is first heard, the losing party can appeal in a state appeals court. Some states have a system of more than one appeals court, while others have a system in which an appeal goes directly to the state's highest court.

3. Many states refer to the highest court as the state supreme court, but some have separate names, including Supreme Court of Appeals or just Court of Appeals. If a case is lost here, it can be appealed directly to the Supreme Court. However, certain requirements must be met before the case can be appealed to the

Supreme Court. A case must involve a federal legal question to be brought before the Supreme Court—such as a treaty, a constitutional question, or a specific violation of a federal law.

Four Ways to Arrive at the Supreme Court

If a case makes it through the federal or state courts and the person who lost the case still wants to move forward, that person can try to get the Supreme Court to hear the case in four ways.

Petition for a Writ of Certiorari

The most frequently used device is filing a petition for a *writ of certiorari*. However, the Supreme Court rules note, "Review on a writ of certiorari is not a matter of right, but of judicial discretion." If the court doesn't agree to hear the case, a petitioner can try again within 25 days for a rehearing.

Inside the Beltway

A written order from a higher court agreeing to review the decision of a lower court is a **writ of certiorari. Per curiam,** meaning "by the court," is a unanimous opinion and, unlike other written opinions, isn't signed by any justice.

When considering whether to issue a writ of certiorari, the court might review whether one court of appeals has rendered a decision that is opposite of another court of appeals' decision in the same type of case, whether a state court has decided a case in a way that conflicts with the decision of a different state court on a similar case, or whether a state or federal court has ruled on a matter that the Supreme Court has not yet ruled on.

Appeal

Another way to have the Supreme Court review a case is through appeal. Anyone who goes this route must prove to the justices that the case qualifies. Typically, appeal cases before the Supreme Court are not tried in oral arguments. Instead, justices decide in private and announce their decision *per curiam*. For example, the landmark case *Brandenburg v. Ohio*, discussed in Chapter 17, was a per curiam decision.

Request for Certification

The third way to achieve a hearing before the Supreme Court is through a request for certification. If a lower court finds that it cannot render a decision itself because of a legal question, it may submit a request for certification to the high court asking it for help. However, Supreme Court rules say that such a petition must be narrow: "Only questions or propositions of law may be certified, and they shall be stated separately and with precision."

Included in the request are the facts of the case and the particular legal question that is troubling to the lower court. The Supreme Court may give instructions to the lower court that must be adhered to, or it may simply decide to hear the case itself.

Petition for an Extraordinary Writ

Finally, the least employed method of bringing a case before the Supreme Court is through a petition for an extraordinary writ. Such writs are difficult to prove and are subject to the wish of the court; therefore, they are used infrequently. In such a petition, the petitioner has a heavy burden.

According to the Supreme Court rules, "To justify the granting of such a writ, the petition must show that the writ will be in aid of the Court's appellate jurisdiction, that exceptional circumstances warrant the exercise of the Court's discretionary powers, and that adequate relief cannot be obtained in any other form or from any other court." Examples of extraordinary writs include a writ of prohibition, which stops a lower court from going outside its jurisdiction; a writ of habeas corpus, which is used to challenge a person's custody; or a writ of mandamus, which orders a lower court or public official to take a certain action and is used only when other judicial options have failed.

Following a Case Through the Process

After one of those four methods is chosen, the clerk of the court receives the documentation and checks to make sure that all necessary information is included. If it is, the petitioner must pay $300 for the justices to even look at the case. However, there are exceptions to the fee for the government and for those whom the court finds cannot afford the expense.

The clerk then numbers the petition and adds it to the court's docket. Justices are supposed to review all the cases on the docket, but because there are so many, justices often pool their resources. In other instances, justices rely on their clerks to read the docket and prepare summaries for them to read.

After justices have reviewed the docket, some of those cases make it to the chief justice's discuss list; others may be added, and the justices vote on which ones they will hear. Specific rules apply in the private conferences at which justices decide which cases they will hear.

Foremost is that these conferences are private—no clerks or court officials are present, and the public is never allowed in. After the chief justice presents the case, other justices comment on the case in order of seniority, including how they might vote. If there is no clear agreement between the justices to take or not to take the case, a vote is taken.

> ## We Hold These Truths
>
> Justices generally do not explain why they have not accepted a case, although one justice may occasionally include a dissent on the list as to why he or she wanted the case to be heard by the high court.

If four or more justices agree to hear the case, it will be heard. If one case is bypassed and one justice clearly wanted to have the case heard, the case can be added to the next conference. Between conferences, the justice can try to convince enough of his or her colleagues to get four approvals at the next conference.

During conferences, the justices also decide whether the case will be decided based on submitted written materials or whether they will hear it themselves in oral arguments. If the justices decide to hear oral arguments, the clerk of the court schedules the case and lets lawyers for both sides know. After the conference, a list is made available to the public detailing cases that have been accepted for review and those that have been rejected.

> ## We Hold These Truths
>
> Lawyers must follow a strict set of rules when they file briefs to the Supreme Court, covering everything from the size of pages to the color of the cover. For example, part of the court rules surrounding briefs filed is as follows:
>
> > Every document, except one permitted to be produced on $8\frac{1}{2}$ by 11-inch paper, shall be produced on paper that is opaque, unglazed, $6\frac{1}{8}$ by $9\frac{1}{4}$ inches in size, and not less than 60 pounds in weight, and shall have margins of at least three fourths of an inch on all sides.
>
> Among the many requirements of the court, each brief cover must be in a specific color, depending on what type of document is being filed, and must also meet a page-limit requirement.

The petitioner or appellant is the one who lost the case in a lower court and is seeking a reversal from the Supreme Court. The respondent or appellee is the one who must defend the original court's decision. Lawyers on both sides then prepare and submit briefs to the court.

Strict time limits are placed on both the appellant and the appellee, although extensions can be granted by the clerk of the court. The appellant must file the brief within 45 days of receiving a writ; the appellee has 30 days after that to file a brief.

Justices then review the materials submitted by both sides, study the case in relation to previous legal precedent, and perhaps formulate questions they plan to ask at oral arguments.

Do's and Don'ts for Lawyers Before the High Court

Like everything surrounding the Supreme Court, there are numerous rules to follow for lawyers who argue before the justices. First, the lawyers' oral arguments should not be a reading; according to the rules, "Oral argument read from a prepared text is not favored."

Lawyers should "emphasize and clarify the written arguments in the briefs on the merits" and "assume that all Justices have read the briefs before oral argument." In addition, unless the court says otherwise, each side will have a half-hour to make its case, but the lawyers are not required to use all the time if they do not need it.

The appellant starts and may choose to conclude after the appellee. Still, the court warns that no points should be left out for rebuttal. In addition, even though court cases that make it all the way to the Supreme Court often have several lawyers on each side, the court wants to hear from only one. If a request is filed for more than one lawyer per side to present arguments, the rules warn, "Divided argument is not favored."

During the oral arguments, when justices interrupt with questions or comments, time is deducted from whichever side is presenting. Lights are used on the lectern where lawyers stand to let them know how much time they have. A white light means that they have five minutes left, but when the red light goes on, the time is up and the lawyer can only complete the sentence he is saying.

Oral arguments are taped and transcribed completely, unless the chief justice or presiding justice asks for an omission. The tapes and transcripts are usually heard by only the justices and their clerks during the term (although the private firm that is hired by the court may sell them before the end of the term). At the conclusion of the term, the tapes and transcripts are sent to the National Archives and Records Administration. Eventually, they are made available through several Internet databases as well as on the Supreme Court's website, www.supremecourtus.gov.

And the Winner Is ...

At conferences to discuss the oral arguments, the justices first debate the merits of each argument and then vote on their decision. Five votes are needed for a majority on a case, and a quorum of six justices must be present for the vote to be taken. If the justices tie, the decision of the lower court stands.

We Hold These Truths

If you see an oral argument before the Supreme Court, don't expect to hear the decision from the justices right after the case has been argued. The court has no time limit on how long it may take to render an opinion: Sometimes it takes only a day, while other times it can take months! However, one time limitation is placed on decisions: All must be rendered before the court adjourns for the summer recess.

After the case is decided, the chief justice or the senior associate justice (depending on which side they are on) decides who will draft the majority opinion. The written opinion is a monumental task that will include citations of relevant cases, legal arguments, and the reasoning for the majority opinion. While one justice writes the draft of the opinion, other justices may pass on information that they want to have included.

We Hold These Truths

Each justice filed a separate per curiam opinion in the Supreme Court case *New York Times Co. v. United States,* which dealt with the publishing of government documents known as the Pentagon Papers. Although the Court ruled that publishing could continue by a 6–3 decision, each justice was compelled to explain the reasoning for his decision.

If a justice who is in the majority disagrees with the reasoning behind the court's majority opinion, that justice may write a concurring opinion giving his reasons. Meanwhile, a dissenting opinion may or may not be rendered by any justices who did not agree with the majority opinion.

After drafts of any written opinions are completed, they are passed to the other judges for input. Agreement is still not a given at this point, as justices review other opinions.

If the case reverses a lower court's decision, there is usually another trial at that level. A court official, the "reporter of decisions," then puts the opinions together. Included is a summary of the decision; the majority, concurring, and dissenting opinions; and a vote tally that shows how each justice voted on the case. The reports are printed and made available to the public and the press. In addition, they are sent to the lower courts involved in the case.

The Least You Need to Know

- ◆ The Court of Appeals was established in 1891 to keep the Supreme Court from having to hear every appeal made from the federal court level.

- ◆ The Supreme Court must render all of its decisions before adjourning for summer recess.

- ◆ There are two types of cases that come before the court. The first is original jurisdiction, which is rare. The more common form is appellate jurisdiction.

- ◆ Attorneys arguing before the Supreme Court must follow a strict set of rules governing their behavior and how they submit their written arguments.

Chapter 17

Setting Precedents

In This Chapter

◆ How the Supreme Court became supreme

◆ The basis of due process

◆ Deciding for (and against!) equal rights

◆ Defining double jeopardy

Each time the Supreme Court hears a new case, it uses previous decisions made by courts in similar cases to render its opinion. This reliance, as you've previously read about, is known as a precedent.

Some of the landmark cases decided by the Supreme Court reverse a precedent. Scholars disagree on the reasoning for this: Is it because the makeup of the court changes? Is it a response to the time period during which a decision is made? How can a case be considered constitutional in one era and unconstitutional in another?

In this chapter, we explore some of the Supreme Court's landmark cases and how they've affected the rights and privileges we enjoy today.

Judicial Review

As you read in Chapter 14, the Supreme Court was the branch of the federal government with the least power in its earliest days. But its actions regarding a civil rights dispute in the early 1800s established it as a force to be reckoned with.

Congress has often legislated the enforcement or enhancement of civil rights, sometimes in response to actions by the Supreme Court. In other cases, the Supreme Court rules on legislation already passed.

Marbury v. Madison

The first such case to go before the court was *Marbury v. Madison*. A complex matter, it set the *precedent* of *judicial review*.

The contentious presidential election of 1800 handed a major defeat to the Federalist Party. Not only did its candidate, John Adams, lose, but it also lost control of Congress. Between the election and Thomas Jefferson's inauguration in March, the Federalists worked to ensure their voice in government by having outgoing President John Adams appoint Secretary of State John Marshall as Chief Justice of the Supreme Court.

Inside the Beltway

A **precedent** is a court decision in a previous case whose facts are considered the rule for a current case under review.

Judicial review is the concept of a review by a court of an act— or failure to act—on the part of a government official or body.

The Senate quickly confirmed Marshall, but he didn't take his new post until Jefferson was sworn in. At the same time, the Federalists, who had enacted the Judiciary Act of 1800, which had created several new judgeships and circuit courts, quickly filled these new posts with members of their own party before Jefferson took office. William Marbury was one of the appointees nominated by the waning Adams administration.

The Senate confirmed all the nominees on the last day of Adams's administration. Because the president must sign each confirmation, Adams spent his final night in office signing them while Marshall, still the Secretary of State, sealed them and sent them off. But several of the completed confirmations, including Marbury's, were never sent.

After Jefferson was sworn in, Marbury asked James Madison, the new Secretary of State, for his confirmation. Madison refused to turn it over, which prompted Marbury to sue Madison and ask the Supreme Court to issue a *writ of mandamus* to compel such action.

Inside the Beltway

A **writ of mandamus** is a measure used to compel a public official to complete an act.

While the Supreme Court had the authority to issue such writs, thanks to the Judiciary Act of 1789, which granted it original jurisdiction in such matters, John Marshall, its new chief justice, knew that the new administration would ignore the writ, which would then significantly weaken the court's authority. But if the Court refused to issue the writ, it might appear as if the justices were backing away from the situation. So Marshall orchestrated a compromise.

In a 5–0 decision, the court ruled in favor of Marbury and said that the withholding of the commission broke the law. However, the court also ruled that the authority given to it by the Judiciary Act to issue writs of mandamus exceeded the authority given to it by the Constitution—in other words, the court decided that the law was unconstitutional and that the Supreme Court didn't have the power to issue such writs.

On the Record

"So if a law be in opposition to the constitution; if both the law and the constitution apply to a particular case, so that the court must either decide that case, conformable to the law, disregarding the constitution; or conformably to the constitution, disregarding the law; the court must determine which of these conflicting rules governs the case; this is the very essence of judicial duty. If, then, the courts are to regard the constitution, and the constitution is superior to any ordinary act of the legislature, the constitution, and not such ordinary act, must govern the case to which both apply."

—Chief Justice John Marshall, in majority opinion for the Supreme Court in *Marbury v. Madison,* 1803

Bush v. Gore

The Supreme Court's position as the ultimate determiner of the law of the land was affirmed by one of its most famous decisions in recent history—*Bush v. Gore.* In the court's main opinion, it said that the president should be elected by the people, but "when contending parties invoke the process of the courts, however, it is our unsought responsibility to resolve the federal and constitutional issues the judicial system has been forced to confront."

How history will judge the Supreme Court's actions in *Bush v. Gore* remains to be seen, even though Gore supporters and those who advocate judicial restraint argue that the justices acted out of their bounds and forever tarnished the reputation of the court. Others contend that the court upheld the rule of law and the Constitution, acting in the only way it could to uphold those ideals of the democracy.

Due Process of Law

The complicated principle of due process of law is one of the most cited concepts in the legal system today. But it wasn't always this way. Before 1866, the Supreme Court used the concept to decide only one case.

In a nutshell, due process protects the right of citizens by prohibiting arbitrary acts by the government and ensures that the laws that affect them will be enforced equally. However, what constitutes due process has been the subject of much debate. At the federal level, its components are more easily ascertainable because the justices can use only the Constitution as a basis for their decisions. At the state level, laws vary widely and there are more of them to consider. However, state laws must be "constitutional" and not overly vague or broad.

We Hold These Truths

The only case to be based on due process before the passage of the Fourteenth Amendment was *Barron v. Baltimore* in 1833, discussed in Chapter 4. That case set the precedent of dual citizenship, meaning that a United States citizen was a citizen of both the nation and the state he or she lived in. But if a right guaranteed by the Constitution was not also guaranteed by a state government, the person was protected as a separate person in each jurisdiction: protected in one or the other, but perhaps not both.

The Fifth and Fourteenth Amendments of the Constitution form the basis of due process at the federal level. The Fifth Amendment, passed in 1791 as part of the Bill of Rights, protects a citizen's life, liberty, and property with due process from the federal government.

As you read in Chapter 4, the Fourteenth Amendment was one of three amendments passed after the Civil War to protect the rights of former slaves. But in its broadest interpretation, it also extends the protections of the Fifth Amendment for all people because it prohibits any state from making or enforcing any law that diminishes an individual's rights or deprives him or her of "life, liberty, or property, without due process of law." It also ensures that individuals will receive equal protection under the law.

Since its passage, the majority of the court's most significant rulings (and almost all of the ones you read about in this chapter) have been related to protecting individual and civil rights under the Fourteenth Amendment. While the amendment extended the rights of citizens under both state and federal governments, how the Supreme Court interpreted it for most of the next century didn't always enforce the amendment that way.

The "Slaughter-House Cases"

In the "Slaughter-House Cases" of 1873, the first Supreme Court interpretation of the Fourteenth Amendment, the court stuck to the amendment's narrowest interpretation: that it was enacted to grant citizenship to African Americans and protect them from discrimination. The case challenged the validity of a Louisiana state law passed in 1869 that gave one company the exclusive right to butcher cattle in New Orleans. It caused outrage among other butchers, who were forced to have their animals slaughtered at the one facility, which would cost them more and potentially bankrupt them.

In the Louisiana State Supreme Court case, the lawyer for the butchers challenged the state law on Fourteenth Amendment grounds (as well as the Thirteenth and the Fifteenth), arguing that his clients had been denied equal protection of the law and deprived of their right to own property without due process.

After losing that case, the group appealed to the Supreme Court, which upheld the prior decision by a 5–4 vote, saying that the butchers were protected only by Louisiana's state constitution and the state courts. The Fourteenth Amendment didn't protect the butchers, the court said, because it protected only certain fundamental rights from state infringement, and the right to property wasn't one of them.

Chicago, Burlington, and Quincy R.R. v. Chicago

Over the years, the court moved away from the rationale it used in the Slaughter-House Cases and eventually abandoned it. In *Chicago, Burlington, and Quincy R.R. v. Chicago,* handed down in 1897, the court reversed its decision in the Slaughter-House Cases and found that the states couldn't take an individual's property without compensation.

The decision was a small step toward guaranteeing other liberties contained in the Bill of Rights. But because it incorporated only the right to property, the court would have to decide cases involving other rights included in the Bill of Rights on a case-by-case basis.

Eventually, as the following chart shows, the justices incorporated into the meaning of the Fourteenth Amendment's due process clause many of the elements of the Bill of Rights. Over time, the court began protecting individual rights against state encroachment by finding that such actions deprived life, liberty, or property without due process of law, forbidden by the Fourteenth Amendment.

How the Bill of Rights Was Incorporated into the Fourteenth Amendment

Selected Provisions	Amendment	When Incorporated	Key Case
Eminent domain	Fifth	1897	*Chicago, Burlington, and Quincy R.R. v. Chicago*
Freedom of speech	First	1925	*Gitlow v. New York*
Freedom of the press	First	1931	*Near v. Minnesota*
Freedom of assembly	First	1939	*Hauge v. CIO*
Freedom from warrantless search and seizure (Exclusionary Rule)	Fourth	1961	*Mapp v. Ohio*
Right to counsel in any criminal case	Sixth	1963	*Gideon v. Wainwright*
Right against self-incrimination and forced confessions	Fifth	1964	*Malloy v. Hogan*
Right to counsel and remain silent	Sixth	1966	*Miranda v. Arizona*
Right against double jeopardy	Fifth	1969	*Benton v. Maryland*

Palko v. Connecticut

In the 1937 case *Palko v. Connecticut*, the Supreme Court set a new precedent for deciding what to incorporate under the due process clause. Frank Palko, who was accused of killing two police officers in a robbery, was brought to trial under charges of first-degree murder but was found guilty of second-degree murder and sentenced to life in prison.

The state appealed the jury's decision and won a second trial when prosecutors introduced new evidence—a confession from Palko—that the first trial judge had disallowed. This time, Palko was found guilty of first-degree murder and faced the death penalty.

Palko's lawyers appealed to the Supreme Court, citing violations of the Fifth Amendment's prohibitions against prosecuting an individual twice for the same crime and the Fourteenth Amendment's guarantee of due process. They also argued that *double jeopardy*, prohibited by the Fifth Amendment, also was protected by state laws.

Inside the Beltway

Double jeopardy holds that no person can be tried twice for the same crime.

In its 8–1 ruling, the court said that certain "fundamental rights" were more central to the well-being of a nation and that those rights were the ones that must be applied equally in state and federal government. Palko's right to not be tried twice was not a fundamental right in the same way the right to life was for the murdered police officers. The *Palko v. Connecticut* case opened the door for rights protected by the Bill of Rights to also be protected by states. While the case didn't allow the entire Bill of Rights to be incorporated into the Fourteenth Amendment, it did allow consideration on a case-by-case basis. Still, the decision on double jeopardy was overturned in 1969 in *Benton v. Maryland*, meaning that states must also comply with the federal system and can't try a person for the same crime twice.

Eventually, though, other civil liberties guaranteed by those amendments were all incorporated into the Fourteenth Amendment under the due process clause.

The Question of Civil Rights

Although the Bill of Rights protects many of the civil rights we take for granted today, they were not always enforced, often thanks to major decisions handed down by the Supreme Court. One of the most noted examples of the court's actions that ended up standing in the way of the rights of African Americans was the 1857 Dred Scott case, or *Scott v. Sandford*.

We Hold These Truths

The Dred Scott decision was set aside in the Fourteenth Amendment, which held, among other things, that all persons born or naturalized in the United States are citizens of the United States and, therefore, are entitled to equal rights and protection under the law.

Scott v. Sandford

Dred Scott was a slave who sued his master for his freedom and his family's freedom, contending that his family had become free when they traveled with their master from Missouri, a slave state, into a free portion of the Louisiana territory. The Supreme Court ruled against Scott on three points. First, the justices said that Scott didn't even have the right to sue because, as an African American, he wasn't a citizen of the United States.

The court could have ended its decision there, but it decided that it wanted to rule on the question of slavery in the territories. The court said that when Scott left the Louisiana Territory, he lost his claim to freedom and that Missouri didn't have to enforce a law outside of its jurisdiction. In addition, the court said that the Missouri Compromise, which banned slavery in certain parts of the Louisiana Territory, was unconstitutional and violated the Fifth Amendment because it deprived slave owners of their property without due process of law.

Plessy v. Ferguson

In another landmark civil rights case, *Plessy v. Ferguson*, decided in 1896, the Supreme Court not only overturned the Civil Rights Act of 1875, which Congress passed to protect African Americans from discriminatory treatment by owners of public businesses, but it also established a dangerous doctrine that supported segregation.

Louisiana had passed a state law requiring whites and African Americans to ride in separate railcars. Homer Plessy, an African American, had bought a first-class ticket and was arrested when he refused to move to a "colored" car. Plessy's attorneys argued two points: that he wasn't afforded "equal protection of the laws" under the Fourteenth Amendment and that the state law violated the Thirteenth Amendment's ban on slavery.

The court ruled that the Fourteenth Amendment protected African Americans only from wrongful actions by the states, not by private citizens, even if they were representing public services or companies. In so doing, the court established the "separate but equal" doctrine that allowed segregation if equal facilities were provided for both races. Segregation was made an acceptable legal standard, and the Supreme Court let it stand for the next half-century.

Brown v. Board of Education

A legal breakthrough on civil rights for African Americans came about in 1954, when the Supreme Court's unanimous decision on *Brown v. Board of Education* overturned *Plessy v. Ferguson* and its separate-but-equal doctrine. Thurgood Marshall, a future Supreme Court justice, represented five African American families who had decided to challenge segregation laws by filing lawsuits against their local school districts. With help from the NAACP, which had brought—and won—similar cases at the Supreme Court level, the five cases headed to the Supreme Court as one.

Marshall argued that under the equal protection clause of the Fourteenth Amendment, segregated schools were not equal and discriminated against people of color. Defense attorney John Davis argued two points: that the Fourteenth Amendment wasn't written to prevent segregation and that the Supreme Court didn't have the right to tell states to desegregate.

In the decision, Chief Justice Earl Warren reversed precedent when he wrote, "We conclude that in the field of public education the doctrine of 'separate but equal' has no place. Separate educational facilities are inherently unequal." And the court went so far as to say that even if all the facilities in the schools were equal (which they weren't), segregation would still be unconstitutional under the Fourteenth Amendment because African American students might always feel inferior in separate facilities.

> **We Hold These Truths**
>
> *Brown v. Board of Education* was named after Linda Brown, an elementary school student in Kansas who was forced to attend a school far outside her neighborhood because she was African American.

Segregated states were furious with the ruling, and many vowed not to desegregate. But the NAACP and other civil rights leaders led by Martin Luther King Jr. pushed for the enforcement of the *Brown v. Board of Education* decision, setting the platform for massive civil rights legislation passed in Congress in the 1960s.

Resistance to desegregation continued for years, even after the passage of civil rights legislation in Congress. In 1968, the Supreme Court said in a ruling on a similar case that segregation must immediately stop.

Freedom of Speech and of the Press

Guaranteed under the First Amendment and reaffirmed by the Fourteenth Amendment, the right to say and print what one believes has always been among the most important freedoms given to Americans. Several Supreme Court cases, most heard within the past 100 years, have defined the parameters of both freedoms.

Schenck v. United States

As you read in Chapter 3, one of the first cases to set the precedent for future freedom of speech cases was *Schenck v. United States* in 1919. In articulating the standard of clear and present danger, the court said that the First Amendment freedom of speech is not always guaranteed and that the government could prohibit certain speech.

Gitlow v. New York

In 1925, the Supreme Court ruled that freedom of speech didn't fall under the protections of the Fourteenth Amendment with its ruling on *Gitlow v. New York*. In a 7–2 decision, the Supreme Court upheld the earlier conviction of Benjamin Gitlow, a member of the Communist Labor Party of the United States who circulated pamphlets advocating the overthrowing of the government. The ruling found that Gitlow didn't have Fourteenth Amendment protection because he broke a state law that made it a crime to invoke violence against the government.

But in its written opinion, the Supreme Court also set the stage for the future expansion of the right to free speech. Even though they ruled against Gitlow, the justices wrote that "for present purposes we may and do assume that freedom of speech and of the press—which are protected by the First Amendment from abridgement by Congress—are among the fundamental personal rights and liberties protected by the due process clause of the Fourteenth Amendment from impairment by the states."

Near v. Minnesota

In the 1931 case of *Near v. Minnesota*, the court was again called on to interpret freedoms guaranteed by the Fourteenth Amendment. Jay Near was the publisher of the newspaper *Saturday Press*, which regularly accused public officials of being incompetent and corrupt. One of the paper's targets, a prosecutor named Floyd Olson, sued

Near under Minnesota's Public Nuisance Abatement Law, which authorized "the abatement ... of a malicious, scandalous and defamatory newspaper, magazine, or other periodical."

Near appealed the state conviction on First and Fourteenth Amendment grounds, arguing the concept of *prior restraint*, which held that laws that authorized censorship of a publication, as Minnesota's did, were unconstitutional.

In a 5–4 decision, the Supreme Court ruled in Near's favor, deciding that the state law was prior restraint and thus violated both the First and Fourteenth Amendments. In their ruling, the justices affirmed the press's right to investigate government as one of the nation's basic tenets and stated that government officials who believed they had been unfairly targeted should use libel laws instead. After *Near v. Minnesota*, the Supreme Court has consistently upheld its ruling on prior restraint, although it has been tested on several occasions.

Inside the Beltway

Prior restraint is the restriction on publication or communication of material before it is published or communicated.

New York Times Co. v. Sullivan

In 1964, the *New York Times Co. v. Sullivan* case expanded the protections provided to the press by the First Amendment. L. B. Sullivan, a police commissioner in Alabama, sued *The New York Times* for libel based on ads placed by two civil rights organizations. Although the ads did not mention Sullivan, they were critical of his police force. Alabama state courts ruled in Sullivan's favor and awarded him $500,000.

In its appeal to the Supreme Court, attorneys for the *Times* argued that the state's libel law allowing restrictions on false statements was unconstitutional. In a unanimous decision, the Supreme Court reversed the state court's decision and said that a major role of the press was to act as a watchdog for the actions of public officials.

The court went on to say that false statements were inevitable in such a debate and must be protected to ensure the best possible debate. Public officials who were the target of a false statement could not be compensated unless they could prove that it was made with the "knowledge that it was false or with reckless disregard of whether it was false or not."

Brandenburg v. Ohio

In 1969, the Supreme Court ruled unanimously in another landmark case that overturned the precedent set by *Schenck v. United States* in 1929.

Clarence Brandenburg, a Ku Klux Klan leader in Ohio, had incited violence against African Americans in a televised KKK rally. Brandenburg was charged and convicted under an Ohio state law, the Criminal Syndicalism Act, which outlawed advocating violence to achieve reform.

In his appeal, Brandenburg charged that his First Amendment rights had been violated—a claim the Supreme Court agreed with. The court said that the government could restrict speech only if there was an obvious and immediate link to breaking the law, overturning the "clear and present danger" precedent earlier established.

The impact of the *Brandenburg v. Ohio* decision further expanded the right of speech under the First Amendment, especially as it relates to political speech.

Rights of Suspected Criminals

Although we've noted significant cases that either granted rights under state law or expanded existing rights, the Supreme Court made numerous other decisions throughout the last century based on how it interpreted the Fourteenth Amendment. Among the issues it addressed are the right to privacy, the right to legal representation, the right to remain silent, and freedom from a police search without a warrant.

Several cases in the 1960s established protection for suspected criminals under the Fourteenth Amendment's due process clause, including *Mapp v. Ohio* in 1961, *Gideon v. Wainwright* in 1963, *Escobedo v. Arizona* in 1964, and *Miranda v. Arizona* in 1966.

Mapp v. Ohio

The first case, *Mapp v. Ohio*, involved Dollree Mapp, whose home was searched by police who said they had a warrant as required under the Fourth Amendment. The officers, who never showed the warrant to Mapp, seized obscene pictures, considered illegal in Ohio. Mapp went to prison.

Mapp's attorney appealed his case to the Supreme Court on the grounds that the search was unconstitutional. In a 6–3 decision, the court overturned Mapp's conviction based on the precedent of the exclusionary rule, which holds that evidence found in an illegal search and seizure can't be used.

Since the *Mapp v. Ohio* case, there has been a narrowing of the exclusionary rule based on cases in which warrants were issued in error. Now, if a warrant is mistakenly issued but is done with the presumption that its issuance was valid, evidence from a search can be used against a suspected criminal.

Gideon v. Wainwright

In the 1963 case *Gideon v. Wainwright*, the Supreme Court set the precedent that ensures a citizen's right to counsel, under both state and federal law. A Florida resident named Clarence Gideon, who was arrested for burglary, asked for a court-appointed attorney on the grounds that he was too poor to pay for one. The court denied his request, forcing Gideon to represent himself. After losing the case and going to prison, Gideon filed an appeal to the Supreme Court, citing protection afforded him by the Sixth and Fourteenth Amendments.

Prior to the case, the Supreme Court had ruled that the only time states were required to provide attorneys to clients was when the death penalty was an option or when there were special circumstances. The court unanimously overruled that precedent and decided that all defendants in criminal proceedings must have access to counsel. Gideon, who received a new trial as a result of the ruling, was found not guilty.

Escobedo v. Illinois

Escobedo v. Illinois, handed down in 1964, and *Miranda v. Arizona*, handed down in 1966, further strengthened the rights of suspected criminals. In Escobedo, the court ruled that a suspected criminal had the right to be informed of his rights, including the right to an attorney and the right to remain silent, before an interrogation.

Miranda v. Arizona

In 1963, Ernesto Miranda was arrested on rape and kidnapping charges at his home in Arizona. After a witness identified him at the police station, Miranda was interrogated for two hours and signed a confession without being informed of his right to have a lawyer present or of his right to remain silent.

During the Supreme Court case, Miranda's attorneys argued that the police had failed to follow the Fifth Amendment when they questioned him; the defense argued that Miranda could have asked for a lawyer any time during the process and that he had given his confession voluntarily.

In a 5–4 ruling, the court overturned Miranda's conviction and decided that the Fifth Amendment ensures that police must first inform suspected criminals of their rights before interrogating them. If police obtain a confession without informing a person of these rights, the evidence cannot be used against that person in court. However, a suspected criminal can waive those rights, the court said.

Miranda v. Arizona dramatically altered the scope of tactics that could be used by law enforcement. Now, whenever a police officer arrests someone, the process of reading the rights to the suspect is known as "Mirandizing" that person.

Right to Privacy and *Roe v. Wade*

The right to privacy contained in the Third, Fourth, and Fifth Amendments was incorporated in the Fourteenth Amendment with the 1973 cases *Roe v. Wade* and *Doe v. Bolton*. *Doe v. Bolton* was decided the same day as *Roe v. Wade* and struck down three regulations on abortion in the state of Georgia.

The historic *Roe v. Wade* decision, which made abortion legal regardless of state law, was based on the right to privacy. In Texas in 1969, the unmarried Jane Roe (whose real name is Norma McCorvey) was denied an abortion because Texas law allowed them only if the mother's life was at risk. In the lawsuit against Henry Wade, a district attorney in Dallas County, Roe's attorneys argued that the Texas law was unconstitutional on the basis of the due process clause and asked for an injunction to stop Wade from enforcing Texas law.

In the 7–2 vote, the Supreme Court said that the right of privacy, found in either the Ninth or the Fourteenth Amendment, ensured that a woman had the right to choose to terminate a pregnancy. However, the majority also went on to make distinctions by breaking a pregnancy into three distinct terms and allowed the states to regulate abortions in the third trimester of a pregnancy.

But the dissent argued that the right to privacy was found nowhere in the Constitution. "A transaction resulting in an operation such as this is not 'private' in the ordinary usage of the word," wrote Justice William Rehnquist in his dissent. "Nor is the 'privacy' which the Court finds here even a distant relative of the freedom from searches and seizures protected by the Fourth Amendment to the Constitution which the Court has referred to as embodying a right to privacy …."

Due to the highly charged nature of the issue, the court has heard several cases that have attempted to overturn or alter *Roe v. Wade*. In *Webster v. Reproductive Health*

Services in 1989, the court nearly overturned *Roe v. Wade* when it upheld part of a Missouri law that restricted abortion. In 1992, another 5–4 decision almost overturned *Roe*. In *Planned Parenthood v. Casey*, states are allowed to place regulations on abortions as long as they don't create an "undue burden." Most recently, in its 2000 decision in *Steinberg v. Carhart*, the court narrowly ruled against state laws banning what opponents call "partial-birth" abortions.

The Least You Need to Know

- The Supreme Court uses decisions from previous cases, called precedents, to render its decisions.

- The court's power when it comes to resolving constitutional issues was established in *Marbury v. Madison*.

- Since the enactment of the Fourteenth Amendment, which extended the rights of citizens under both state and federal governments, most of the Supreme Court's landmark decisions have related to the individual and civil rights the amendment protects.

- The court continues to hear cases that challenge its landmark decision in *Roe v. Wade*, which asserted that the right to privacy found in both the Ninth and Fourteenth Amendments give women the right to terminate a pregnancy.

Part 5

Follow the Money

Before the Constitution was ratified, each state had the authority to levy and collect taxes, coin its own money, and establish its own trade relationships with foreign nations. After ratification, those authorities transferred to the legislative branch of the government.

To this day, members of Congress spend a significant amount of their time exercising their financial authority on behalf of the U.S. government and its citizens. It takes a lot of money to run the United States, and it takes a lot of time, not only to make sure the funds go where they should, but also to determine that they're spent as they were intended to be.

Getting to Congress—or to any other political office, for that matter—is another thing that takes a lot of money. In this part, you'll learn more about how candidates raise money, how the government spends money, and where all that money comes from.

18

Fed Money

In This Chapter

- ◆ Doling out the dough
- ◆ Players in the process
- ◆ Passing the pork
- ◆ Watching how the money's spent

Congress's power comes down to the "power of the purse"—or control over how all federal dollars are spent. No federal agency can spend any money without Congress approving it. The federal budget process is confusing, complicated, and 100 percent necessary to run the government. Congress is given the leading role in deciding how much money should be spent on various programs and by various agencies, as well as what it should be spent on—an enormous power.

This chapter explores the federal budget process and explains the path it takes from the White House through Congress and to the agencies that use the funds to run the federal government.

The Federal Budget Process

As set out by the Constitution, Congress has the power to do two things: to originate *revenue* through taxes, tariffs, and similar means and to borrow money from itself through the U.S. Treasury. Most revenue raised by the government comes from individual taxes, corporate income taxes, and payroll taxes.

The founders placed few requirements on the federal budget process, only calling for all funding measures to originate in the House of Representatives. In fact, the Constitution doesn't even require a federal budget. Over time, however, lawmakers have developed an intricate system of rules and laws that govern the budgeting process and have given the executive branch a much stronger role in the budgeting process.

During the country's early history, one single *appropriation* funded everything. The first appropriation in 1789 was $689,000.

Inside the Beltway

Revenue is the government's income, from various sources, used to pay for public programs.

An **appropriation** is a measure setting aside public funds for a specific purpose.

Congress gradually split the large appropriations pool into smaller amounts, beginning with separate appropriations used to fund military operations. By 1865, there were 10 separate appropriations measures (there are 13 today). Until then, the House Ways and Means Committee controlled all appropriations measures. But in 1865, Congress separated the banking powers from the appropriations powers and created two new committees—the Appropriations Committee and the Banking and Currency Committee.

The first appropriations bill reported out of the new committee—for fiscal year 1867—totaled $357,542,675. In contrast, President George W. Bush's federal budget spending in fiscal year 2005 was about $2.4 trillion. The federal budget has increased dramatically during times of war because the government has had to increase defense spending and social programs. However, the end of the Korean War in 1954 marked the last time the federal budget decreased.

Two types of spending are included in the federal budget. Discretionary spending includes the annual "must-pass" funding for federal agencies, such as the Defense Department, that is provided in the form of appropriations bills. Mandatory spending, which comprises two thirds of the federal budget, arises from permanent laws and includes entitlements such as funding for Social Security and Medicare. Congress and the president can change the laws regarding mandatory spending, but they aren't required to.

Major Budget Laws

Several laws passed during the twentieth century govern the way the federal budget is created. The Budget and Accounting Act of 1921 requires the president to submit his official budget—known as the Budget of the United States Government—to Congress by the first Monday in February.

We Hold These Truths

The president's budget outlines his priorities and recommendations for spending in relation to his legislative priorities. Congress isn't required to stick to the president's budget, although the president's requests are generally taken under strong consideration. Certainly, if the president's party controls the House or Senate, his budget priorities are given stronger consideration and generally are moved forward.

The 1921 law also created the OMB, which helps the president develop his budget and ensures that the various agencies are sticking close to their budget outlines, and the General Accounting Office (GAO), which helps Congress track programs.

The Congressional Budget Act of 1974 requires that the House and Senate agree and approve a concurrent resolution on the budget, which then serves as an outline for Congress in developing the budget. The act also created specific budget committees in the Senate and House, which create the budget outline and enforce its spending limits. It also created the Congressional Budget Office (CBO) to help Congress with the multitude of budget information it needs to compile its outline.

Gramm-Rudman-Hollings Act

The Emergency Deficit Control Act of 1985, also known as the Gramm-Rudman-Hollings Act, was named after the three senators who originally co-sponsored it: Republican Phil Gramm, from Texas; Republican Warren Rudman, from New Hampshire; and Democrat Ernest Hollings, from South Carolina. It was passed to decrease the large deficits that the government was operating under by that time. To do so, a process was developed that would allow for across-the-board cuts if federal spending was more than the targets set in the law. Estimates for the cuts fall under the jurisdiction of the comptroller general, who developed the figures with the help of reports from the OMB and GAO. The comptroller general's recommendation then goes to the president, who issues a *sequestration* if the amounts are higher than the targets.

Inside the Beltway

Sequestration is a writ ordered by the president that cancels budget resources.

Inside the Beltway

PAYGO stands for "pay as you go" and refers to the requirement that any new mandatory spending be deficit-neutral, either through revenue increases or spending cuts elsewhere.

This law was challenged in the 1986 Supreme Court case *Bowsher v. Synar*, named for Comptroller General Charles Bowsher in the Reagan administration and Rep. Michael Synar, a Democrat from Oklahoma who challenged the law's constitutionality. The Supreme Court agreed that a separation of powers issue was in play and said that the comptroller general, whose role falls under the legislative branch, could not act with powers under the executive office. The law was then revised to have the sequestration power fall under the OMB director, who operates under the jurisdiction of the executive branch.

Laws passed in 1990 and 1995 further amended the budget process. The Budget Enforcement Act of 1990 placed limits on discretionary spending and on *PAYGO* requirements.

The Unfunded Mandates Reform Act of 1995 placed limits on mandated programs that could cost state, tribal, or local governments more than $50 million a year unless the federal government paid for it, and it included a detailed report from the CBO on the cost impact of a mandated program.

The Federal Budget Timeline

The federal budget process follows a timeline that contains all sorts of projected deadlines (although Congress rarely, if ever, meets the majority of them). Here's how it breaks down.

The first deadline is the first Monday in February, which is when the president must submit his budget to Congress.

We Hold These Truths

The first Monday in February is actually near the end of the process for the executive branch in terms of all the work it must do to complete its budget. Except in inauguration years, the president's budget outline is worked on for nearly a year prior to its unveiling. (If a new president is being inaugurated, the outgoing president usually submits a budget in January and the new president submits his own later.)

Federal agencies also develop their estimated budgets for the upcoming fiscal year, which runs from October 1 through September 30, anywhere from nine months to a year before the president submits his budget. Rather than working with the president's staff in developing budgets, the agencies work closely with the OMB staff, which keeps tabs on the agencies' work as well as economic forecasts as the budgets are developed.

Creating a Framework

By February 15, after the president's budget has been presented, the CBO gives its economic outlook report to the House and Senate budget committees. Each committee has six weeks from when the president submits his budget to develop its own budget estimates, which may or may not incorporate the president's recommendations.

Next, the House and Senate budget committees hold hearings to create the concurrent budget resolution. Federal agencies send representatives instead of OMB officials to defend their budget estimates during the hearings. However, the OMB director or other high-level OMB official usually testifies at a few budget committee hearings each year. In general, the budget committees let most program-specific budget requests be worked out in the proper appropriations subcommittee, focusing instead on the overall makeup of the budget.

The CBO assists the budget committees with its own estimates and economic reports, which can conflict with the estimates from the OMB's research and predictions. The CBO is also responsible for developing baseline budget projections, or projections of future estimated

We Hold These Truths

The concurrent budget resolution is not a bill; therefore, it is not sent to the president for his approval or veto. The resolution is merely an outline that is referred to as a budget framework.

revenues with an economic forecast if funding for a certain program remains the same. These baseline projections are carefully considered throughout the budget process.

After the House and the Senate pass their individual budget resolutions, it's usually necessary to convene a conference between the two chambers to work out the major differences in the two measures. The leadership of each chamber appoints the conferees, usually budget committee members who have worked extensively on the legislation.

Preparing the Budget on Time

By April 15, the House and the Senate are supposed to have agreed on and passed the concurrent resolution on the budget. The House begins work on the 13 appropriations measures around May 15, even if the concurrent budget resolution has not yet been passed.

About a month later, the House Appropriations Committee should have reported all 13 appropriations bills. By the end of June, the House is scheduled to have completed any work on the 13 appropriations bills as well as any required reconciliation bills, which are used to balance revenue with the figures set by the budget resolution. This rarely happens on this timetable, however.

During the appropriations process, it is the primary responsibility of the House and Senate budget committees to keep lawmakers within budgetary limits. To do this, budget committee members rely on points of order to block procedural actions that would go over the budget. Because the concurrent resolution is only an outline, though, lawmakers can and do exceed budgetary limits.

The president can submit an update to his budget proposal any time during the year, if he wants, and he might alter his projections based on a changed economic climate or other legislative priorities. He is required to submit one update to his budget by July 15. This update is known as the Midsession Review.

Federal agencies deliver their estimated budgets to OMB staff in the fall, with detailed information on nearly every program the money requested is used for.

Appropriations

At the same time that the House and Senate budget committees are doing their work, members of the appropriations committees in each chamber are doing theirs.

After the president submits his budget to Congress, government agencies submit supporting materials that are much more detailed to members of the powerful House and Senate appropriations committees.

The Power of 13

As the following list details, 13 regular appropriations bills must be passed each year to fund government agencies and keep the government running:

Appropriations Subcommittees and Annual Appropriations

◆ Agriculture, Rural Development, Food & Drug Administration, and Related Agencies

◆ Departments of Commerce, Justice, State, and Related Agencies

◆ Department of Defense

◆ District of Columbia

◆ Energy and Water Development

◆ Foreign Operations, Export Financing, and Related Programs

◆ Department of the Interior Related Agencies

◆ Departments of Labor, Health and Human Services, Education, and Related Agencies

◆ Legislative Branch

◆ Military Construction

◆ Department of Transportation

◆ Treasury, Postal Service, and General Government

◆ Departments of Veterans Administration and Housing and Urban Development, and Independent Agencies

> **We Hold These Truths**
>
> The 26 appropriations subcommittee chairmen are referred to as cardinals.

The appropriations committees in each chamber are the largest committees in each body. The House Appropriations Committee currently has 65 members; the Senate Appropriations Committee has 29 members. The 13 subcommittee chairmen of the appropriations committees are some of the most influential members of Congress, and the posts are highly sought after. Frequently, states with members of Congress on the appropriations committee benefit disproportionately from states without members of Congress on those committees in terms of the federal dollars they receive.

Appropriations Timeline

The House Appropriations Committee begins work on the proposals outlined in the president's budget first, divided among 13 subcommittees that coincide with the agencies funded through the 13 must-pass appropriations bills. After the relevant subcommittee completes its work, the entire appropriations committee passes the measure—often with few changes—and the measure goes to the House floor after May 15.

The Senate Appropriations Committee begins work on the appropriations measures around the same time as the House does, but its proposals are held up on final passage until a House appropriations measure has been considered. When the Senate considers a House appropriation on the floor, it is frequently changed by amendments. After an appropriations measure has passed the Senate and the House in some form, a House-Senate conference is convened to iron out the often extensive differences. Both chambers must pass the conference report before it can be sent to the president for his signature or veto.

Although the Constitution doesn't specify a time frame for when appropriations should be made, appropriations have always been done on an annual basis. Spending measures are required to originate in the House, according to the Constitution.

Funds appropriated by Congress are good only for the fiscal year in which they are designated, unless lawmakers provide a special exception in the appropriation.

Three different types of appropriations measures exist:

- Regular appropriations.

- Continuing appropriations acts. These are used (almost on a yearly basis) when Congress does not finish its appropriations work by the start of the next fiscal year, October 1, to keep federal agencies running in the interim.

- Supplemental appropriations acts. These are used when the regular appropriations are used up or for new programs not provided for in the regular appropriations measure.

Pass Me the Pork!

Members of Congress are elected by their districts, and their number-one job is to make their constituents happy. One of the most common ways to do that is to get federal funding for local projects, such as a badly needed bridge or highway reconstruction, that will make the folks back home happy. Neither of those necessarily sounds like a bad thing—but their meaning becomes more negative when they are called "pork-barrel spending." Lawmakers typically refer to them as earmarks.

To ensure their ability to secure pork projects, members often resort to sneaking them into a much larger appropriations bill. The wrangling over a set amount of funds can often come down to which members are facing a tough re-election bid: If they get the pork project, they can remind their constituents during the campaign of their effectiveness in bringing home money from Washington, D.C.

Pork projects add up to billions of dollars a year in the 13 spending bills, and by most estimates, such spending continues to grow. In 2000, Citizens Against Government Waste, a government watchdog group, estimated pork spending at $18.5 billion. By 2003, the figure was up to at least $22 billion, despite a budget deficit and the war on terrorism.

Arizona Sen. John McCain has spent years railing against pork spending and typically compiles a list each year of what he considers the most egregious examples of it. Those against pork spending also frequently disparage the fact that members who sit on the appropriations committees are better able to secure pork dollars. The disproportionate spending also takes away from other needed programs, according to opponents.

But many of McCain's colleagues defend pork and argue that because taxpayers are funding them, they should expect to get the earmarks in return. Many of the projects are truly necessary and fund programs such as increased special education funding for children in a certain district that might not otherwise be able to have such a program.

But some pork projects are often considered less necessary. For example, in 2001, one bill provided $250,000 for seaweed control in Hawaii. In 2003, $1 million was added for the Young Patriots Program, where the money was earmarked to help "expand the Young Patriots Program to include a video which promotes the significance of National Patriotic Holidays." Another 2001 bill provided more than a half-million dollars for agricultural waste in West Virginia.

Because pork projects are stuck inside must-pass appropriations bills, it is very difficult for lawmakers to vote against a bill, especially if it has been the work product of many committees and a House-Senate conference. On many appropriations bills, few lawmakers would ever vote against them for that reason alone.

Agency Implementation

After appropriations have been made, often less attention is focused on how the money dedicated to certain programs is actually spent than on the entire budget process, which is closely monitored by the press and lawmakers. But Congress does keep tabs on the appropriated funds in several ways.

House and Senate committees and subcommittees can use their oversight authority to investigate how federal programs—and the money spent on them—work at any time they want. Included in their oversight power are the abilities to subpoena witnesses and extensively investigate how an agency has used appropriations. Often these oversight hearings are held in the beginning of the appropriations process, when lawmakers are beginning the process of funding for the next fiscal year. Other times, oversight hearings are held in response to a specific problem with a program reported in the media.

Inside the Beltway

Apportionment is the distribution of funds from appropriations bills to agencies.

After Congress has appropriated funds for agencies, the OMB decides how each agency will be able to access those funds through *apportionment*. Often agencies are given access to one quarter of their funds for each quarter of the fiscal year.

Another way that Congress can track the funds it appropriates arises if an agency wants to use money for another purpose, through either a transfer of funds or a reprogramming of funds. A transfer of funds moves them to another account entirely and requires Congress to pass a law approving the transfer. Reprogramming shifts funds only within the same account, so no law is required, although the Appropriations Committee has typically set up rules that agencies must follow if they use reprogramming.

Finally, when Congress passes an appropriation, the entire funding is expected to be used up. But if an agency does not use all of an appropriation, the remaining funds can be impounded—delayed or stopped—under the Budget and Impoundment Control Act of 1974.

The passage of this law was a response to then-President Richard Nixon's attempt to use frequent impoundments to stop domestic programs he opposed. Nixon lost every lawsuit filed against his proposed impoundments, and Congress passed the measure to clarify the president's power of impoundment. The House and Senate then had to approve the impoundment—whether it was a deferral or a rescission—and stated that the president did not have a constitutional power of impoundment. The president cannot impound funds based on policy reasons.

When funds appropriated go unused, the executive and legislative agencies have two options. The president can ask Congress either to delay the use of funds through a deferral or to pass a rescission—or cancellation—of funds by changing the law. Funds can be deferred only through the fiscal year. In both cases, the president sends a proposal to Congress detailing the reasons for his request and the affected programs.

The Least You Need to Know

- No federal agency can spend any money until Congress approves it.

- To provide funds to federal agencies, Congress goes through a long and arduous budgetary process, after which money is appropriated to various agencies.

- Getting pork-barrel projects included in larger appropriations bills is one way for members of Congress to curry favor with their constituencies.

- If an agency doesn't use all its appropriated money during its budget year, it can lose the remaining funds.

Chapter 19

Campaigns and Money

In This Chapter

- ◆ How campaigns are financed
- ◆ Rules governing campaign financing
- ◆ Contributions other than money
- ◆ "PAC"ing it in

Before candidates decide to run for election, one of the first things they have to decide is whether they have enough money—or can raise enough money—to compete with their potential opponents. Doing so is becoming increasingly difficult as the cost of campaigns at all levels continues to sky-rocket.

Before anyone decides to give money to a potential candidate, or even before a candidate decides to make a run for political office, it is necessary to understand the rules of the process. In this chapter, we discuss the many rules and regulations surrounding political money, what nonmonetary items count as contributions, and what the average citizen can do to support candidates.

War and Chests

The way the current political system runs, it is increasingly necessary for candidates to be well financed. A campaign for Senate typically costs millions. On the highest level, the cost of running a winning presidential race costs in the hundreds of millions of dollars. The total amount of money spent in the presidential and congressional races in the 2004 cycle was near the staggering $4 billion mark.

One of the first tasks on a potential candidate's agenda is to find someone to keep track of the war chest—or treasury. The treasurer solicits and keeps track of all contributions that a candidate receives and where that money is spent. The treasurer is responsible for making sure that the contributions are legal as well.

> ### We Hold These Truths
>
> Sen. Jon Corzine, a Democrat from New Jersey, broke a record when he spent some $60 million (including much of his own money) to win a Senate seat in 2000.

Following the Rules

Running for a political office costs money—usually a lot of it. But the rules and regulations surrounding campaigns and elections in the United States are highly complex. The Federal Election Commission (FEC) is the agency responsible for the bulk of the rules and regulations—and everything has a deadline. Aside from the FEC rules, candidates must also follow local and state laws and Internal Revenue Service (IRS) laws.

> ### Inside the Beltway
>
> **Political action committees,** or **PACs,** are organizations designed to raise and spend money for candidates or party committees they support.

One of the easiest ways for the average citizen to get involved in the election process is to donate money. But federal campaign finance laws limit the amount of money that can be given from one individual, corporation, or *political action committee (PAC)* to a candidate. Organizations known as *527's* (for the part of the tax code they fall under) are similar to PACs. The key difference is that 527's are not regulated by the FEC and therefore do not fall under the same limits. 527 organizations are required to report to the IRS on their funding and spending.

> ### Inside the Beltway
>
> **527's** are organizations that engage in political activity, often through the use of soft money for issue advocacy efforts that back or refute a candidate. They are named for the part of the tax code they fall under.

Certain sources are prohibited from giving money at all. When discussing federal candidates, we are referring to candidates for president, vice president, or Congress.

Complicated Contributions Rules

Individuals can give $2,000 to each federal candidate per election and $5,000 to each PAC or state or local party per election. For example, if an individual gives money to a candidate who is running for Congress but who first must win a primary, the individual can give $2,000 to the primary campaign and another $2,000 for the general election if the candidate wins the primary.

For the most part, individuals do not have to file detailed reports with the FEC. But the recipient of the money—if it's over $200—does have to report certain information about contributors. Basic information, such as the contributor's name and address and the amount and date of the contribution, must be reported.

Let's say that you want to donate funds to someone who might become a candidate but who hasn't decided whether to run for office. If that person does decide to run, your money would be counted as a contribution. Therefore, the same limits are placed on donations made to someone who may become a candidate.

Federal party organizations have the highest limit of funds that can be received from individuals: $25,000 per year. However, an individual could give a $25,000 donation to a federal party organization one year and $25,000 to a Senate party organization in the same year.

> **We Hold These Truths**
>
> PACs are required to return cash donations of more than $100 from an individual. But what happens if someone sends an anonymous contribution that exceeds the limit? Since they can't return the money, any amount over the $50 limit can be used for other purposes, as long as they are not used in relation to a federal election.

Rules also govern how the money is transmitted to the candidate, PAC, or party. An individual who wants to donate money anonymously can do so only up to $50. Any contribution that is more than $100 must be in writing—by check or money order, or with "written consent." For every two-year cycle, an individual is limited to spending $95,000 in total.

Critical Deadlines

The biennial limit of $95,000 spans the two-year period from January 1 of an odd-numbered year to December 31 of the following even-numbered year. For example, donations to federal candidates and a national party could not exceed the limit from January 1, 2003 through December 31, 2004.

We Hold These Truths

Sometimes individuals contribute money to help candidates after the election. Whether they win or lose, candidates often have a tremendous debt from their campaigns. If a campaign is already over and a contributor wants to help with their candidate's debt, the individual must designate the past election on the contribution, under FEC rules.

To help keep the contribution deadline process clear, the FEC encourages contributors to indicate on the check, money order, or other donation which election their money for the candidate is intended for. Likewise, if two or more individuals want to make a contribution from a joint account, they must all sign the check or money order, or attach a written consent to their contribution.

Who Can't Give?

Two categories of people cannot give individual contributions to federal candidates under FEC rules: foreign nationals and individuals working under a federal government contract. The rule does not apply to foreign nationals who already have a green card. Foreign nationals cannot give money to support any local or state campaigns, either.

In the case of federal contracts, if an individual is the sole owner of a business with the federal contract or is consulting with a federal agency, that person is prohibited from making contributions. But someone who works for a company that has a federal government contract can make a contribution, as long as the money comes from his or her personal funds.

The FEC also prohibits funds from corporate accounts and labor unions from an individual. For example, a small business owner cannot make a contribution from a business account to a federal account but can do so from a personal account. An individual who works for a corporation can make a contribution from a personal corporate account that is nonrepayable, such as one in which the person takes money against his or her salary.

Contributions can never be made to federal candidates in someone else's name, according to FEC rules. A parent cannot make a contribution in a child's name.

A person cannot loan funds to someone to give to a specific candidate. Corporations cannot use bonuses or other similar methods to entice their employees to contribute to a certain candidate.

In-Kind Contributions

Perhaps surprisingly, money is not the only way to contribute to a federal candidate. Anything that is considered to have value is also a contribution, according to the FEC. These types of contributions are called in-kind contributions and might include services or materials provided to a federal campaign. For example, donating the space for a candidate to speak instead of charging a fee is an in-kind contribution. So is the free printing of brochures, ads, and other campaign-related materials or the donation of furniture to a campaign headquarters. Even giving a discount on the normal cost of a service is considered an in-kind contribution.

Every time an individual purchases a ticket to a fundraiser for a candidate or party, the face value of the ticket counts as a donation against that person's yearly limit. The same goes for the purchase of a candidate's bumper sticker, T-shirt, or other fundraising paraphernalia.

> **We Hold These Truths**
>
> Loans made to candidates or committees from an individual also count as contributions.

Volunteering for Campaigns

Like many of the FEC rules, there are exceptions. Volunteering on a campaign is not considered an in-kind contribution—even though someone might donate time or a car to drive the candidate—because volunteers are not paid for their work. Any travel that an individual volunteer makes on behalf of the candidate and pays for personally must be $1,000 or less per election for a candidate, or $2,000 or less per year for a national party. If the individual is reimbursed from some other source, the source's payment is considered a contribution in the yearly limit.

If an individual makes a church or community room available to the candidate for a speech or reception, that is not considered an in-kind contribution if the space is regularly offered for use without charge. Individuals may also use their homes to host receptions, which falls under volunteering. Any refreshments or other expenses at a home event for a federal candidate are not considered contributions, as long as they fall under certain limits. For a federal candidate, a husband and wife can spend up to

$2,000 per election; for a party committee, they can spend up to $4,000 per year. But if they co-host a party with a nonresident of the home, that individual's money spent is considered a contribution.

A corporation or a labor union's facilities can be used by an employee for a federal candidate (if the employer allows it in its own rules) as long as it does not interfere with the employee's work or the company's regular schedule. But if the usage of the facility is more than one hour a week or four hours a month, the employee must reimburse the corporation or labor union. Likewise, any equipment used by the employee to aid the federal candidate must be paid to the corporation or labor union and counts as a contribution in the individual's yearly limits.

Just as foreign nationals are prohibited from giving money to political races, foreign corporations are forbidden from giving money to any U.S. political races. However, there are ways around this through the use of soft money, which you'll read about in Chapter 20.

If a food or beverage vendor wants to help a federal candidate, the vendor can provide products to a campaign or candidate at cost, as long as the discount does not exceed $1,000 per candidate per election or $2,000 per party committee per year. The vendor could provide $2,000 in products to both the Republican and Democratic parties, for example, for a total of $4,000 in one year.

A business can help a federal party committee without making a contribution, too. If a business wants to donate legal services to a committee on employees' time, it can do so as long as the reason is to help the committee follow the complicated federal elections laws, the business does not hire additional outside people to do the work, the work does not directly help one federal candidate, and the business reports to the FEC what the services would have cost.

Inside the Beltway

Independent expenditures are funds from an outside group donated independently of a campaign to support a candidate.

Finally, *independent expenditures* can be used by individuals to help the federal candidate they want to see elected. They are not considered contributions, either, and are one reason many people support campaign finance reform. An independent expenditure is frequently an advertisement supporting the candidate or criticizing the candidate's opponent. Individuals cannot coordinate in any way with their favored candidate when making an independent expenditure, and must indicate that the campaign did not coordinate the effort and that the individual paid for the ad. If the independent expenditure costs more than $250, the individual must file a special report with the FEC detailing what the money was spent on.

If a group of individuals decides to raise money for a federal candidate or party, those people may become a political committee. If they raise or spend more than $1,000 a year on their activities, they must register with the FEC and file reports on their group's activities.

Campaign Committees, PACs, and 527's

Just as individual contributions to political candidates have increased exponentially, the same has happened with spending from campaign committees, PACs, and 527's.

Some PACs' viewpoints are easily distinguishable, such as the Planned Parenthood PAC and the National Rifle Association Victory Fund. But others, like EMILY's List, have more ambiguous names. EMILY's List supports pro-choice Democratic women candidates for political office, and it gave more money than any other PAC in the 2000 election cycle: $430,100. The best way to find out a PAC's position is to find out whom it contributes money to.

Ten days after a group is designated as a PAC, it must file a Statement of Organization with the FEC—which is the first of many required forms tracking the money. Just as individuals are limited in whom they can give funds to, campaign committees, national party committees, and PACs are all limited in the amount of funds they can contribute to candidates.

A party committee, such as the National Republican Congressional Committee, can give $1,000 per candidate per election, $5,000 to another political committee, and $20,000 to another national party committee, such as the Republican National Committee.

> **We Hold These Truths**
>
> In the 2004 election cycle, PACs raised a whopping $629.3 million by the end of June—a figure that the FEC estimates increased by 24 percent over the 2002 campaign. Meanwhile, 527's raised $115 million in soft money during the 2002 election cycle. In the 2004 election cycle, 527's spent at least $386 million in federal races.

A PAC can give $1,000 per candidate per election, $20,000 to a national party committee, and $5,000 to any other political committee. A multicandidate PAC—one that has more than 50 contributors—can give $5,000 per candidate per election, $15,000 to a national party committee, and $5,000 to another political committee.

The treasurer of each PAC, campaign committee, or candidate campaign committee must file regular reports, either with the FEC or, if the candidate is running for the House or Senate, with the Clerk of the House and the Secretary of the Senate. The reports include the total cash on hand for the candidate, receipts, loans, and other financial information. Any contributions over $200 should include detailed information about the contributor.

If a treasurer believes that a contribution is illegal, he or she must either return or deposit the contribution within 10 days. If the contribution is deposited, the treasurer must detail why he or she thinks it is illegal, must have enough in the campaign fund in case a refund becomes necessary, and must report that the contribution may be illegal when filing his or her report. Likewise, if the treasurer receives a contribution that he or she believes exceeds the contributor's limit, the treasurer must check on it. If the limit is exceeded, the treasurer must either ask the contributor to redesignate the check for another election or refund the money.

PACs, candidates, and congressional committees must also follow laws of the Federal Communications Commission (FCC) when advertising on television or the radio. The FCC rules are more lax than those of the FEC; in fact, disclosures about the candidate or organization paying for the ads are given to the station on which the ads are run rather than to the FCC.

The IRS regulates another type of group that is not subject to the same campaign finance laws as PACs or campaign committees. These groups are referred to by their tax code numbers and are called 527's or 501(c)(3) and (4)'s. In English, they are non-profit issue advocacy organizations that engage in political activities. The groups, which are one of campaign finance reformers' top criticisms, are required to make public through the IRS their annual tax returns and tax status. You'll read more on this in Chapter 20.

Presidential Coffers

The presidential war chests are the largest of any political campaign coffers. How they are filled and how presidential campaigns are financed are as highly regulated as every other political campaign.

One area that differs in these war chests is public funding, which has been available to presidential candidates since the 1974 election. Public funding of presidential elections was a reaction to the Watergate scandal that resulted in President Nixon's resignation. Many of the illegal activities exposed were financed by funds for which there was no paper trail. The first year public funds were available, qualified candidates received $21 million in the general election. That amount rose to about $74 million for qualified candidates in the 2004 election.

If a primary candidate for president raises $5,000 from individuals in denominations of $250 or less in 20 or more states, those donations can be matched with federal money. The federal matching funds must be less than half of the primary spending limit. In the general election, a nominee from the Democratic or Republican parties is eligible for a $20 million grant, which is adjusted for the cost of living, if they agree to spend under the limit and do not accept private donations. If a presidential candidate decides to accept public funding, the candidate can contribute up to $50,000 to his or her own campaign.

> **We Hold These Truths**
>
> Checking the Yes or No box on your tax form for the $3 does not increase or decrease your federal taxes!

Where does the money to finance presidential candidates come from? A question on your federal income tax form helps answer the question. Everyone who fills out the form is asked if they would like to give $3 of their federal tax to the Presidential Election Campaign Fund. More than 30 million people check the Yes box every year—all of that money goes to presidential campaign financing and the two major parties.

The money is divided every four years and is given to the candidates who qualify. If money is left in the fund, it remains there until the next presidential election. The nominees for the general election from the two established parties, the Republican and Democratic parties, automatically receive the funds. Other nominees from other parties may qualify if they received 5 percent of the vote in the previous presidential election. (The amount an outside nominee will get is based on a ratio comparing his or her party's popular vote to the two major parties in the previous election.)

Funds are also provided to the Republican and Democratic parties to hold their national convention, where their nominee is chosen. Presidential primary candidates can receive matching funds—which come out of the Presidential Election Campaign Fund—if they reach the standards detailed previously.

Many candidates use the public financing only in the general election. For example, candidates who use the public funding for the general election are barred from raising money from PACs or individuals. (Individuals and PACs are not barred from independent expenditures on behalf of their candidate, though.) They must also agree to a spending limit. Because of the rules, a candidate can choose not to use the public funds.

After the election, the FEC checks on the use of the public funds. Any unused money from the campaign must be returned to the U.S. Treasury and goes into the next Presidential Election Campaign Fund.

Tracking the Money

You can find out and keep track of the massive amounts of money that flow into political campaigns in numerous ways. The most reliable way is to contact the office that regulates the local, state, or federal campaign and find out how information is released to the public. For example, the FEC provides its reports in several forms: Records can be requested and mailed to a person, and the FEC also maintains a website at www.fec.gov that provides specific filing information about federal candidates and PACs.

Many think tanks and organizations, particularly those pushing for stronger campaign finance laws, also provide large databases of information on campaign contributions in report form or on the Internet. Some groups, such as Common Cause, are non-profit nonpartisan organizations that track money in government.

If an individual believes that a candidate or committee has broken a campaign finance law, he or she can file a complaint with the FEC. A notarized letter should explain the alleged violation as well as whether the individual has inside information about the potential violation or whether it is based on public knowledge. All the complaints received by the FEC are called Matters Under Review, or MURs. A candidate or committee accused of potential violations receives a copy of the alleged violation and has the opportunity to respond to the FEC, which may or may not conduct an investigation. Until the FEC makes a decision on the MUR, the entire process is kept confidential. The information becomes public after a decision has been made and both parties have been notified.

The Least You Need to Know

◆ Candidates raising money for their campaigns are governed by the rules and regulations of the Federal Election Commission (FEC), as well as local and state laws and Internal Revenue Service laws.

◆ Individuals who want to contribute to federal political campaigns can give $95,000 every two years.

◆ Presidential candidates who raise $5,000 from individuals in 20 states in denominations of $250 or less can receive federal matching funds in the primary, and a $20 million grant is available for the general election to the two major parties' candidates, if they agree to a limit and do not accept private donations.

◆ Individuals can keep track of political spending by reviewing financial reports at the local and state level, or for federal candidates, with the FEC.

20

Campaign Finance Reform

In This Chapter

◆ The difference between hard and soft money

◆ Early attempts at finance reform

◆ Impact of scandals on campaign financing

◆ Where reform is now

You've probably heard lots about campaign finance reform in the last few years. Even with recent overhauls on campaign financing, including the Bipartisan Campaign Reform Act (BCRA) of 2002, many campaign finance reform advocates say there is more to be done. But there are still many people who don't realize that the notion of reforming the political financial system has been around nearly as long as campaigns have had to raise money.

In this chapter, you learn about the types of money that influence campaigns, the history of campaign finance reform, and how the latest laws on campaign financing affect how money is raised.

Soft and Hard Money

The high cost of political campaigns has had a huge influence on American politics, and there is a long history of calls for reform in the funding of elections. Much of the debate over campaigns comes from the definitions of two types of contributions: *hard money* and *soft money*. Most of the funds described in Chapter 19 were so-called hard money. That type of money includes funds that go directly to support the election of a specific candidate, whether it is through an individual, a campaign committee, or a PAC contribution.

Inside the Beltway

Hard money is money raised and spent by individuals, PACs, or party committees for specific political candidates; it is subject to strict regulations by the FEC, the IRS, and other entities. **Soft money** is money raised and spent by organizations that are not coordinated directly with a candidate, such as 527's. BCRA banned federal candidates or party committees from using soft money.

On the other hand, soft money in campaigns is much more controversial. Soft-money funds are used in a more ambiguous manner and are not subject to most campaign finance laws. PACs and 527's might use soft money for a "nonpartisan" purpose—except that the underlying purpose truly is partisan and could directly help one candidate.

Soft money is used in this way most frequently in issue-oriented ads. An issue-oriented ad typically supports a candidate without an explicit endorsement. For example, an education group organization might run an ad against legislation that funds school vouchers and note that Candidate X voted against the measure. Without directly stating "Vote for Candidate X," the ad could have just that effect on a voter who opposes school vouchers.

Before the passage of BCRA, a major reason for the uproar against soft money stemmed from the more lenient rules and regulations surrounding disclosure of soft money. That problem has proliferated through 527's, which do not fall under the FEC, but do have to file disclosure information with the IRS.

What's the Beef?

As long as money and politics are so deeply entwined, there will probably be a politician who finds a way around the rules. Nearly every time a major financial scandal has received public attention, there has been some reform of the role of money in politics. Today there are continuing calls for an even greater upheaval in the way the system is run. But understanding how money and politics became so entangled is critical to comprehend the current efforts for campaign finance reform.

The Federal Election Campaign Act of 1971 (FECA) and ensuing amendments to the law are considered the grandfather of campaign finance laws and are the ones the political money machine operates under today. But that law was by no means the first attempt at campaign finance reform. Nearly every political campaign has involved some money, but the amounts were fairly insignificant until the mid-nineteenth century. By the time Abraham Lincoln ran for president in 1860, he doubled the amount his opponent raised, with $100,000. Calls for reform, however, had already been made by Lincoln's time because of the spoils system. In place for years, party officials regularly required donations from government officials who had been beneficiaries of the spoils system in the 1830s.

In response to the long-running spoils system, Congress passed a relatively insignificant law in 1867 that made it illegal for a government employee at a Navy yard to be required to pay contributions to party officials. In addition, a government employee at a Navy yard could not be removed from his post because of political opinions. Regardless of its insignificance, the law is considered the first campaign finance reform enacted in America.

The law did little to quell the rise of political money or the manner in which parties raised their funds. But a major scandal in Congress that resulted in an increasingly cynical view of politicians and the censure of two members prompted another look at reforming the system. Throughout the mid-nineteenth century, many railroad companies competed for funding and land grants from Congress to build railroads. How they gained influence was revealed through the Credit Mobilier scandal. Rep. Oakes Ames, a Republican from Massachusetts, was a lobbyist for the railroad company who sought favors from members of Congress and gave company stock to his colleagues in exchange for support of the company.

After the furor over that scandal subsided, another reform, known as the Pendleton Civil Service Act, was enacted in 1883. An attempt to limit the spoils system, the measure required some federal government workers to take a test to qualify for certain high-level jobs. Those who qualified could not be solicited for political contributions, causing the national parties to shift their fundraising from government workers to other areas. From the passage of the Pendleton Act on, major industries became huge benefactors to political parties.

As the financial stakes rose, so did the persistent calls for further reform. The arguments used then regarding political money are remarkably similar to those used today by politicians advocating campaign finance reform. Reformers charged that the big donors were reaping favors and influence—in effect "buying" their way into the running of the government.

> ### We Hold These Truths
>
> At the turn of the century, railroads and steel were some of the top political donors, drastically changing the amount of money in campaigns in a relatively short period. By the time William McKinley ran for president in 1896, he raised approximately $3 million—quite a leap from Lincoln's $100,000 almost 40 years earlier.

Congress did nothing at first to appease the reformers. But President Theodore Roosevelt's challenger in 1904, Alton Parker, was direct in his criticism of Roosevelt and his fundraising. Parker accused Roosevelt of all kinds of abuses, including blackmailing potential donors. Incredibly, after winning the election, Roosevelt listed campaign finance reform as a priority in three consecutive State of the Union addresses, 1905–1907. In the first, Roosevelt advocated a law that would end "bribery and corruption in Federal elections."

Each year his proposal grew. In 1906, Roosevelt asked Congress to enact a ban on contributions from corporations. Roosevelt's message on campaign finance reform in 1907 even included a recommendation that the government provide some type of public financing because the cost of campaigns was running so high.

After the third try in 1907, Congress acted that year and passed a measure sponsored by Sen. Benjamin Tillman, a Democrat from South Carolina. The Tillman Act made it illegal for corporations to give money directly to federal election candidates.

Another provision, called the Federal Corrupt Practices Act, was passed in 1910 and required U.S. House candidates to disclose some financial information and placed limits on total spending from national party committees. But the law had loopholes: Parties didn't have to report their contributions before elections, and candidates themselves didn't have to report anything.

After the 1910 election, control of the House shifted from Republicans to Democrats, who raised the Federal Corrupt Practices Act again in an attempt to require filings of contributions before elections. The amendments to the law, passed by both chambers, now required House and Senate candidates to file reports before and after elections and placed limits on campaign spending.

A precursor of what was to follow, the law limiting contributions was challenged in the 1921 Supreme Court case *United States v. Newberry*. In a strict constitutional ruling, the court said that because parties and primaries were not covered in the Constitution, Congress could not regulate them. The decision weakened the campaign finance rules, in effect saying that the spending limitations were illegal. Yet another financial scandal followed close on the heels of the court decision, prompting Congress to enact more campaign finance rules.

Teapot Dome

During the Calvin Coolidge administration in the 1920s, the public was made aware of a scandal that had taken place during the previous administration of Warren G. Harding, who died in office in 1923. Dubbed "Teapot Dome," the scandal was made public after a Senate investigation revealed that Republican officials had secretly leased oil reserve lands owned by the Navy to private companies. (The reserves were supposed to be kept intact for use by the Navy in an emergency.) Secretary of the Interior Albert Fall, a former senator, was even charged with bribery, fined $100,000, and sentenced to a year in prison. Other officials involved in the scandal received lesser penalties, and some resigned from office.

After most of the information about the Teapot Dome scandal came out in 1924, Congress passed the Federal Corrupt Practices Act the following year. The measure was similar to previous laws on the books. It expanded disclosure requirements in an effort to stem events such as the Teapot Dome scandal. Now reports had to be filed quarterly by political parties active in more than one state, even in years in which there was not an election. The law also limited Senate and House campaigns to spend specific amounts on their campaigns: $25,000 and $5,000, respectively. But little changed in the fundraising aspect of campaigns because the filed reports were vague in the law, and there was no enforcement system to deal with penalties.

Political spending increased dramatically during the New Deal and World War II eras as the federal government grew. Many workers hired by the federal government during President Franklin Roosevelt's reforms did not fall under the Pendleton Act, which prevented workers from being solicited for political money. The Clean Politics Act was passed in 1939, covering all other federal workers not covered under the Pendleton Act.

As a result, the amount of political money donated by labor unions grew. In 1943, Roosevelt's opponents in Congress passed the War Labor Disputes Act of 1943, which prohibited funds from labor unions directly to federal candidates. (The act was supposed to retire six months after the war but was made permanent.)

Meanwhile, labor unions found their own loophole in the law and created the first PAC in 1943: the Congress of Industrial Organizations Political Action Committee. As other organizations caught on, the number of PACs and the money they spent grew, but not as rapidly as they would after the major campaign finance laws passed in the 1970s.

Another major change in political fundraising in the mid-twentieth century arose due to the changing way candidates had to run their races with the advanced media available to them to "get out the message." Going directly to the voter was not always a viable operation, and television and radio ads cost a lot of money. But those candidates who learned to use the new media to their advantage first were often highly successful.

FECA: Reform for Real

The 1971 FECA law tried to solve the growing problem of financing campaigns in the savvy new media age. The law established limits for candidates' contributions to their own campaigns and the amount they could spend on media, including radio, television, telephone banks, and print advertising. Rules on disclosure from both candidates and committees were increased and refined. Now candidates had to file more information on contributors donating $100 quarterly, as well as additional reports just before and after an election.

But the law's reforms did not appear adequate after the Watergate scandal. The public uproar over the break-in at the Democratic Party national headquarters and the subsequent cover-up by President Richard Nixon during the 1972 presidential campaign unveiled numerous campaign contribution violations in the resulting congressional hearings. Remember the spoils system? Some officials charged that the practice was back in full force in the Nixon scandal and that government positions had been the gift to major contributors.

In 1974, Congress amended the 1971 FECA law. The approved legislation was more stringent than any campaign finance reform ever enacted. With the legislation, Congress established the Federal Election Commission (FEC) to enforce the campaign finance rules for the first time. Now candidates would be held accountable for their fundraising practices. The law also devised the presidential public financing system that you read about in Chapter 19. New contribution limits were established, limiting individuals to $1,000 per election per candidate. PACs were limited to $5,000 per election per candidate.

> **We Hold These Truths**
>
> Who is in charge of the FEC? The independent panel has six members, who are appointed by the president and confirmed by the Senate. Terms for the members are six years, with two slots being open every two years. No more than three members can be from the same political party, and the chairman switches every year between members.

Constitutional Questions Arise

Many people involved in the political process questioned the constitutionality of some of the reforms put in place in 1974. Sen. James Buckley, a Republican from New York, and presidential candidate and former Sen. Eugene McCarthy, a Democrat from Minnesota, were two of the leaders who charged that the law was unconstitutional on the grounds of violating a person's First Amendment rights. After they lost their case in district court and the U.S. Court of Appeals, they filed with the Supreme Court, which decided the case in January 1976.

The landmark Supreme Court case *Buckley v. Valeo* set the standard on campaign finance reform. In the decision, the court ruled that contributions are considered a form of free speech. In its decision, the court said, "This is because virtually every means of communicating ideas in today's mass society requires the expenditure of money." That is, most limits on contributions to candidates would violate an individual's constitutional right to free speech. The provision limiting the amount a candidate could spend on his or her own campaign was completely shot down by the court, unless a candidate took part in the public funding program.

But the court did set some limits for the amount an individual can spend, in order to avoid the impression of money in politics equaling corruption. The $1,000 limit to federal candidates from the 1971 law was upheld. The court also upheld the provisions of the 1971 law requiring disclosure of campaign financing.

The court's decision was handed down before the 1976 election, forcing Congress to again revise the law if it wanted the campaign finance reforms to apply to the election. The amendments passed in 1976 included revisions in the amounts that a candidate could contribute to his or her own campaign if public funds were accepted, restructured the way FEC commissioners were appointed (to the current system), and restructured disclosure requirements.

In the late 1970s, another scandal involving congressional financing came to light. Referred to as Koreagate, the scandal involved more than 20 members of the House and the Senate. The Korean government, through businessman Tong Sun Park, was connected to several lawmakers by giving them money in exchange for political favors. The scandal, although useful in pointing out the potential corruption in government with high contributions to lawmakers, had relatively little effect in changing the process itself.

Following Koreagate, minor changes were made to the FECA law, partially to fix some loopholes that had arisen during the law's implementation, including a provision that prohibited candidates from converting campaign funds that they did not use into personal funds.

Even with the reforms enacted in the 1970s as a result of political financial scandals, the influence of spending from special interest groups and PACs has continued to grow at an incredible rate. The following table lists the top fundraising PACs in the 2002 election cycle:

Top Fundraising PACs in the 2002 Election Cycle*

No.	PAC	Funds Raised
1.	National Association of Realtors	$3.6 million
2.	Laborers Union	$2.8 million
3.	Association of Trial Lawyers of America	$2.8 million
4.	National Auto Dealers Association	$2.6 million
5.	American Medical Association	$2.5 million
6.	American Federation of State-County-Municipal Employees	$2.4 million
7.	Teamsters Union	$2.4 million
8.	United Auto Workers	$2.3 million
9.	International Brotherhood of Electrical Workers	$2.3 million
10.	Carpenters & Joiners Union	$2.2 million

Center for Responsive Politics

The following table lists the top 10 527 organizations raising soft money in the 2004 election cycle:

Top 10 527 Organizations in the 2004 Election Cycle*

No.	Organization	Funds Raised
1.	Joint Victory Campaign 2004	$42 million
2.	Media Fund	$28 million
3.	America Coming Together	$27 million
4.	Service Employees International Union	$16.7 million
5.	American Federation of State-County-Municipal Employees	$13.7 million
6.	MoveOn.org	$9 million
7.	New Democrat Network	$7.2 million
8.	Club for Growth	$5.5 million
9.	EMILY's List	$4.2 million
10.	AFL-CIO	$4.1 million

Center for Responsive Politics, according to data from the IRS as of September 12, 2004.

Close to $500 million was spent by the parties in soft money in the 2000 election cycle. According to the Center for Responsive Politics (CRP), a campaign watchdog group, there were only 608 PACs in 1974; that number rose to 4,000 by 1984. Although the CRP says that the number of PACs has decreased slightly, the amount they spend has not.

Two major scandals in the early 1990s contributed to the increasing public attention on the need for closer accountability of money in politics. One financial scandal that exploded in 1991—referred to as the Keating Five—involved five senators who were accused of intervening with federal bank regulations on behalf of a banker named Charles Keating. All five had received large campaign contributions from Keating, but an investigation by a Senate committee resulted in criticism of their judgment and a reprimand for one senator. Ironically, Sen. John McCain, a Republican from Arizona, currently one of the top proponents of campaign finance reform, was a member of the Keating Five.

A year later, public and media attention was focused on a scandal in the House bank that involved more than 300 members of Congress! Until that time, members were allowed to write checks out of a personal account operated by the House. But an investigation found that more than 300 members had bounced those checks and did not have to face any penalties for their actions. The bank was closed, and many members involved in the scandal retired or were defeated that year.

Bipartisan Campaign Reform Act of 2002

The continuing rise of spending in campaigns has renewed campaign finance reform efforts, especially the rise in the less accountable soft-money spending. One campaign finance reform law passed in 2000 did close a loophole allowed for 527 organizations, making it a requirement that such groups now must make financial disclosures if they bring in more than $25,000 a year. The law was passed after a 527 group took out more than $2 million in campaign ads against John McCain in his 2000 Republican presidential primary bid against George W. Bush. Known as the Republicans for Clean Air, the group was financed by businessman Sam Wyly, a strong Bush supporter.

A significant campaign finance bill—sponsored by Sen. McCain and Sen. Russ Feingold, a Democrat from Wisconsin—was signed into law by President Bush in 2002. Its counterpart measure in the House—sponsored by Rep. Christopher Shays, a Republican from Connecticut, and Rep. Marty Meehan, a Democrat from Massachusetts—faced fierce opposition from top House Republicans, but passed in 2002 after the Enron scandal. The McCain-Feingold and Shays-Meehan bills eliminated most soft-money political fundraising and since its passage has resulted in a major shift in political fundraising. In addition, the bill raised limits on contributions and strengthened disclosure requirements of political advertising.

In an effort to bypass the House GOP leadership's unwillingness to schedule a floor vote, supporters of campaign finance reform worked to force a rare discharge petition on the measure. With 218 signatures, the House leadership was forced to bring the issue to the floor for a vote. Calls for campaign finance reform increased following the investigation into the demise of the nation's seventh largest company, Enron Corp., which also gave significant contributions of political money to both Democrats and Republicans.

The U.S. Supreme Court upheld major portions of BCRA in December 2003. After *Buckley v. Valeo*, another Supreme Court decision, *Colorado Republican Party v. Federal Election Commission*, in 1996 upheld the constitutionality of the use of soft money.

The Least You Need to Know

◆ Hard money is money that directly supports the election of a specific candidate.

◆ Soft money also helps support the election of a specific candidate, but in a more indirect manner. Soft money is money raised and spent by organizations that are not coordinated directly with a candidate, such as 527's.

◆ Soft-money spending in political campaigns has increased significantly in recent elections.

◆ The most comprehensive campaign finance reform signed into law in decades—the Bipartisan Campaign Reform Act of 2002—banned federal candidates or party committees from using soft money.

Chapter 21

Fundraising

In This Chapter

◆ Pitching for dollars

◆ Heavy hitters in the fundraising arena

◆ Fundraising on the web

◆ The Hollywood connection

Fundraising is repeatedly cited as the key to winning a political campaign. But how is it done? What mistakes do candidates frequently make? What separates candidates who can outpace their opponents in the race for dollars? The challenge is even more difficult for a first-time candidate and for anyone who challenges an incumbent.

In this chapter, we describe how successful candidates raise funds, who donates the most money to political campaigns, and what effect major industries such as businesses and labor unions have on the political process.

Fundraising Strategies

Getting a head start on the money game is critical in any political campaign. But there are several strategies that anyone can learn about fundraising. First, candidates need to decide who their audience is and what their message is. The targeted audience for political fundraising should be a core group who is motivated to give money to a campaign based on their message. Identifying that group and creating a database of potential givers is necessary.

Major parties have lists of people who have given funds in the past, and it's a good idea for candidates to acquire as many of those lists as possible to include in their databases. Another way candidates acquire lists of potential donors is to ask area organizations with a similar political belief. For example, Republican candidates might ask the local Chamber of Commerce for donor lists. Democrats might ask the local Sierra Club for similar lists.

Next, candidates must decide how they will reach their audience and ask for money. Direct fundraising letters mailed to potential donors is a frequent starting point. Typically, the most successful fundraising letters are those that are personal (as much as a mass mailing can be) and those that are brief. Envelopes containing the solicitation should look as distinguishable from junk mail as possible—using real stamps or addressed in handwriting.

Asking for a specific amount and a date by which the money is "needed" is also a good idea. Sometimes potential candidates need to raise a certain amount of money by a filing deadline with the FEC to prove that they are viable candidates. In other cases, they might request the money to help pay for a specific event or campaign need. In direct mail solicitations, candidates should include an envelope that has the information required by the FEC for reports on contributions from donors, including name, address, phone number, and employer.

> ### We Hold These Truths
>
> George W. Bush got an easy head start when he began fundraising for a potential presidential run when he was still governor of Texas. Bush's parents, former President George Bush and Barbara Bush, had a large donor base that their son tapped into, including a Christmas list with 35,000 people, according to numerous media reports.

> ### We Hold These Truths
>
> Instead of simply calling the event "Fundraiser for Candidate X," campaigns often tie the event into another holiday or theme, such as "Help Candidate X celebrate his or her forty-first birthday." In 2001, Maryland Lt. Gov. Kathleen Kennedy Townsend, a Democrat, held a grand total of four 50th birthday fundraisers—and her run for governor in 2002 wasn't even official yet!

A general fundraising appeal might also be sent early in the campaign to every voter in the candidate's party who voted in the last election. Those lists are usually available from county clerks or the person responsible for maintaining the lists of registered voters. That appeal is also the time campaigns solicit for campaign volunteers.

Following direct mail solicitations are fundraising events for candidates. A common way candidates begin fundraising is to hold a function in the home of a well-known person in the community who is supporting the campaign.

Invitations to the fundraiser often are sent to potential donors along with a return envelope for people to send money to the campaign, even if they cannot attend the event. Included on the invitation is information on the hosts, the time, the place, and the cost (or range of costs) for attendees. To save money, candidates often create a host committee for fundraisers. Each of the hosts contributes something to the event, such as food or decorating assistance. Members of the host committee also are included on the fundraiser invitation. Follow-up fundraising letters then go out to the same list of people about a month after the event—many people who intended to donate may have simply forgotten.

Other important fundraising strategies include the following:

♦ Making contacts with PACs early in the campaign. If the candidate is an unknown, the selling job to potential donors is all the more difficult. But there are several ways to get PACs to support even unknown candidates. Demonstrating the capacity to run an organized campaign is crucial. Candidates often provide PACs that they believe might support them with a detailed campaign plan that includes explaining how they plan to win.

♦ Asking current lawmakers for money. Many lawmakers do not have difficult races and usually have campaign money that they are more than willing to give out to a new face that holds the same beliefs. Both PAC representatives and lawmakers constantly must be apprised of a candidate's campaign—through mailings, calls, and personal visits, time permitting.

Perhaps most important, though, is thanking all campaign donors. This thank-you is a traditional thank-you note (preferably signed personally by the candidate) or a follow-up phone call. Separate fundraising appeals are sent to everyone who has already contributed to a campaign, thanking them first for their previous contribution.

Thinking Outside of the Box

Creativity is the most important aspect of fundraising. Successful candidates often tap new donors in fundraising by trying a new approach that inspires their base. To think creatively in campaigns, campaign staff members keep careful tabs on what the opponent does well and what he or she misses. They routinely try new tactics and repeat those that work later in the campaign. Candidates ask supportive current or former elected officials from the area what methods they used to raise funds and ask if they have any new ideas that might work.

For example, a letter from a candidate's mother might work wonders in a small town in North Dakota but could look unprofessional to voters in a city in California. When trying out new ideas, candidates keep their target audiences in mind. During the 2004 presidential campaign, Democratic vice-presidential candidate John Edwards of North Carolina told donors they could receive the recipe for his mother's peanut butter pie.

Every candidate event usually includes some type of fundraising appeal, whether it's subtle or explicit. But as much as possible, they all try to vary the way in which the money is asked for. No event is too insignificant to try to raise money.

Variety Is Key

Candidates hold a variety of fundraising events—some meet-and-greet receptions, some at restaurants and some tied to a sporting event or other activity. Instead of a stated fundraiser at a person's home, a smaller intimate potluck dinner might raise just as much money as a large fundraiser with the right group of attendees. If a person has a reason to attend an event other than to give money, that person might be more likely to go.

Fundraisers might also be more successful if headlined by the right name. In 2000, Sen. John McCain, a Republican from Arizona, agreed to campaign on behalf of about 30 House and Senate candidates across the country after his failed presidential bid. McCain's appeal was based on the success of the "Straight Talk Express" message that resonated with a broad range of independent and moderate Republicans. He also campaigned with President George W. Bush and Vice President Dick Cheney after endorsing their campaign. In many cases, a challenger's long-shot campaign was given a much-needed boost by a visit from McCain.

Fundraisers are held in a wide variety of locations. If a fundraiser is in the home of a well-known doctor, the next home fundraiser might be held by a supporter who is in another line of work. Fundraisers are often tied to local events, such as a corn roast or Fourth of July celebration. Bake sales can be organized in the community to tap into different markets—at area churches, at school sporting events, and at senior citizens events, to name just a few.

Raising Money Online

Candidates don't forget to raise funds from their websites, either. Although the technology behind political campaign websites is behind other successful web ventures, the influence and success of fundraising from the web is improving. Candidates who do not have a lot of money can easily compete through online fundraising.

The necessary aspects to raising funds via a candidate's website are fairly simple. First, campaigns must ensure that the website address is known to the target audience. Second, the website must give voters the option of either submitting a payment via credit card through a secure transaction online or printing out a form and mailing it in with a campaign donation. Political e-mail campaigns can also keep a candidate's core group of supporters informed of campaign progress at a significant savings to direct mailings.

Several key groups are heavily involved in raising money for political candidates, often in an attempt to influence public policy. Just a few of those are organized labor, Hollywood, big business, and single-issue organizations, including religious influences.

> **We Hold These Truths**
>
> Democratic presidential candidate John Kerry broke the online fundraising record in early 2004—raising $26.7 million in the first quarter. The Kerry campaign also broke the single-day record for online fundraising with more than $2.6 million on March 4, 2004.

Single-Issue Influences

Thousands of special-interest groups donate money to political campaigns every year, and their numbers continue to grow. Nearly $135 million was donated to political candidates in the 2002 election by single-issue organizations.

The following table lists the top 10 single-issue political contributors and their contributions for the 2002 election period.

Top 10 Single-Issue Political Contributors and Their Contributions in the 2002 Election Cycle*

No.	Single-Issue Political Contributor	Contribution
1.	Texans for John Cornyn	$3.1 million
2.	EMILY's List	$2.3 million

continues

Top 10 Single-Issue Political Contributors and Their Contributions in the 2002 Election Cycle* (continued)

No.	Single-Issue Political Contributor	Contribution
3.	Jon Corzine/US Senate	$2.1 million
4.	National Rifle Association	$2 million
5.	Governor Bush Committee	$1.7 million
6.	New Republican Majority Fund	$1.5 million
7.	Center for Middle East Peace/Econ Coop	$1.5 million
8.	DASHPAC	$1.3 million
9.	Republican Majority Fund	$1.3 million
10.	Americans for a Republican Majority	$1.3 million

Center for Responsive Politics

The number of special-interest and single-issue groups has grown rapidly throughout the last 30 years. The growth occurred for several reasons but coincided with increased government regulation in various industries. Other special-interest groups that claimed to be public-interest groups also grew exponentially during the Vietnam War and afterward. Those groups were tied to specific efforts, such as the women's movement that led to the creation of the National Organization for Women.

This group is a broad category that includes pro- and anti-gun rights groups, pro-choice and pro-life groups, and leadership PACs formed by members of Congress to support other candidates with similar ideologies. Specific-ideology single-issue groups tend to grow in number in relation to the party's success in the political arena as well. For example, the number of conservative single-issue groups increased dramatically after former President Ronald Reagan left office. Former Reagan administration officials founded or organized the start of many groups themselves, such as the conservative group formed by activist Grover Norquist, Americans for Tax Reform.

As you read in Chapter 20, the general public's growing sentiment that special-interest groups overly influence lawmakers that they contribute to increases with every financial-political scandal. But although the framers never envisioned today's vast expansion of special-interest groups, they did believe in a political system that allowed special interests to compete against one another. Today that often means that whichever group can raise the most money is heard over other interests (you'll read more about this in Chapter 22).

Republicans and Democrats were fairly split in the amount of funds received from single-issue groups. But the real winners were incumbents, who received 88 percent of funds from the organizations.

Going to the Stars (for Money, That Is!)

Celebrities campaigning for politicians is nothing new. John F. Kennedy snagged Frank Sinatra for a performance at his inaugural ball in 1960. Bruce Springsteen hit the campaign trail for John Kerry's presidential bid. The association might not be the reason a person votes for a candidate, but having a celebrity campaign for a candidate might just tip the balance in key swing states.

Part of the reason for Hollywood's high political contributions has to do with industry issues that Congress regulates, including the marketing of violence to children in movies, television, and video games. Many donations from Hollywood industry groups are likely used as part of their effort to stop any excessive regulation.

Hollywood insiders gave nearly $40 million to federal political candidates in the 2002 election cycle, according to the following list. In general, the majority of Hollywood money went to Democrats over Republicans. Of the nearly $40 million contributed during that cycle, about $31 million went to Democrats and about $9 million went to Republicans. Former Democratic presidential hopeful and Rep. Richard Gephardt, a Democrat from Missouri, was the top recipient from Hollywood, receiving almost $230,000 from Hollywood in 2002.

The following table lists the top 10 Hollywood political contributions in the 2002 election cycle:

Top 10 Hollywood Political Contributions in the 2002 Election Cycle*

No.	Contributor	Contribution
1.	Saban Capital Group	$9.3 million
2.	Shangri-La Entertainment	$6.7 million
3.	Viacom Inc.	$2 million
4.	AOL Time Warner	$1.5 million
5.	Walt Disney Co.	$1.2 million
6.	Vivendi Universal	$1.2 million
7.	Sillerman Companies	$1 million

Top 10 Hollywood Political Contributions in the 2002 Election Cycle*   (continued)

No.	Contributor	Contribution
8.	National Association of Broadcasters	$1 million
9.	National Cable & Telecommunications Associations	$1 million
10.	YankeeNets	$895,300

Center for Responsive Politics

Most people remember former President Bill Clinton's close ties to Hollywood, including a going-away bash thrown by Hollywood stars for Clinton just before the start of the 2000 Democratic National Convention in Los Angeles. The event was a fundraiser for then-first lady Hillary Rodham Clinton's Senate campaign. The next morning, Barbra Streisand hosted a fundraiser for Clinton's presidential library that raised $10 million. Whoopi Goldberg, Jimmy Smits, Quentin Tarantino, Kevin Costner, and numerous other celebrities all held fundraisers or addressed Democrats at their convention as well.

Because Republicans usually have fewer ties to Hollywood than Democrats, their chances of celebrities campaigning for them are much slimmer. For example, movie star Ben Affleck campaigned as a part of John Kerry's bus tour immediately following the 2004 convention. Bush, on the other hand, had several less-well-known actors appear on his behalf at the Republican convention, but did not campaign with them afterward. Regardless of political affiliation, candidates usually make an effort to contact celebrities' representatives and ask for a signed item to use at an auction. (Candidates also ask high-ranking lawmakers in their party for memorabilia donations to auction off.) This is a creative and fun moneymaker for any political campaign.

Union Influence

As you read in Chapter 20, labor unions formed the first political action committee. Organized labor's political contributions have long been the backbone of Democratic fundraising. In the 2002 election cycle, organized labor unions contributed nearly $97 million, according to the following list. Ninety-three percent of labor unions' political contributions went to Democrats in 2002, and 7 percent went to Republicans. The top individual recipient from labor unions was U.S. Senator Mary Landrieu, a Democrat from Louisiana.

The following table shows the top 10 labor unions' political contributions in the 2002 election cycle:

Top 10 Labor Unions' Political Contributions in the 2002 Election Cycle*

No.	Labor Union	Contribution
1.	American Federation of State-County-Municipal Employees	$9.5 million
2.	Service Employees International Union	$6.9 million
3.	Carpenters & Joiners Union	$6.2 million
4.	Communications Workers of America	$5.6 million
5.	Laborers Union	$5.5 million
6.	American Federation of Teachers	$5.3 million
7.	International Brotherhood of Electrical Workers	$3.9 million
8.	United Food & Commercial Workers Union	$3.6 million
9.	National Education Association	$3.5 million
10.	United Auto Workers	$3.3 million

Center for Responsive Politics

Workplace issues dominate unions' agendas, including worker safety, health care, and equitable awarding of federal contracts. Organized labor's less-than-cordial relationship with the GOP may be shifting slightly in George W. Bush's administration because Bush has made an effort to reach out to union leaders. But there may be a backlash for Republicans from labor because of several anti-union measures that passed through Congress during the first months of the Bush administration.

Corporate Influence

Just as organized labor has long been active in Democratic fundraising, business has financially supported Republican candidates. But the split is not as distinct in giving between the parties from business groups as it is for labor. Sixty-five percent of money from business groups went to Republicans in the 2002 election, as opposed to 35 percent to Democrats, according to the CRP numbers. The following table shows who donated what during the 2002 election cycle.

Top 10 Business Political Contributions in the 2002 Election Cycle*

No.	Contributor	Contribution
1.	National Beer Wholesalers Association	$2.6 million
2.	Anheuser-Busch	$2.3 million
3.	Wal-Mart Stores	$1.5 million
4.	Sunland Park Racetrack & Casino	$1.3 million
5.	General Electric	$1.3 million
6.	Cintas Corp	$1.1 million
7.	Outback Steakhouse	$1.1 million
8.	LA Avengers/Bleu Penguin	$1 million
9.	National Restaurant Association	$977,000
10.	Marriott International	$975,000

Center for Responsive Politics

Big business favors fewer regulations, and its agenda is frequently dominated by what it believes to be excessive regulations placed on business owners, as well as health-care cost issues and tax issues.

One major battle fought between business and organized labor arose over the repeal of an ergonomics standard in the workplace. The measure was signed into law by former President Bill Clinton, but business groups wanted the law repealed. Both sides organized an intensive grass-roots campaign involving their statewide branches, but Congress repealed the ergonomics law and President Bush signed the measure into law.

But for all that business and organized labor disagree about, there are some campaigns that they both support. Both are part of a broad coalition of groups that actively fight to stop passage of campaign finance reform.

The Least You Need to Know

- It takes money—a lot of money—to run a political campaign, especially at the national level.

- Successful fundraising campaigns start with the basics—identifying key audiences, coming up with a strategic plan, and so on.

- Coming up with new fundraising approaches is a key aspect in reaching previously untapped donor pools.

- Online fundraising is gaining in popularity as the functionality of such websites improves.

Chapter **22**

The Right to Petition

In This Chapter

♦ The art of the lobby

♦ Lobbying versus bribery

♦ Characteristics of top lobbyists

♦ The revolving door

Every special-interest group has something it wants included in some piece of legislation. But how do these groups reach the right member of Congress? Who has more access to a member, and why? How do these groups use their influence to get the provision they want in a piece of legislation? Do lobbyists and members of Congress have to follow certain rules in their interactions? How did Washington, D.C., end up with thousands of lobbyists in the first place?

Many Americans have negative perceptions of Washington lobbyists. They might imagine lobbyists in slick business suits handing money to lawmakers over "three-martini" lunches. While those perceptions might hold true for a few select lobbyists, the vast majority of highly successful lobbyists have an intricate, valuable knowledge of the way government works and follow the rules of the game when they do their job.

In this chapter, we discuss the complex art of lobbying, which lobbyists have the most influence on public policy, and what rules lobbyists and lawmakers must follow.

What Is a Lobbyist?

Lobbyists are people who advocate a specific policy or measure to an elected lawmaker, and they can be found at every level of government. Professional lobbyists are paid by special-interest groups, advocacy groups, and just about anyone who wants to see something happen on Capitol Hill, to actively pursue agenda items from members of Congress. Businesses, labor unions, trade associations, religious groups, universities and colleges, states, and public-interest organizations all employ lobbyists, many on a full-time basis. A lobbyist might want a lawmaker to support one provision in a bill or might want a lawmaker to pressure another member of Congress to do the same.

We Hold These Truths
More than 12,000 active lobbyists work in Washington today.

Lobbyists have existed for as long as the United States has—although the term was not used in America until the mid-nineteenth century. The word *lobbyist* (first used in Britain) refers to the lobbies and corridors that lobbyists often spend hours in waiting for lawmakers.

The framers of American government even ensured a provision for lobbying in the First Amendment: "Congress shall make no law … abridging the freedom of speech … or the right of the people peaceably to assemble, and to petition the government for a redress of grievances." But the line between lobbying and bribery was blurred, to say the least, in early American history. Sen. Daniel Webster of Massachusetts once wrote to powerful banker Joseph Biddle that if he wanted to keep his relationship with the Bank of the United States intact, he would have to send him a retainer. Biddle eventually sent Webster more than $30,000.

The negative image the general public has of lobbyists was reinforced over the years when scandal after scandal involved a lawmaker, a political favor, and a sizable amount of money (see Chapter 20). Even the common reference to where lobbyists stand in Congress and their affinity for expensive items (and ample money to pay for them) has a negative connotation: "Gucci Gulch." But as the calls for campaign finance reform increased, lobbyists made sure their pleas for protection under the First Amendment were remembered, resulting in greater regulation of lobbying.

Today individuals often act as lobbyists themselves. Sometimes individuals "lobby" their member of Congress or someone who sits on a panel related to a specific legislative proposal. On other occasions, citizens are brought in to lobby members from a specific district to assist Washington-based professional lobbyists.

Ordinary citizens are often brought to Washington in larger groups for specially planned "Lobby Days" on Capitol Hill. On many occasions, the Lobby Day is planned into an organization's annual conference in Washington, D.C. Members of the organization travel from around the country but might meet in smaller groups with members from their congressional district or state delegation to press their organization's cause.

For example, the American Hotel & Lodging Association holds a Legislative Action Summit every year in Washington, D.C. During the summit, hotel and lodging industry insiders from around the country converge on the capital to discuss their legislative agenda. Once that's decided, they head to Capitol Hill to lobby their members of Congress, combining Washington lobbyists and a grass-roots network of real people.

But what is lobbying like for the average citizen who wants to get involved in the process? Lobbying is essentially a small, polite debate. A constituent sets up the meeting with his or her member of Congress, visits the office, and frequently has to make a case in about 10 minutes. When a citizen lobbyist is making the case at the behest of an organization, he or she typically has much of the groundwork done by that group and comes armed with plenty of facts and statistics to back up the case. The following pointers from Common Cause suggest the best approach.

Pointers for an Effective Lobby Visit with Your Elected Official*

Before the Meeting

- ◆ **Set up an appointment.** Call your elected official's office to request a meeting. Inform the office of the issue(s) that you would like to discuss. It is unlikely that the staff person will be able to schedule a meeting on the spot. You will likely need to follow up on this initial request with another phone call or a letter. Don't be afraid to be persistent.

- ◆ **Determine who will join you in the meeting.** You may visit your elected official alone or with other like-minded people in your community. If you do go as a group, be sure to establish in advance the person who will be the principal spokesperson for the group.

- ◆ **Do your homework.** You do not need to be a policy expert to lobby your elected officials, but you should be familiar with the issue you want to discuss with them and the basic provisions of the bill you would like them to support or oppose. You should also be familiar with the legislative status of the bill.

During the Meeting

- ◆ **Establish common ground.** Start the meeting in a positive way by thanking your elected official for a recent vote he or she cast that you favored, or for other positive actions he or she has taken on behalf of your community. It is particularly effective to thank your elected official for a positive action taken in support of the issue you are planning to discuss in the meeting. You might also mention something else you share in common or a common acquaintance.

- ◆ **Make a short presentation.** Briefly lay out your case (no more than five minutes). Be polite but persuasive. Make it clear what you would like your senator or representative to do, and ask what actions he or she intends to take in response to your request.

- ◆ **Be a good listener, but don't allow your elected official to evade the issue.** Let your elected official ask questions and express her or his opinions. Be responsive to questions, concerns, and comments. If your elected official changes the subject or evades your questions, don't be afraid to tactfully press for specifics. Remember that you are not expected to be an expert—if you cannot answer a question, let the elected official know that you will get the relevant information and get back to him or her.

- ◆ **Thank your elected official for the time and support.** End the meeting on a positive note by thanking your elected official for taking the time to meet with you and for any actions he or she agreed to take in support of the issue you discussed. Reiterate your position once again before leaving.

After the Meeting

- ◆ **Let us know what happened.** Please report to us on your meeting by phone, e-mail, mail, or fax. The information you provide is critically important to us as we work to lobby your elected officials in Washington.

- ◆ **Send a thank-you note to your elected official.** Send a quick thank-you note to your elected official and to the staff member who arranged the meeting. Restate your understanding of the positions your elected representative took on the issue during the meeting. Include a summary of your position, answers to any questions your representative raised, and any new information that supports your case.

*Courtesy of Common Cause

Recipe for Success

So what makes an effective professional lobbyist? Why do some organizations get their favored proposal through to completion while others are shut out of the legislative process? In general, lobbyists do not need a specific degree or background to do their jobs. But many lobbyists are lawyers or have extensive government experience and have worked "inside" Washington for years.

Like many professions, lobbyists have their own professional association, known as the American League of Lobbyists (ALL). ALL is a nonprofit group that works to explain the profession of lobbying in a more positive light to the general public, and it also provides training services and support to its members. ALL notes that lobbying is much more than convincing legislators to support a certain proposal. It also involves having excellent communication skills, being able to do extensive research (and absorb it), and being able to disintegrate massive amounts of details into a succinct pitch.

> **We Hold These Truths**
>
> Because lobbying relies heavily on personal relationships and communication skills, many lobbyists adhere to a philosophy of "pounding the pavement." Those lobbyists argue that the most effective lobbying can be done only in person. In those instances, access to lawmakers becomes a critical issue.

From ALL's perspective, some of the best lobbyists are those who have held staff positions on Capitol Hill. They understand the legislative process from start to finish, and they often have extensive contacts with other staffers and lawmakers. They also understand the value of a Capitol Hill staffer's or a lawmaker's time, having been through the grueling days themselves. Because politicians often work on a variety of topics, they are less likely to be experts in every area. In that sense, lawmakers frequently rely on lobbyists for up-to-date and detailed information in a specialized area.

Gerald Cassidy, the founder, president, and chief executive officer of one of Washington's top lobbying shops, told *The Hill* newspaper that a good lobbyist is someone with a "strong working knowledge of the legislative process and an in-depth research capability." Cassidy went on to say that good lobbyists are persistent, plan strategically, and "possess strong advocacy skills along with presentation and reasoning skills."

Aside from all those traits, lawmakers are especially favorable to those lobbyists they trust. If a lobbyist has come through before on a promise, the lawmaker will be all the more inclined to listen to them during the next 10-minute pitch.

Influence of Lobbyists

At the heart of downtown Washington is K Street, home to many of the city's top professional lobbying firms and home to plenty of money. More than $1.45 billion was spent on lobbying in 1999 alone, according to the most recent figures available from the Center for Responsive Politics. The top firms in 2000 raised almost as much—$1.42 billion. All of the top 10 had multimillion-dollar contracts representing a variety of interests, as seen in the following table.

Top Billing Firms Through 2000*

No.	Firm	Lobbying Receipts
1.	Cassidy & Assoc.	$27,380,000
2.	Verner, Liipfert et al.	$20,460,000
3.	Patton Boggs	$19,870,000
4.	Akin, Gump et al.	$15,895,000
5.	Van Scoyoc Assoc.	$10,760,000
6.	Preston, Gates et al.	$10,550,000
7.	PricewaterhouseCoopers	$9,900,000
8.	Barbour, Griffith & Rogers	$9,250,000
9.	Williams & Jensen	$9,200,000
10.	Podesta/Mattoon	$7,870,000

Center for Responsive Politics

Which firms make the most money usually coincides with which party controls Congress and the White House. When Republicans took over control of Congress in 1994, their influence and power grew. Likewise, when Democrats took back the Senate in 2001, many GOP-heavy firms scrambled to fill their ranks with seasoned Democrats.

On an issue-by-issue basis, several industries top the long list of lobbying interests. A quarter of lobbyists work on tax policy for clients, often trying to decrease regulations or provide loopholes for clients to save money in taxes. In terms of industries that spent the most on lobbying, health-care products and pharmaceutical companies were far in front of other industries, as seen in the following table.

Industry Breakdown of Money Spent on Lobbying in 2000*

No.	Industry	Amount Spent
1.	Finance, Insurance & Real Estate	$229 million
2.	Miscellaneous Business	$224 million
3.	Health	$209 million
4.	Communications & Electronics	$201 million
5.	Energy & Natural Resources	$159 million
6.	Transportation	$138 million
7.	Other	$103 million
8.	Ideological/Single Issue	$85 million
9.	Agribusiness	$78 million
10.	Defense	$60 million

Center for Responsive Politics

At the same time lobbyists are working for their clients, they know that a member of Congress's top priority is getting re-elected to office. The connection between campaign contributions from lobbyists to lawmakers has long been a battle cry for those who believe that big money owns public policy.

Lobbyists spend nearly as much time at fundraisers in Washington as lawmakers do. Lobbying firms contribute millions of dollars to political campaigns every year. While lawmakers and lobbyists alike insist that a political contribution does not constitute an allegiance, public-interest groups and average citizens frequently suggest the likelihood of a *quid pro quo*.

Inside the Beltway

Quid pro quo is an exchange for something of equal value, such as a vote in exchange for a financial contribution.

Still, it is not uncommon for individual lobbyists or lawyers' PACs to contribute more money to lawmakers who have jurisdiction over areas they lobby on. For example, former President Bill Clinton was accused of a quid pro quo—or "money for pardons"—when he granted a pardon his last day in office to billionaire fugitive Marc Rich. Denise Rich, Marc's ex-wife, is a top contributor to the Democratic Party.

On the other hand, grass-roots lobbying can often be just as effective for re-electing lawmakers as money. While organized labor contributes heavily to Democratic candidates, their efforts in getting out the vote for their candidates is also a reason for the close alliance between union lobbyists and lawmakers.

Rules of the Game

While lobbyists must follow many regulations, a few major pieces of legislation include the bulk of the rules.

Lobbyists remained unregulated in any significant way until the passage of the Federal Regulation of Lobbying Act in 1946. The measure simply required lobbyists to disclose whom they lobbied for and how much they received. No limits were placed on the lobbying, though, and enforcement of the law was weak, at best. Furthermore, the Supreme Court decision *U.S. v. Harriss* decreased the types of lobbying that had to be disclosed. Even though political financial scandals continued, few major reforms were enforced on the lobbying community until late in the twentieth century (see Chapter 20).

When Republicans took control of Congress in 1994, one of their major overhauls in government the following year took place in the area of lobbying. Known as the Lobbying Disclosure Act of 1995, the measure increased the disclosure requirements for lobbyists. Lobbyists now must register with the Clerk of the House or the Secretary of the Senate, depending on whom they lobby. The disclosure also makes public the areas in which a lobbyist works for a client, who the client is, and how much the lobbyist is compensated for the work. The law also made it illegal for some groups that receive federal funds to use those monies to lobby the government.

Lobbyists are required to register under the law if they meet these three conditions: They receive more than $5,000 from a client for lobbying over a six-month period; they have frequent contacts with congressional staff, members, or executive branch officials; and more than 20 percent of their time working for a client involves lobbying. (Of course, some lobbyists can skirt registration by not meeting all the criteria.) Any group that has its own lobbyists in-house must register once expenses on lobbying exceed $20,500 in six months.

To enforce the law, an individual can be fined up to $50,000 if he or she does not register with the appropriate office after being granted a 60-day warning period. Some areas are left out of the 1995 law, though. Most notably, all the grass-roots lobbying done by organizations (such as Lobby Days) does not have to be registered under the law. In 2001, the records kept by the House clerk and the Senate secretary were made even more accessible to the public and can now be obtained online.

Lobbyists who represent the interests of foreign nations on Capitol Hill or with the executive branch are also subject to disclosure regulations under the Foreign Agents Registration Act (FARA), which falls under the jurisdiction of the Justice Department. Foreign commercial interests that meet all the criteria under the Lobbying Disclosure Act must register with the House or the Senate rather than FARA.

Other restrictions outside the Lobbying Disclosure Act dictate the types of acceptable relationships between members and lobbyists. For example, a member cannot accept any gift from a lobbyist that is greater than $50 in value, including meals. Total gifts cannot be more than $100 in one year. While members can accept gifts from those deemed to be personal friends, any gift over $250 must be reported and approved by the House or Senate ethics committees. In addition, if a member of Congress accepts a payment of travel by a lobbyist or a firm, some element of official business must be associated with the trip.

Lobbyists must familiarize themselves with many other gift rules, to avoid any embarrassing situations or ethical breaches.

The following table shows the top individual group spenders of 1999.

> **We Hold These Truths**
>
> Part of the lobbying tab for many major firms pays for members to travel to exotic locations to hold "legislative planning sessions" or other meetings. Sometimes these official occasions are an afternoon of meetings sandwiched between a long weekend of activities at a ski resort or at major sporting events such as the Super Bowl.

Top 10 Individual Group Spenders on Lobbying in 1999*

No.	Organization/Company	Amount Spent
1.	U.S. Chamber of Commerce	$18.8 million
2.	American Medical Association	$18.2 million
3.	Philip Morris	$14.8 million
4.	American Hospital Association	$12.5 million
5.	Exxon Mobil Corp.	$11.7 million
6.	Edison Electric Institute	$11.6 million
7.	Blue Cross/Blue Shield	$11.2 million
8.	SBC Communications	$9.6 million
9.	Schering-Plough Corp.	$9.2 million
10.	AT&T	$8.6 million

Center for Responsive Politics

Blurring the Lines

Many members of Congress head straight to K Street when they retire instead of returning to their congressional districts. Former staffers also make frequent career changes that include lobbying once they leave Capitol Hill.

More than 100 former members of Congress are currently lobbyists, in what is usually a very lucrative career move compared to their congressional salaries. The split between Democrats and Republicans who leave Congress to lobby is fairly even. Many lobbying firms actively recruit retiring members to become lobbyists—who has the same access to Capitol Hill as someone who was just there?

We Hold These Truths

To represent the White House on Capitol Hill, the president hand-picks his own chief lobbyist, whose official title is Director of the Office of Legislative Affairs. This lobbyist's job is to make sure that the president's top proposals have the support of enough lawmakers on Capitol Hill to pass. Nicholas Calio, a long-time lobbyist who was a partner at the firm O'Brien Calio, returned to the White House in the chief lobbyist role in 2000 under President George W. Bush. He was in the legislative affairs shop in the first George Bush White House as the liaison to the House of Representatives.

A former member or staffer faces limited restrictions on lobbying former colleagues under the 1995 law. A member is not allowed to directly lobby colleagues for one year after leaving office. The same ban is placed on former administration officials. Some high-level staffers are also barred from lobbying former bosses or, if they were committee staff, members of the committee, for one year.

Even though firms might pay a hefty salary for one year in which a former member is barred from lobbying, that member's understanding of legislative strategy as a consultant can be just as valuable. In addition, former members are allowed on the House and Senate floors, which can be another powerful lobbying presence. For example, former House Appropriations Committee Chairman Bob Livingston, a Republican from Louisiana, made more than $1 million lobbying his first year out of office. His firm grew even more following the death of former Rules Committee Chairman Gerald Solomon, a Republican from New York, when The Livingston Group absorbed The Solomon Group in 2002.

In addition to former members and staffers who become lobbyists, many relatives of current lawmakers make their living in Washington, D.C., as lobbyists—sometimes working for clients that have interests in front of their spouse's or relative's interests. For example, Linda Hall Daschle, the wife of former Senate Majority Leader Tom Daschle, a Democrat from South Dakota, is a prominent aviation lobbyist.

Even though there are restrictions on lobbying former colleagues, many examples of blurring those lines are argued by foes of corporate lobbyists. Another area that some people argue should be included in the lobbying registrations involves public relations firms that put together elaborate campaigns on a particular piece of legislation.

The Least You Need to Know

◆ Lobbyists, people who advocate specific policies or measures, can be found at every level of government.

◆ Successful lobbyists possess excellent communication skills and the ability to conduct and absorb extensive research; they are skilled at distilling massive amounts of detail into a succinct pitch.

◆ Lawmakers often rely on lobbyists for up-to-date and detailed information in specialized areas.

◆ Health-care and pharmaceutical companies spend the most money on lobbyists.

◆ Many lawmakers and top staffers become lobbyists after leaving Capitol Hill.

Part 6

State and Local Government

While the entity created by the framers of the Constitution is the central feature of American government, there are thousands of smaller governmental units, ranging from state governments all the way down to the boards and councils that govern counties, cities, towns, and villages.

These smaller entities were the building blocks of American government, and the framers wisely left them in place. While they believed that some functions should be placed under the jurisdiction of the centralized government they had created, they also believed that citizens should have more direct contact with the officials in charge of important local functions.

This multilayered governmental system not only brings government to the people, it provides many opportunities for citizens to get involved. From registering to vote to running for public office, American government is definitely by the people, of the people, and for the people.

Chapter 23

Governors and Other State Leaders

In This Chapter

◆ Heads of states

◆ What governors do

◆ The role of the lieutenant governor

◆ Other state officials (elected and not)

The governor of your state has no federal authority, meaning that he or she answers to just your state, not to Washington, D.C. Congress can call each governor in for hearings and ask him or her about issues concerning the given state, a task that governors are usually happy to comply with. But have you ever wondered what your governor does? What about the lieutenant governor and the secretary of state? This chapter goes into detail about what these jobs entail and how they work.

From Figurehead to Elected Official

When the colonies were first established, governors were largely figure-heads. They were appointed by the king to represent royal interests in the new land. Because of this appointment, relations between the governors and the legislatures, which were elected by the people, were often strained. The legislatures and the colonists themselves didn't trust the governors, so the power of the office was relatively weak.

When the United States declared its independence from Great Britain in 1776, state constitutions were drawn up to establish a representative government in each of the newly formed states. In large part because of the earlier distrust between the governors and the legislatures, the governors in all but two states were appointed and not elected. Early governors served for one year and had limited powers.

The U.S. Constitution set a precedent that all the states soon came to follow. Soon afterward, the states began to draft similar constitutions with their own version of the federal document that gave like powers to both the legislative and executive branches.

As the governors began to gain more trust from their legislatures, they also began to gain more control. By the late nineteenth century, state governors began to wield unprecedented powers. As the heads of their states, and effectively the heads of their state political parties, governors began to control more of the agenda and more people. They also gained the authority to convene special sessions of the legislature in the event of an emergency, as well as submit budgets for review. With all these changes, however, formal reorganizations of state constitutions were necessary to meet the growing needs of states and their executives.

This reorganization took place over several years, and the process and control of the governor varies from state to state. Today most governors have extensive powers within their states and are very influential at the state level—and even at the federal level, when they come to lobby Congress on behalf of their state's interest.

We Hold These Truths

Illinois was the first state to radically change its executive branch, doing so in 1917. Rather than having hundreds of different agencies with various heads reporting to the governor—and, in some cases, to no one—the agencies were consolidated into nine new departments with one administrative head who reported directly to the governor. Other states soon followed suit, reducing the number of elected officials—which had ballooned during the Jacksonian era of the early nineteenth century—and handing the governor new authority.

Going to Higher Ground

Over time, the office of governor has been a stepping-stone to higher political positions. Twenty-three presidents and vice presidents have served as governor before ascending to higher office.

> ### We Hold These Truths
>
> Like most other aspects of American politics, the office of governor was limited to white men for much of the country's history. The first woman elected governor was Nellie Tayloe Ross of Wyoming, elected in 1925. It didn't take long for her to get female company at the highest level, though. Fifteen days after Ross was sworn in, Miriam L. Ferguson was sworn in to the first of her two terms as governor of Texas. It would be 64 years later, in 1989, that Virginia elected the first African American governor, L. Douglas Wilder.

Four of the last five presidents served as governor before becoming president. Jimmy Carter was governor of Georgia, Ronald Reagan was governor of California, Bill Clinton was governor of Arkansas, and current President George W. Bush was governor of Texas.

Getting to Gov

Governors were first appointed, initially by the king and then later by the legislature. Over time that has changed, and today all states elect their governors by popular vote. Most state constitutions set minimum requirements for a person to be governor, such as age and length of residency.

Formal requirements help a candidate enter a race. But it takes a lot more than just attaining a certain age or having lived in a state for a certain number of years to be elected governor. Money is a very important consideration. Other considerations, such as personal integrity, honesty, and strength of character, also come into play. In 1998, a former wrestler seemingly came from nowhere to win the governorship of Minnesota. Jesse Ventura was elected in large part because the people weren't interested in the "political

> ### We Hold These Truths
>
> Only two states—Ohio and Kansas—do not set formal requirements for holding the office of governor.

speak" of the major party candidates and liked what they heard from Ventura during the campaign.

In most states, the governor and the lieutenant governor run together on the same ticket and are selected during party primaries. In some states, such as Republican-dominated Virginia or Democratic-dominated California, the primary is the real battle because one party has majority control. In the general election, all the parties put forward their candidates; whoever wins the majority of votes, even if it is just a plurality, wins the election. In Georgia and Louisiana, if no candidate wins a clear majority, a run-off election is held. In Mississippi and Vermont, if there is no clear winner, the legislature decides.

Campaigning for governor can be a grueling experience. Like running for the U.S. Senate, the candidate must travel the entire state. In small states such as Rhode Island and Hawaii, that is not too hard, but for larger states with diverse populations, such as California, Texas, and New York, it can be increasingly demanding. For example, the citizens in Beaumont, Texas, a small town in the north-central part of the state, have very different needs from those people living in El Paso or Brownsville, which are larger communities that border Mexico. Meeting the needs and demands of these different constituents can pose quite a difficult challenge for a candidate.

One of the main reasons it's so expensive to run for statewide office is the length of time the average campaign takes. Although the general election for most governors is not until November, some campaigns can begin as early as June of the year preceding the election year—a full 17 months in advance! Chances are, while most people are not even aware that an election year is fast approaching, most of the major decisions of who will run have already been made.

In most states, the governor serves a four-year term. About half the states impose a term limit on how long a governor may serve; the other states don't. The salaries also vary from state to state, but governors are generally well paid—usually more than $100,000 per year—and are also provided with an expense account and an official residence to call home.

Once a governor is elected, it is hard to remove that person from office, but not impossible. As with the presidency, in every state except Oregon, the governor can be impeached by the legislature. The lower house must bring the charges against the official, and the upper house holds the trial.

We Hold These Truths

In the last 100 years, four governors have been impeached from office: William Seltzer of New York (1913), James E. Ferguson of Texas (1917), J.C. Walton of Oklahoma (1923), and Henry Johnston, also of Oklahoma (1929).

In at least 15 states, citizens have the authority to remove their governor by holding a *recall.* To be successful, the group needs to circulate a petition to get enough signatures to hold a recall. This method has been used only twice in the last 100 years. Gov. Lynn Frazier of North Dakota was recalled in 1921 and Gov. Gray Davis of California was recalled in 2003.

Inside the Beltway

A **recall** is a procedure to remove elected officials from office by way of gathering signatures and calling for a special election.

Governing

Governors have numerous roles that they must fulfill during their tenure. The three most important fall into distinct categories: executive, legislative, and judicial.

Executive Role

The executive powers of the governor are limited in many ways by checks and balances incorporated in various state constitutions. One of the most important responsibilities that the governor has, however, is submitting the state budget at the beginning of the year. In this budget, which the governor usually submits at the beginning of the legislative term of the state legislature, the governor outlines the spending priorities of the state. These priorities usually mirror those of the governor and what he or she campaigned on. For example, if Candidate Jones stressed education as an important issue while running for office, education spending likely will receive an increase under Gov. Jones's administration.

The legislature has the power to amend the state budget and must eventually pass the budget before any money can be spent. Often it amends the proposals of the governor, but the final product usually is similar to that of the original document. The state budget says what money will be spent where and how. It can support programs and initiatives that the governor thinks are important, and it can also serve as the cutting board for programs that the administration opposes. It also dictates whether taxes will be raised to meet the spending needs of the state. It can also call for a decrease in taxes or even a tax rebate if there is a surplus in state funds.

The governor also has certain military powers. While the president is commander in chief of the entire military, the governor is the commander in chief of the National

Guard in the state. As such, the governor is responsible for ensuring civil defense in the event of an attack against the United States. In the event of a natural disaster, such as a hurricane or a tornado, the governor can deem a particular region of the state to be in a "state of emergency." This enables the state to apply for federal assistance to help recover from the event.

Legislative Role

The second area in which the governor has authority is legislative. The governor can be viewed as the representative of the wishes of the entire state before the legislature.

Inside the Beltway

The **State of the State address** is the annual address given by the governor to the legislature, usually at the beginning of the term, outlining the state's priorities.

With this in mind, the governor often will propose legislation. More often than not, this comes during the *State of the State address.*

During the State of the State address, the governor outlines his or her priorities for the coming year. If the governor just won election by a large margin, he or she has a mandate and could use this to influence the legislature to enact legislation that it might otherwise be disposed against.

If the legislators don't get the hint—or don't take it—during this address, governors can and do meet informally with legislators throughout the session to do some arm-twisting. If this doesn't work, the governor can (and usually does) make public appeals to constituents to get them to write or call their legislators and put pressure on them to support the governor's initiative.

In some states the legislature and the governor are from different parties. While in an ideal world Democrats and Republicans would always get along and find bipartisan solutions, it is possible that the legislature can pass laws that the governor does not support. When this happens, in all but one state (North Carolina), the governor has the authority to veto legislation. While it is often easy to override legislation by simply threatening to do so, the governor has enormous influence over what the legislature does—and, in some cases, *doesn't* do.

Judicial Role

The governor also has broad judicial authority in the state. One example in which this comes into play concerns convicted felons. This power comes through certain *executive clemency* rules that give the governor the right to lighten or even overturn sentences. A governor can also choose to pardon a criminal and set the person free. The best example of this is when a death row inmate appeals to the governor to spare him or her from execution.

Inside the Beltway

Executive clemency is the power to lighten or overturn the sentences of criminals.

When it comes time for a state to go to the federal government for assistance on any of a wide range of issues, including monetary and protection concerns, the governor is the acting spokesman for the state. He or she comes to Washington, D.C., and testifies before Congressional panels about the needs of the state. What might the governor be asking for, you wonder? Well, the local interstate that runs through your town requires federal funds from the Department of Transportation. If the roads are poor, the governor will ask for assistance for improvements.

The governor is also viewed as a political leader, for both the state and the party. Just by virtue of the office, every news conference and public appearance that the governor holds is likely to receive coverage. This guaranteed media coverage enables governors to focus attention on the issues they see as important.

In addition to being a political leader, governors are in many ways party leaders. While they might have to fight a U.S. senator or large city mayor for the attention, as heads of their states, governors are likely to be viewed as the leaders of their parties. At national conventions, it is not unusual for the governor to make the announcement of delegates for a given candidate if the governor is of the same party affiliation as the nominee.

Second in Command: The Lieutenant Governor

Varying from state to state, the role of the lieutenant governor is similar to that of the vice president. In many ways this person is elected solely for the purpose of fulfilling the term of the elected governor in the event that he or she cannot complete the term. How a lieutenant governor is elected varies.

In some states, such as New York, the governor and lieutenant governor run together as a team. The selection process for the lieutenant governor is as hotly debated on the local level as the veepstakes are at the national level. If a gubernatorial candidate is from one region of the state, he or she may select a running mate from a different part of the state to help carry the region. Or, if the candidate is from one ideological wing of the party, he or she may pick someone who represents a different part of the party, so that all interests are represented. When you vote for Jane Smith for governor, you also vote for her running mate.

Other states, such as Rhode Island, have the governor and lieutenant governor run separately. Often the state parties make sure that the two candidates can work together and have a solid relationship before putting both names on the ballot. This can net both positive and negative results. For example, if you're a moderate Democrat and you vote for your nominee for governor but you like the Republican nominee for lieutenant governor, you're liable to face a divided government. However, by electing the lieutenant governor directly, the individual also has a mandate from the people and can therefore wield more influence—and hopefully allow for open dialogue in the event of a stalemate.

> **We Hold These Truths**
>
> In Texas, the lieutenant governor is actually as powerful (and, in some respects, more powerful) than the governor. The lieutenant governor is responsible for committee assignments in the legislature and the agenda in the upper house.

Sometimes the lieutenant governor is given authority over certain jurisdictions within state government, depending on what his or her own priorities are. If the lieutenant governor was once a teacher, he or she may deal with primary oversight of educational matters. On the other hand, if crime is a big concern, overview of the state's detention centers could fall under his or her authority.

The Attorney General

The attorney general is the primary legal official in the state. It's the attorney general's responsibility to represent state affairs in issues before the courts, and this official has important law enforcement duties. In most states, this is an elected position, but seven states allow the governor or the legislature to appoint the official.

The attorney general serves as the primary legal advisor to the state. He or she reports to the governor, the legislature, and various state agencies. Perhaps most important, the attorney general has the authority to set the legal interpretations of state law—so what the attorney general says, goes! And unless a court intervenes, this official has the force of law in state affairs.

The Secretary of State

Don't confuse the responsibilities of the secretary of state on the federal level with the secretary of state at the state level. Their respective responsibilities could not be more different. The secretary of state at the state level is the person in charge of all the official documents and records. He or she issues business licenses and corporate charters.

The other main responsibility of the secretary of state is to act as the state's chief election officer. This means that he or she administers the election laws and also prepares and distributes ballots and receives election results. Ultimately, he or she also certifies the election. In most states, this position is elected; only Alaska and Hawaii do not have one.

We Hold These Truths

Before 2000, the position of secretary of state was mostly unheard of and was largely ignored. That changed with the presidential election and the controversial results in Florida. Secretary of State Katherine Harris became one of the most well-known and either beloved or hated—depending on your political stripes—people in America. She was the one responsible for certifying the election results for George W. Bush. Many questioned her objectivity. She had worked on Bush's campaign as a state representative, and Bush's younger brother, Jeb, was essentially her boss—the governor of Florida.

In the end, Harris certified Bush as the winner by fewer than 600 votes. As you have read in previous chapters and undoubtedly remember from the election itself, the Supreme Court ultimately declared Bush the winner. Numerous recounts, sponsored by various media outlets from around the country, came to the same conclusion—with only the margin of victory changing.

State Treasurer and Comptroller

The person in charge of collecting money from you is either your state treasurer or comptroller, depending on where you live and the rules established by your constitution. This person is responsible for investment of state money and performs the duty of state paymaster. In some states, he or she is responsible for the collection of taxes.

The treasurer or comptroller is also considered the state's monetary watchdog. It's up to this individual to determine whether the spending by the various state agencies is authorized by law.

The Least You Need to Know

◆ Governors started out as royal figureheads, representing the interests of the king instead of the people.

◆ After the adoption of the Constitution, many states drafted similar constitutions.

◆ Some governors can serve unlimited terms, meaning that they can run as often as they want. Others are term-limited. Virginia, for example, says that the governor can serve only one term.

◆ Like the vice president at the federal level, lieutenant governors hold the backup position and stand ready to serve if their governors are unable to do so.

24

Reapportionment and Redistricting

In This Chapter

◆ Counting the populace

◆ Ensuring equal representation

◆ Concentrating and diluting power

◆ The politics of reapportionment

When you vote for your member of Congress, your state senator, or even your county council member, do you ever wonder why you are voting for that specific person? Why do you live in District 5 when your sister three blocks over lives in District 6?

Every 10 years, the U.S. government conducts a census. The census is done to find out the geographic makeup of the country. Where is everyone living? What areas are people moving to? Why are they leaving a certain area? These are just some of the questions the census answers. When the totals come in, federal and state officials are given the task of redrawing the congressional and legislative maps. County councils and city governments use the figures as well, and thus the decennial process of redistricting begins.

In this chapter, you learn about how the process began and what it's like today. What does this mean for you and the representation you receive in your capital or in Washington, D.C.? Are you getting a fair deal? What can you do to ensure your voice is heard?

The Census

Before any lines are drawn, the federal government takes a snapshot of the demographic lines that make up the United States. This process is known as the census. Article 1, Section 2, of the Constitution says that the government is responsible for conducting a census. Taken every 10 years, the census is a profile of the American republic. The next census will be taken in 2010.

The census compiles statistics of what the American people are doing. The census is not just numbers and percentages; the census details real people. It does this through demography, which is the statistical study of a population. The census is conducted by the Bureau of the Census, which is a division of the Department of Commerce.

The most important function of the census is to determine the apportionment of congressional seats, which is discussed in greater detail later in this chapter. However, there are other responsibilities of the census. One of the most important uses of the census is to determine the distribution of federal funds to state and local governments. The distribution of these funds is based on several factors, including population and per capita income.

> ### We Hold These Truths
>
> The first census was taken in 1790 under the direction of then-Secretary of State Thomas Jefferson.

Another purpose of the census is to help political scientists analyze government policy. They study and compare the shifts in voting patterns as well as public opinion and changes in the character of the population.

Redistricting

The number of members in the U.S. House of Representatives is set at 435. Every 10 years after the census has been completed, the allotment from the 435 seats that each state receives for representation is debated. Some states lose seats because of a change in demographics and a decrease in population. Ohio, Michigan, and even New York were a few of the states that lost seats as a result of the 2000 census. The census found that people were moving south and west; consequently, states such as Florida, Texas, and California all gained representation. This process is known as *reapportionment*.

Under the "one man, one vote" principle, each person is entitled to equal representation under the law. Legislative and congressional districts should be roughly the same throughout the state, with comparable figures to the other like districts, to accomplish this goal. Unfortunately, this is not always practical. To ensure that the lines drawn pass constitutional muster, legislators are given approximately a 5 percent leeway in this matter. As long as the lines are as close in population totals as possible and a good faith effort by the legislatures has been made to ensure relative equality within the lines, the districts are considered acceptable.

Inside the Beltway

Reapportionment is the periodic redistribution of congressional or legislative seats based on changing census figures, as required by the Constitution.

Each congressional district has an average of 600,000 people. The sizes of legislative districts differ from state to state, depending on the structure of the legislature itself.

Drawing the Lines

After the government determines what states will keep their congressional seats, which will get more seats, and which will lose seats, it's up to the states themselves to determine the lines. And determining these lines can sometimes be a contentious battle. It isn't as simple as just dividing the districts into nice, neat little boundaries. Instead, it's usually a battle for party superiority, and the lines that come out very rarely look like anything other than random lines dividing up states.

Walk into your congressperson's office on Capitol Hill (or, in some cases, district office), and you will see a big blue map provided by the U.S. Geological Society. It gives the exact location of that district, from street corner to street corner. This map is not like anything you have ever seen (unless you study maps), and it was designed to help (or hurt) a candidate, even if that candidate is not the one holding office today.

Government officials will tell you that they want to ensure the best representation for the state. But what does best representation really mean? Unfortunately, it often means which party can get the most out of it, even if it is not in the best interests of the state.

On the Record

"I think he deserves to be complimented for his focus and his achievements politically. I don't think it's good for the country, but he certainly accomplished his goals ... The personal destruction that they set out to do on me is something that I'll have a hard time forgetting the rest of my life."

—Democratic U.S. Rep. Nick Lampson of Texas, in a November 2004 interview with the *Dallas Morning News*, on his defeat as a result of controversial redistricting in his home state of Texas. Lampson was not alone; six other Texas Democrats lost their seats as a result of the plan orchestrated with the guidance of U.S. House Majority Leader Tom DeLay, Republican of Texas. The new district lines placed the incumbent Democrats—many of whom were conservative—in Republican-leaning districts, and they lost in part because of the letter that followed their name: D.

You can do something about it, though. It isn't hopeless. Different states have different rules. Depending on what state you live in, the redistricting map for both the congressional and legislative (meaning state boundaries) is open to debate at a number of public hearings across the state. Here, members of a commission with the sole responsibility of redrawing the lines listen to the concerns of the citizens. They travel around the state and hear from concerned citizens what they want. Some minority citizens might want to see an increase in their representation or would prefer to have the lines drawn so that they can have a different representative.

Even if you don't like the plan that your commission approves, in most states the legislature has the final authority to approve the plan by the governor or the commission. Lobby your delegate or state senator to vote the way you want. Remind them that they will have to pay the price in the voting booths come the next election if they forget to pay attention to your needs.

Unequal Districts

From the beginning of time, the process of drawing boundaries for districts has been primarily political. When the lines of a district have been drawn so that they overwhelmingly favor one group at the expense of another, malapportionment occurs. While the Constitution requires that the lines of congressional districts be redrawn every 10 years to reflect the changing demographics of states, there are no guidelines to reflect the changing demographics within a state.

As America has grown over the years, more people have moved into urban areas. Unfortunately, these changes were not reflected in the drawing of congressional lines. In some instances, one district had less than 200,000 people, while another in the same state had more than a million. This allowed for disproportionate representation for rural voters at the expense of urban voters.

In the 1960s, this changed. In a series of court decisions, most notably *Wesberry v. Sanders* in 1964, the Supreme Court ruled that district lines must be drawn so that each contains roughly the same number of people. *Wesberry v. Sanders* revolved around the citizens of the Fifth District in Georgia and their representation. After redistricting, the district contained twice as many voters as the other districts around the state. A group of citizens filed a class action suit to stop future elections until the district lines were redrawn with equitable representation. The district court refused, saying the issue was a political one, not a judicial one.

The citizens took their case to the Supreme Court. In a 7–2 verdict, the court ruled that the states were responsible for fair and equitable representation for all citizens. The vote of one person in Congress should not be worth more than that of anyone else, the court said, with the aim of political equality. If legislators make a "good-faith effort" to do this, the lines will likely withstand a court challenge.

 On the Record

> "While it may not be possible to draw congressional districts with mathematical precision, that is no excuse for ignoring our Constitution's plain objective of making equal representation for equal numbers of people the fundamental goal for the House of Representatives. That is the high standard of justice and common sense which the Founders set for us ...."
>
> —Justice Hugo Black, in the majority opinion of the Supreme Court in *Wesberry v. Sanders*, 1964

Unusual Boundaries

While malapportionment has been addressed, the issue of bizarre land lines continues. The party in power in a state usually draws the district lines to its favor. In Republican-leaning states such as Florida, the GOP hopes to pick up seats. But this pick-up will be balanced with Democratic pick-ups in states such as California.

Still, when the lines are drawn, legislators have to be careful that they are not charged with *gerrymandering*. The goal of gerrymandering is to get as many seats as possible for one party at the expense of another. This goal is achieved in two ways. The first way is to clump all the registered voters of the minority party into an odd-shaped district so that their influence in the other districts is limited. This might enable the minority party to get one or two seats out of a state in which it otherwise may have gotten more. By joining all the minority voters into one district, the other districts become safe for the majority party.

Inside the Beltway

The name **gerrymander** comes from maneuvers that Massachusetts Democrats pulled in 1812 to secure more representation for themselves over their political rivals, the Federalists. That year, lawmakers from the state, most of whom were Democrats, passed a bill that strengthened the Democratic party. It created odd-shaped districts to ensure Democratic victory. One of the odd-shaped districts looked similar to a salamander. When one Federalist saw the map and made this observation, another piped up that it instead looked like a gerrymander, after Gov. Elbridge Gerry, who had signed the bill. The name stuck. The first "gerrymander" was considered a huge success. Despite receiving only 1,000 more votes than the rival Federalists, the Democrats were able to elect 29 state senators compared to 11 for the Federalists.

The other way to go about gerrymandering involves the exact opposite strategy. Instead of giving the minority party something, the majority party works to ensure that it does not get anything. This is done by spreading out the minority party voters through as many districts as possible, to ensure that their power is diluted.

Gerrymandering is totally unfair. No one will argue against this point. If you live in a state that is overwhelmingly controlled by one party, of course the voters from the other party will be disenfranchised. This is not something the framers had in mind, but little can be done to prevent it. Should legislation state that all River Valley residents must live in the same district? Or should urban and rural voters never be placed in the same jurisdiction? Of course not. But there is no easy answer, and it is something that commissions, judges, and legislatures have grappled with for years, with no clear-cut solutions in sight. Sure, the minority party will fight when it believes that its representation is limited, but the fight is usually long, bitter, and expensive.

The Least You Need to Know

- The Constitution stipulates that a census of the United States' population is to be taken once every 10 years.

- The Bureau of the Census, a division of the Department of Commerce, is the entity responsible for conducting the census.

- States use census figures to draw district lines for congressional and state legislative boundaries.

- The reapportionment process is almost always political, yet the results affect everyone.

- Gerrymandering, or the uneven distribution of voters created to give one party greater influence in a certain area, is an old and unfair practice that still takes place today.

Chapter 25

Another House, Another Senate, and What They Do for You

In This Chapter

◆ Lawmaking at the state level

◆ One house or two?

◆ Powers of the state legislature

◆ Where state money goes

Just as Washington, D.C., is the capital of the United States and all laws are made in the Congress, each state has a capital and a legislature where its laws are passed. Each state has a constitution, which stipulates the powers of the legislature. Any power that is not specifically granted to another entity in the state or that is not outlined in the U.S. Constitution is thereby granted to the state legislature.

Many similarities exist between your state government and the federal government. You will learn more about them in this chapter.

State Legislatures and Constitutions

Legislatures played a prominent role in colonial times and continue to do so today. When the early colonies and the states started writing constitutions, the legislature was an outlet where the local leaders could come together and voice their opinions. Over the course of American history, legislatures have varied in their degree of relevance and importance in society. Some legislatures are very important, while others have gone through periods of relative obscurity.

The statehouse, where the legislature meets, is in the state capital. Unlike the U.S. Congress, what goes on in a statehouse is often not very exciting. Legislators elected to the statehouse spend most of their time debating issues that, while important to the daily lives of some people, are quite possibly irrelevant in the lives of many others. How often do you think about the width of your sewer system pipes or the amount of space between a new monument and the street? If you're like most people, not very often. For state legislators, however, this is a part of the job.

On the Record

"I arrived at our new marble Capitol expecting to spend most of my time considering momentous issues—Social Security, taxes, conservation, civil liberties. Instead we devoted long hours to the discussion of regulations for labeling eggs. We have argued about the alignment of irrigation ditches, the speed of motorboats on mountain lakes, the salaries of the justices of the peace, and whether or not barbers and beauty parlor attendants should be high school graduates. For two days we wrangled about a bill specifying the proper scales for weighing logs and lumber ...."

—Oregon legislator Richard L. Neuberger, on his experience after he was first elected in 1941, from *American Government: The Republic in Action*, 1986

Inside the Beltway

A **bicameral** legislature is composed of two chambers. **Unicameral** legislatures have just one.

All 50 states have a legislature, and 49 of them are *bicameral*. Only Nebraska has a *unicameral* legislature. Like their big brother in Washington, the state legislatures have an upper house and a lower house. The upper house is referred to as the Senate. Depending on the state, the lower house is known by a variety of names, including House of Representatives, House of Delegates, or General Assembly.

The People Who Serve

The majority of people who serve in the state legislature do so on a part-time basis. The salary for a state legislator is small, and often the legislative session runs for only a few months out of the year. Because the salaries are based on part-time work, and because the sessions are not conducted on a full-time basis, there is a high rate of turnover for state representatives. Many who choose to serve do so for one term and then return to their private-sector jobs. It is difficult to afford living on a part-time salary, and few people can afford to take three or six months off each year and then return to their other lives.

In another similarity to the U.S. Congress, most states have a rule stating how old a person must be to serve in the state legislature, with the average age being 21. If you want to get an early start on a political career, entering the state legislature is the way to go. For many congressmen, governors, and senators, the formative years of their political experience were developed in a statehouse.

In the bicameral legislative setup, the upper house has fewer members. Often these senators represent an entire area of a state that might simultaneously be represented by two or more delegates from the lower house. As with their counterpart in the U.S. Congress, state senates usually are more refined and reserved than the people's house. The lower houses typically have more members, and there is a much more collegial atmosphere among them.

We Hold These Truths

Over the years, several states have considered making their legislatures unicameral instead of bicameral institutions. Proponents of the change argue that the Congress in Washington, D.C., represents a confederation of states, which explains why there are two houses; in a state capital, however, only one state is involved, so only one house should be sufficient. Opponents of this argument say that just as the U.S. Congress is a group of diverse states coming together, a state legislature brings together a group of diverse counties. Different parts of a state, particularly a large one, have different needs, they say, so the two-house structure is better.

Many people get involved in state government because they really do care about the size of parking lots or the number of trees in their backyard. They are community activists who want to make a difference or improve a given situation. While most who serve in state legislatures are lawyers, there are also a large number of teachers, bankers, and engineers, as well as a growing number of doctors. Unlike the U.S. Senate Majority Leader and the Speaker of the House, who cannot go out in public in their home states without being instantly recognized, these people are average citizens whom you can see in your grocery store or at the local mall. Chances are, they'd be flattered if you said that you recognized them. And if you said you wanted to work on a given issue, they likely would take a keen interest in helping you.

We Hold These Truths

At the state level, grass-roots organization is key, in large part because of the accessibility of local legislators. Here's a test: Look up your U.S. senator's home number. Chances are, it is not listed. But if you look up your state senator, more often than not his or her number *is* listed. The address might be blocked for security reasons, but legislators often keep their numbers public so that citizens can get in touch with them if they want to.

The size of state legislatures varies from state to state. Some states, such as New Hampshire, have a relatively large assembly, with more than 400 members representing a state whose population is roughly 1.25 million. The flip side is larger states with greater populations and less representation, such as Nevada, which has 60 members for a population of roughly 2.3 million. When a state legislature exercises its right to establish new laws or amend older ones, it is acting in a legislative manner. This can be done in a wide range of areas, including education, transportation, public health, and welfare. The state legislature also has the power to raise and lower taxes.

The states also have different constitutions. These do not outweigh the federal constitution in terms of power, but instead they establish the rules for the state. Like the U.S. Constitution, state constitutions have been amended over time. To change a state constitution, a constitutional convention must be called.

In all but seven states, the legislatures have the power, with the advice and consent of the people, to call a constitutional convention. These conventions are similar to national conventions. Delegates are selected, and once the work of the delegates is completed, the voters decide whether to approve the new document.

The leadership setup for the House and the Senate in most state legislatures is similar to that of the House and the Senate in the U.S. Congress, as detailed in Chapter 9 and Chapter 10. In the House, the Speaker is the most powerful member and comes from the majority party. There are also majority and minority leaders, as well as majority and minority whips for the House. On the Senate side is a president, who wields enormous influence, and majority and minority leaders.

Powers of the State Legislature

Two important legislative powers of the legislature include the police powers and the power of the purse.

Police Powers

While it is not written anywhere in state constitutions or in the U.S. Constitution, the state legislatures effectively have the ability to maintain civility in the state. They are ultimately responsible for the health, safety, morals, and welfare of the people who live within their borders.

On the surface, this might appear to just be law enforcement, but in reality it goes much deeper than that. Civil rights for homosexuals are guaranteed through the actions of some state legislatures. Some state legislatures have strongly considered the rights of their citizens to use marijuana for medicinal purposes, while others have okayed assisted suicide for someone dying as the result of a terminal disease. Everything from affirmative action to state holidays to the contractors building a bridge in the state is fair game for debate within the state legislature. If you turn on C-SPAN, chances are good that you will not see the same sort of debate on the floor of the U.S. Senate.

> **We Hold These Truths**
>
> California is the only state that requires a super-majority—that is, a two-thirds vote—in its Assembly and Senate to pass a budget, without exception.

Power of the Purse

The power of the purse is fairly obvious. Without approval from the state legislature, the governor—or anyone else, for that matter—cannot spend money.

The procedure for passing legislation in state legislatures is also similar to that of the U.S. Congress. Legislators introduce legislation that they feel is important to their communities. Community newspapers are more likely to cover these proposals than big dailies, but with many small communities depending on the weeklies for news, the word eventually gets out. Legislators become fast friends with their colleagues—while in session, they spend more time with them than with their own families—and lobbying begins.

State Spending

When the governor of your state announces on television that the budget for the coming year is $3 billion, what exactly does that mean? Where does he or she plan to spend the money? Your state government works to improve the daily lives of its citizens in numerous areas. Some of the more notable ones are mentioned here. While the federal government offers assistance for all of these programs, the state is ultimately responsible for a large portion of their financing.

Education

This is the largest item in every state budget. Roughly one third of all money allocated by the states goes toward improving education. The reason for this is simple: Who will openly oppose education spending? What state senator will stand up and say that he thinks education is not that important? No one who wants to get re-elected, at least.

Most of the funds that the state government allocates for education spending go toward colleges and universities. Tuition for state schools, such as Michigan State, UCLA, Morgan State (MD), and the University of Rhode Island, is considerably lower than that of private schools. This is because the state sponsors the schools and taxpayer money goes toward the needs of each school. For this reason, tuition for out-of-state students is considerably higher than for in-state students.

> **We Hold These Truths**
>
> The University of Georgia was the first state-sponsored school. It was chartered by the state legislature in 1785.

Tuition at state schools is notoriously less expensive than their private counterparts. State schools are viewed by many to be a relatively (note the word *relatively*) inexpensive way to receive a quality education. But what if you want to go to a well-known state school such as the University of Wisconsin or the University of North Carolina and you are not a resident? The answer is that you are going to have to come up with the dough. Annual out-of-state tuition rates can be four and even five times what state residents pay.

Why is there such a difference between in-state and out-of-state tuition? Because state residents want the majority of their tax dollars to go toward educating their own. While the responsibility for operating your local elementary and secondary schools is left primarily up to your county and town governments (you'll read more about this in Chapter 26), the state government—and, therefore, the state legislature—often plays an important supervisory role. For example, the state legislature can determine how many days a year the schools must meet. It can also establish a set of guidelines each school must follow in order to graduate students. These guidelines can be in the form of statewide tests or can mandate a particular curriculum. While the state does set these guidelines, it is traditionally the local government's responsibility to see that they are implemented.

Education spending can be a thorny issue at times. Some people who do not have children object to having taxpayer dollars go toward a program they are not using. Another debate centers on the use of state money to provide anything, even if it is transportation or secular books, to any student attending a private or religious school. Often these issues are settled in the courts.

Highways and Byways

Another of the state's main responsibilities is the construction and maintenance of roads. While this is smaller in comparison to the size of education allotment—transportation is about 10 percent—few people do not use roads at some point during the day. What does it mean to maintain the roads? Well, if you live in Buffalo, New York, it means getting the snow off the roads as soon as possible. In Seattle, it means installing and maintaining reflectors and other devices so drivers can see where they're going in the rain and fog. These are just weather-related examples. But maintenance goes beyond Mother Nature. Urban areas that are experiencing rapid growth, such as San Francisco, need more roads to get people to and from their jobs, families, and livelihood. It is the state's responsibility to help free up congestion so that commuters can get in and out of a city and work in a timely fashion.

It is not just the construction of these roads that is the state's responsibility. The states also set minimum and maximum driving speeds for the highways, as well as other driving laws and safety standards, such as mandatory use of a seat belt.

Finally, and perhaps most obvious to teenagers, the state is responsible for administering driving tests and driver's licenses. Your local department of motor vehicles has the course, the computer test, and sometimes even the schools that help give licenses to new drivers. The driving age in the states varies. Check with your local DMV to find out what the rules are, or just ask a typical high school sophomore—chances are, they know!

Public Health and Welfare

Approximately one third, and sometimes even more, of all state budgets go toward administering health and welfare benefits. Welfare benefits are offered to those who have been laid off work or who cannot find work. They offer cash benefits as well as counseling and other services to those in need. In 1997, Congress passed and President Bill Clinton signed the Welfare-to-Work bill. This legislation said a person can't receive welfare benefits for more than five years. Its results have been mixed, but for the first time in American history many people are finding and keeping jobs with the help of the states.

State health agencies administer a wide range of programs to promote personal and environmental health. The states operate more than 500 hospitals around the country. Often these hospitals are run in conjunction with a state-sponsored medical university. With this cooperation, the students receive practical training and the hospitals can administer basic health benefits to those in need.

Immunization, child health care, and control of communicable diseases fall under the jurisdiction of the state. The state must also regulate medical practices. All doctors, dentists, and nurses must be licensed by the state they want to practice in. Hospitals and nursing homes must do the same.

In recent years, environmental health has become a concern of the states as well. People have been encouraged to keep their communities cleaner in order to decrease the likelihood of disease. States also have sponsored cleanups of polluted shorelines and forests so that wildlife is not threatened.

Conservation

The United States is a huge country. If you look at some state maps, such as New Hampshire, New York, Wyoming, Montana, and most certainly Alaska, you will see that vast amounts of land are open and not populated. Some of this land has been federally protected. Over the last 100 years, states have taken a growing role in making sure that land is set aside for conservation purposes. While this often puts them at odds with developers, the end result is beautiful, pristine wild areas for all to enjoy.

State parks systems across the country have worked to preserve millions of acres of unspoiled land.

Citizens can work together with their state (and federal) government to preserve land. As an example, in March 2002, more than 170,000 acres of land in Northern New Hampshire were sold. The price tag: $42–44 million. The financers: state and federal governments, and about $8 million from a coalition of state residents who wanted to preserve the land from developers. The land will still be available for hunting, fishing, and logging, but it will have state protection. As a result of the efforts of the state and the citizens, there will be no large shopping malls or exclusive clubs in this region north of the White Mountains.

> **We Hold These Truths**
>
> Florida was the first state (in 1935) to appropriate funds for the use of preserving land. Since that time, more than 200,000 acres have been set aside in that state alone.

If you hunt or fish, you are well aware of the state's interest in preserving wildlife. States impose deer seasons and certain times and days when a person can fish. If there is concern over dwindling populations of a certain species in a region, a state can also impose a moratorium on catching or hunting that particular fish or animal. The reverse is true, too: If there are too many deer or bears, a state may call for an expanded hunting season to protect area residents.

The state legislature can also enact some laws that you might not even realize pertain to conservation, such as the use of motor vehicles in certain areas, for fear of noise or ecological pollution.

Law Enforcement and Corrections

All 50 states have a police system to maintain law and order. The first police operation in a state was the Texas Rangers, established in 1835, when the territory was still a republic. In 1903, Connecticut became the first state to have a regular police department. It might seem surprising that it took so long to establish state police departments, but remember that the automobile (a staple in all police departments, state and local) was not invented until the late nineteenth century—in many ways, there was no need for a state police department.

State police departments vary in authority from state to state. In most states, they are responsible for enforcing the laws outside major cities. They also keep a central file with fingerprints, prisoner histories, and crime lab information that can be utilized at a moment's notice.

The states all have their own corrections systems as well, including juvenile detention centers.

The Least You Need to Know

♦ Any power that is not specifically granted to another state entity, or is not outlined in the U.S. Constitution, is thereby granted to the state legislatures.

♦ State legislatures differ little in structure, with the majority having two chambers, but they vary a great deal in size, ranging from 400 members in New Hampshire to 60 in Nevada.

♦ Because salaries for state legislators are low and legislative sessions generally run for just a few months a year, most state legislators hold other jobs.

♦ Like Congress, state legislatures are responsible for setting budgets and allocating funds to state agencies.

Chapter 26

Local Government

In This Chapter

- ◆ How local government is structured
- ◆ County mounties and other local officials
- ◆ Towns versus townships
- ◆ Charter me a city

The United States has more than 80,000 governmental jurisdictions. These include the aforementioned state and federal governments, but that only totals 51. When you factor in counties, municipalities, townships, school districts, and a variety of other jurisdictions, the total is a staggering 82,688.

In this chapter, you read about the different types of local governments and learn how you can take part in their actions to make a difference.

Counties

Throughout the country, the 50 states are divided into more than 3,000 counties. Counties have always been a part of American culture and government. It was only after World War I, however, with cars, electricity, and other modern conveniences, that suburbs came into existence and the real purpose of counties began to be seen and utilized. Thirty years later, after World War II, with the baby boom generation in full swing and suburbia becoming a household word, changes at the state government level began to affect how counties did their jobs. In the last 50 years, counties have begun to receive more autonomy and power from their state legislatures and are now providing even more services to their citizens than in past years.

The main function of counties is to administer the rules of state governments. Counties must abide by state rules and, when applicable, can also enact their own legislation. How influential a county government is rests predominantly on whether it is an *incorporated* or *unincorporated* area. Rural counties, which are always unincorporated, are responsible for building and maintaining local roads. They also assess the value of property and collect taxes. When a new baby is born, they issue the birth certificate, and when it comes time to vote, they open the polls. In urban counties, the responsibilities for these functions are often shared with the city governments.

The county seat is the town in the county where all the government business takes place. The courthouse is located here, and most of the business and social activities of the county take place here as well.

> **We Hold These Truths**
>
> Forty-eight states have county jurisdictions. Rhode Island and Connecticut are the only ones that do not. In Louisiana, the counties are known as parishes, and in Alaska they are referred to as boroughs.

> **Inside the Beltway**
>
> The process that a city goes through that allows it to become a legal body that can administer laws is known as **incorporation**. When a city is incorporated, it has boundaries and has the ability to govern itself, depending on the powers granted by the state constitution. If a region is outside the boundaries of this area, it is **unincorporated**.

County Duties

For the most part, counties perform duties delegated to them by the state government. These duties include but are not limited to property assessment, vital statistics, maintenance of rural roads, and poverty relief.

County government can take several forms:

◆ **Commission** In a commission government, an elected commission of a board of supervisors mutually exercises the legislative and executive powers. The legislative authority enacts regulations and adopts budgets, while the executive delineates the policies and appoints county employees.

◆ **Commission-administrator**   With a commission-administrator form of government, the county board of commissioners selects an administrator who serves at its pleasure. The amount of power given to this administrator varies. He or she could be nothing more than a figurehead. At the same time, this person could be given a broad range of powers, including the ability to hire and fire those in charge of various departments, as well as assemble a budget.

◆ **Council-administrator**   Finally, with the council-administrator form of government, a county executive is the chief administrator in this locality. The county executive, who is elected by the county at large, has the ability to veto legislation passed by the county council. He or she also can hire and fire department administrators.

Demands on local county administrators are growing. Over the last 10 years, jobs that were traditionally completed by the federal and state government are now being handed down to the counties. For example, on September 11, 2001, when tragedy struck New York, Virginia, and Pennsylvania, the county (and, in the case of New York, city) fire and police departments were the first to arrive on the scenes. Federal operators later joined these county agencies, but dialing 911 doesn't get the U.S. Department of Justice; it's the local police department that receives the call.

On the Record

"When that plane crashed into the Pentagon, it was the local fire department, not the federal, and the local police department, not the federal, that were first on the scene."
—Prince George's County (Maryland) Executive Wayne Curry, whose jurisdiction is across the river from the Pentagon, on the demands of local emergency personnel in the event of a crisis. Interview with *The Washington Times*, January 25, 2002.

The structure of county government varies from state to state, but there are many common themes. The county board is administered by a group of elected officials. Depending on where you live, this board is known by a variety of names, including the board of commissioners, the board of supervisors, the fiscal court, the county board, and even the police jury. Elected boards also vary in size; some are as small as 3 members, while others are as large as 80.

Most county boards are small, averaging fewer than a dozen members. These individuals are known as the county commissioners. Terms on the county commission are usually four years in length, and pay for this position is minimal. Members of the larger county boards are known as the county supervisors. These people are elected from smaller subsections of the county, called townships. Each supervisor is usually an officer in the township as well. The powers of these county boards are both legislative and executive. The boards have the ability to levy taxes (who doesn't?) as well as appropriate funds for the jurisdiction. Like their state counterparts, they, too, administer programs for the health and well-being of their citizens.

We Hold These Truths

It is the responsibility of counties to administer the education needs of the state. Sometimes this can get counties in hot water. In 2001, the Supreme Court ruled that Milford Central School District in New York was violating the First Amendment rights of students who wanted to partake in a religious-themed club after school. The district had said that the Good News Club, a national organization with chapters across the country and whose message is that Jesus Christ is the savior, could not use school facilities. The court ruled that by not allowing the club but allowing other clubs to use the facilities after school, the school district was violating the rights of the students and the organization to free speech.

Other County Officials

In addition to the county board members and the county executive/commissioner (or whatever his or her title is in your area), several other elected officials in the counties have important positions:

♦ **Sheriff**   The sheriff is responsible for police protection in the unincorporated areas of the county. He or she also maintains the jail and is responsible for summoning jurors and enforcing court dates. In some states, the sheriff also serves as the tax collector, process server, or collector of judgments!

♦ **County attorney**   The attorney responsible for the legal needs of the county can go by several different names, including the district attorney, the county attorney, the state's attorney, and the prosecutor. This person is the lead lawyer for the county in all civil suits against the jurisdiction. He or she also conducts criminal investigations and prosecutes those who break the law.

♦ **County clerk**   The county clerk is responsible for registering deeds to homes, as well as registering all births, deaths, marriages, divorces, and adoptions. This person also oversees elections and may issue licenses.

◆ **County assessor**   The assessor is responsible for determining the value of your home for tax purposes.

◆ **County treasurer**   The county treasurer collects county funds.

Other elected officials at the county level include the auditor, who keeps track of the financial records of the county and the tax rolls, and approves expenditures; and the coroner, who investigates deaths when a physician is not available. Finally, the county superintendent of schools oversees the public schools, both elementary and secondary, in your area. This is the person who decides whether it is a snow day.

Some people believe that county governments are not conducive to real change and democracy. They point to four problems. First, many people are unaware that a county government exists, much less how it affects their lives. Second, with so many different officials, the government structure is fractionalized and confusing. If you know you have a county government, you might not know whom you have to meet with to solve your problem. In a similar vein, when you go to vote, the list of whom you can vote for is often so long that the names mean nothing and the job titles likely seem unclear.

These problems, however, have not stopped citizens from taking a stand when they are opposed to development in their area. *NIMBY* has become an everyday expression when discussing local government issues. Short for "not in my back yard," NIMBY is now used to describe any number of local civic-minded groups that come together to oppose development in their area. Whether it is opposition to construction of a new electrical tower or an extension of a local highway, NIMBY advocates can and do make a difference in their county governments.

Inside the Beltway

"Not in my back yard," or **NIMBY**, has come to stand for resistance to projects that directly affect the people who live near them.

Towns and Townships

While county governments are important in some regions of the country, town governments play a critical role in others, with New England being a prime example. Except for the areas immediately surrounding an incorporated area, a town includes one or more villages and the surrounding countryside. The town provides most of the same services that cities and counties do in other jurisdictions.

A town meeting is the form of government most commonly used in New England towns, and it is the modern version of direct democracy that the first settlers incorporated into their own daily lives. These meetings are typically held once a year and are open to all qualified voters. At these meetings, the voters sign off on a budget, decide on taxes, and pass new laws. A town clerk, a tax collector, a constable, a road commission, and even a school board are all elected here. Voters also elect a board of advisors, known as the selectmen—usually three to five people—to manage the day-to-day affairs of the town between the meetings.

In twenty-first-century America, however, few problems can be resolved in just one day, and few people have the time or the energy to devote to an event such as the town meeting. In the larger towns of New England, delegates are selected by the people to attend the town meeting on their behalf. And the selectmen, whose original job was just to maintain the town in the event of catastrophe, now make many of the decisions on behalf of the townspeople.

In 16 states, mostly ranging from the Midwest to New York, some counties are divided into townships. In most cases, these townships were the original units measured for the purpose of surveying the land. The average size of the townships is 6 square miles. Some townships hold meetings every year to keep current and conduct business. All of these townships have elected board members. Other members of the council include a supervisor, a clerk, an assessor, a treasurer, and a justice of the peace.

You are probably wondering, what exactly is the difference between a town and a township? One big difference is that a township does not include villages. Any village that falls within the area of a township has its own form of government. Township functions are typically the same as those of a county. A township is responsible for the roads and the weeds, as well as local law enforcement. Like many aspects of Americana, townships are a dying breed. Their responsibilities have essentially been transferred to counties.

Special Districts

As if government could get any more fractionalized, there is another jurisdiction known as the *special district*, which can be created for fire prevention or sewer care in regions that are sparsely populated and need these services. These districts are also created to help serve airports and assist with conservation, irrigation, and even mosquito or locust control. Special districts are established under state law and are governed by small elected boards. They have the power to impose taxes to pay for the services they provide.

The most common type of a special district is a school district. Can you guess when the first local ordinance was passed to require towns to provide education to children? It was 1647 in Massachusetts. Just over 200 years later, mandatory education became standard in the states. It was New York, however, that first established school districts in 1812 to define where students should attend classes.

Inside the Beltway

A **special district** is created to address a single problem or a small group of problems that affect people living in the same region, regardless of boundary lines.

Today, in states (about half) that do not administer their schools through the cities or counties, school districts watch over the educational needs of the citizens. School districts come in all shapes and sizes. Furthermore, they do not have to follow the same lines as some counties or cities. In an effort to centralize school districts and to consolidate powers, the number of school districts across the country has decreased in the last 50 years. At one point, there were more than 100,000; now there are approximately 15,000.

An elected school board generally administers school districts. This board makes the policy decisions for the jurisdiction and also appoints a superintendent to administer the system. Those that operate under state laws also have the ability to tax, to borrow money, and to build new schools.

In January 2002, President George W. Bush signed legislation that some consider the greatest reform in public education in more than 30 years. The measure was an overhaul of the 1965 Federal Elementary and Secondary Education Act. The 2002 law, known as "No Child Left Behind," established numerous reforms, including yearly testing and increased accountability, as well as greater flexibility for local governments in spending some federal funds.

Cities, Small and Large

There are big cities, such as New York, Los Angeles, and Chicago, and then there are smaller cities, such as Providence, Baltimore, Cleveland, and San Diego. What do all these cities have in common? Well, first and foremost, these *municipalities* are the most important form of local government in the country.

Inside the Beltway

Municipalities are cities or towns with local self-government.

When the nation was born, most people lived out in the rural areas, the backwoods. Today the opposite is true, with more than 75 percent of all Americans living near a metropolitan area. A central city is defined as an area that has at least 50,000 people residing inside its borders. Throw in an additional 50,000 (or 25,000, if you live in the New England states) in the surrounding areas, and you have a metropolitan area. Usually these areas are clumped together by the term "greater"—for example, the Greater Atlanta area.

The term "city" itself can mean a wide variety of things, depending on what state you live in. In some states, a city is any municipality, no matter how large or small. In other states, larger municipalities are called cities, while smaller ones are villages, boroughs, or towns. Originally, because cities were few and far between—and before counties or other jurisdictions came into play—they received most of their powers from the state legislatures. Over time, however, conflicts arose and power struggles ensued. Eventually, control of the cities shifted from the legislatures to the cities themselves. State constitutions spell out the powers and privileges of the cities in great detail. The constitutions also discuss incorporation.

One big difference—although there are many—between a city and a county is how both are formed. The citizens form a city as the result of a request. Once it is formed, it has been officially incorporated. Requirements for incorporation are often outlined in the state constitution with standards such as size and population mandates.

We Hold These Truths

While most cities are the result of people gradually coming together and forming a local community, some cities are planned communities, in which developers build homes and businesses and try to convince people to move into the area. One such example is Columbia, Maryland. This small city, nestled off I-95 between Baltimore and Washington, was built in the 1970s and today is a thriving community with people working in both of the major cities to its north and south.

City Charters

For a city to be incorporated, it must have a charter. A charter is equivalent to a constitution. It names the city and outlines the power structure of the government. Elections and the appointment of city officials are outlined in this document, and the responsibilities of the elected officials are delineated as well. But guess what? Just like so many other aspects of local government, these charters are also differentiated. There are four types: special, general, optional, and home rule.

The home rule charter is the most popular way that cities can incorporate themselves. A home rule charter can be done legislatively or through the state's constitution. Which route a city receives its home rule charter from can make a significant difference. A home rule charter that is granted by the constitution is more secure to the city because the rights that it outlines are guaranteed. On the other hand, a home rule charter that is given by the legislature can be revoked at any time. What the legislature giveth, it can taketh away.

A home rule charter allows citizens to elect a group of individuals to draft a city charter, like a constitution. The proposed charter is then put before the voters for their approval or rejection. Also like a constitution, the voters must approve any future amendments that are made to the charter.

Home rule charters can be a double-edged sword. While a home rule charter allows a city to have some power to manage its own affairs, the laws must meet the provisions outlined in the state constitution. When the two are in conflict, the state constitution pulls rank. As mentioned earlier, some problems go beyond arbitrary land lines and can extend past a jurisdictional boundary and create conflict between the state and local governments.

The special charter was the first type of charter granted by state legislatures to the cities. Each time a new city was created, a new charter was granted. In recent years, special charters have been abandoned, however, because they are too time-consuming. Furthermore, any changes that the city might want to make to a special charter must first be approved by the legislature.

A common type of charter today is the general charter. Many states classify a city based on its size and mandate a specific charter based on the size. This is more time-saving than the special charter, and it allows for equal treatment of smaller cities and larger ones. Opponents have one complaint about the general charter: Two cities that are the same size, thus qualifying for the same charter, may have very little else in common.

The final type of charter, one that sprung from the complaints associated with the general charter, is the optional charter. Under an optional charter, cities can choose from several different types of charters allowed by state law. Typically, the city voters must approve whatever choice is made, but this allows citizens to take part in a direct democracy affecting their lives and also permits an individualized approach to the needs of the cities.

Once the charter issue is settled, there is another topic to be grappled with in the formation of a city: its structure. There are three types of city government structure—the mayor-council plan, the council-manager plan, and the commission plan.

Mayor-Council Cities

The most common type of city government structure is the mayor-council plan. This plan is similar in idea and sometimes in practice to the legislative makeup of a state. The voters elect both the mayor and the council. The council is traditionally unicameral and is composed of members from the various neighborhood districts, also known as wards in some jurisdictions, from around the city. Most city councils have fewer than a dozen members. Because the district representatives have the interest of their section at heart, opponents said that the needs of the entire city were ignored. This gave rise to an at-large system as well. In addition to voting for a neighborhood representative, citizens elect an at-large rep (sometimes more than one) to address the needs of the entire city.

The power structure of the mayor-council plan varies from city to city. Some have a strong mayor plan. Under this plan, the mayor has the authority to veto legislation passed by the council and can also hire and fire city administrators as well as prepare a budget. The success of this type of program depends largely on the abilities of the mayor. If the mayor is a strong one with a solid mandate from the voters, he or she can lead the city through great prosperity. If the mayor is weak, however, conflict can arise between the executive and the council, and little gets accomplished.

If the city has a weak mayor, the mayor is nothing more than a figurehead. He or she cannot veto legislation and does not have the ability to hire and fire administrators. Instead, this authority is given to the council. The council also has the authority to budget the city's finances.

Council-Manager Cities

The mayor-council form was the original plan for dealing with city government. Over time, as issues and problems evolved, another form was established: the council-manager plan. This form allows an elected city council to appoint a professional administrator known as the city manager. He or she is responsible for running the day-to-day operations of the city, but the city council has the authority to fire this person. Furthermore, the city council is responsible for city policy.

The city manager serves in a nonpolitical fashion, without regard to party affiliation. A mayor is either elected by the citizens of the city or chosen from the council, but he or she is usually no more than a figurehead. While the council makes policy, the city manager has an influential role over the council and has the ability to hire and fire city employees. He or she also prepares the budget and spends the money appropriated by the council.

The council-manager plan is most popular in the smaller cities because it encourages cooperation and a businesslike mentality of the administrators, ensuring that the needs of the citizens are met. It has been rejected by larger cities, however, because it does not allow for strong political leadership, offers limited representation for special interests and minorities, and has no channels through which bargaining can occur.

Commission Cities

The final plan for the structure of city government is the commission plan. This type of plan was developed as a reform mechanism in the early twentieth century and is in use today in only about 100 cities nationwide.

Under the commission plan, the operations of a city are under the control and watchful eye of a board of commissioners elected by the city voters. These commissioners oversee the city departments and agencies and have legislative and executive authority. A mayor is chosen from the sitting commissioners, but this position is largely ceremonial.

The problems with the commission plan are obvious. With no single authority, there is a lack of leadership and confusion over who is in charge. Over the years, minorities have voiced opposition to this type of government structure because they often find it difficult to elect a single representative to address their needs, and therefore feel shut out of the process.

The Least You Need to Know

- ◆ Counties are one of the oldest and most basic forms of local government in the United States.

- ◆ In some parts of the country, most notably New England, towns provide most of the same services that cities and counties do in other areas.

- ◆ What constitutes a city depends on the state you live in.

- ◆ The commission style of city government, one of the newer forms, is also one of the most ineffective because leadership and authority are split among many individuals instead of resting with one.

Chapter 27

The Power of One

In This Chapter

- Finding your political home
- Understanding party differences
- Getting out the vote
- Speaking out

So now that you know all about the American political structure and your federal, state, and local governments, how do you turn that knowledge into action? Are you a Democrat or a Republican? Do you favor a limited or active government? This chapter helps to explain the differences between the major parties and some of the third parties that are trying to make inroads on the political arena.

This chapter also explains registration, voting, and absentee ballots, as well as how you can get involved to make a difference.

The Major Parties

Twenty-first-century America is divided into two major parties—Democrat and Republican—and they have little in common. The two parties differ with regard to the role of government in matters of taxation, regulation of business, personal rights, and other issues.

Democrats tend to support government programs that directly impact the daily lives of Americans. Social programs such as welfare and Medicare are major issues that Democrats advocate more vocally than Republicans. It isn't that Republicans don't want to help with societal problems—they do. But most prefer letting private companies and individuals make decisions on their own.

We Hold These Truths

Political parties have been a part of American government since its beginning. Although George Washington argued against their formation, two parties were already in place by the time he was elected to his second term. The Federalists were the conservatives, led by John Adams and Alexander Hamilton. Thomas Jefferson headed up the more liberal Democratic-Republicans.

Reviewing arguments between major issues will illustrate this point. Reforming education is one such example. Democrats want a national system in which standards would be the same in New York City as in Bozeman, Montana. They argue that all American students should be treated and viewed equally. Programs geared toward drug prevention, alcohol abuse, and sexual education should be equally administered across the country, Democrats argue, with little difference.

Republicans, on the other hand, argue that the needs of New York City students, who live in an urban environment with incredible diversity and high crime, among many other factors, are very different from the needs of students in Bozeman, Montana. Bozeman is a small rural town with minimal diversity, and hunting is a way of life. Bozeman has crime, but not the same as New York City. Problems such as alcoholism and drug abuse are common, but for different reasons than in New York City; therefore, programs should be administered according to the individual needs of a community, Republicans argue.

In other words, Democrats, in broad terms, believe in greater governmental involvement. In their mind, the government knows what's best. Republicans believe in less governmental control and want to help you help yourself. They believe you know what is best for you, not the government.

Well, broad terms are great, but what does this mean for issues that directly affect you, such as the minimum wage, gun control, and abortion?

Minimum Wage

The Fair Labor Standards Act of 1938 established protections against unfair employment practices of employers. It established a maximum work week of 40 hours, restricted the use of child labor, and instituted a minimum wage for any work.

In 1938, the minimum wage was 25¢ per hour. In 2005, it is $5.15 per hour. To discourage employers from mandating service over the maximum 40 hours, overtime pay is set at time and a half, meaning full-time salary ($5.15) plus half (approximately $2.60). Originally the law protected only workers engaged in interstate or foreign commerce. Over the years, it has been expanded to include nearly all professions.

Democrats are almost always trying to increase the minimum wage, while Republicans are always trying to keep it at its current level—whatever that level may be. Democrats argue that if you increase the minimum wage, you raise the living standards of those on the minimum wage, help keep them out of poverty, and also ensure they are not dependent on any government subsidies.

Republicans argue that if an employer is forced to pay employees more, one of two things will happen: Either the employer will be unable to hire as many employees, thus being forced to let go current staff, or he or she will have to raise prices to help fund the additional payment for the current staff.

Most minimum-wage earners tend to vote Democratic, while most of their employers tend to vote Republican.

Abortion

Under the 1973 *Roe v. Wade* Supreme Court decision, abortion was declared legal, and a constitutional right of American women to have an abortion during the first and second trimester without government interference was granted. This decision, however, didn't end the debate on what many consider the most controversial and divisive issue to face the nation since slavery.

Those who favor abortion call themselves pro-choice, and this group includes most Democrats. They argue that the government shouldn't have the right to tell a woman what to do with her body, and that the decision to terminate a pregnancy should be made between a woman and her doctor. Because they believe this is a private matter, pro-choicers oppose virtually all legislation that in any way infringes on the right of a woman to have an abortion, such as parental notification laws and 24-hour waiting period laws.

Those who are opposed to abortion call themselves pro-life, and this includes most Republicans. They believe that life begins at conception or shortly thereafter and, therefore, that life must be protected. Abortion is murder in their eyes. While most pro-life supporters allow for exceptions in the case of rape and incest, they are opposed to most laws that allow for greater access to abortion.

Few supporters on either side believe that abortion on demand or an outright ban on all abortions will ever come about. Instead, most of the battles in this debate are fought over middle-of-the-road issues, such as the current fight over what abortion opponents call partial-birth abortion. This procedure, a late-term abortion by which the fetus is partially delivered alive and then terminated, is incredibly divisive. Most pro-choice supporters agree the procedure should be illegal, but they support exceptions for the life and health of the woman; most pro-lifers are opposed to any exceptions.

The House and the Senate passed an outright ban on the procedure and President George W. Bush signed it into law. However, the issue is now working its way through the courts and it could be years before a definitive answer is reached on the constitutionality of the procedure.

Gun Control

The Second Amendment to the Constitution says, "A well-regulated Militia, being necessary to the security of a free State, the right of the people to keep and bear Arms, shall not be infringed."

Most Republicans support a narrow interpretation of this amendment, believing that any legislation that limits the availability of guns to free American citizens is a violation of the Second Amendment. Currently more than 20,000 laws are on the books around the country, and they argue that these laws should be sufficient—and should be properly enforced—to curb gun violence.

We Hold These Truths
The National Rifle Association, which is opposed to most laws restricting the use of guns, is considered one of the most influential groups in America. Its endorsement can make or break a candidate. An example: In the 2001 governor's race in Virginia, the NRA withheld an endorsement of Republican Mark Earley because it was satisfied that Democrat Mark Warner would not take away the rights of gun owners to own and use guns. Virginia is an overwhelmingly Republican state, but Warner was able to win by portraying himself as a moderate. Many Republicans quietly argue that if the NRA had put its name behind Earley, he would have won.

Most Democrats support tighter rules concerning gun use. They argue that the Second Amendment was written during a different time and refers only to "militia," not to individual citizens. The United States has an alarming rate of deaths due to gun violence, and Democrats often use tragic school shootings such as the 1999 case at Columbine High School in Colorado to illustrate their point.

This is another hotly contested issue, with lobbies on both sides attempting to persuade members of Congress to vote a certain way.

Other Issues

Note that all the issues previously discussed were preceded by the word *most*. You do not have to take a test to be a member of one party or the other. The following table illustrates several other issues that Democrats and Republicans often disagree on. Remember, however, that these are the general rules—and in politics, there are always exceptions!

Issue	Democrats Usually ...	Republicans Usually ...
Abortion	Support	Oppose
Gay marriage	Support	Oppose
Tax cuts	Oppose	Support
Voluntary prayer in school	Oppose	Support
Gun control	Support	Oppose
Minimum wage hike	Support	Oppose
Amendment banning flag burning	Oppose	Support
Affirmative action	Support	Oppose

Other Parties

Not sure you agree with either the Republicans or the Democrats enough to call yourself one? That's okay. Several nationwide third parties have chapters in most states.

In recent years, the Green Party has had the most influence as a third party. The Green Party is a liberal, people-power-oriented party that has more in common with the Democrats than with the Republicans.

At the core of this party is a belief that grass-roots politics is best and that all politics should be kept in the hands of the common man. Greens argue that big corporations and the wealthy in America have too much control. On both social and fiscal issues, they are on the far left end of the spectrum.

The Libertarian Party could be considered the Republican equivalent to the Green Party. It is more fiscally conservative than the Republican Party, and it believes that the government should have no say in citizens' lives. Libertarians believe that the answer to America's problems include a free-market economy, a dedication to civil and personal liberties, and a foreign policy of nonintervention, peace, and free trade. Unlike the Green Party, however, it is not as large and has not had the effect on elections that the Green Party has.

Still not feeling bonded to one of these parties? That's fine, too. You can always register as an independent, meaning that you are not affiliated with anyone. The only downside is that declaring yourself as an independent might affect your ability to vote in primaries, depending on your state's election laws. Call your local board of elections for more details.

> **We Hold These Truths**
>
> In 2000, Green Party presidential candidate Ralph Nader took enough votes away from Al Gore, the Democratic nominee, to give George W. Bush the election.

If you're still searching and want to be a part of some political party, check out www.politics1.com/parties.htm, which is a virtual bible of American political parties, their views, and websites. If you really want to find something you will like, here is where it would be!

Registration Requirements

So now you know that you want to sign up to be a member of one of the given parties, or you have decided to be an independent. Whatever the case is, you are ready to register and are eager to get your voter's card!

> **We Hold These Truths**
>
> Under most circumstances, a person born in the United States, regardless of his or her parent's origin, is considered an American citizen. If a person immigrates to the United States from another country, that person must take a test to become a citizen.

When the United States was first founded, only white men could vote. Obviously times have changed, and the only requirements for voting in an election are that you must be at least 18 on the day of the election and must be a resident of the state you are registering in. Finally, while it is not formally written in the Constitution, anyone wanting to vote must be an American citizen. Some local jurisdictions, however, including Washington, D.C., have begun considering proposals that would allow legal residents who are not U.S. citizens to vote in local races such as school board and city council. Supporters of such proposals argue that these legal residents pay taxes and are affected by the decisions made, so therefore should have a vote.

Most states require that you register to vote at least 30 days prior to the date of the election. A few states, such as Wisconsin, allow you to register to vote on the day of the election. And North Dakota is in a league of its own: It does not require any voter registration! To find out more information about your specific state, call your state board of elections and ask for specific rules and timelines.

Registering to Vote

The electoral process has come under intense criticism in the past, especially in light of the controversy surrounding the election of 2000. Some criticize the process as too complicated and time-consuming. As a result of the Motor Voter bill, also known as the National Voter Registration Act of 1993, the process has become a little bit easier.

Signed by President Clinton, the act says that people must be given the opportunity to register to vote, if they choose, when they go to apply for a driver's license. The premise is that because most people get a driver's license, the process will be more accessible to ordinary people. Most people who don't vote don't claim that they are apathetic; they say they just did not have the time to register in the first place.

In addition to registering when you get a license, under this bill, the government is required to allow you to have the chance to register when you apply for state or public assistance, whether it is through food stamps, Medicaid, or welfare, and to give you the chance to register at Armed Services recruiting stations. Through the Motor Voter bill, the government has made it very easy for those who want to vote.

Also, several states and jurisdictions have begun to post their registration forms online. Check with your local Board of Elections. Registering to vote could be as easy as downloading a form and mailing it in. How easy is that?

Remember, the Constitution gives you the right to vote, but it also gives you the right *not* to vote. However, if you don't vote, you have no one to blame but yourself for the status of the country or the poor garbage removal in your town!

Election Day

After months of campaigning and an almost endless stream of candidate commercials, the day to go out and vote arrives. Schoolchildren are usually ecstatic for this day because, in many districts, the schools are closed to allow the polls to set up. Other locations for polling include churches and firehouses.

When you registered, you most likely received a voter registration card. This card should state where your polling location is for your district. You can't just go to any polling station; instead, you have to go to the one assigned to you by your local jurisdiction. This way, the government can check off that you voted and ensure that no one votes in your place and that you don't vote twice.

On Election Day, most polls are opened early in the morning and stay open for much of the day. Other than two small communities in the state, which have their own rules, New Hampshire's polls open the latest of any state, at 11 A.M. New York polls are open from 6 A.M. to 9 P.M., the longest of any state. Kentucky, Indiana, and Hawaii's polls close the earliest, at 6 P.M.

On the days preceding an election, your local paper will run reminders that the election is coming up (in addition to a plethora of articles on the last-minute campaigning of the candidates). In the reminders will be the times and sometimes even the places, depending on the size of your precinct.

Different states and even different counties have different methods for voting once you get behind the voting booth. No one can forget the butterfly ballot from the disputed Florida election in 2000, but that is not the only type. Some states have lever-booths, in which you go behind a curtain and pull several levers for the different offices, but your vote is not cast in stone until you pull the big lever at the top (and sometimes even at the bottom), which finalizes everything.

Other states have ballots that are like the childhood game of connect the dots, except it involves connecting arrows. You are given a special type of pen or pencil that can be read from a machine, and then you individually fill in each person you want to vote for.

As a result of the disputed election and the confusion surrounding the ballots in Florida, lawmakers in Congress are attempting to pass election reform. Some of these election reforms call for uniform voting machines and modern equipment.

When you go to vote, you may be asked to present your voter identification card, or you may not. Chances are, you will have to show a license, a passport, or something other than a Blockbuster Card to prove that you are who you say you are. Volunteers check your name off the list and then escort you to the booth. You can ask for assistance at any point during the voting process if you are unsure how to vote, but these volunteers cannot in any way encourage you to support one candidate over another or be seen as anything other than fair and impartial.

Now you are there at your assigned polling place—preparing to vote. No one knows whom you vote for, unless you choose to tell. You can stay in there as long as you like, or you can go in and out in 35 seconds. Sometimes there are long lines for voting; other times it seems as if you are the only person in the entire area who has decided to vote. If you live in some states, while you were walking in you were bombarded with literature from candidates or issue-advocacy groups supporting a certain candidate, but the time has finally come, and X marks the spot. Congratulations, you have taken part in the American system!

Voting Away from Home

What if you will be away from home on the day of the election? Maybe you work in an area far from where you would vote, or maybe you go to school out of state. Maybe you're in the military. Whatever the reason, you can still vote by absentee ballot.

As soon as you find out that you won't be available to go to your polling station on Election Day, call your local board of elections and ask for an absentee ballot application. You will be sent a document with a wide range of reasons for why you can't vote in person on Election Day. You must check the one that applies to you and then sign it saying that you will be away, that no one will vote for you in person, and that you want to receive a ballot in the mail. Then send it back.

About a month before the election, you will receive your ballot in the mail. You have plenty of time to fill it out; as long as it is postmarked by the day of the election, and not a second after the polls closed, your vote will be counted. As the election of 2000 proved, every vote counts, and not just at the presidential level. U.S. Reps. Mike Rogers of Michigan and Mark Kennedy of Minnesota both won their elections in 2000 by fewer than 200 votes, and absentee ballots played a big role in their victories.

Get Involved

You can get involved in an election in many ways to help your candidate or cause win. Most candidates are always looking for volunteers for their campaigns. Volunteering could be something as simple as copying and pasting articles into massive e-mails for supporters to read, or it could mean that you are responsible for driving the candidate all around and ensuring that he or she is not terribly late. (Most candidates and politicians, however, are notoriously at least a half hour late to scheduled functions. The flip side is that they are rarely more than an hour late, but then they stay for only a few minutes.) You can always make signs or place calls reminding people to get out and vote.

On Election Day, you can volunteer to work the polls to convince any last-minute voters to switch to your side. These volunteers do not go into a booth with voters or watch them fill out their ballots. Instead, they stand outside the polling place and hand out pamphlets for last-minute undecided voters to read, in hopes of swaying them to vote for a particular candidate. (Some states do not allow politicking within a certain area outside polling places.)

And you can also be any age. You don't have to even be old enough to vote to help out on a campaign. One of the best ways to get your foot in the door if you're interested in a career in government or public service is to volunteer early for a candidate. If the candidate wins, you might be able to intern in his or her office during school breaks, or you might even get a job once you're out of college!

Inside the Beltway

A **referendum** is a particular law or issue put before voters for a decision. The people then vote either to support a law passed previously or to turn it down. It can also be used to allow for tax increases, among many other issues. Traditionally, a set number of signatures are required to bring an issue to a referendum.

Issue-advocacy groups are always looking for volunteers. There are advocacy groups for just about every issue, from abortion to zoos! All you have to do is find one that espouses a cause that you support, and you're set. Something as simple as being a neighborhood contact for the organization can do wonders for the cause and can raise your profile as well as the profile of the organization.

Some issues, such as the aforementioned abortion or gun control, are national issues with chapter organizations for and against them all across the country. Other issues are more localized. *Referendums* can be held in your city or state on issues such as how to spend county money or where a new jail or school should be constructed.

If your local jurisdiction has decided to build a mass-transit metro system through your backyard, you and your neighbors can join forces to explain to the rest of your community that, while the metro might be a good idea for the region, it does not necessarily need to be built in your backyard. Not in my back yard, or NIMBY, has become a part of the political lexicon in recent years, as neighborhood groups have banded together to successfully oppose the construction of a wide variety of projects proposed for their region.

One of the more notable NIMBY cases in recent years was the work of the citizens of Lake Placid, New York. Lake Placid, home of the 1932 and 1980 Olympics, is a small village in upstate New York (about 45 miles from the Canadian border) that depends on tourism for a great deal of its survival. The citizens, however, are fiercely protective of their way of life and like the fact that things are a bit calmer in this not-so-fast-paced town. When Wal-Mart, one of the nation's largest retailers, wanted to open a store in Lake Placid, the citizens protested, saying that this store would ruin their way of life.

While the battle is ongoing, as of this printing, the citizens of Lake Placid have successfully blocked the permit for Wal-Mart. They argue they have nothing against the store; they just don't want it in their backyard! It's pretty impressive for a small community in rural New York to take on one of the giants of American commercialism and win. This truly shows the power of one!

The Least You Need to Know

- Figuring out how your philosophies align with those of the major political parties is the best way to determine which party to support.

- Exercising your right to vote is one of the best ways to ensure that your voice is heard.

- Volunteering for political campaigns and working with activist groups are two other ways to make your opinions and beliefs heard.

- Every person has the right to be heard and can make a difference.

Glossary

amicus curiae brief   A legal brief submitted to the court by a group with some stake in the outcome of the case being argued.

apportionment   The distribution of funds from appropriations bills to agencies.

appropriation   A measure setting aside public funds for a specific purpose.

articles   Sections of a legal document that deal with particular points.

balancing doctrine   The belief that the rights guaranteed by the First Amendment are no more valuable than other freedoms.

bicameral   A legislature composed of two chambers.

bill of rights   A set of agreed-upon freedoms granted to a people that can never be taken away by their government.

Bill of Rights   The first 10 amendments to the U.S. Constitution.

broad constructionists   Those who interpret the Constitution by applying the intentions of the framers to a changing society.

bully pulpit   The term Teddy Roosevelt used to refer to the power and influence given to him as a holder of public office.

carpetbagger   An outsider whose only interest in coming to a place is to win it as a political seat.

caucus   A group that unites to promote a particular policy or interest.

caucuses   Held when local party officials or delegates gather to vote on behalf of all the registered voters in that state to select the winner.

censure   Expressing official disapproval or condemnation of somebody or something, usually by vote.

charter   A formal written statement describing the rights and responsibilities of a territory or a state and its citizens.

checks and balances   Branches of government keeping watch over each other's powers.

cloture   The only way to stop debate in the Senate without unanimous consent.

delegates   Party loyalists selected by their local parties to represent their states at the national convention.

direct veto   The measure used by the president when nixing a bill while Congress is in session. The president has two options for nixing legislation.

discuss list   A list of potential cases to be heard by the Supreme Court, drawn up by the chief justice.

double jeopardy   Prosecuting someone for the same crime twice, which is prohibited by the Constitution.

due process of law   Usually referred to simply as due process, it guards individual rights from infringement by state or federal governments.

dugouts   Press conferences held by political party leadership to discuss a broad range of topics.

equal protection clause   A constitutional clause stipulating that no state can deny equal protection of the law to any of its citizens.

excise tax   An internal tax levied on the manufacture, sale, or consumption of a commodity within a particular country.

executive clemency   The power to lighten or overturn criminal sentences.

executive privilege   The practice of withholding presidential information from Congress or other entities.

federalism   The ability of both state and federal governments to make their own laws.

filibusters   Delaying or blocking votes on legislation by delivering long speeches.

frank   A mark used by members of Congress instead of postage when sending newsletters or other official materials to their constituents.

franking privilege   Allows members of Congress free postage for official mailings, but prohibits them from using the system for personal mail or for campaign literature.

grandfather clause   A clause in some southern states' constitutions that waived electoral literacy and poll tax requirements for descendants of those who had been allowed to vote before 1867.

grass roots   The power of ordinary people in influencing their political leaders.

hard money   Money raised and spent from individuals, PACs, or party committees for specific political candidates that is subject to strict regulations by the FEC, the IRS, and other entities.

implied powers   Powers assumed by Congress under the Constitution, even if not explicitly stated there.

incorporation   The process a city goes through to become a legal lawmaking body.

independent expenditures   Funds from an outside group donated independently of a campaign to support the candidate.

judicial review   The power given to the federal courts system to declare laws passed by the government or approved by lower courts unconstitutional.

laissez-faire constitutionalism   The idea that the government should take a hands-off approach to business and industry in regard to contracts and legal agreements.

litigant   A person actively involved in a court case. He or she can be either the plaintiff or the defendant.

litmus test   A test in which a single factor determines the outcome.

markup   The phase of the legislative process during which committee and subcommittee members refine a bill through amendments and debates.

municipalities   Cities or towns with local self-government.

narrow constructionists   Those who interpret the Constitution based on the framers' intentions. Also known as strict constructionists.

New Deal, The　Franklin Delano Roosevelt's legislative response to the Great Depression, during which a number of measures were launched and federal agencies were created to help bolster the country's flagging economy.

NIMBY　Acronym for "not in my back yard," which refers to resistance to projects that directly affect the people who live near them.

nonbinding　Legal opinions that do not create legal or moral obligations.

off-year elections　Elections held in years when the president is not up for re-election.

Office of Legislative Counsel　Senate offices composed of attorneys who offer nonpartisan advice and assistance on crafting legislation, resolutions, and amendments. Both the Senate and the House have these offices.

oral arguments　Arguments made before a court that augment briefs already filed by each side.

original jurisdiction　The power to hear and decide on a case for the first time.

PAYGO　Acronym for "pay as you go," which refers to the requirement that any new mandatory spending be deficit-neutral, either through revenue increases or spending cuts elsewhere.

per curiam　Meaning "by the court," this is an unsigned, unanimous opinion delivered by the entire Supreme Court.

plurality　The number of votes the leading candidate obtains over his or her nearest rival.

pocket veto　The measure used by the president to nix a bill after Congress has adjourned and can't override his decision.

political action committees　Organizations designed to raise and spend money in support of candidates or party committees they support.

poll taxes　Fees levied at polling places used to raise money and stop poor people from voting.

pork　From the term pork barrel, the millions of dollars attached to spending bills for individual projects in the home districts of members of Congress.

precedent　A court decision in a previous case whose facts are considered the rule for a current case under review.

primary   Elections in which registered members of political parties choose among candidates in their own party.

prior restraint   Restricting publication or communication of material before it's published or communicated.

pro hac vice   Meaning "for this turn," this is a legal term granting a lawyer temporary admission to the bar for a specific case only.

quid pro quo   Exchanging something of equal value, such as a vote for a financial contribution.

reapportionment   The periodic redistribution of congressional or legislative seats based on changing census figures, as required by the Constitution.

recall   Removing elected officials from office by gathering signatures and calling for a special election.

recess appointments   Appointments authorized by the president when Congress is in recess.

referendum   A particular law or idea put before voters to decide.

revenue   The government's income, from various sources, used to pay for public programs.

roll call votes   Votes during which each member's name is called and recorded.

rules committees   In both the House and the Senate, these committees set the rules and procedures for legislation coming to the floor.

scutage   A fee paid in lieu of military service.

sequestration   A writ ordered by the president that cancels budget resources.

soft money   Money raised and spent by organizations that are not tied directly to a candidate and, therefore, are not subject to many regulations.

special district   A district created to address a single problem or a small group of problems that affect people living in the same region, regardless of boundary lines.

State of the State address   The annual address given by the governor to the legislature, usually at the beginning of the term, outlining the state's priorities.

State of the Union address   The annual speech given by the president to a joint session of Congress, usually in January or February.

states' rights The theory that each state should have the right to interpret federal laws to suit its individual needs.

stay Delaying an execution.

strict construction The interpretation of the Constitution that holds that powers not explicitly mentioned there belong to the people.

suffrage The right to vote. Also known as franchise.

Super Tuesday The second Tuesday in March, when ten states—California, Connecticut, Georgia, Maryland, Massachusetts, Minnesota, New York, Ohio, Rhode Island, and Vermont—hold primaries and caucuses to determine who their nominee is.

swing districts Areas that could support candidates of either party.

term limits Legislation dictating the number of years that elected officials may serve.

unanimous consent Agreements that allow generally routine motions to pass.

unicameral Legislatures composed of just one chamber.

unincorporated Regions located outside of incorporated areas.

veep The slang term often used when referring to the vice president.

writ of certiorari A written order from a higher court agreeing to review the decision of a lower court.

writ of mandamus A measure used to compel a public official to complete an act.

Branches of the Federal Government

The Legislative Branch

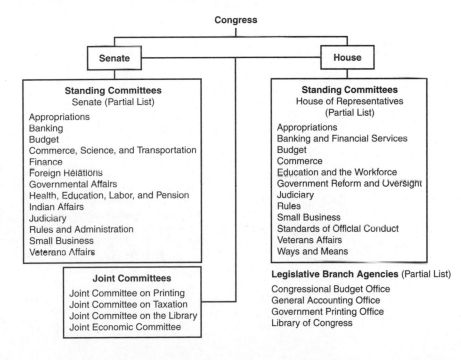

Congress

Senate — House

Standing Committees
Senate (Partial List)

Appropriations
Banking
Budget
Commerce, Science, and Transportation
Finance
Foreign Relations
Governmental Affairs
Health, Education, Labor, and Pension
Indian Affairs
Judiciary
Rules and Administration
Small Business
Veterans Affairs

Standing Committees
House of Representatives
(Partial List)

Appropriations
Banking and Financial Services
Budget
Commerce
Education and the Workforce
Government Reform and Oversight
Judiciary
Rules
Small Business
Standards of Official Conduct
Veterans Affairs
Ways and Means

Joint Committees

Joint Committee on Printing
Joint Committee on Taxation
Joint Committee on the Library
Joint Economic Committee

Legislative Branch Agencies (Partial List)

Congressional Budget Office
General Accounting Office
Government Printing Office
Library of Congress

The Executive Branch

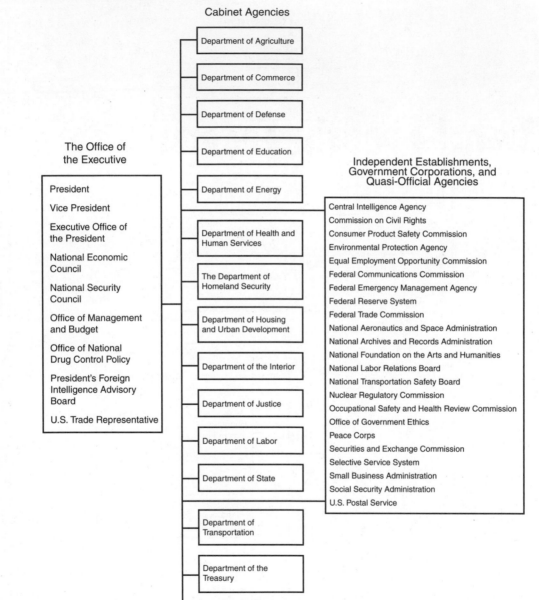

Cabinet Agencies

- Department of Agriculture
- Department of Commerce
- Department of Defense
- Department of Education
- Department of Energy
- Department of Health and Human Services
- The Department of Homeland Security
- Department of Housing and Urban Development
- Department of the Interior
- Department of Justice
- Department of Labor
- Department of State
- Department of Transportation
- Department of the Treasury
- Department of Veterans Affairs

The Office of the Executive

- President
- Vice President
- Executive Office of the President
- National Economic Council
- National Security Council
- Office of Management and Budget
- Office of National Drug Control Policy
- President's Foreign Intelligence Advisory Board
- U.S. Trade Representative

Independent Establishments, Government Corporations, and Quasi-Official Agencies

- Central Intelligence Agency
- Commission on Civil Rights
- Consumer Product Safety Commission
- Environmental Protection Agency
- Equal Employment Opportunity Commission
- Federal Communications Commission
- Federal Emergency Management Agency
- Federal Reserve System
- Federal Trade Commission
- National Aeronautics and Space Administration
- National Archives and Records Administration
- National Foundation on the Arts and Humanities
- National Labor Relations Board
- National Transportation Safety Board
- Nuclear Regulatory Commission
- Occupational Safety and Health Review Commission
- Office of Government Ethics
- Peace Corps
- Securities and Exchange Commission
- Selective Service System
- Small Business Administration
- Social Security Administration
- U.S. Postal Service

The Judicial Branch

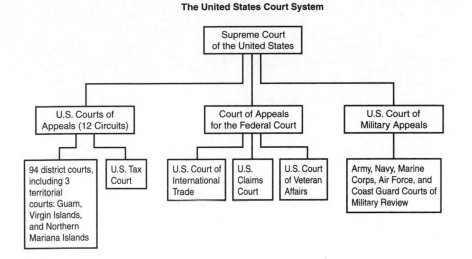

The United States Court System

Supreme Court of the United States

- U.S. Courts of Appeals (12 Circuits)
  - 94 district courts, including 3 territorial courts: Guam, Virgin Islands, and Northern Mariana Islands
  - U.S. Tax Court
- Court of Appeals for the Federal Court
  - U.S. Court of International Trade
  - U.S. Claims Court
  - U.S. Court of Veteran Affairs
- U.S. Court of Military Appeals
  - Army, Navy, Marine Corps, Air Force, and Coast Guard Courts of Military Review

Recap of the 2004 Elections

The 2004 presidential election pitted the incumbent president, Republican George W. Bush, against Democratic candidate Sen. John Kerry of Massachusetts. On the ticket with President Bush was Dick Cheney, his 2000 running mate. Senator Kerry chose former presidential candidate John Edwards, a one-term senator from North Carolina, to share his ticket.

Ralph Nader, who ran as the Green Party candidate in 2000, also threw his hat into the ring for 2004, running as an independent candidate endorsed by the Reform Party.

Both main party candidates campaigned long and hard, and spent more money doing it than any other candidates before them (Bush raised $273 million, compared with Kerry's $249 million), despite new laws designed to limit the influence of political donations.

Senator Kerry had to first best nine other possible candidates in a series of primaries across the United States. While George W. Bush ran for his party's nomination unopposed, he was by no means a shoe-in, with public sentiment against the war in Iraq and concerns about the economy mounting throughout the election season.

Concerns such as these drove the highest voter turnout since the 1968 presidential election. Interestingly, however, exit polls revealed that voters put a premium not on terrorism or the economy, but on "moral values."

Republicans not only retained control of the House, Senate, and the White House, but increased their margins of control. And unlike the debacle that was the 2000 presidential election, a clear winner was established within hours of the last poll closing.

The Race to the White House

While George W. Bush ran unopposed for his party's nomination, 10 individuals vied for the Democratic spot, among them a former general, a religious leader, a doctor, and a trial attorney.

Those competing for the chance to occupy the top seat in the land included …

- ◆ Carol Moseley Braun. The only female presidential hopeful, Braun was the first African American woman to win election to the U.S. Senate, doing so in 1992. She represented Illinois for one controversy-filled term, lost her bid for re-election, and was subsequently appointed ambassador to New Zealand by President Clinton. Largely overlooked by the media and contributors, she lagged behind the other candidates from the start and withdrew from the race early in the primary season.

- ◆ Wesley Clark. Clark, a retired general, was the supreme commander of NATO during the 1999 war in Kosovo and brought a distinguished 34-year military record to the table. While a latecomer to the race, announcing his candidacy more than a year after the rest of the challengers, he quickly gained support. However, his statement regarding how he might have voted on the 2002 congressional resolution that authorized the war on Iraq (he said he "probably" would have voted for it) took away any viable chance for the nomination.

- ◆ Howard Dean. Dean, a medical doctor and former governor of Vermont, was an early front-runner and garnered substantial attention as the first candidate to mount a successful fundraising campaign on the Internet. However, concerns that he leaned too far to the left, his sometimes unbridled, often abrasive manner, and several disastrous appearances before the media ultimately undermined his bid for the nomination.

- ◆ John Edwards. The young (49 when he began his campaign), charismatic senator from North Carolina had served only one term in the Senate (and chose to forgo a second term so he could focus all of his attention on the presidential race) before deciding to take a stab at the presidency. Smart and ambitious, the trial lawyer's ability to connect with voters and his excellent debating skills helped him land the vice-president's spot on the Democratic ticket.

◆ Richard Gephardt. After an unsuccessful run for the White House in 1988, Missouri Rep. Richard Gephardt gave it another try in 2004. A member of Congress for more than a quarter-century, Gephardt is a familiar face and has high name recognition. Long a strong proponent of organized labor, he nevertheless failed to capture voter support and was one of the first candidates to drop out of the running, doing so after he placed fourth in the Iowa caucuses.

◆ Bob Graham. Graham had extensive experience in both the executive and legislative branches of government, having served in Florida's state legislature and as the state's governor before being elected to the U.S. Senate in 1986. While hailing from a crucial swing state was in Graham's favor, he entered the race late and his stumping skills were rusty. His campaign failed to gain any momentum, and he was the first candidate to drop out.

◆ John Kerry. From the get-go, the Massachusetts senator was considered the candidate to beat by many political observers. In comparison to almost every other candidate, Kerry's campaign was well funded from the beginning, which gave him a decided advantage. A decorated war veteran—he was the only candidate in either party who saw active military duty—Kerry's service in Vietnam was thought to be one of his candidacy's strengths; however, his service record became the focus of attack by the Republican party. Noted as a ferocious campaigner, Kerry chalked up early primary and caucus wins and captured his party's nod at the Boston convention.

◆ Dennis Kucinich. Kucinich was the longest shot in a field of many dark horses. He was Cleveland's mayor in 1978 when the city became the first since the Depression to default on its debts. Although Kucinich's role in the collapse is still debated, it remained a significant black mark on his record in voters' minds. Nevertheless, Kucinich went on to serve four terms in the U.S. House before running for the Democratic presidential nomination. Interestingly, as a devout Catholic Kucinich was a long-time opponent of abortion but promised to appoint only judges who backed *Roe v. Wade*. However, even this stance failed to capture much support.

◆ Joe Lieberman. The three-term senator from Connecticut and 2000 vice-presidential nominee, Lieberman was an early leader in national polls but failed to do well in the Democratic primaries and caucuses. He also lacked support from the Democrats for splitting from the party line on such key issues as the death penalty, the war in Iraq (Lieberman supported Bush's authority to wage the war, as did Gephardt, Kerry, and Edwards), and tort reform.

◆ Al Sharpton. Sharpton, a civil rights activist and Pentecostal minister from New York City, was without a doubt the campaign's most entertaining figure. Positioning himself as a voice for the alienated and disaffected, he nevertheless failed to gain much support among the electorate.

Race Results

John Kerry won the Iowa caucuses and the New Hampshire primary in January. Howard Dean, who many believed would pose a serious threat to Kerry, finished third in Iowa and second in New Hampshire.

In February, Kerry continued to amass solid wins with victories in five of the "Super Seven" states as well as Maine, Michigan, Washington, Virginia, Tennessee, and Wisconsin. His wins in Tennessee and Virginia were especially encouraging, as they showed he could attract southern voters.

Howard Dean, who failed to win even one primary, pulled out of the race after Wisconsin. Joe Lieberman withdrew after Delaware, as did Wesley Clark, even after a win in Oklahoma.

In March, Kerry sealed his nomination as the Democratic candidate, winning nine of the 10 Super Tuesday states including New York and California. There were a number of primaries to come; however, with Kerry's bid virtually locked up, they were considered more an indication of public sentiment than anything else.

In April, George W. Bush's campaign took some serious hits with negative publicity over bloodshed in Iraq. Kerry was subsequently attacked as being inconsistent and weak on security.

Kerry accepted the Democratic nomination at the party's convention, held in Boston in July. He chose former rival John Edwards as his running mate. Post-convention polls reflected growing support for the ticket after Kerry's strong performance during the convention.

The Republican party affirmed George W. Bush's candidacy at its August convention in New York. Both sides took a bit of a breather for the remainder of the summer, but things heated up again in September. During the first of three presidential debates, Kerry seemed to best the commander in chief.

The war in Iraq, national security, and the economy emerged as key issues in the campaign, with both sides launching aggressive attack ads centered on these issues.

In two more presidential debates, the candidates slugged it out over domestic policy and security; however, neither emerged as a clear front-runner. In the sole vice-presidential debate, incumbent Dick Cheney seemed to best challenger John Edwards.

By October, the race between Bush and Kerry was a statistical dead heat. While various polls painted one or the other as the potential winner, margins of error made the race too close to call.

Election Day

After 2000, various media organizations had pledged to work on a better system for reporting future elections to avoid embarrassment when votes were counted. As such, most outlets played it safe in 2004 and took pains to not make any predictions based on exit polls.

However, this didn't stop them from internally reporting the results of exit polls, and these results became public knowledge almost instantaneously thanks to bloggers (web loggers). By midday, the polls showed Kerry with significant leads over Bush in key states. One had him winning the battleground state of Pennsylvania by 20 points (he eventually won the state by 2 percent).

By 11 P.M., however, Kerry's 20-point lead in Pennsylvania had evaporated. Still to be decided, however, was Ohio, whose 20 electoral votes made it a key battleground for both candidates. The popular vote totals remained excruciatingly close throughout the night and into the following morning. At that point, Kerry, realizing there weren't enough provisional ballots to erase his opponent's lead, conceded the race.

By 11 A.M. on Nov. 3 it was all over, with George W. Bush garnering 51 percent of the vote to John Kerry's 49 percent. It was the first time since 1988, when George H.W. Bush, the president's father, defeated Massachusetts Gov. Michael Dukakis, that a presidential candidate received more than 50 percent of the vote.

Exit polls showed that national security was a major concern for many voters. They did not differentiate between the war in Iraq and Afghanistan. At the end of the day, voters felt safer keeping Bush in office than having Kerry face problems they had not been convinced he knew how to solve.

Kerry was widely criticized for saying he "had a plan" but rarely offering specifics. Bush, on the other hand, acknowledged that people were likely to disagree with his approach but, unlike with Kerry, they would always know where he stood. It was this ability to paint Kerry as a "flip-flopper" that helped carry Bush to victory.

Another issue that captured voter attention was something characterized as "moral values." Voters in 11 states, including the blue (Democratic) states of Michigan and Oregon, passed measures banning same-sex marriage. The inclusion of these referendums on ballots led many to speculate that voters cared more about the private sex lives of two men or two women than they did about national security. But opponents to this conclusion pointed out that while 22 percent of voters said moral values was their key issue, 19 percent said the economy and jobs were key—making it a statistical dead heat.

And since there is no definition of what moral values are, they have been left open for interpretation. Some will argue opposition to abortion and gay marriage are moral values, while others will argue that opposition to the war in Iraq and support for greater social programs are moral values.

The debate over moral values has led many Democrats to wonder where their party will go in the next four years. The number-one question Democrats are facing is how to convince red state (Republican) voters that they share their values, while at the same time not alienating their blue state base.

Republicans, particularly social conservatives, feel galvanized as a result of the election. They believe they helped Bush win a second term, and are expecting to be rewarded with lower taxes, as well as appointments of conservative justices to the Supreme Court. Bush is likely to appoint at least one—and possibly four—justices during his second term.

Congressional Elections

Congressional control didn't change in the 2004 elections, but Republicans made gains in both chambers. The GOP picked up four seats in the U.S. Senate for a 55–44–1 majority and two seats in the U.S. House.

Bolstered by redistricting and a lack of highly competitive seats, incumbency ruled the day, although many also attributed GOP gains to riding President George W. Bush's coattails in key races.

Notable Senate races included …

- ◆ Senate Minority Leader Tom Daschle's loss to former U.S. Representative John Thune. It was the first time a Senate leader was unseated since 1952, when Barry Goldwater of Arizona defeated Senate Majority Leader Ernest McFarland.

◆ Illinois State Sen. Barack Obama's win over Republican Alan Keyes to take back the seat for the Democrats. His victory makes him the only black member of the Senate and only the third since Reconstruction.

◆ Democrat Ken Salazar's narrow win over Republican beer magnate Pete Coors in Colorado in a contest over retiring Republican Sen. Ben Nighthorse Campbell's seat. Salazar will be the first Democratic Hispanic senator in more than 25 years.

◆ Former Housing and Urban Development Secretary Mel Martinez's win over Democrat Betty Castor in Florida. Martinez becomes the first Cuban American to serve in the U.S. Senate.

All 435 House seats, including 36 open seats, were up for grabs in the 2004 election. Nineteen of the open seats were held by Republicans, 14 by Democrats. A controversial redistricting plan in Texas, pushed by U.S. House Majority Leader Tom DeLay, resulted in three new seats and a more Republican-friendly map, and helped the party pick up five Democratic seats from the Lone Star state.

The final two races to be decided were in Louisiana, which were run-off elections held in early December. Both parties had something to celebrate as they each won one of the races, bringing the final total in the House to 231 Republicans, 202 Democrats, and 1 Independent, who caucuses with the Democrats.

Notable House races included:

◆ In Illinois, Democrat Melissa Bean ousted Republican Phil Crane, the longest-serving member in that chamber.

◆ In Kentucky, Republican Geoff Davis won out over Nick Clooney, father of actor George Clooney.

◆ In Wisconsin, Democrat Gwen Moore became the first African American elected to Congress from the Badger State.

At the State Level

There were 11 gubernatorial races in 2004, with six of them involving incumbents. Republicans maintained their control of the majority of governorships with 28; the Democrats hold 21. Interestingly, two states switched from Democrats to Republicans during the 2004 elections; two others traded Republican governors for Democrats.

In Washington State, the seat appeared to tip to Dino Rossi, the Republican candidate. More than a month past the election, a second statewide recount by hand was underway after a machine recount gave Rossi a 42-vote margin of victory over Democrat Christine Gregoire. The state's chief elections officer certified the machine recount and declared Rossi the official governor-elect. However, Gregoire raised enough funds to demand and receive a hand recount, which she won.

In Montana, Brian D. Schweiter's win changes the governorship from Republican to Democrat, as is also the case in New Hampshire, where Democratic challenger John Lynch defeated incumbent Republican Governor Craig Benson. In Missouri, the governorship changes from Democrat to Republican with Matt Blunt's win over outgoing Democrat Bill Holden. Indiana also joins the roster of states with Republican governors with Mitch Daniels's defeat of incumbent Democrat Joe Kernan.

In the Legislatures

Eighty percent of state legislative seats were up for election in 2004. Election results show major party control changes in several states, including …

- ◆ Colorado, where Democrats took control of both the House and the Senate for the first time in 40 years.

- ◆ Georgia, where Republicans are now in control of the House. This gives Republicans full party control in Georgia for the first time.

- ◆ Indiana, where Republicans took control of the House. Coupled with a newly elected Republican governor, this win gives Republicans full control.

- ◆ Montana, where the loss of six Republican seats in the Senate put that chamber under Democrat control. This, coupled with the election of a Democratic governor, changes Montana from full Republican control to split control.

- ◆ Washington, where Democrats took control of the Senate. This gives them control of both the governor's office and the legislature.

Ballot Initiatives and Referendums

Issues ranging from health care and tort reform to gambling and same-sex marriage were among the ballot initiatives and referendums that voters were asked to decide during the 2004 election.

There were 162 different ballot measures in 34 states across the United States. California, perennially the leader in this area, came out on top again with no fewer than 16. Of these, voters approved a proposal that calls for collecting DNA samples from felons; a criminal justice measure relaxing the state's existing "three-strikes" law, requiring the third strike to be a serious or violent crime; and a proposal to fund embryonic stem cell research. It became the first state to publicly fund such research.

Voters in 11 states—Arkansas, Georgia, Kentucky, Michigan, Mississippi, Montana, North Dakota, Ohio, Oklahoma, Oregon, and Utah—were asked to weigh in on same-sex marriage. In some states, the issue at hand was the definition of marriage as being a union between a man and a woman. In other states, initiatives included wording stating that a legal status substantially similar to marriage, such as a civil union, would not be recognized between same-sex partners. The measures passed by large margins in all 11 states.

Tort reform measures met with mixed results before voters in six states. Florida voters passed a package of three medical malpractice measures. Nevada residents voted against an initiative that would punish attorneys for filing frivolous lawsuits but approved a measure limiting non-economic damages in malpractice cases. A similar measure failed in Wyoming. In California, voters put limits on unfair business practices suits. Coloradoans voted against a measure that would repeal limits brought against homebuilders for construction defects.

Six states—California, Florida, Michigan, Nebraska, Oklahoma, and Washington—voted on gambling measures. In California, two tribal-related measures failed to win approval. One would have required tribes to pay 25 percent of their gaming revenues to the state, and would have authorized the establishment of non-tribal casinos if they refused. The other would have granted tribes exclusive gaming rights in the state and would exempt them from making any payments to the state if non-tribal gaming was approved.

Voters in Michigan voted to require voter approval of any future casino gaming. In Oklahoma, voters approved a state lottery to fund education. Florida voters approved a measure allowing slot machine gaming at race tracks. In Washington, voters nixed a plan that would have used revenues from non-tribal slot machine gaming to offset property taxes. Nebraska voters voted against all four gambling initiatives put before them.

Medical marijuana programs were on the ballots in several states. While Oregon voters elected not to expand the state's existing program, Montana voters approved one for their state. In Alaska, an initiative that would legalize marijuana use for all adults failed.

The Cabinet Shuffle

Appointing new cabinet members is common following a president's re-election, as people get burned out after four years of heavy workloads demanded by high-level government service. While turnover is expected, the pace of change in George W. Bush's cabinet was rapid compared to some administrations, with six of the 15 cabinet-level officials announcing their resignations within two weeks of the election.

Of the resignations, at least half were reported to be of the cabinet member's own volition. As of this printing, those who have resigned and the nominees to replace them include ...

◆ Secretary of State Colin Powell. Powell always said he would serve only one term. National Security Advisor Condoleezza Rice was nominated for the post.

◆ Attorney General John Ashcroft. White House counsel Alberto Gonzales was nominated to replace him.

◆ Secretary of Agriculture Ann Veneman. Nebraska Governor Mike Johanns has been tapped as her replacement.

◆ Secretary of Commerce Don Evans. Evans cited his desire to move back to Texas as the reason for his resignation. Carlos Gutierrez, chief executive of the Kellogg cereal company, was nominated to replace him.

◆ Secretary of Education Rod Paige. Margaret Spellings, a domestic policy adviser in the White House, was nominated to fill the post.

◆ Secretary of Energy Spencer Abraham. Bush nominated Samuel W. Bodman to the position. Bodman is a business executive who served at the deputy level in both the Departments of Commerce and Treasury during Bush's first administration.

◆ Secretary of Homeland Security Tom Ridge. Ridge was the first secretary of the newly created department. Judge Michael Chertoff, who serves on the 3rd Circuit Court of Appeals in Philadelphia, was nominated as Ridge's replacement.

◆ Secretary of Veterans Affairs Anthony Principi. Principi resigned in December. Bush nominated Jim Nicholson, the Ambassador to the Vatican, to fill the post.

◆ Secretary of Health and Human Services Tommy Thompson. Thompson is expected to enter the private sector after a lengthy career as a public servant. Environmental Protection Agency chief Michael Leavitt will replace him.

Cabinet members who have said they will stay on include Secretary of Defense Donald Rumsfeld, Interior Secretary Gale Norton, Labor Secretary Elaine Chao, Transportation Secretary Norman Mineta, Treasury Secretary John Snow, and Housing and Urban Development Secretary Alphonso Jackson.

The Senate must confirm all Cabinet nominations.

With Republicans holding a larger majority in the Senate, opposition to most of Bush's appointments is expected to be minimal. The week after his re-election, Bush told reporters he had "political capital" as a result of his victory and intended to use it. As of this printing, none of his nominations for cabinet posts have garnered partisan opposition the way some have in the past.

Appendix D

Resources

Bibliography

Abraham, Henry J., and Barbara A. Perry. *Freedom and the Court: Civil Rights and Liberties in the United States.* New York: Oxford University Press, 1998.

Barone, Michael, Richard E. Cohen, and Charles E. Cook Jr. *The Almanac of American Politics 2002.* Washington, D.C.: National Journal Group Inc., 2001.

Birnbaum, Jeffrey H. *The Lobbyists: How Influence Peddlers Work Their Way in Washington.* New York: Times Books, 1993.

Bowen, Catherine Drinker. *Miracle at Philadelphia: The Story of the Constitutional Convention May to September 1787.* Boston: Little Brown and Company, 1986.

Brands, H. W. *TR: The Last Romantic.* New York: Basic Books, 1997.

Gillies, Nicola. *The First Ladies of the United States.* New York: Dovetail Books, 2001.

Greenberg, Ellen. *The Supreme Court Explained.* New York: W. W. Norton & Company, 1997.

Hardgrave, Jr., Robert L. *American Government: The Republic in Action.* Orlando: Harcourt Brace Jovanovich, 1986.

Irons, Peter, ed. *The First Amendment.* May It Please the Court Series. New York: The New Press, 1997.

Klapthor, Margaret Brown, with contributor Allida M. Black. *The First Ladies of the United States of America.* Washington, D.C.: White House Historical Association, 2001.

Koempl, Michael L., and Judy Schneider. *Congressional Deskbook 2000.* Alexandria: The Capitol.Net, 2000.

McCloskey, Robert G. *The American Supreme Court, Second Edition.* University of Chicago Press, 1994.

Office of the Historian, U.S. House of Representatives. *Women in Congress: 1917–1990.* Washington, D.C.: U.S. Government Printing Office, 1991.

Paddock, Lisa. *Facts About the Supreme Court of the United States.* New York: The H. W. Wilson Company, 1996.

Patrick, John J., Richard M. Pious, and Donald A. Ritchie. *The Oxford Guide to the United States Government.* New York: Oxford University Press, 2001.

Price, David E. *The Congressional Experience, Second Edition.* Boulder: Westview Press, 2000.

Serow, Ann G., W. Wayne Shannon, and Everett C. Ladd, eds. *The American Polity Reader.* New York and London: W. W. Norton & Company, 1993.

Waldman, Tom. *The Best Guide to American Politics.* Los Angeles: Renaissance Books, 2000.

Wasby, Stephen L. *The Supreme Court in the Federal Judicial System.* New York: CBS College Printing, 1984.

Woodward, Bob, and Scott Armstrong. *The Brethren: Inside the Supreme Court.* New York: Avon Books, 1979.

Yalof, David Alistair. *Pursuit of Justices: Presidential Politics and the Selection of Supreme Court Nominees.* Chicago: The University of Chicago Press, 1999.

News Sites

National

Below are links to suggested websites for national news. The list includes both print and electronic media. These sites are constantly updated, and provide the latest news from around the world, as well as national news affecting all Americans.

ABC News: www.abcnews.com

Boston Globe: www.boston.com/globe

CBS News: www.cbs.com

CNN: www.cnn.com

Cybercast News Service: www.cnsnews.com

The Drudge Report: www.drudgereport.com (compiles stories and columns from hundreds of media sources in the United States and around the world)

Fox News: www.foxnews.com

Los Angeles Times: www.latimes.com

MSNBC: www.msnbc.com (mirrors the MSNBC cable channel and provides links to other news sources)

New York Times: www.nytimes.com

Salon.com: www.salon.com (an online magazine with 10 content areas updated daily or more frequently, including politics, news, arts and entertainment, books, life, and technology)

Washington Post: www.washingtonpost.com

Washington Times: www.washingtontimes.com

Washington, D.C.

The links below provide the reader with in-depth behind-the-scenes news on what is happening in and around Washington, D.C. These sites provide the "inside baseball" news items that the hard-core political junkie cannot do without. Well known inside the beltway, these sites are often the first to break the hard news stories that all of Capitol Hill is talking about.

Congressional Quarterly: www.cq.com

National Journal Group publications: www.NationalJournal.com

Roll Call: www.RollCall.com

The Hill: www.TheHill.com

Government Sites

The sites listed below are key government sites. Several are useful when researching legislation currently pending before Congress, as well as for finding upcoming scheduled events on Capitol Hill. Several sites also contain historical information on their respective topics.

Federal legislative information: http://thomas.loc.gov

First Lady: www.whitehouse.gov/firstlady

Library of Congress: www.loc.gov

U.S. House of Representatives: www.house.gov

U.S. Senate: www.senate.gov

U.S. Supreme Court: www.supremecourtus.gov

Vice President: www.whitehouse.gov/vicepresident

White House: www.whitehouse.gov

Political Information

This list provides links to national party organization sites.

Democratic Congressional Campaign Committee: www.dccc.org

Democratic National Committee: www.democrats.org

Democratic Senatorial Campaign Committee: www.dscc.org

Green Party: www.greenparty.org

Libertarian Party: www.lp.org

National Republican Congressional Committee: www.nrcc.org

National Republican Senatorial Committee: www.nrsc.org

New Democrat Network: www.newdem.org

Republican Main Street Partnership: www.republicanmainstreet.org

Republican National Committee: www.rnc.org

Interest Groups

This listing provides information about just some of the thousands of active interest groups. Their websites are regularly updated to provide viewers a behind-the-scenes look at what their organization hopes to accomplish.

American Association of Retired Persons
www.aarp.org
202-434-2277
1-800-424-3410

American Civil Liberties Union
www.aclu.org
202-544-1681

American Conservative Union
www.conservative.org
703-836-8602

American Israel Public Affairs Committee
www.aipac.org
202-639-5200

American League of Lobbyists
www.alldc.org
703-960-3011

American-Arab Anti-Discrimination Committee
www.adc.org
202-244-2990

Children's Defense Fund
www.childrensdefense.org
202-628-8787

Christian Coalition
www.cc.org
202-547-3600

Citizens Against Government Waste
www.cagw.org
202-467-4253

Coalition to Stop Gun Violence
www.gunfree.org
202-530-0340

Concerned Women of America
www.cwfa.org
202-488-7000

Michael J. Fox Foundation for Parkinson's Research
www.michaeljfox.com

NAACP
www.naacp.org
410-486-9100
877-NAACP-98

National Abortion and Reproductive Rights Action League
www.naral.org
202-973-3000

National Council of La Raza
www.nclr.org
202-785-1670

National Gay and Lesbian Task Force
www.ngltf.org
202-332-6483

National Organization for the Reform of Marijuana Laws
www.norml.org
202-483-5500

National Right to Life Committee
www.nrlc.org
202-626-8800

People for the Ethical Treatment of Animals
www.peta.org

Public Citizen
www.citizen.org
202-588-1000

Tracking the Money: Where to Start

These sites are valuable for researching financial disclosure information related to federal candidates. In addition, several of the sites track Capitol Hill, general political happenings, or offer information about past politicians.

Common Cause: www.CommonCause.org (a nonprofit, nonpartisan citizen's lobbying organization promoting honest and accountable government)

Federal Election Commission: www.FEC.gov

Open Secrets: www.OpenSecrets.org (a comprehensive guide to federal campaign contributions and lobbying sponsored by The Center for Responsive Politics)

PoliticalMoneyLine: www.politicalmoneyline.com (inside information on campaigns, PACs, individual donors, and lobbyists)

Politics.com: www.politics.com (a comprehensive online guide to all things political, including elections, financing, organizations, and more)

The U.S. Cabinet

Department of Agriculture: www.usda.gov

Department of Commerce: www.doc.gov

Department of Defense: www.defenselink.mil

Department of Education: www.ed.gov

Department of Energy: www.doe.gov

Department of Health and Human Services: www.hhs.gov

Department of Homeland Security: www.dhs.gov

Department of Housing and Urban Development: www.hud.gov

Department of Interior: www.doi.gov

Department of Justice: www.usdoj.gov

Department of Labor: www.dol.gov

Department of State: www.state.gov

Department of Transportation: www.dot.gov

Department of Treasury: www.treasury.gov

Department of Veterans Affairs: www.va.gov

Cabinet-Level Agencies

Office of National Drug Control Policy: www.whitehousedrugpolicy.gov

Environmental Protection Agency: www.epa.gov

Office of Management and Budget: www.omb.gov

Office of the U.S. Trade Representative: www.ustr.gov

Index

A

abortion, debate over, 329-330

absentee voting, 335

ACLU (American Civil Liberties Union), 200

Adams, John, 54, 64, 66, 129, 210, 328

Adams, John Quincy, 124

Adarand Constructors, Inc. v. Pena, 191

advice-and-consent powers (Senate), 127-128

Affleck, Ben, 270

AFL-CIO, 259

agency implementation, federal budget process, 236-237

Albright, Madeleine, 75

Agriculture Department, 78

ALL (American League of Lobbyists), 277

Allgeyer v. Louisiana, 184

Amendments (U.S. Constitution)

Eighteenth Amendment, 46

Eighth Amendment, 39

Eleventh Amendment, 42

failed amendments, 32, 49-50

Fifteenth Amendment, 44

Fifth Amendment, 36, 38-39

First Amendment, 34-37

Fourteenth Amendment, 36, 43-44

Fourth Amendment, 38

Nineteenth Amendment, 5, 34, 47-48

Ninth Amendment, 40

Second Amendment, 37

Seventeenth Amendment, 33, 45

Seventh Amendment, 39

Sixteenth Amendment, 45

Sixth Amendment, 39

Tenth Amendment, 40

Third Amendment, 38

Thirteenth Amendment, 43

Twelfth Amendment, 42-43

Twentieth Amendment, 46

Twenty-fifth Amendment, 46

Twenty-first Amendment, 46

Twenty-fourth Amendment, 48

Twenty-second Amendment, 46

Twenty-seventh Amendment, 48

Twenty-sixth Amendment, 48

Twenty-third Amendment, 48

America Coming Together, 259

American Civil Liberties Union (ACLU), 200

American Federation of State-County-Municipal Employees, 259
political contributions, 271

American Federation of Teachers, political contributions, 271

American Government: The Republic in Action, 306

American League of Lobbyists (ALL), 277

Americans for a Republican Majority, 268

Americans for Tax Reform, 268

Ames, Oakes, 253

amicus curiae briefs, 200

Anheuser-Busch, political contributions, 272

Animal and Health Plant Inspection Service, 78

Anthony, Susan B., 47

Anti-Federalists, 15-16

AOL Time Warner, political contributions, 269

appeals, Supreme Court, 202

appellate jurisdiction, Supreme Court, 199-200

appointments
federal courts, 173-174
Senate, 162-163

apportionments, federal budget process, 228, 232-237

Arthur, Chester, 66

Articles, U.S. Constitution, 21
Article 1, 22-24, 45
Article 2, 24-27
Article 3, 27-28
Article 4, 28-29
Article 5, 29
Article 6, 30
Article 7, 30

Articles of Confederation, 9, 19
land claims, 11
ratification of, 10
weaknesses of, 10

Ashcroft, John, 163

assignments, House committees, 112

associate justices, 189-195

Attorney General, 77

attorney general (state government), 294

B

balancing doctrine, First Amendment to the U.S. Constitution, 35

Bankruptcy Court, U.S., 170

Barbour, Griffith & Rogers, lobbying receipts, 278

Barkley, Alben, 69

Barron v. Baltimore, 44, 212

Bayard, James, 43

BCRA (Bipartisan Campaign Reform Act) of 2002, 251, 260

Benton v. Maryland, 214-215

Bentsen, Lloyd, 71

bicameral legislatures, 306

Biddle, Joseph, 274

Bill of Rights, 32-34
Eighth Amendment to the U.S. Constitution, 39
Fifth Amendment to the U.S. Constitution, 38-39
First Amendment to the U.S. Constitution, 34-37
Fourth Amendment to the U.S. Constitution, 38
Ninth Amendment to the U.S. Constitution, 40
Second Amendment to the U.S. Constitution, 37
Seventh Amendment to the U.S. Constitution, 39
Sixth Amendment to the U.S. Constitution, 39
Tenth Amendment to the U.S. Constitution, 40
Third Amendment to the U.S. Constitution, 38

bills, 135
committees, 137
concurrent resolutions, 136
floor debates, 140-142
hearings, 138-139
joint resolutions, 135

legislative process, 133-135

mark-up phase, 139-140

passing, 142-143

resolutions, 136

sponsorships, 136

Bipartisan Campaign Reform Act (BCRA) of 2002, 251, 260

Black, Hugo, 35, 37, 301

blanket primaries, 159

Boland, Veronica Grace, 104

Bork, Robert, 191, 194

Bowsher, Charles, 230

Bowsher v. Synar, 230

Brandenburg, Clarence, 220

Brandenburg v. Ohio, 202, 220

Breed's Hill, Battle of (U.S. Revolutionary War), 7

Brennan Center for Justice at New York University Law School, 200

Breyer, Stephen, 190, 194

broad constructionists, 129

Brooks, Preston, 120

Brown, Linda, 217

Brown v. Board of Education, 44, 186, 217

Brutus, Anti-Federalist essayist, 16, 32

Buchanan, James, 93, 124

Buchanan, Patrick, 57

Buckley, James, 257

Buckley v. Valeo, 257, 260

Budget and Accounting Act of 1921, 229

Budget and Impoundment Control Act of 1974, 236

Budget Enforcement Act of 1990, 230

budget process (federal), 228-229

apportionments, 236-237

appropriations, 228, 232-234

Budget and Accounting Act of 1921, 229

Budget Enforcement Act of 1990, 230

Congressional Budget Act of 1974, 229

discretionary spending, 228

Emergency Deficit Control Act of 1985, 229-230

mandatory spending, 228

PAYGO (pay as you go), 230

pork spending, 235-236

sequestration, 230

timeline, 230-232

Unfunded Mandates Reform Act of 1995, 230

bully pulpit, 95

Bunker Hill, Battle of (U.S. Revolutionary War), 7

Bureau of Alcohol, Tobacco, and Firearms (ATF), 76

Bureau of Engraving and Printing, 75

Bureau of the Census, 298

Burger, Warren, 186-187

Burr, Aaron, 42, 64-65, 88

Bush v. Gore, 188, 192, 200, 211-212

Bush, Barbara, 264

Bush, George H. W., 57, 68, 70-71, 124, 192-193, 264

Bush, George W., 27, 53, 56, 59, 61, 68, 75, 79, 81, 161, 188, 192, 260, 264, 266, 271-272, 282, 289, 295, 321, 330

Bush, Jeb, 295

C

cabinet, presidential, 73

Attorney General, 77

establishment of, 73

expansion of, 77

Secretary of Agriculture, 78

Secretary of Commerce, 78-79

Secretary of Defense, 76

Secretary of Education, 81-82

Secretary of Energy, 81

Secretary of Health and Human Services, 80

Secretary of Homeland Security, 82-83

Secretary of Housing and Urban Development, 80

Secretary of Labor, 79

Secretary of State, 75

Secretary of Transportation, 81

Secretary of Treasury, 75

Secretary of Veterans Affairs, 82

selection process, 74

Calhoun, John C., 63, 91-92, 119

campaigns, political
  527's, 245-246
  committees, 245-246
  contributions, 252-260
  financing, 240-243
  fundraising, 263-267
  money, tracking, 248
  PACs, 245-246
  presidential, 59
  presidential war chests, 246-248
  volunteering for, 243-245, 335-337

Campbell, George W., 125

Caraway, Hattie, 122

Card, Andrew, 83

Carnahan, Jean, 163

Carnahan, Mel, 163

Carpenters & Joiners Union, political contributions, 271

carpetbaggers, 105

Carter, Jimmy, 67, 124, 194, 289

case workers, congress, 153-154

cases, Supreme Court,
  see also specific cases
  appeals, 202
  petitions for an extraordinary writ, 203
  procedure, 200-202
  process, 203-205
  requests for certification, 203
  rules, 205-206
  rulings, 206-207
  writ of certiorari, 202

Cassidy, Gerald, 277

Cassidy & Assoc., lobbying receipts, 278

caucus chairmen, House of Representatives, 109

caucuses, House of Representatives, 57, 109-110

CBO (Congressional Budget Office), creation of, 229

celebrities, political campaign contributions, 269-270

censures, 23

census, 297-298

Center for Disease Control, 80

Center for Middle East Peace/Econ Coop, 268

Center for Nutrition Policy and Promotion, 78

Chao, Elaine, 79

charters, 6
  city charters, 322-324

Chase, Salmon P., 42, 183

checks and balances, U.S. Constitution, 21-22

Cheney, Richard, 61, 68-69, 266

Chicago, Burlington, and Quincy R.R. v. Chicago, 213-214

chief justices of Supreme Court, 180-189

chiefs of staff, congress, 152-153

Chisholm, Alexander, 42

Chisholm v. Georgia, 42, 181

Cintas Corp, political contributions, 272

circuits, federal court system, 171

Citizens Against Government Waste, 235

city government, 321-325
  city charters, 322-324
  commission plan, 325
  council-manager plan, 324-325
  mayor-council plan, 324

civil disobedience, 36

Civil Rights Act of 1875, 216

Civil Rights Act of 1957, 130

Civil Rights Act of 1964, 123

civil rights cases, Supreme Court, 215-217

Civil War Amendments, U.S. Constitution, 43-44

Clay, Henry, 118-119

Clean Politics Act of 1939, 256

"clear and present danger," concept of, 35

clerks, Supreme Court, 196

Clinton, Bill, 58, 68, 81, 136, 143, 161-162, 187, 194-195, 272, 279, 289, 333

Clinton, Hillary Rodham, 122, 270

closed primaries, 159

cloture, 130

Club for Growth, 259

Coercive Acts of 1774, 6-7

Coke, Sir Edward, 5

Colorado Republican Party v. Federal Election Commission, 260

Commerce Department, 78-79

commission city governments, 325

commission governments, counties, 316

commission-administrator government, counties, 317

Committee of Style and Arrangement, Second Constitutional Convention, 20

committees, congress, 110-112, 131

  appropriations sub-committees, 233

  assignments, 112

  bills

    hearings, 138-139

    mark-up phase, 139-140

    reviewing, 137

  divisions, 113

  hearings, 150

  leadership, 113

  political campaigns, 245-246

  sizes, 112

  staffs, 113, 155-156

    case workers, 153-154

    chiefs of staff, 152-153

    communications directors, 153

    interns, 154-155

    press secretaries, 153

communications directors, congress, 153

Communications Workers of America, political contributions, 271

Compromise of 1850, 119

Compromise Tariff of 1833, 92

concurrent resolutions, 136

Condit, Gary, 164

conference chairs, House of Representatives, 108

confirmation hearings, 150

congress

  creation of, U.S. Constitution, 22-24

  daily schedule, 149-152

  election process, 157-158, 162

    candidate selection, 158-159

    primaries, 159-160

  federal budget process, 228-229

    apportionments, 236-237

    appropriations, 228, 232-234

    Budget and Accounting Act of 1921, 229

    Budget Enforcement Act of 1990, 230

    Congressional Budget Act of 1974, 229

    discretionary spending, 228

    Emergency Deficit Control Act of 1985, 229-230

    mandatory spending, 228

    PAYGO (pay as you go), 230

    pork spending, 235-236

    sequestration, 230

    timeline, 230-232

    Unfunded Mandates Reform Act of 1995, 230

House of Representatives, 101
  caucus chairmen, 109
  caucuses, 109-110
  committees, 110-113
  conference chairs, 108
  election process, 102-104
  fiscal responsibilities, 113-114
  leaders, 106-107
  majority leaders, 108
  majority whips, 108
  membership, 102
  minority leaders, 109
  minority whips, 109
  requirements, 105-106
  Speaker of the House, 107-108
  women serving in, 104-105
job perks, 146-149
legislative process, 133-135
  committees, 137
  concurrent resolutions, 136
  floor debates, 140-142
  hearings, 138-139
  joint resolutions, 135
  legislation types, 135
  mark-up phase, 139-140
  Office of Legislative Counsel, 134
  passing, 142-143
  resolutions, 136
  sponsorships, 136

lobbyists, 160-161
reapportionment, 298-299
redistricting, 299-302
Senate, 117, 122
  committees, 131
  early compromises, 119-120
  election process, 126
  establishment of, 118
  evolution of, 118-119, 121-124
  leadership, 129-130
  minority membership, 121-122
  New Deal agenda support, 122
  policy shifts, 123
  powers, 126-129
  presidential candidates from, 124
  procedures, 129-130
  requirements, 125
  terms and limits, 125
  weekend schedule, 152
Congressional Black Caucus, House of Representatives, 109
Congressional Budget Act of 1974, 229
Congressional Budget Office (CBO), creation of, 229
Constitution, U.S., 22
  amendments
    allowance for, 31-33

Eighteenth Amendment, 46
Eighth Amendment, 39
Eleventh Amendment, 42
failed amendments, 32, 49-50
Fifteenth Amendment, 44
Fifth Amendment, 36, 38-39
First Amendment, 34
Fourteenth Amendment, 36, 43-44
Fourth Amendment, 38
Nineteenth Amendment, 5, 34, 47-48
Ninth Amendment, 40
Second Amendment, 37
Seventeenth Amendment, 33, 45
Seventh Amendment, 39
Sixteenth Amendment, 45
Sixth Amendment, 39
Tenth Amendment, 40
Third Amendment, 38
Thirteenth Amendment, 43
Twelfth Amendment, 42-43
Twentieth Amendment, 46
Twenty-fifth Amendment, 46

Twenty-first Amendment, 46

Twenty-fourth Amendment, 48

Twenty-second Amendment, 46

Twenty-seventh Amendment, 48

Twenty-sixth Amendment, 48

Twenty-third Amendment, 48

articles, 22-30, 45

checks and balances, 21-22

debate regarding, 15-17

preamble, 21

ratification of, 17

signing of, 14

strict constructionist interpretation, 88

Constitution Party, 160

Constitutional Convention, 11, 14

constitutions, state, 306

contributions, political campaigns, 252-260

controllers, 295

conventions, parties, 58

Coolidge, Calvin, 72, 255

Cornwallis, Sir Charles, 10

corporations, political campaign contributions, 271-272

Corzine, Jon, 240, 268

Costner, Kevin, 270

council-administrator governments, counties, 317

council-manager city governments, 324-325

county assessors, 319

county attorneys, 318

county clerks, 318

county government, 315-319

county treasurers, 319

Court of Appeals (U.S.), 171

Court of Appeals for the Federal Circuit (U.S.), 171

Court of Federal Claims (U.S.), 171

Court of International Trade (U.S.), 171

Court of Military Appeals (U.S.), 171

Court of Veteran's Appeals (U.S.), 171

court system

appointments, 173-174

establishment of, 170

jurisdictions, 172-173

regional circuits, 171

terms, 174-175

trial courts, 170-171

Cox, Eugene, 155

Credit Mobilier scandal, 253

Crittenden, John, 120

Crittenden Compromise, 120

Cruzan, Nancy, 187

Cruzan v. Director, Missouri Department of Health, 187

Curry, Wayne, 317

Curtis, Charles, 122

Cushing, William, 182

D

daily schedule, congress, 149-152

Daschle, Linda Hall, 283

Daschle, Tom, 283

DASHPAC, 268

Davis, Gray, 291

Davis, Jefferson, 120

Davis, John, 217

DCCC (Democratic Congressional Campaign Committee), 158

Declaration of Independence, 8, 16

Declaration of Rights and Grievances, 6-7

"Declaration of Sentiments," 47

Defense Department, 76

DeLay, Tom, 300

delegates, presidency, 58-59

Democrat Party, 327-328

congressional candidates

election process, 162

primary process, 159-160

selection process, 158-159

DCCC (Democratic Congressional Campaign Committee), 158

DSCC (Democratic Senatorial Campaign Committee), 158

fundraising, 158

Democratic Congressional Campaign Committee (DCCC), 158

Democratic Senatorial Campaign Committee (DSCC), 158

Department of Agriculture, 78

Department of Commerce, 78-79

Department of Defense, 76

Department of Education, 81-82

Department of Energy, 81

Department of Health and Human Services, 80

Department of Homeland Security, 82-83

Department of Housing and Urban Development, 80

Department of Labor, 79

Department of State, 75

Department of the Treasury, 75

Department of Transportation, 81

Department of Veteran Affairs, 82

direct fundraising letters, 264

discretionary spending, congress, 228

discuss list, Supreme Court, 198

districts, swing, 160

dockets, 198

Doe v. Bolton, 222

double jeopardy, 215

Douglas, Stephen, 93, 118-119

DSCC (Democratic Senatorial Campaign Committee), 158

"due process clause," Fifth Amendment to the U.S. Constitution, 38-39

"due process clause," Fourteenth Amendment to the U.S. Constitution, 44

due process of law, 212-215

dugouts, 151

Dukakis, Michael, 58, 71

E

"E Pluribus Unum," 75

Eagleton, Thomas, 70

Earley, Mark, 330

Eaton, John H., 125

Education Department, 81-82

Edwards, John, 266

EEOB (Eisenhower Executive Office Building), 67

Eighteenth Amendment to the U.S. Constitution, 46

Eighth Amendment to the U.S. Constitution, 39

Eisenhower Executive Office Building (EEOB), 67

Eisenhower, Dwight D., 25, 72, 80

invocation of executive privilege, 25

"elastic clause" (Article 1, U.S. Constitution), 24

electoral college, 14, 59

creation of, 26

Elementary and Secondary Education Act of 1965, 321

Eleventh Amendment to the U.S. Constitution (1798), 42

Elizabeth I, queen of England (1588-1603), 5

Ellsberg, Daniel, 35

Ellsworth, Oliver, 182

Emancipation Proclamation of 1863, 93

Emergency Deficit Control Act of 1985, 229-230

EMILY's List, 160, 245, 259, 267

Energy Department, 81

Energy Research and Development Administration, 81

"equal protection clause," Fourteenth Amendment to the U.S. Constitution, 44

Equal Rights Amendment, failure of, 49

Escobedo v. Illinois, 221

Espionage Act of 1919, 35

"establishment clause," interpretation of, 37

excise taxes, 86-87

executive branch, creation of, 24

executive clemency, 292-293

executive privilege, 25-26

F

failed amendments to the U.S. Constitution, 49-50

Fair Labor Standards Act of 1938, 328

Fall, Albert, 255

FARA (Foreign Agents Registration Act), 281

Farquhar, Robert, 42

FDA (Food and Drug Administration), 80

FECA (Federal Election Campaign Act), 253, 256-257

federal budget process, 228-229

  apportionments, 236-237

  appropriations, 228, 232-234

  Budget and Accounting Act of 1921, 229

  Budget Enforcement Act of 1990, 230

  Congressional Budget Act of 1974, 229

  discretionary spending, 228

  Emergency Deficit Control Act of 1985, 229-230

  mandatory spending, 228

  PAYGO (pay as you go), 230

  pork spending, 235-236

  sequestration, 230

  timeline, 230-232

  Unfunded Mandates Reform Act of 1995, 230

Federal Corrupt Practices Act of 1910, 254-255

Federal Corrupt Practices Act of 1924, 255

federal court system

  appointments, 173-174

  establishment of, 170

  jurisdictions, 172-173

  regional circuits, 171

  terms, 174-175

  trial courts, 170-171

Federal Election Campaign Act of 1971 (FECA), 253, 256-257

Federal Energy Administration, 81

Federal Power Commission, 81

Federal Regulation of Lobbying Act in 1946, 280

federalism, 28

  Constitutional definition of, 29

Federalist Papers, The, 15, 21-22

Federalists, 15-16

Feingold, Russ, 260

Felton, Rebecca Latimer, 122, 163

Ferguson, James E., 290

Ferguson, Miriam L., 289

Ferraro, Geraldine, 71

Fifteenth Amendment to the U.S. Constitution, 44

Fifth Amendment to the U.S. Constitution, 36, 38-39

filibusters, 130

Fillmore, Millard, 66

financing, political campaigns, 240-243

First Amendment to the U.S. Constitution, 34-37

First Continental Congress, 6-7

Fong, Hiram, 122

Food and Nutrition Service, 78

Food and Safety Service, 78

Ford, Gerald, 68-69, 124, 190, 192

Foreign Agents Registration Act (FARA), 281

Fourteenth Amendment to the U.S. Constitution, 36, 43-44

Fourth Amendment to the U.S. Constitution, 38

Frankfurter, Felix, 35

Franklin, Benjamin, 9

Frazier, Lynn, 291

"free exercise clause," interpretation of, 37

freedom of assembly, establishment of, 36

freedom of religion, establishment of, 36-37

freedom of speech, establishment of, 35-36

freedom of speech and press cases, Supreme Court, 218-219

Frost, Martin, 134

Fuller, Melville, 184

fundraising, 151, 158, 263-267

    527's, 245-246

    PACs, 245-246

G

Garner, John Nance, 66

Gates, Bill, 154

General Electric, political contributions, 272

George III, King of England (1760-1820), 6, 8, 54

Gephardt, Richard, 269

Gerry, Elbridge, 63, 302

gerrymandering, 302

Gideon, Clarence, 221

Gideon v. Wainwright, 214, 221

Gingrich, Newt, 109

Ginsburg, Douglas, 192

Ginsburg, Ruth Bader, 194

Gitlow, Benjamin, 218

Gitlow v. New York, 214, 218

Glass v. The Sloop Betsy, 181

Goldberg, Arthur, 190

Goldberg, Whoopi, 270

Gonzales, Elian, 138

Gore, Al, 27, 53, 55, 59, 68, 188, 192

governors, 287-289

    election process, 289-291

    requirements, 289-291

    responsibilities, 291-293

Gramm, Phil, 229

Gramm-Rudman-Hollings Act of 1985, 229-230

Grand Inquests: The Historical Impeachments of Justice Samuel Chase and President Andrew Johnson, 188

grandfather clauses, 103

Grant, Ulysses S., 66, 94

grass-roots campaigns, 33

Great Compromise, 13

Great Seal of the United States of America, 75

Green Party, 160, 331

Green, Mark, 153

Griswold v. Connecticut, 186

Guinn and Beale v. United States, 103

gun control, debate over, 330-331

H

Hamilton, Alexander, 15-16, 20, 31, 64-65, 86, 328

Hamlin, Hannibal, 70

Hancock, John, 16

hard money contributions, political campaigns, 252-260

Harding, Warren G., 46, 124, 255

Harlan, John Marshall, 184

Harris, Katherine, 295

Harrison, Benjamin, 124

Harrison, William Henry, 66, 92, 124

Hatch, Orrin, 134

Hauge v. CIO, 214

Health and Human Services Department, 80

hearings, 150

Henry, Patrick, 16-17

Henry III, king of England (1216-1272), 4

Hepburn v. Griswold, 183

Hill, Anita, 193

Hispanic Caucus (House of Representatives), 110

Hollings, Ernest, 229

Hollywood, political campaign contributions, 269-270

Homeland Security Act of 2002, 83

Homeland Security Department, 82-83

Hoover, Herbert, 122

House of Representatives, 101

    average terms, 146

    caucuses, 109-110

    committees, 110-112

        assignments, 112

        divisions, 113

hearings, 150

leadership, 113

sizes, 112

staffs, 113

creation of, 22-24

daily schedule, 149-152

election process, 102-104, 157-158, 162

  candidate selection, 158-159

  primaries, 159-160

expulsions, 164

federal budget process, 228-229

  apportionments, 236-237

  appropriations, 228, 232-234

  Budget and Accounting Act of 1921, 229

  Budget Enforcement Act of 1990, 230

  Congressional Budget Act of 1974, 229

  discretionary spending, 228

  Emergency Deficit Control Act of 1985, 229-230

  mandatory spending, 228

  PAYGO (pay as you go), 230

  pork spending, 235-236

  sequestration, 230

  timeline, 230-232

Unfunded Mandates Reform Act of 1995, 230

fiscal responsibilities, 113-114

job perks, 146-149

leaders, 106-107

  caucus chairmen, 109

  conference chairs, 108

  majority leaders, 108

  majority whips, 108

  minority leaders, 109

  minority whips, 109

  Speaker of the House, 107-108

membership, 102

reapportionment, 298-299

redistricting, 298-302

requirements, 105-106

seating, 108

special elections, 163

staffs, 152-156

  case workers, 153-154

  chiefs of staff, 152-153

  communications directors, 153

  interns, 154-155

  press secretaries, 153

weekend schedule, 152

women serving in, 104-105

Housing and Urban Development Department, 80

Huck, Winnifred Mason, 104

Hughes, Charles Evans, 184-185, 187

Humphrey, Hubert, 27

I

Immigration and Naturalization Services v. Chadha, 187

impeachment powers, Senate, 128-129

  rules of, 23

implied powers, 24

income tax, adoption of, 45

incorporated areas, 316

Innocent II (Gregorio Papereschi), 4

Interagency Council on the Homeless, 80

Internal Revenue Service (IRS), 75

International Brotherhood of Electrical Workers, political contributions, 271

interns, congress, 154-155

Intolerable Acts of 1774, 6-7

investigative hearings, 150

Iredell, James, 42

"Ironclad Test Oath," 121

J

Jackson, Andrew, 73-74, 90-92, 119, 124, 182

  invocation of executive privilege, 26

Jay, John, 15, 86, 127, 181

"Jay's Treaty," 127

Jefferson, Thomas, 8, 32, 42, 54, 61, 64-65, 88-89, 210, 298, 328

John, king of England (1199-1216), 4

Johnson, Andrew, 66, 70, 72, 94-95, 121, 124-125, 129

Johnson, Lyndon, 70, 103, 124

Johnson, Richard Mentor, 43, 65

Johnson, William Samuel, 20

Johnston, Henry, 290

joint committees, House of Representatives, 112

joint resolutions, 135

Joint Victory Campaign 2004, 259

judicial review, 28
Supreme Court, 210-212

judicial system
appointments, 173-174
establishment of, 170
jurisdictions, 172-173
regional circuits, 171
terms, 174-175
trial courts, 170-171

Judiciary Act of 1789, 86, 211

Judiciary Act of 1800, 210

jurisdictions
federal courts, 172-173
Supreme Court, 199-200

Justice Department, 77

K

Kansas v. Colorado, 200

Kansas–Nebraska Act of 1854, 119

Kennedy, Anthony, 191-192

Kennedy, John F., 27, 54, 56, 70, 124, 269

Kerry, John, 161, 267, 269-270

King, Martin Luther, Jr., 217

King, Rufus, 20

King, William R., 66

"kitchen cabinet," 91

"Koreagate," 258

L

LA Avengers/Bleu Penguin, political contributions, 272

Labor Department, 79

labor unions, political campaign contributions, 270-271

laissez-faire constitutionalism, 184

Lampson, Nick, 300

Landrieu, Mary, 270

Langdon, John, 129

Larrazolo, Octaviono, 122

law clerks, Supreme Court, 196

League of Nations, establishment of, 96

Lee, Richard Henry, 8, 16

Lee, Robert E., 94

Legal Tender Act of 1862, 183

legislative process, 133-135

committees, 137
floor debates, 140-142
hearings, 138-139
legislation types, 135
concurrent resolutions, 136
joint resolutions, 135
resolutions, 136
mark-up phase, 139-140
Office of Legislative Counsel, 134
passing, 142-143
sponsorships, 136

Legislative Reorganization Act of 1946, 155

legislatures, state government, 306-308
bicameral, 306
fiscal powers, 309-314
police powers, 309
unicameral, 306

Levy, Chandra, 164

Libertarian Party, 160, 332

Lieberman, Joe, 56

lieutenant governors, 287, 293-294

limited government, theory of, 16

Lincoln, Abraham, 70, 74, 78, 93-94, 121, 183, 253-254

Lincoln, Mary Todd, 93

litigants, 173

Livingston, Bob, 282

Lobbying Disclosure Act of 1995, 280

lobbyists, 160-161, 273-275
ALL (American League of Lobbyists), 277
former legislators, 282-283
influence, 278-280
meetings, planning, 275-276
personal interaction, importance of, 277
regulations, 280-281
successful, 277

local government
cities, 321-325
city charters, 322-324
commission plan, 325
council-manager plan, 324-325
mayor-council plan, 324
counties, 315-319
special districts, 320-321
townships, 319-320

loose constructionists, 129

Louisiana Purchase, 89

Lovell v. City of Griffin, 185

M

Madison, James, 11-12, 15, 20-22, 24, 28, 32-33, 211

Magna Carta, 4-5

Magna Carta and Its American Legacy, The, 4

majority leaders, House of Representatives, 108

majority whips, House of Representatives, 108

malapportionment, 300

Malloy v. Hogan, 214

mandatory spending, congress, 228

Mapp, Dollree, 220

Mapp v. Ohio, 214, 220

Marbury, William, 210

Marbury v. Madison, 210-211

Maritime Disaster Family Assistance Act of 2001, 154

mark-up phase, legislative process, 139-140

Marriott International, political contributions, 272

Marshall, John, 24, 182-184, 210-211

Marshall, Thomas, 69

Marshall, Thurgood, 193, 217

Martin, Luther, 13

Martinez, Mel, 80

Mason, George, 13-14

Matters Under Review (MURs), 248

Mayflower Compact, 5-6

mayor-council city governments, 324

McCain, John, 235, 260, 266

McCarthy, Eugene, 257

McCarthy, Joseph, 25

McCorvey, Norma, 222

McCulloch, David, 24

McCulloch v. Maryland, 24

McGovern, George, 70

McKinley, William, 54, 67, 95, 254

Media Fund, 259

Medicare, 80

meetings, lobbyists, 275-276

Mineta, Norman, 81

minimum wage debate, 328-329

Minor v. Happersett, 183

Minor, Virginia, 47

minority leaders, House of Representatives, 109

minority whips, House of Representatives, 109

Miracle at Philadelphia, 13-14

Miranda, Ernesto, 221

Miranda v. Arizona, 186, 214, 221-222

Missouri Compromise of 1820, 119

Mondale, Walter, 67, 71

Monroe, James, 89-90, 124

"Monroe Doctrine," 89-90

Morris, Gouverneur, 20

MoveOn.org, 259

municipalities, 321

Munn v. Illinois, 183

Murkowski, Frank, 163

MURs (Matters Under Review), 248

Murtha, John, 107

N

Nader, Ralph, 55, 332

narrow constructionists, 129

National Association of Broadcasters, political contributions, 270

National Beer Wholesalers Association, political contributions, 272

National Cable & Telecommunications Associations, political contributions, 270

National Education Association, political contributions, 271

National Law Party, 160

National Organization for Women (NOW), 268

National Republican Congressional Committee (NRCC), 158, 245

National Republican Senatorial Committee (NRSC), 158

National Restaurant Association, political contributions, 272

National Rifle Association (NRA), 160, 268, 330

National Rifle Association Victory Fund, 245

National Voter Registration Act of 1993, 333

National Weather Service, 79

National Women's Party, 160

Near, Jay, 218

Near v. Minnesota, 36, 214, 218-219

Neuberger, Richard L., 306

New Deal programs, 123

New Democrat Network, 259

New Jersey Plan, 12

New Republican Majority Fund, 268

New York Times Co. v. Sullivan, 219

New York Times Co. v. United States, 206

NIMBY (not in my back yard), 319, 336

Nineteenth Amendment to the U.S. Constitution, 5, 34, 47-48

Ninth Amendment to the U.S. Constitution, 40

Nixon, Richard M., 27, 36, 67-70, 95, 124, 186, 190, 237, 246, 256

   executive privilege, invocation of, 26

No Child Left Behind Act of 2002, 321

nonbinding opinions, 136

Norquist, Grover, 268

not in my back yard (NIMBY), 319, 336

NOW (National Organization for Women), 268

NRA (National Rifle Association), 160, 268, 330

NRCC (National Republican Congressional Committee), 158

NRSC (National Republican Senatorial Committee), 158

O

O'Connor, Sandra Day, 190-191

Obama, Barack, 58

off-year elections, 162

Office of Legislative Counsel, 134

Office of the Solicitor General, 77

Olson, Floyd, 218

online fundraising, 267

open primaries, 159

oral arguments, Supreme Court, 198

Orders List, Supreme Court, 198

original jurisdiction, Supreme Court, 199-200

Outback Steakhouse, political contributions, 272

oversight hearings, 150

P

Packwood, Robert, 164

PACs (political action committees), 245-246, 258

   fundraising techniques, 265

pages, Congress, 154-155

Palko, Frank, 215

Palko v. Connecticut, 215

Park, Tong Sun, 258

Parker, Alton, 254

Parker, John, 122

partial-birth abortion, 330

parties

    choosing, 327-328

    congressional candidates

        election process, 162

        primary process,
           159-160

        selection process,
           158-159

    fundraising, 158

    registration requirements,
        332-333

    third parties, 160, 331-332

party conventions, 58

Patent and Trademark
    Office, 79

Paterson, William, 12

Patriot Act, 40

Patton Boggs, lobbying
    receipts, 278

PAYGO (pay as you go), 230

Pelosi, Nancy, 105, 136

Pendleton Civil Service
    Act of 1883, 253

"Pentagon Papers," printing
    of, 35

Pepper, Claude, 125

per curium decision, 202

Perkins, Frances, 79

Perot, H. Ross, 5, 55, 160

petitions for an extraordinary
    writ, Supreme Court, 203

Pierce, Franklin, 66, 124

Pilgrims, 5

*Planned Parenthood of
    Pennsylvania v. Casey*, 191, 223

Planned Parenthood PAC, 245

Plessy, Homer, 216

Plessy v. Ferguson, 44, 182, 216

plurality, 159

Podesta/Mattoon, lobbying
    receipts, 278

police powers, state legisla-
    tures, 309

political campaigns

    527's, 245-246

    committees, 245-246

    contributions, 252-260

    financing, 240-243

    fundraising, 263-267

    money, tracking, 248

    PACs, 245-246

    presidential war chests,
        246-248

    volunteering for, 243-245,
        335-337

poll taxes, 48

*Pollock v. Farmers' Loan &
    Trust Company*, 45

pork spending, 149

    federal budget process,
        235-236

Powell, Colin, 75

Powell, Lewis, 191

preamble, U.S. Constitution,
    21

precedents, 209-210

presidency

    annual salary, 60

    campaigning, 59

    candidates, 55-56

    chain-of-command, 60-61

    delegates, 58-59

    electoral college, 59

    establishment of, 54

    party conventions, 58

    primaries, 56-58

    requirements, 55

    youngest presidents, 54

Presidential Succession
    Act of 1947, 61

press secretaries, congress, 153

Preston, Gates et al., lobbying
    receipts, 278

PricewaterhouseCoopers,
    lobbying receipts, 278

primaries, 57

    blanket primaries, 159

    closed primaries, 159

    congressional candidates,
        159-160

    open primaries, 159

    presidency, 56-58

prior restraint, 219

pro hac vice, 177

Pro-Life Caucus (House
    of Representatives), 109

Publius, 15

Q-R

Quayle, Dan, 63, 68, 70
quid pro quo, 279

Rainey, Joseph, 103
Randolph, Edmund, 12
Rankin, Jeanette, 104
Reagan, Ronald, 67, 71,
  98, 124, 187, 190-191,
  230, 268, 289
reapportionment, 298-299
recalls, 291
redistricting, 298-302
referendums, 336
Reform Party, 160
registration requirements,
  332-333
Rehnquist, William,
  187-188, 222
*Reno v. American Civil
  Liberties Union*, 35
Republican Majority Fund,
  268
Republican National
  Committee (RNC), 245
Republican Party, 327-328
  congressional candidates
    election process, 162
    primary process,
      159-160
    selection process,
      158-159
  fundraising, 158

NRCC (National
  Republican Congressional
  Committee), 158
NRSC (National
  Republican Senatorial
  Committee), 158
requests for certification,
  Supreme Court, 203
resolutions, 136
Revels, Hiram, 122
revenue, 228
Revolutionary War (U.S.),
  7, 10
Rich, Denise, 279
Rich, Marc, 279
right to privacy cases,
  Supreme Court, 222-223
rights of suspected criminals
  cases, Supreme Court,
  220-222
RNC (Republican National
  Committee), 245
Roe v. Wade, 187, 222, 329
Rogers, Edith Nourse, 105
roll-call votes, 150-151
Roosevelt, Franklin D.,
  66, 69, 72, 79, 97-98,
  122-123, 185, 255
  "court-packing" proposal,
    27
Roosevelt, Theodore, 54, 63,
  66, 72, 95-96, 122, 254
Rosenberg, Ethel, 28
Rosenberg, Julius, 28
Rosenberger, Ronald, 192

*Rosenberger v. University of
  Virginia*, 192
Ross, Nellie Taylor, 289
Rudman, Warren, 229
Rules Committees, 140-141
Rutledge, John, 182
Rutledge, Wiley B., 190

S

Saban Capital Group, political
  contributions, 269
Scalia, Antonin, 191, 194
Schenck, Charles, 35
Schenck v. United States, 35,
  218
Scott, Dred, 120, 216
Scott v. Sanford, 216
scutages, 4
Second Amendment to the
  U.S. Constitution, 37
Second Bank of the United
  States, creation of, 24
Second Constitutional
  Convention, 20
Secret Service (U.S.), 76
Secretary of Agriculture, 78
Secretary of Commerce, 78-79
Secretary of Defense, 76
Secretary of Education, 81-82
Secretary of Energy, 81
Secretary of Health and
  Human Services, 80
Secretary of Homeland
  Security, 82-83

Secretary of Housing and Urban Development, 80

Secretary of Labor, 79

Secretary of State, 75

secretary of state (state government), 295

Secretary of Transportation, 81

Secretary of Treasury, 75

Secretary of Veterans Affairs, 82

select committees (House of Representatives), 111

Seltzer, William, 290

Senate, 117, 122

  appointments, 162-163

  committees, 131

    hearings, 150

  creation of, 22-24

  daily schedule, 149-152

  direct election of, adoption of, 45

  early compromises, 119-120

  election process, 126, 157-158, 162

    candidate selection, 158-159

    primaries, 159-160

  establishment of, 118

  evolution of, 118-119, 121-124

  expulsions, 164

  job perks, 146-149

  leadership, 129-130

  minority membership, 121-122

  New Deal agenda, support for, 122

  policy shifts, 123

  powers, 126-129

  presidential candidates from, 124

  procedures, 129-130

  requirements, 125

  staffs, 152-156

    case workers, 153-154

    chiefs of staff, 152-153

    communications directors, 153

    interns, 154-155

    press secretaries, 153

  terms and limits, 125

  weekend schedule, 152

Seneca Falls Convention (1848), 47

sequestration, 230

Service Employees International Union, 259

  political contributions, 271

sessions, Supreme Court, 197-199

Seventeenth Amendment to the U.S. Constitution, 33, 45

Seventh Amendment to the U.S. Constitution, 39

Shakespeare, William, 20

Shangri-La Entertainment, political contributions, 269

Shays, Christopher, 260

sheriffs, county, 318

Sherman, Roger, 13

Sherman Compromise, 13

Shriver, Sargent, 70

Sillerman Companies, political contributions, 269

Sinatra, Frank, 269

single-issue political contributors, 267-269

Sixteenth Amendment to the U.S. Constitution, 45

Sixth Amendment to the U.S. Constitution, 39

"Slaughter-House Cases," 213

Smits, Jimmy, 270

soft money contributions, political campaigns, 252-260

Solicitor General, 77, 195

Solomon, Gerald, 282

Souter, David, 192-193

"speakeasies," 46

Speaker of the House of Representatives, 107-108

special districts, local government, 320-321

special elections, House of Representatives, 163

special-interest groups, 160-161

"spoils system," 91, 253

sponsorships, bills, 136

Springsteen, Bruce, 269

staffs, congress, 152-156
  case workers, 153-154
  chiefs of staff, 152-153
  committees, 155-156
  communications directors, 153
  interns, 154-155
  press secretaries, 153
Standard Oil v. United States, 184
standing committees, House of Representatives, 110-111
Stanton, Edwin, 94, 121
Stanton, Elizabeth Cady, 47
State Department, 75
state government
  attorney general, 294
  constitutions, 306
  controller, 295
  governor, 287-289
    election process, 289-291
    requirements, 289-291
    responsibilities, 291-293
  legislatures, 306-308
    bicameral, 306
    fiscal powers, 309-314
    police powers, 309
    unicameral, 306
  lieutenant governor, 293-294
  secretary of state, 295
  treasurer, 295

State of the State addresses, 292
State of the Union addresses, 61
Steinberg v. Carhart, 223
Stevens, John Paul, 190, 196
Stone, Harlan, 186
Streisand, Barbra, 270
strict construction interpretation of Constitution, 88
strict constructionists, 129
suffrage, 47
Sullivan, L.B., 219
Sumner, Charles, 120
Sunland Park Racetrack & Casino, political contributions, 272
"Super Tuesday," 57
"supremacy clause" (Article 6, U.S. Constitution), 30
Supreme Court, 179
  amicus curiae briefs, 200
  associate justices, 189-195
  case procedure, 200-202
  cases
    appeals, 202
    petitions for an extraordinary writ, 203
    process, 203-205
    requests for certification, 203
    rulings, 206-207
    writ of certiorari, 202
  chief justices, 180-189
  civil rights cases, 215-217

  clerks, 196
  creation of, 27-28
  discuss list, 198
  due process of law cases, 212-215
  freedom of speech and press cases, 218-220
  judicial review cases, 210-212
  jurisdictions, 199-200
  oral arguments, 198
  Orders List, 198
  precedents, 209
  requirements, 175
  right to privacy cases, 222-223
  rights of suspected criminals cases, 220-222
  rules, 175-177, 205-206
  Solicitor General, 195
  terms, 197-199
Swift Boat Veterans for Truth, 161
swing districts, 160
Synar, Michael, 230

T

Taft, William Howard, 184-185
Taney, Roger, 182-183
Tarantino, Quentin, 270
Tariff Act of 1832, 92
"Tariff of Abominations," 92
Tax Court (U.S.), 171

Taylor, Gene, 107

Teapot Dome scandal, 255-256

Tenth Amendment to the U.S. Constitution, 40

Tenure of Office Act, 121

term limits, 146

terms
   federal judges, 174-175
   House of Representatives, 146
   Supreme Court, 197-199

Texans for John Cornyn, 267

Texas v. White, 42

Third Amendment to the U.S. Constitution, 38

third parties, 160, 331-332

Thirteenth Amendment to the U.S. Constitution, 43

Thomas, Clarence, 193

Thompson, Tommy, 61

"three-fifths compromise," 14

Thurmond, Strom, 125, 130

Tillman, Benjamin, 254

Tillman Act of 1907, 254

timeline, federal budget process, 230-232

Tinker v. Des Moines Independent Community School District, 36

Townsend, Kathleen Kennedy, 264

townships, government, 319-320

Traficant, James, 107

Transportation Department, 81

treason, Constitutional definition of, 28

treasurer (state government), 295

Treasury Department, 75

treaties, senatorial power over, 126

Treaty of Versailles, 127

Triumph of the American Nation, 91

Truman, Harry S, 69, 72, 124, 186

Twelfth Amendment to the U.S. Constitution, 42-43

Twentieth Amendment to the U.S. Constitution, 46

Twenty-fifth Amendment to the U.S. Constitution, 46

Twenty-first Amendment to the U.S. Constitution, 46

Twenty-fourth Amendment to the U.S. Constitution, 48

Twenty-second Amendment to the U.S. Constitution, 46

Twenty-seventh Amendment to the U.S. Constitution, 48

Twenty-sixth Amendment to the U.S. Constitution, 48

Twenty-third Amendment to the U.S. Constitution, 48

Tyler, John, 66, 92, 124

U

unanimous consent agreements, 130

Unfunded Mandates Reform Act of 1995, 230

unicameral legislatures, 306

unincorporated areas, 316

unions, political campaign contributions, 270-271

United Auto Workers, political contributions, 271

United Food & Commercial Workers Union, political contributions, 271

United States Constitution. *See* Constitution, U.S.

United States v. Curtiss-Wright Export Corp., 123

United States v. Harriss, 280

United States v. La Vengeance, 182

United States v. Newberry, 255

United States v. Nixon, 186

V

Van Buren, Martin, 43, 65, 92, 124

Van Scoyoc Assoc., lobbying receipts, 278

veeps, 64

Ventura, Jesse, 160, 289

Verner, Liipfert et al., lobbying receipts, 278

Veteran Affairs Department, 82

Viacom Inc., political contributions, 269

vice presidency, 64
 annual salary, 71
 duties, 64
 evolution of, 67-68
 irrelevancy of, 66-67
 offices, 71
 selection process, 69-71
 staff, 72

Vinson, Fred, 186

Virginia Plan, 12

Vivendi Universal, political contributions, 269

volunteering for political campaigns, 243-245, 335-337

voting, 333-335
 absentee voting, 335
 registering for, 333

Voting Rights Act of 1965, 103

W–X–Y–Z

Wade, Henry, 222

Waite, Morrison, 183

Wal-Mart Stores, political contributions, 272

Walt Disney Co., political contributions, 269

Walton, J.C., 290

War Department, 76

War Labor Disputes Act of 1943, 256

War Powers Act of 1973, 124

Warner, Mark, 330

Warren, Earl, 186, 217

Washington, Bushrod, 32-33

Washington, George, 28, 32-33, 54, 61, 64, 86-88, 127, 182, 328
 commander in chief, naming of, 7

Watson, Thomas, 163

Webster, Daniel, 118-119, 274

Webster v. Reproductive Health Services, 223

weekend schedule, congress, 152

Wesberry v. Sanders, 301

Wheeler, William, 63

Whiskey Amendments, 46

"Whiskey Rebellion," 86-87

White, Byron, 194

WIC (Women, Infants, and Children) program, 78

wide-open primaries, 159

widows, congressional appointments, 163

Wilder, L. Douglas, 289

Williams & Jensen, lobbying receipts, 278

Williamson, Hugh, 54

Wilson, Henry, 66

Wilson, Woodrow, 61, 69, 72, 96, 122, 127, 185

Wolff Packing Company v. Court of Industrial Relations, 185

Women's Caucus, House of Representatives, 109

Woodhull, Victoria, 56

Woolsey, Lynn, 137

writ of certiorari, 202

writ of mandamus, 211

Wyly, Sam, 260

YankeeNets, political contributions, 270

Yates, Robert, 16

Yates v. United States, 186

Yorktown, Battle of (U.S. Revolutionary War), 10